D0215069

WITHDRAWN
UTSA LIBRARIES

THE LABOUR LEFT 1945—51

Also from Unwin Hyman

A BEVERIDGE READER
edited by Karel Williams and John Williams

THE DEVELOPMENT OF TRADE UNIONISM IN GREAT BRITAIN AND
GERMANY, 1804–1914
edited by Wolfgang J. Mommsen and Hans-Gerhard Husung for the *German
Historical Institute, London.*

THE ENGLISH–SPEAKING ALLIANCE
Britain, the United States, the Dominions and the Cold War 1945–51
Ritchie Ovendale.

LABOUR AND THE LEFT IN THE 1930s
Ben Pimlott

LAW, SOCIALISM AND DEMOCRACY
Paul Q. Hirst

MARXISM, CLASS ANALYSIS AND SOCIAL PLURALISM
Les Johnston

LABOUR'S CONSCIENCE
THE LABOUR LEFT 1945–51

JONATHAN SCHNEER

Georgia State University

Boston
UNWIN HYMAN
London   Sydney   Wellington

© Jonathan Schneer, 1988
This book is copyright under the Berne Convention. No reproduction without
permission. All rights reserved.

Allen & Unwin, Inc.,
8 Winchester Place, Winchester, Mass. 01890, USA

Published by the Academic Division of
Unwin Hyman Ltd
15/17 Broadwick Street,
London W1V 1FP

Allen & Unwin (Australia) Ltd,
8 Napier Street, North Sydney, NSW 2060, Australia

Allen & Unwin (New Zealand) Ltd in association with the Port Nicholson Press Ltd,
60 Cambridge Terrace, Wellington, New Zealand

First published in 1988

Library of Congress Cataloging in Publication Data

Schneer, Jonathan.
  Labour's Conscience.
  Bibliography: p.
  Includes index.
  1. Labour Party (Great Britain) 2. Socialism—Great
Britain. 3. Great Britain—Politics and government—
1945–1964. I. Title.
JN1129.L32S36 1988   324.24107   87-17470
ISBN 0-04-942193-X (alk. paper)

British Library Cataloguing in Publication Data

Schneer, Jonathan
  Labour's conscience : the Labour Left,
    1945–51
  1. Labour party (Great Britain)—History
  I. Title
  324.24107'09   JN1129.L32
  ISBN 0-04-942193-X

Typeset in 10 on 12 point Bembo by Word Capture, Salford, and printed in Great
Britain by Biddles of Guildford.

Library
University of Texas
at San Antonio

To my father

Contents

Preface

Labour's Conscience: The Labour Left, 1945–51 analyzes the attitudes and activities of a critical force in modern British politics during a period that proved decisive in the history of Labour and the British Left generally. Inevitably it emphasizes events in Westminster, but it attempts to indicate the role of the Labour Left in the trade unions and constituencies as well.

Perhaps I should state at the outset that I am aware of the difficulties in using the term "Labour Left." During 1945–51 the Labour Left never was an organized force. It had no formal membership. For the most part the men and women who may be said to have "belonged" to it considered themselves first and foremost members of the Labour Party. If they were critical of some of the policies laid down by their party's leaders, often they were equally critical of each other. Moreover there were periods during Attlee's premiership when the Labour Left was inactive and virtually silent—when, in fact, some might have been tempted to question whether it existed at all. It is one of the main purposes of this book, however, to show that it did exist—as a tendency, if not as a coherent, easily delimited political group—and that its experiences and evolution during the early postwar era constitute a vital chapter in the history of the British Left and of the Labour Party as well.

My interest in the subject flows from my previous scholarly work which focused on the labor and socialist movements in Britain during the late nineteenth and early twentieth centuries. Few of Labour's pioneers lived to see the Attlee governments, and while researching and writing a biography of the dockers' leader, Ben Tillett, I often wondered what he and his contemporaries would have thought of them. The present volume, which, of course, makes no attempt to provide answers to such anachronistic musings, nevertheless was sparked by them.

If my interest in the early postwar years stemmed in part from my studies of a previous generation of Labour leaders, I was led to examine them too by my efforts to understand the continuing drama which the Labour Party has offered up for public viewing ever since I began to follow British politics. As a result of my studies I have come to believe that the thoughts and actions of the Labour Left of 1945–51 offer crucial insights into Labour history of the pre- and post- World War II eras.

Over the years during which I have been occupied with this project, so many people have helped me that it is impossible to mention them all by name. I want at the outset to express my gratitude to Yale University, Georgia State University and the American

Council of Learned Societies for financial assistance and for making possible time off from my teaching responsibilities. Without their support this book could never have been written.

While carrying on my research, archivists and librarians all over Britain provided me with unstinting assistance. I wish particularly to thank Stephen Bird, the Labour Party archivist; Norman Higson of Hull University; Tommy Marshall, local history librarian of the Gateshead Public Library; Dr Angela Raspin of the British Library of Political and Economic Science; and Richard Storey of the Modern Records Centre at Warwick University. Professor John Saville and Dr Joyce Bellamy generously opened the files of their *Dictionary of Labour Biography* to me; and Andrew Roth and Judy Tench most generously permitted me to use their own "Parliamentary Profiles" files which they have compiled over the years. Theirs is not an archive usually available to historians, and I am most grateful to them for permitting me to benefit from their hard work.

Then there were many who experienced at first hand the events described in this volume, and who proved willing to tell me about them. I learned much from interviews with Austin Albu, Lord Brockway, Lord Davies of Leek, Michael Foot, Lord Hale, E. R. Millington, Ian Mikardo and Lord Strauss. I am particularly grateful to Mr Albu and to Lord Hale for allowing me to view papers of the period which were in their possession, and for their hospitality. I wish, too, to acknowledge the generosity of Stephen Solley, who made his father's scrap-book available to me, and of Inigo Bing, who shared memories and insights into his father's political career with me. And I will never forget the helpfulness of Jim Murray, who induced some veterans of the Gateshead labor movement to reminisce in my presence about their first postwar Labour MP, Konni Zilliacus. I want, too, to acknowledge in print my gratitude to John Grigg, with whom I have often discussed various aspects of this work, and from whose insights and knowledge I have never failed to profit.

Many veterans of the period with whom I was unable to schedule an interview were nevertheless most helpful to me. I am very grateful to John Platts Mills, who sent me excerpts from his unpublished autobiography. Tony Benn, MP, astonished and flattered a young American historian by finding time to read and comment upon an article about the third force movement which later became the basis of Chapter 3 of the present volume. I have corresponded too with Lord Bruce, Barbara Castle, Lady Jeger, John Freeman, Jo Richardson, MP, Lyall Wilkes, Woodrow Wyatt and Michael Young.

My debt to historians is equally great. I wish to thank the participants in Gareth Stedman Jones's social history seminar at King's College, Cambridge, and in Pat Thane's, Jonathan Zeitlin's, Ben Pimlott's and Alice Prochaska's seminars at the Institute of Historical Research, University of London, for their comments and suggestions on early drafts of what proved, eventually, to be Chapter 1 of the present volume. I wish also to thank Jim Cronin, John Field, Gary Fink, Pat Hilden, David Howell, Paul Kennedy, Standish Meacham, R. K. Webb and Peter Weiler, who have read and commented upon portions of the manuscript, and in some cases the entire work. I have tried to follow their suggestions. Needless to say, however, where errors of fact or interpretation remain, they are mine alone.

My most profound debt as a historian is to my former teacher and friend, Stephen Koss, who died suddenly in October 1984. I miss his guidance more than it is easy to express.

Finally I must thank my wife, Margaret Hayman, for bearing with me over the years during which this manuscript has been in preparation.

Acknowledgments

The author and publishers would like to express their gratitude to the following for permission to reproduce photographs:

BBC Hulton Picture Library, the Labour Party, Syndicational International and the TUC.

Abbreviations

ADA	Americans for Democratic Action
AEU	Amalgamated Engineering Union
BLPES	British Library of Political and Economic Science
CEEC	Committee of European Economic Coordination
CLP	Constituency Labour Party
CPGB	Communist Party of Great Britain
DLP	Divisional Labour Party
EC	Executive Committee
ETU	Electrical Trades Union
FIB	Fabian International Bureau
FO	Foreign Office
GMC	General Management Committee
ILP	Independent Labour Party
NEC	National Executive Committee
NUDAW	National Union of Distributive and Allied Workers
NUM	National Union of Mineworkers
NUR	National Union of Railwaymen
PLP	Parliamentary Labour Party
PPS	Parliamentary Private Secretary
SDF	Social Democratic Federation
SLP	Socialist Labour Party
TUC	Trades Union Congress
UDC	Union of Democratic Control
USDAW	Union of Shopworkers, Distributive and Allied Workers
USSE	United Socialist States of Europe
VfS	Victory for Socialism

Introduction

In July 1945 the Labour Party scored its greatest electoral victory. With 393 seats in the House of Commons, it had converted a deficit of approximately 233 against the Tories into a majority of 146 over all parties combined. No parliamentary combination could block its legislation. For the first time Labour had the power to embark upon the socialist project which, since 1918, had been its declared aim.[1]

Under Prime Minister Clement Attlee, Labour held office until October 1951. During those six years it carried many far-reaching reforms. It fulfilled its election promises to nationalize the Bank of England, the mines, railways, gas, electricity, aviation, road haulage, and iron and steel. Despite the crippling economic burdens imposed by World War II, it provided for the first time diverse forms of social insurance to all Britons, "from the cradle to the grave." Unlike previous administrations it actively promoted Indian independence, which was achieved in 1947. No wonder that many Labour supporters believe these great accomplishments imparted to the Attlee governments a luster which time has only burnished. During the 1983 general election, Labour Party leader Michael Foot held up Attlee's governments as his ideal. Historian Kenneth Morgan notes that right- and left-wing Labourites, who agree on little else, concurred with Foot. Morgan himself concludes in his widely acclaimed study, *Labour in Power, 1945–51*, that Attlee's were "without doubt the most effective of all Labour Governments, perhaps amongst the most effective of any British Government since the passage of the 1832 Reform Act."[2]

Although many Labourites today perceive the early postwar era as an almost mythic, golden and all too short-lived moment, Attlee's governments had numerous critics at the time. Of course Conservatives found much to oppose during Attlee's tenure as Prime Minister. For the first few years of peace, however, they lacked confidence and impact, and after 1947 they found many of Labour's policies to their liking, especially in foreign affairs. Party conflict was sharp enough at mid-century, but observers from every political perspective thought the 1950 and 1951 general elections relatively tame. As Richard Crossman, the Labour Member for Coventry East and future Cabinet minister under Harold Wilson, remarked, "The mood of this 1951 election is quiet, even quieter than in 1950, and the voter is watching the two contestants with a cool and reserved detachment." This is not, perhaps, what might have been expected after the first six years of the transition to socialism which Labour had promised in 1945.[3]

In fact, some of Attlee's sharpest and most effective critics were on the Left, and belonged to his own party. As wartime gratitude and respect for the Soviet Union waned, British communists found themselves increasingly isolated and on the defensive. British Trotskyists were still a negligible force. Left-wing Labourites, however, while lacking formal organization, were perhaps more in tune with public opinion than ever before or since. The war had generated a popular radicalism which found expression in unprecedented support for the Left. In 1945 Labour reaped the electoral benefits, in part because it seemed the most effective vehicle for promoting "one hundred per cent Socialism," as an important left-wing candidate put it almost immediately after the election. When later it became evident that Attlee's government was following a less militant path than they had expected, left-wing Labourites appeared strategically placed to criticize its policies and to attempt to change them.[4]

The alienation of Labour's left wing was a gradual and painful process. Because the Labour Left was extraordinarily heterogeneous it responded to the government's policies in diverse and occasionally conflicting fashions. Uneven and multifaceted as it was, however, that response proved to be of great significance in the history of both the Labour Party and the British Left as a whole. The government's unprecedented parliamentary majority meant that for five crucial years the Labour Left had the opportunity of voting its conscience in the House and, in the trade unions and constituencies, of agitating for change without worrying about contributing to the downfall of Labour rule. Moreover, for the first time in history, the Labour Left could consider realistically, not hypothetically, how to implement its ultimate aims. The result, as I hope to demonstrate, was an extraordinary burst of creativity, in which the Labour Left sought to provide blueprints for the party leadership to follow. Perhaps at no other time in history had so many people attempted to think about, and to solve, the problems British socialists would encounter during "the transition" period.

As the Labour Left grew disillusioned with the government, another dynamic became evident. Precisely because it expected more far-reaching measures from a government with so massive a majority in the House, the Labour Left was forced to consider more seriously than ever before its place in the Labour Party and its relationship to the leaders. A searching reassessment of Labour's commitment to socialism and of its ability to achieve it replaced the early optimism. The party's wafer-thin parliamentary majority during the second Attlee administration (1950–1) gave added point to this rethinking. Now the Labour Left was forced to choose between the socialist yardstick it had fashioned during the previous five years, and the government which it had charged with failing to measure up. This situation forced the Labour Left to define more self-consciously than ever before its role as keeper of what it considered to be the party's conscience. Simply as a result of the political balance in Parliament, therefore, the period 1945–51 is among the most revealing in Labour's history and in what might be termed the intellectual history of the British Left.

Another factor enhanced its importance for Labour. The cold war fractured the alliance between communists and democratic socialists which had helped to defeat fascism. Grimly, inexorably, the world divided into massive, hostile blocs. In Britain, as throughout Europe, libertarian and Marxist socialists came into portentous collision.

The Labour Left, refashioned by this clash, took on its modern lineaments. The postwar Labour Party derives essential characteristics from that remaking. In this respect, too, 1945–51 were watershed years for Labour and the British Left generally.

The period has rarely been treated as such, however. Naturally historians of Labour's foreign policy during the postwar era have emphasized the duel with Stalin, the development of the Marshall Plan, the creation of NATO. These historical works pay scant attention to the evolution of attitudes within the Labour Party or Labour movement. Equally, diplomatic historians who have considered Labour's internal debates have tended to stress the negligible significance, or the questionable motives, of the left-wing critics. More recently, Alan Bullock has traced Foreign Secretary Ernest Bevin's patient and successful tutelage of the Labour Party in anti-communism. It is the partial burden of this study, however, to suggest that the Labour Left was both more important, and came to hold views more nuanced, than Bevin could accept or than Bullock records.[5]

Historians of the 1945–51 Labour governments, and even of the Labour Left itself, likewise either have minimized the significance and scope of left-wing disaffection with the government or have emphasized the political ascendancy of the Labour center and right wing. By way of contrast, this book seeks to place the Labour Left at the heart of Britain's postwar experience and to demonstrate that 1945–51 were crucial years for it and, therefore, for the party and the movement to which it belonged. The resignations from the government of Aneurin Bevan, Harold Wilson and John Freeman in 1951 because they objected to taxing the National Health Service in order to help pay for rearmament marked the culmination of the Labour Left's disenchantment with Attlee's administrations. Labour's subsequent history, notably the battles between Gaitskellites and Bevanites, unilateralists and multilateralists, "Europeans" and "little Englanders," Tribunites and Bennites, even perhaps Militants and Kinnock supporters, is rooted in that fatal fracturing.[6]

The main themes of this book, then, are the centrality of the Labour Left during 1945–51, the broad implications of its early postwar experience and its enduring, if ambiguous, significance.

II

The Labour Left has been a critical force in British politics since the foundation of the Labour Party in 1900. At that time there were three main socialist groupings in Britain: the Fabians, the Marxist Social Democratic Federation (SDF) and the Independent Labour Party (ILP). None of these were capable of competing with the two great established political parties, the Liberals and Conservatives. Indeed, the Fabians initially thought it more realistic to attempt "permeating" them with socialist ideas than to run candidates against them in elections. By the turn of the century, however, enough trade unions believed in independent labor representation to join with the socialist groups in a working-class political party. This was Labour. It did not adopt a socialist platform, however, because many trade unionists would not accept one, and therefore socialists constituted its left wing.[7]

The socialist wing of the Labour Party played a crucial role in the organization's early history. The ILP leader, Keir Hardie, became known as the "father of the Labour Party," because he provided the formulation which made possible its establishment. "Let us have done," Hardie intoned at the founding conference in 1900, "with every 'ism that is not Labourism." In 1901 the Marxist SDF concluded that this was not enough. It left Labour in pursuit of purer politics and after many splits and schisms eventually evolved into the British Communist Party. The ILP and the Fabians, however, were more constant. A member of the ILP, James Ramsay MacDonald, became Labour Party leader. Other Fabians and ILP members—Keir Hardie, Philip Snowden and Sidney Webb, for example—had influence on Labour Party policy out of all proportion to socialist numerical strength within it. They and others spoke for ideals with which Labour has been identified ever since: the brotherhood of man regardless of national frontiers, women's rights, the immorality and inefficiency of unrestrained capitalism and, often from a pacifist perspective, opposition to armaments and war.[8]

World War I greatly strengthened the socialist element of the Labour Party, although initially it seemed as though the war would have quite the opposite effect. A xenophobic wave swept the country. Keir Hardie died, of a broken heart, it was said. MacDonald was driven from his position as Labour Party leader, because he would not unambiguously endorse British participation in the conflict. The ILP, almost alone, stood out bravely against the nationalist tide. By 1917 the ILP was less isolated. The war of attrition on the western front horrified almost everyone. The Russian Revolution revitalized egalitarian and internationalist sentiments. The famous "secret treaties" which the Bolshevik regime discovered and published, and which a left-wing Labour newspaper edited by George Lansbury, the *Herald*, printed in Britain, seemed to make a mockery of everything British soldiers had thought they were fighting for. Although victory in war generated a second patriotic upsurge which Lloyd George, the Prime Minister, unscrupulously exploited during the 1918 "khaki election," it proved ephemeral. MacDonald was re-elected Labour Party leader. By 1922 almost all the old ILP-ers were back in Parliament. Labour had a future. Lloyd George did not.

Two developments during this period were of the utmost significance for the Labour Left. Their ranks had been augmented by a body of new recruits, former radical Liberals who opposed their party's position on the war and who, typically, joined first the Union of Democratic Control, an anti-war body, and then the Labour Party. These ex-radicals were a critical addition. Their internationalism, rooted in the old Gladstonian sympathy for "subject peoples struggling to be free," was as deep seated as that of the socialists. Their devotion to civil liberties was, if anything, stronger than that of many collectivists for whom social equality, not freedom, was the touchstone of belief. Ever since World War I old-fashioned radical liberalism has found a more or less congenial home on the left wing of the Labour Party.

Another consequence of the war proved even more significant for the Labour Left. It won the battle it had been fighting since the party's inception. Labour's constitution was rewritten so that its fourth clause finally committed the party to secur[ing] for the producers by hand or brain the full fruits of their industry and the most equitable distribution thereof that may be possible, upon the basis of the Common Ownership of the Means of Production and the best obtainable system of popular administration and control of each industry and service.

Since 1918 Labour has been one of the world's leading democratic socialist political parties.[9]

The new constitution was profoundly important to members of Labour's left wing and not only because it seemed to endorse their long-standing goals. Previously the Labour Party had made little provision for individual membership. Rather it had accepted affiliated bodies, for example trade unions and various socialist and professional societies. After 1918, however, the basis for a mass membership was laid. Local Labour parties were established in virtually every electoral district, and their members belonged to the national party. Although not appreciated at the time, this provision was bound to erode ILP influence in the Labour Party as a whole. The ILP sponsored its own parliamentary candidates, held its own annual conferences and issued its own programs, while attempting to convince the rest of the Labour Party to share its goals and personnel. It really was a "party within a party" and could be accused, legitimately, of acting like a competing organization. After 1918 militant socialists discovered increasingly that if they wished to influence Labour they could do so more effectively through their local parties than through the ILP. During Labour's periods of office, in 1924 and especially during 1929–31, the diminution of ILP strength was evident. Ramsay MacDonald, though still a nominal member of the ILP, ignored it. In 1932 the ILP despaired of influencing the party in a socialist direction, and voted to disaffiliate. Like the SDF in 1901 it chose the purer and perhaps psychologically satisfying but politically unwise path of "no compromise."

Nineteen thirty-two was a crucial moment in the history of Labour's left wing, teaching it a negative lesson. Although ILP militants argued that the decision to separate from Labour would spark a massive upsurge of popular radicalism which they could steer in a socialist direction, it led the other way—to a catastrophic lessening of ILP membership and effectiveness. A young MP from a Welsh mining district had foreseen this. "I tell you what the epitaph on you Scottish dissenters will be," Aneurin Bevan warned one ILP loyalist, his future wife, Jennie Lee. "You will be pure all right. But . . . at the price of impotency. I tell you," Bevan is reported to have said, striding back and forth in Jennie Lee's Guilford Street flat in London,

> it is the Labour Party or nothing. I know all its faults, all its dangers. But it is the party that we have taught millions of working people to look to and regard as their own. . . And I am by no means convinced that something cannot yet be made of it.

These words have served, ever since, as a sort of unofficial credo of the Labour Left.[10]

In order to avoid the political wilderness Bevan had predicted for the separatists, a group of Labour Party militants founded the Socialist League. This new organization was designed to carry on ILP traditions within the Labour Party. It had its own officers, membership and program, but no MPs. Still it ran into the same problems which had debilitated the ILP. Socialists who hoped to influence Labour now had to belong primarily to it, not to other organizations, however much these insisted that their purpose was to complement and not to criticize the parent body. In 1937 the Socialist League voted to disband. "This is not a funeral," one member argued in justification of the decision, "but a deliberate political tactic." The speaker was Barbara Betts, who as Barbara Castle became a prominent Labour leftist in the postwar period, a Bevanite and, finally, a Cabinet minister under Wilson.[11]

The dissolution of the Socialist League marked the end of an era. There never has been, since then, a formally constituted, organized, "loyal opposition" within the Labour Party.

III

During the interwar period, political discussion on the Left was dominated by two momentous issues: whether socialism could be achieved in Britain primarily by parliamentary means, and whether democratic socialists and communists could cooperate with each other. The first issue was fought out, primarily, before about 1935. The second, though significant during the 1920s, attained paramount importance after the Nazi seizure of power in Germany in 1933.

The Labour Left did not unanimously favor the parliamentary road to socialism during the early postwar period. Profoundly alienated by the "khaki election" because they believed that its results did not truly reflect public opinion, many left-wing Labourites demanded industrial action on behalf of political goals. They supported threats of a general strike in 1920 to oppose British intervention against the Russian Bolsheviks and, although it never was called, the famous "triple alliance" strike in 1921, on behalf of the miners who opposed decontrol of the coal industry. During the General Strike of 1926 and the lock-out of miners which followed, the ILP was conspicuously tougher than the Labour Party itself, both in the localities and in Parliament. During these years the "Red Clydesiders" James Maxton, John Wheatley and David Kirkwood, all members of the ILP, cemented their reputations for militancy, which they had earned as outspoken critics of the war.

Militants in the industrial wing of the labor movement were defeated during 1918–26. Yet the extra-parliamentary path to power which they and their PLP allies had broached was not completely discredited. This was because Labour's parliamentary experiences, especially during 1924 and 1929–31 when it formed the government, inspired deep suspicion.

In the first instance, Labour was the second largest party in the House, but the Conservatives, who had the most seats, did not command a majority. The Liberal leader, Herbert Henry Asquith, concluded that this was an opportune moment for Labour to form the government. Without Liberal support it could not pass legislation. MacDonald accepted the dubious honor of attempting to lead the country in these circumstances. Insisting that Labour must prove that it was "fit to govern," whatever that might mean, he ignored left-wing calls for the party to live up to its socialist constitution and program. Despite this moderate agenda, however, Asquith, the king-maker, withdrew Liberal support nine months later, and MacDonald's first Labour government fell ignominiously.[12]

Labour's second stint of "power," which coincided with the depression, was even worse. This time the government was overwhelmed by economic problems, the most important of which was unemployment. Again the Left pushed for a more radical and imaginative approach than either MacDonald or Snowden, who was Chancellor of the Exchequer, or J. H. Thomas, who was initially the responsible minister, was willing to contemplate. In the end, this triumvirate accepted Conservative-inspired suggestions for significant decreases in unemployment benefits and other programs for the poor. MacDonald resigned as Labour Prime Minister, only to reappear with the King's commission to form a "National government." This "betrayal" as many called it led to his expulsion from Labour. Snowden and Thomas were the only important party members to follow him.[13]

From this debacle many among the Labour Left concluded that the parliamentary road to socialism was at least as problematic as the extra-parliamentary one. At the heart of the ILP decision in 1932 to disaffiliate from Labour was its conviction that the disaster of the previous year could not be explained by reference to the apostasy of individuals and that it stemmed, in part, from the party's exclusive emphasis upon electoral politics. The Labour Party itself remained divided over the issue. A new generation of leaders had already begun to emerge—Clement Attlee, Herbert Morrison, Hugh Dalton—all of whom were strict parliamentarists. But Harold Laski, a professor at the London School of Economics and, after 1937, a member of Labour's National Executive Committee, warned that establishment forces might violently oppose a Labour government that carried out its election promises. John Strachey, in *The Coming Struggle for Power*, agreed. He and Laski were among Britain's most prominent left-wing intellectuals. Stafford Cripps, a wealthy lawyer and former member of the 1929–31 government, gained the greatest notoriety for predicting violent revolutionary struggle. The son of the great Conservative Lord Parmoor, Cripps foresaw Conservative counter-revolution if a determinedly socialist Labour government took power, and argued that such a government would be justified in taking sweeping emergency measures to protect itself.[14]

Prewar debates over parliamentarism continued to resonate during the postwar era. More relevant for the Labour Left after 1945, however, was the ongoing discussion about cooperation with communists. This issue had first divided Labourites in 1920 when Welsh and Scottish sections of the ILP briefly advocated membership in the communist Third International. The ILP rejected this proposal, but relations between communists and Labourites remained uncertain. When Lenin recommended that his British followers strive for revolution from within Labour's ranks, supporting the party "as a rope supports a hanged man," Labour's leaders determined to settle the matter permanently. In 1924 they persuaded the annual party conference to prohibit communists from membership. Many on the Labour Left, however, rejected this solution. During 1926-7 twenty-three CLPs were disaffiliated for refusing to expel communist members.

The issue of cooperation between the two wings of the Labour movement in Britain became supremely important during the 1930s when the communists, who in accordance with the 1929 "new line" had been denouncing democratic socialists as social fascists, reversed themselves and called for a popular front of all forces opposed to fascism. Left-wing Labourites who had withheld support from the earlier Labour Party ban on communists fervently embraced this appeal, while the Labour Party leadership, with equal vehemence, denounced the possibility of an alliance with representatives of a totalitarianism they found as loathsome as Hitler's.[15]

The Labour Left favored the popular front for a variety of reasons. For many the ban on cooperation with communists contradicted common sense. Communists were effective allies in the trade unions. Indeed often they had been effective allies in the Labour Party against what later became known as "MacDonaldism"—until they had been expelled. At any rate they were essentially on the same side of the great divide which separated the working class from its enemies. The Labour Left admired the agitation carried on by communists on behalf of the unemployed and believed that their party should cooperate in it. To the dismay of Labour's leaders, left-wing Labour members frequently participated in demonstrations organized by the communist-led National Unemployed Workers' Movement. Perhaps more important, the Labour Left agreed with the communists that only a popular front could effectively combat fascism both at home and abroad.

The Labour Left held a darker view of the National government than the party leadership did, especially after Chamberlain became Prime Minister. Such a government, according to Cripps, might slide into a sort of "country gentleman's fascism." Cripps was as much worried by Chamberlain's foreign as by his domestic policies. After 1935, when the pacifist George Lansbury resigned as Labour Party leader, Transport House favored rearmament so that Britain could deal with the fascists from a position of strength. Cripps and many others on the Labour Left, however, believed that the government might strike a deal with fascist leaders in Germany and Italy. British "neutrality" during the Spanish Civil War, which could not help but benefit Franco, seemed to confirm such fears. Therefore the Labour Left opposed giving weapons to Chamberlain on the grounds that they were as likely to be used against the international labor movement as against international fascism. The answer of the Labour Left to the threat of fascism was not rearmament, but collective security based primarily upon a strengthened League of Nations and alliance with the Soviet Union.[16]

Labour Left agitation for this alliance grew more intense, as the aggressive and insatiable nature of Hitler's regime became evident. The agitation was conducted primarily on two fronts. Cripps, Bevan and George Strauss, the Labour Member for North Lambeth, founded a newspaper, *Tribune* (which still exists), to press it in the country as a whole, while the Socialist League, during its brief existence, acted as spearhead for the campaign within the Labour Party. The party leadership, however, remained rocklike in its opposition. And the leaders commanded the big battalions. Labour's annual conferences, dominated by the trade-union bloc vote, decisively repudiated the popular front. In 1939 Cripps was expelled for continuing to speak from platforms on which communists were present. Bevan and Strauss, who had been expelled with Cripps, were readmitted only after promising to toe the line.

This unequal struggle was a formative political experience for the generation which constituted the postwar Labour Left. Michael Foot, Richard Crossman, Konni Zilliacus, Geoffrey Bing and Barbara Castle, to name only a few in the postwar Parliamentary Labour Party, Walter Padley, Bob Edwards and Jack Tanner among the non-communist left-wing trade-union leadership, and Laski and the Oxford don G.D.H. Cole among the intelligentsia affiliated with Labour, carried memories of the campaign for a popular front into the postwar period. From it they gained knowledge of the party hierarchy's power, but also of the methods and tactics of carrying on an agitation. The "class of '45," as Labour Members who entered Parliament in the first postwar general election often were called, gained their primary education during the 1930s.

They went to secondary school during World War II. Its impact upon them was at least as profound as the crusade for a popular front with the communists. Russian neutrality during the first year and a half of the conflict caused great bitterness on the Labour Left both at the time and during the cold-war era. During most of the war and its immediate aftermath, however, the Labour Left thought not of the Nazi–Soviet Pact, but of the Anglo-Russian alliance, which represented the popular front at government level and seemed to vindicate the Labour Left's earlier agitation for such an arrangement. Equally, the conflict confirmed many postwar Labour leftists "in the belief," as one of them put it, "that planning by the state was not only desirable but practicable." The history of the Labour Left during 1945–51 is, in large part, the history of its evolving attitudes towards these two ideals.[17]

Moreover, the experience of total war, and revulsion against the British politicians who so poorly prepared their country for it, led many Britons to support the Left generally. For once the Left rather than the Right could convincingly claim to wear the patriotic mantle. This reversal, unprecedented during modern British history, was encapsulated in the publication in 1940 of *Guilty Men*, a pamphlet pseudonymously co-authored by three radical journalists, one of whom was Michael Foot. The heroes of *Guilty Men* were Churchill and Lloyd George. In biting prose Foot and his co-authors contrasted the stature of these giants with that of the "pygmies" who, in keeping them from power during the interwar years, had left the country nearly defenseless against the fascists. Yet the Left was as much the beneficiary of the pamphlet as were the former and current occupants of 10 Downing Street. Labour's leaders and policies also had been ignored during the 1930s. Now Labour entered Churchill's coalition government. A wise move, it enabled Attlee and his lieutenants to prove, finally, that Labour *was* fit to govern. In the 1945 general election they reaped their reward.

During the war, however, the party's official conduct seemed tame to some. Left-wing activists called for an end to the political truce which went hand in hand with participation in the coalition. They demanded that a second front be established in western Europe to relieve pressure on Russia in the East, that the government commit itself to implementing the famous Beveridge Report, that civil liberties be maintained even during wartime. As the party leaders demurred, prewar divisions reappeared. This time the clash produced a new political party altogether, Common Wealth.[18]

The politics of Common Wealth were vague and inspirational. Members advocated a confusing and often contradictory mix of Christian, radical Liberal and Marxist principles and goals. The party appealed, above all, to middle-class "progressives" who looked forward to a new beginning in Britain and who believed in cooperative, selfless, ethical standards of conduct. Some left-wing intellectuals like Laski and Strachey were suspicious of the organization, because it lacked a theory of society and a working-class base. Nevertheless, like the ILP and the Socialist League, Common Wealth was a training school for the postwar Labour Left. Its founder, Richard Acland, became a Labour MP in 1947. Its general secretary and chairman, R. W. G. Mackay, gained entrance to the House of Commons as one of the Labour Members for Hull in 1945. Both Tom Driberg, an independent socialist standing in Maldon in 1942 and endorsed by Acland, and E. R. Millington, a Common Wealth candidate in Chelmsford, won their by-elections and later joined the Labour Party, becoming prominent on its left wing. Equally important were those among the rank and file who, radicalized and politically energized by the war, came to share Common Wealth's crusading socialist spirit. They supported the new party in by-elections that Labour refused to contest. When Labour finally repudiated the political truce at the end of the war, these new recruits tended to gravitate in its direction. Such men and women played their part in the party's great victory in 1945 and afterwards, in the Labour Left's struggle to push Attlee's governments along a more radical path than they wished to follow.[19]

IV

Who belonged to the Labour Left in 1945? How may their mental universe be described? The views and social composition of this critical force within the Labour Party will emerge in the body of the text. Nevertheless several fundamental and unchanging aspects of Labour's left wing deserve emphasis at the outset.

Most striking is the Labour Left's ideological heterogeneity. This single section of the Labour Party brought together socialist fundamentalists who had been inspired by Keir Hardie, Christians and pacifists in the mold of George Lansbury, former radical Liberals for whom, perhaps, the young Lloyd George was a model, trade unionists who had been influenced by the preachers of "direct action" immediately before and after World War I, and Marxists who admired Lenin and Stalin, or Lenin and Trotsky. Its own left wing included communist sympathizers (four of whom were later expelled from the PLP for being "fellow-travellers") and former ILP crusaders who were equally militant but objected to communist discipline and connections with Moscow. Its right wing was composed of pacifists who usually supported the party leadership, but whose objection to the use of force was based upon a powerful British tradition which authority ignored at its peril. The Labour Left brought together an array of dissenters, reformers and revolutionaries. It was more a "militant tendency" than an organized, disciplined movement.

Diversity of outlook was promoted by diversity of experience. In the constituencies, trade unions and even the PLP there were left-wing Labourites who remembered the struggle to found a national working-class political party before the turn of the century and who had attempted, once the party was organized, to push it in a more radical direction than its leaders favored. Others could recall the anti-war movement of 1914–18 and the industrial conflicts of the early 1920s. Many had participated in the prewar battle to establish a popular front between Labour and the communists against fascism, while yet another cohort had come to socialist politics during World War II. Age was rarely a factor in the divisions which beset the Labour Left after 1945, but each generation was capable of speaking with a distinctive voice. The slogans and rallying cries of earlier battles conducted by the Labour Left echoed and re-echoed during 1945–51.

Class differences further divided left-wing Labourites. The parliamentary combinations which they developed during the early postwar era usually lacked significant proletarian representation. A Labour Left Member of Parliament elected in 1945 was more likely to come from a middle-class than a working-class family. Michael Foot, Richard Crossman, Ian Mikardo, Stephen Swingler, Geoffrey Bing, Woodrow Wyatt, Leslie Hale and Konni Zilliacus, for example, were more typical of the postwar parliamentary Labour Left in this regard than say a working-class trade unionist like the pacifist Tom Scollan, who belonged to the National Union of Distributive and Allied Workers (NUDAW), or Fred Lee of the Amalgamated Engineers (AEU).

Middle-class preponderance was less overwhelming in the left-wing constituency Labour parties, although Chapter 7 will argue that Labour Left CLPs tended to have a disproportionately high number of non-working-class members. In some instances inter-class communication in left-wing CLPs may have been a problem. Coventry alderman Reverend Richard Lee, for example, had "worked in past days with the SDP [Social Democratic Party, as the SDF briefly called itself during 1910], the ILP and the SLP [Socialist Labour Party, a pre-1914 DeLeonite group] as well as the CPGB." Yet this devoted and experienced socialist could address the working class only from outside, complaining (almost from above) at one point that the "Socialist spirit" did not yet "permeate the mass of the workers. They have got to realise that in working for civic and State enterprise they are working for themselves and the common people." Compare this with the exhortation delivered by Ernie Roberts, president of the Coventry Amalgamated Engineers, to his "Fellow trade unionists, socialists and comrades that they urge that the things we at the bottom know to be necessary should be done." Roberts and Lee were equally prominent in Coventry during the early aftermath of the war as Labourites demanding a more resolute socialist program from Attlee's government. Yet they spoke nearly a different language.[20]

Roberts's role in Coventry underlines another point about the Labour Left in the early postwar era. Commentators tended naturally to concentrate on the highly visible activities of the Labour Left at Westminster. Yet Chapter 6 will argue that a non-communist left was powerful not only in Roberts's own AEU but also in the National Union of Railwaymen (NUR), the Chemical Workers' Union and the National Union of Distributive and Allied Workers (which amalgamated with the Shop

Workers and Journeymen Butchers' Federation in 1946 to become USDAW).

Divided as the postwar Labour Left was, its disparate experiences could also serve as a common resource upon which all might draw. "What has now become of [our] great pioneering enthusiasm?" a left-wing Labour Member who had participated in the movement's early struggles in Liverpool asked rhetorically in 1950. "Why are we not stepping forward with the old vigour?" And she answered herself: "I believe it is because the rank and file do not make the programme any more." In 1949 the relatively young Ian Mikardo (he was forty-one) wrote a pamphlet whose opening lines might have been composed by a working-class advocate of the "religion of socialism" half a century earlier: "Socialism is not a system of economics but a system of ethics, not a piece of machinery but a way of life. Its fulfilment depends . . . not merely on socialising things but also on a revolution in men's minds." Labour Left members consciously looked backwards for inspiration, as Mikardo did in his pamphlet. One could cite many similar appeals to the spirit of "the pioneers," and many additional examples of the postwar Labour Left speaking and writing in a language which would have been familiar to their forebears.[21]

No single person could claim to define the Labour Left vision of socialism, as I will argue in conclusion. Yet Mikardo's refusal to limit his definition of the great goal merely to state intervention on behalf of the poor or to government "planning," and his emphasis on the intangible aspects of socialism, were common among postwar left-wing Labourites, cutting across class boundaries and uniting trade unionists with former radical Liberals and members of Common Wealth. "Our cause includes at its very centre the outright preaching of the spirit of a new age," Richard Acland wrote in *Reynolds News* of 23 September 1945, upon joining the Labour Party. "We aspire to high ideals," NUDAW president Percy Cotrell reminded his union's annual conference at about the same time, "ideals in which beauty can play its part." To this Michael Foot made a crucial addition in a debate with communist leader Harry Pollitt. Democratic socialism must "combine the maximum of economic planning of the resources of the nation with maximum political and civil liberty." It was when the Labour government appeared to ignore these cherished convictions of the Labour Left that men like Foot, Cotrell and Mikardo began to voice the criticisms and alternative policies with which this book is concerned.[22]

Another fundamental precept shared by members of the Labour Left was that socialism could be brought to Britain only by Labour. "Looking down from the gallery on the crowded floor of delegates" to Labour's annual conference in 1944, Fenner Brockway, who had bolted the party twelve years earlier, finally concluded that Labour "was the movement of the common people of Britain from whom a changed society will come." Only personal loyalty to ILP leader James Maxton kept him from applying for readmission, and when Maxton died in 1946 Brockway quickly rejoined. Despite many criticisms of Labour's postwar performance, few on the Labour Left doubted the rightness of Brockway's position.[23]

Thus for all their diversity Labour Left members shared a heritage and a belief in the destiny of the larger party to which they belonged. Moreover the vexatious issues which soon would cause them to divide publicly and bitterly were not visible in 1945.

Rather, for the only time in history, the Labour Left was confident in the devotion of Labour Party leaders to socialism (which it did not trouble yet to define in any detail), optimistic about the continuation of a popular front with communists at home and abroad, and certain that reconstruction from the devastation of World War II would proceed along socialist lines not only in Britain but throughout Europe. In retrospect, the Labour Left in 1945 appears singularly naive.

And yet it was poised for its greatest victory. When, on 23 May 1945, Churchill announced the end of the coalition, the establishment of a temporary "caretaker government" composed of Conservatives and a three-week general election campaign with a polling date of 5 July (though results would not be announced until 26 July to give time for the collection and counting of service votes from overseas, and to take account of some local holidays), both the Labour Party and its left wing were better prepared and enjoyed greater popular support than at any previous time. Indeed, for reasons to be examined in Chapter 1, the Labour Left believed, during the spring and summer of 1945, that its hour finally had come.

Notes and References

1   In the 1935 general election Labour won 154 seats, Conservatives 387, National Liberals 33, Liberals 21.
2   Kenneth O. Morgan, *Labour in Power, 1945–51* (Oxford, 1984), pp. 3–4, 503.
3   *Sunday Pictorial*, 14 October 1951.
4   Richard Acland in *Reynolds News*, 23 September 1945.
5   Among the standard diplomatic histories: F. S. Northedge, *Descent from Power, British Foreign Policy 1945–73* (London, 1974); C. M. Woodhouse, *British Foreign Policy since the Second World War* (London, 1961); M. A. Fitzsimons, *The Foreign Policy of the British Labour Government* (Notre Dame, Ind., 1953); Terry Anderson, *The United States, Britain and the Cold War, 1944–47* (Columbia, Mo., 1981). Those which consider Labour's internal debates include: Michael Gordon, *Conflict and Consensus in Labour's Foreign Policy, 1914–65* (Stanford, 1969); Eugene Meehan, *The British Left Wing and Foreign Policy* (New Brunswick, NJ, 1960); Alan Bullock, *Ernest Bevin: Foreign Secretary, 1945–51* (London, 1983).
6   The two best and most recent histories of the 1945–51 Labour governments are Morgan, *Labour in Power*, and Henry Pelling, *The Labour Governments, 1945–51* (London, 1984). Historians who have considered the Labour Left include: Ralph Miliband, *Parliamentary Socialism* (London, 1972); David Howell, *British Social Democracy* (London, 1976); David Coates, *The Labour Party and the Struggle for Socialism* (Cambridge, 1975); Mark Jenkins, *Bevanism: Labour's High Tide* (London, 1979).
7   Among the many excellent studies of Labour's early period, see particularly Henry Pelling, *The Origins of the Labour Party* (London, 1954).
8   See F. Bealey and H. Pelling, *Labour and Politics, 1900–1906* (London, 1958), and Ross McKibbin, *The Evolution of the Labour Party, 1910–24* (Oxford, 1974), among others.
9   See, for example, G. D. H. Cole, *A History of the Labour Party since 1914* (London, 1948), and McKibbin, *The Evolution of the Labour Party*.
10   See Michael Foot, *Aneurin Bevan 1897–1945*, Vol. 1 (London, 1962), especially p. 147 for the discussion with Jennie Lee.
11   For the Socialist League, see, among many excellent studies, Ben Pimlott, "The Socialist

League: intellectuals and the Left,'' *Journal of Contemporary History*, Vol. VI, no. 3 (1971), pp. 12–39.

12   For the 1924 Labour government, see R. Lyman, *The First Labour Government* (London, 1957); for the events leading to its formation, see M. Cowling, *The Impact of Labour, 1920–24* (London, 1971).

13   See especially R. Skidelsky, *Politicians and the Slump* (London, 1967).

14   For Laski's views, see H. Laski, *The Crisis and the Constitution* (London, 1932); G. Eastwood, *Harold Laski* (London, 1977); Kingsley Martin, *Harold Laski, A Biographical Memoir* (London, 1953). For Strachey's, see Hugh Thomas, *John Strachey* (London, 1973). For Cripps, see Colin Cooke, *The Life of Richard Stafford Cripps* (London, 1957).

15   For the popular front, see, among many fine studies, Ben Pimlott, *Labour and the Left in the 1930s* (Cambridge, 1977, London, 1986).

16   Cripps, quoted in Miliband, *Parliamentary Socialism*, p. 220. For the Labour Left view, see, among many excellent studies, John Saville, ''May Day 1937,'' in Asa Briggs and John Saville (eds), *Essays in Labour History, 1918–1939* (London, 1977), pp. 232–340.

17   Woodrow Wyatt, *Into the Dangerous World* (London, 1952), p. 80. Wyatt soon began a slow drift to the Right which has led him, finally, to become an advocate of Margaret Thatcher.

18   For Labour during World War II, see, among many excellent studies: Foot, *Aneurin Bevan*; Angus Calder, *The People's War* (London, 1971); Paul Addison, *The Road to 1945* (London, 1977).

19   For Common Wealth, see Angus Calder, ''The Common Wealth Party, 1942–45,'' D.Phil. thesis, Sussex University, 1968.

20   *Coventry Tribune*, 15 May 1948, 1 November 1947, 20 September 1947.

21   Bessie Braddock in *Socialist Outlook*, June, 1950, Ian Mikardo, *The Labour Case* (London, 1949), p. 1.

22   BBC Written Archives, Reading, ''London Forum,'' 12 December 1947.

23   *Daily Herald*, 10 January 1947.

1

The Labour Left in the General Election of 1945

THE GENERAL ELECTION campaign of 1945 was among the most important of the century. It was the prelude to one of the great upsets in British political history. It registered the impact of the world's most destructive war upon a politically sophisticated electorate. It gave real power to the Labour Party for the first time. And it was a formative experience for the postwar Labour Left.[1]

Unsurprisingly, the campaign has been subjected to much expert scrutiny. In its immediate aftermath, two psephologists, R. B. McCallum and Alison Readman, recapitulated the main issues of the contest and summarized the points of view of the political parties which participated in it. Since then historians have delved more deeply into the underlying causes of Labour's unexpected victory. Naturally they have emphasized different factors in accounting for it, for example the "swing of the political pendulum," the importance of the service vote, even the ignorance of electors who thought they could vote Labour and yet retain Churchill as Prime Minister. Over the years, however, a general consensus has emerged. It owes much to Paul Addison's brilliant study of British politics during World War II, *The Road to 1945*. In his concluding chapter Addison argues that Labour's general election victory affirmed a new "Butskellite" consensus based upon Keynesian economic policies at home and collective security (mainly with the Americans) abroad. The new consensus had been forged during the war, experience of which converted a majority of the intelligentsia to belief in the virtues of "planning," and a majority of the working class to insistence upon government guarantees of vastly improved economic and social conditions, while convincing both sectors of the population of the need for collective security against dictatorships and the threat of war. To an extent all the main parties shared these ideals and aspirations in 1945, but because Labour espoused them most forthrightly it reaped its reward in the general election of that summer. In so doing it set the seal upon British politics for more than a generation.[2]

Helpful as previous work on the general election has been, we may push our knowledge further by focusing upon the Labour Left during the campaign. On the most basic level this helps fill a gap in the literature; since, despite its significant role during the contest, historians never have considered the Labour Left's impact. Moreover, the lessons and conclusions which many left-wing Labourites derived from the general election were to influence significantly their later behavior. In fact, when one views it in the refracted light of subsequent Labour Left disillusionment with Attlee's governments, the 1945 election takes on new meaning. That light endows the campaign with a poignancy and irony missing from other accounts. It makes a more nuanced interpretation of this crucial event possible. The paradox of 1945, as I hope to demonstrate, is that it set the stage for Labour's great achievements under Attlee's Prime Ministership—but also for Bevan's climactic Labour Left rebellion of 1951.[3]

II

The background to the general election is uncontroversial, but there is one point of significance which often has been forgotten. The flat-out contest for supremacy between Labour and Conservatives which took place during the campaign might not have occurred, had it not been for the Labour Left.

When Churchill announced the general election neither he nor a majority of his Cabinet wanted an end to the political truce that had been more or less in effect in Britain since the beginning of the war. Most of the Labour ministers continued to hope that the coalition government would remain in power at least until victory over Japan had been won; not knowing of the atomic bomb, they thought this victory might take several years to achieve. That Labour fought the general election not to improve its position against the Conservatives in the coalition, but in hopes of achieving outright victory, was largely a result of pressure emanating from the party rank and file, most forcefully articulated by Harold Laski, Aneurin Bevan and Emanuel Shinwell, representatives of the Left on Labour's National Executive Committee. They convinced Herbert Morrison and William Whitely, Labour's chief whip in the House of Commons, that the party would not accept continued coalition government. Attlee, Bevin and Dalton, who argued to the contrary, were outvoted at a meeting of Labour's National Executive Committee. Thus the most successful general election in Labour Party history was due in part to a victory of the rank and file, and of the Labour Left, over the party leaders.[4]

There is general agreement about the course of the campaign. Labour was quickest off the mark, having been meeting in annual conference while the decision was being made to terminate the coalition. Labour candidates fanned out into the constituencies with the exhortation of retiring party chairman Ellen Wilkinson ringing in their ears, "Fight clean, fight hard, and come back with a solid majority for a Labour government." Once the campaign was on, the leadership, though it doubted victory, showed no signs of its previous indecision. The Conservative leadership, which, if anything was suffering from over-confidence, appeared at least equally determined. Churchill made a notable, if rash, intervention in a radio broadcast of 5 June, predicting that a Labour victory would lead to Britain being governed by a socialist Gestapo. This and other charges he leveled during the campaign—for example, that the Post Office savings of the poor would be jeopardized if Labour won—generally are held to have been counter-productive. On the other hand, many observers believed that his cross-country auto tour was a triumphal progress. If Churchill the party leader was not universally admired, it seemed that Churchill the national symbol and great wartime statesman was.[5]

A critical moment in the campaign came on 15 June when Churchill invited Attlee to accompany him to Potsdam for the pending Three-Power talks. Harold Laski, who had replaced Ellen Wilkinson as chairman of Labour's NEC, intervened. If Mr Attlee attended the conference, Laski warned, he should do so only as an observer: "The Labour Party and Mr Attlee can hardly . . . accept responsibility for agreements which . . . will have been concluded by Mr Churchill as Prime Minister." This was the first Labour Left intervention in the campaign to receive national publicity.[6]

Laski's statement provided the Conservatives with two openings which they were quick to exploit. First they pointed out that the professor, although a member of Labour's executive, was not responsible to the general electorate. Thus his presumed directive to Attlee, the party leader, was evidence that an undemocratic caucus controlled the Labour Party. If Labour should win the election, it would control Britain too. Secondly, they held that Churchill's position at Potsdam would be weakened if it became known that Britain was divided over foreign policy. Therefore, Laski's comments had been unpatriotic.

When they have written about this episode and its immediate aftermath, historians have agreed unanimously that Attlee used it to show that Labour would not abandon the principle of "continuity in foreign policy" and to demonstrate the dismissive manner with which he would confront pressure from Labour's left wing. At the same time Attlee chided Tories for their ignorance of his party's constitution. In a series of public letters to Churchill, he argued that the NEC had no power over the party leader in such matters. He accepted the Prime Minister's invitation: "There seems to me to be great public advantage in preserving and presenting to the world at this time that unity on foreign policy which we maintained throughout the last five years." The discrediting of Laski, it generally is held, could not have been more complete.[7]

The basis for the common understanding of this incident seems to be, first, the Labour government's traditional approach to foreign policy after the general election and, second, the famous last line of a private letter which the new Prime Minister sent to Laski on 20 August: "a period of silence on your part would be welcome." It is tempting to read back into June 1945 tensions within the Labour Party which became explicit only later. No doubt they were implicit at the time. But people interpret politics mainly on the basis of some kind of public record. On that basis a reasonable person (especially of the Labour Left) could have concluded that neither Attlee nor the party leadership had repudiated Laski's doubts about Conservative foreign policy. In fact, it would have been reasonable to think that they had been endorsed.

Laski opposed "continuity in foreign policy," on the grounds that the approach of a socialist party to international affairs must be different from that of the Conservative Party. Later the Labour Left fiercely criticized Attlee's Foreign Secretary, Ernest Bevin, for following the main lines of Churchill's traditional foreign policy, rather than embarking upon a new "socialist" one. Like any other phrase, however, "continuity in foreign policy" was subject to more than one interpretation, perhaps especially during that politically charged summer. A close reading of Labour campaign speeches suggests that in June and July 1945 the phrase could have held connotations quite the opposite of what eventually became its generally accepted meaning.

The three most publicized elements of the coalition's foreign policy had been total defeat of the Axis powers, alliance with America and the Soviet Union and support of a new and powerful United Nations Organization to keep peace after the war. During the summer of 1945 Labourites often maintained that a purely Conservative government would be unlikely to continue striving for a strong UNO or close relations with Russia. They even suggested that total victory could not be assured if the "men of Munich" were returned to power. In this context the meaning of "continuity in foreign policy" is far from clear.

Its ambiguity seems most obvious with regard to Anglo-Soviet relations. As Tom Braddock, Labour candidate for Mitcham and a future critic of the government's anti-Soviet alliance with America, put it in his election address, "It is impossible not to see that Russia is unpopular with big business cartels and monopolies, and with the Tory Government. It is only natural that it should be so. Russia is not run for the profit makers." Under Labour, Braddock predicted, Great Britain would not be run for profit either. Labour, then, was better qualified than the Conservative Party to maintain the coalition's policy of friendship with the Soviets. The party leadership agreed, explicitly and on numerous occasions. Here is one instance taken from many— Stafford Cripps, who recently had rejoined the party and immediately catapulted to the top, speaking at Oxford on 26 June:

> We must have a progressive, forward looking Government if we are to enter into the reconstruction of Europe hand in hand with the Soviet Union. Mr Churchill's and Mr Eden's policy has been good, but it has been the outcome of a Government of all parties. It would be a completely different proposition were we to have a Tory Government in power.

Which party, then, was opposed to "continuity in foreign policy"? Already on 23 June the *New Statesman* had concluded that "if there is a breach in the continuity of the policy of good relations with Russia, it is far more likely to come from a Tory administration" than from Labour.[8]

It was not only with regard to Russia, however, that such conclusions about continuity could be drawn. For example Attlee argued vigorously for maintaining coalition support of UNO which, according to him, the Conservatives might abandon. This was also the burden of Philip Noel-Baker's BBC election broadcast on 18 June. Before the war, he argued, Conservatives had weakened the League of Nations. Only with the advent of Labour in the coalition government had support for UNO and the principle of collective security become a major theme of British foreign policy. Ernest Bevin, too, seemed to argue on the BBC that "continuity in foreign policy" meant continuation of Labour's ideals, including support of UNO, which Churchill and the Conservatives might jettison. "I repeat," Bevin declared, "the foreign policy being pursued at the moment was devised by the Coalition Government, not by the Tory Members alone but by a combined effort, and is based upon collective security, a policy for which Labour has always stood." Such statements, though emphasizing the tripartisan nature of the coalition's approach to international affairs, were by no means necessarily repudiations of Laski's warnings about continuity. It all depended on what was being continued. Laski himself, while reiterating that "the Socialist Party has principles different from Tory policy," professed himself content with these and similar Labour pronouncements.[9]

What, then, of Attlee's reaction to Churchill's attempts to pin him down on the "continuity" issue? On 16 June, as we have seen, he informed the Prime Minister that he hoped to maintain "that unity on foreign policy" which had characterized party relations during the war. He then added:

> I do not anticipate that we shall differ on the main lines of policy which we have discussed together so often. I understand, of course, that responsibility must rest with the government, but I take it that we should consult together upon the issues that arise in order to present a policy consonant with the views of the great majority of the people of this country.

Laski's response to this statement should be noted. "Now that the sphere of responsibility has been defined the position is entirely satisfactory."[10]

In retrospect it is clear that the professor was indulging in wishful thinking. But the question is what Labour supporters and particularly the Labour Left might have thought *at the time*, and thus what Labour's electoral victory meant to them. We must not read cold war tensions and suspicions of the Soviets among rank-and-file Labour voters into the Britain of 1945. Perhaps the Russian threat and the overriding need to maintain friendly relations with America were the issues which, in fact, Attlee and Churchill had "discussed together so often." In June or July 1945, however, it would have been reasonable to infer from Attlee's statements that, during the war, the coalition government had carried out a foreign policy to which Labour had made a distinctive contribution, and that he was attending Potsdam to ensure that it continued to do so.

At the close of the campaign, Attlee responded again to Churchill over the "continuity" issue:

> it is obvious that a Labour Government will follow a policy in accordance with the principles in which it believes, and on which its members in the House of Commons have been elected . . . The fact that in the late Government members of all parties were in accord on the main lines of our foreign policy does not alter the fact that the complexion of the new House of Commons will decide the course of future policy.

This seems almost an explicit endorsement of Laski's argument that Labour would strive for different international objectives than the Conservatives. Attlee's meaning hinges upon the phrase, "main lines of our foreign policy." In retrospect, we can see that he may have meant suspicion of Soviet intentions, the need to maintain a "special relationship" with the United States and continuation of Britain's world role. These, in fact, became the principal themes of Labour's foreign policy. At the time, however, an intelligent voter could reasonably have thought that Attlee meant complete victory over fascism, development of the UNO and the maintenance of friendly relations with America and the Soviet Union. This *was* the conclusion reached by the *New Statesman* on 14 July. According to its editor, Kingsley Martin, the Three-Power meeting would provide Attlee with an opportunity to "indicate what continuity of foreign policy will really mean if interpreted in terms of 1945," namely, the "evolution from inter-Allied war planning to inter-Allied planning for reconstruction." Far from opposing Attlee's presence at Potsdam, then, the Labour Left had come to endorse it.[11]

All accounts of this episode have emphasized Laski's utter defeat and repudiation by Attlee. In fact, the Labour Left had reason to think that the party leader had come to Laski's support. It was satisfied, not unhappy, with the outcome of this incident.[12]

Of what else did the Labour Left believe a "socialist foreign policy" would consist? Again, Laski was prominent in formulating objectives. He believed that World War II was not primarily a defensive struggle of the democracies against rapacious fascism, as commonly was maintained. Rather, in his opinion, it was a positive revolutionary war in which the European working classes could succeed, finally, in defeating capitalism. The primary aim of a British Labour government, therefore, must be to establish friendly relations with new, revolutionary regimes, where they had already taken power, and to aid revolutionary movements in those countries where victory had not yet been achieved. During the general election this became a common Labour Left theme. Konni Zilliacus, a former staff member of the League of Nations in Geneva who now was standing for Labour in Gateshead, said:

> Throughout Europe the resistance movements . . . are largely under Socialist and Communist leadership. Their reconstruction programmes are based on sweeping advances toward Socialism . . . Only a British government friendly to Socialism can join effectively in making peace in Europe.

The young Denis Healey, soon to be appointed Labour's international secretary, concurred. As he told Labour's annual conference at Blackpool in 1945, "The Socialist revolution has already begun in Europe and is already firmly established in many countries in Eastern and Southern Europe. The crucial principle of our own foreign policy should be to protect, assist, encourage, and aid in every way that Socialist revolution, wherever it appears."[13]

In these sentiments, too, the Labour Left thought it heard agreement in speeches of the party leadership. Cripps was, perhaps, most explicit. As he explained at Oxford, "If we are to have any hope of a peaceful reconstruction of Europe it must be on the basis of the Left Governments that are arising in Europe today." He professed to be "terrified of the result if the old Conservative clique got back into power." He had not forgotten —nor, Labour candidates made certain, had the electorate—Churchill's counter-revolutionary zeal after 1917. "Was there not a danger," Cripps asked an audience in Cardiff, "that a Tory Government would try to reimpose the reactionary governments which would endanger the whole reconstruction of Europe?" There is no evidence that the Labour leadership sought to restrain this sort of rhetoric, despite its implication that, unlike the Conservatives, Labour would support foreign revolutionaries. Perhaps the most famous line to come from Labour's annual conference in 1945 was Bevin's, "Left understands Left but Right does not." This was commonly understood to mean that a Labour government could work more easily and productively with the Soviets and other European left-wing governments and movements than the Conservatives. Bevin encouraged this assumption again, on 26 July at Central Hall, Westminster, where his audience was composed of Labour MPs from the metropolis and outlying areas. Expecting Attlee to appoint him Chancellor of the Exchequer, he described how, as master of England's finances, he would assist every anti-fascist organization in Europe (including the communists) which had contributed to the defeat of Hitler, thus completing the socialist revolution launched on the Continent in the anti-Nazi resistance. He received an ovation.[14]

One does not want to go too far with this line of reasoning. It is not meant to suggest that Labour's leaders held revolutionary sentiments in 1945. On the other hand, one can see that the Labour Left had grounds for thinking that the party leadership shared its main foreign policy goals. In that case, however, the Butskellite consensus of 1945 appears problematic. At the least, different wings of the Labour Party might read different meanings into their great electoral victory. The Labour Left in 1945 was mistaken, but it had reason to suppose that its government would cooperate with the Soviets and with continental revolutionary movements in reconstructing Europe on a socialist basis.[15]

III

The Labour Left attitude towards the party's domestic program likewise was based upon mistaken, but hardly groundless, expectations. Before the opening of the election campaign it had greeted the party platform with restraint. *Let Us Face the Future* was a "well written, simply worded document," according to the *New Statesman*, "embodying a clear, if limited policy of immediate objectives." Such judiciousness, however, did not survive Churchill's rapid and unexpected conversion from national to Conservative Party leader. The Prime Minister's "Gestapo" charge, and the attack upon Laski, even upset some of his own party. "Who could tell," Robert Boothby queried Kingsley Martin, "that Winston would descend to such unfathomable depths?" Among the Labour Left the response was an almost instinctive rallying behind the party leadership and a natural inclination to identify its own attitudes with those of the party as a whole.[16]

Polarization between the two main political parties led the Labour Left to accept, perhaps uncritically, a belief in the epochal nature of the contest. As one Labour Left candidate, Dr Santos Jeger of South-East St Pancras, put it, "It is not a simple question of Box replacing Cox. We have to settle by our votes who is to control the wealth and resources of Britain and in whose interests." In Wales, Aneurin Bevan was sharper.

The election was, in his view, "a real struggle for power . . . between Big Business and the People." This was the line taken by the leadership to which Bevan soon would be promoted. As Herbert Morrison, the number-two man in the party, after Attlee, put it on 29 June on the BBC:

> The election is about who is going to organise the producing power of our country, and how, and for what ends. It's about whether a great national plan can win the peace as it won the war, or whether the speculators, the buccaneer barons of Fleet Street, the sluggish leaders of big business, monopolies and cartels, are to sit comfortably—on our backs—for another shameful period of national decline.

Given the circumstances of the campaign, for Morrison to pose the antithesis so starkly may have suggested to the Labour Left that he favored measures more radical than the party leadership usually advocated.[17]

This reading of the leadership's intentions may have prompted Labour candidates to voice assessments and aspirations which, probably, the party's highest officials neither shared nor intended to fulfill. "I believe," said Stanley Awberry, Labour candidate for Bristol Central, that "the time has arrived for the present economic and social system to be entirely changed." Richard Acland, speaking on behalf of the Common Wealth Party but already on the verge of joining Labour, spelled out on the BBC what such a transformation would mean:

> All the resources of our country, the banks, the land, the mines, railways, insurance companies, shipping lines and all substantial industries and factories of any kind, must cease to be owned by big business and must be owned by all of us in common; run to meet the human needs of the many, not to make the profits of the few.

This, of course, went beyond Labour's official program. The Labour Left was confident, however, that eventually its party would enact such measures. As Walter Monslow put it in Barrow-in-Furness:

> Only a complete Socialist transformation of society can solve the economic problems of our age. . . We can no longer patch and tinker . . . A Socialist government with the firm backing of the common people will introduce Socialist measures that would pave the way for a new classless society from which poverty and insecurity would be forever banished.

Perhaps such predictions appear utopian or naive to a later generation. They seemed to many in 1945, however, to follow from the terms in which Labour's leadership approached the general election in the first place.[18]

Throughout the campaign, Labour Party leaders expressed themselves in language which the Left could reasonably consider its own. It was not, as often has been argued, simply "planning" which the leadership endorsed (and which Liberals and some

Conservatives advocated as well) but, seemingly, the socialist promise of democratic control of the economy. Attlee himself was capable of warning:

> if the community did not control the powerful economic forces . . . it would be controlled by them. The fight for economic freedom had yet to be won. The control over men's lives by great trusts and combines could be as oppressive as the rule of the barons in the past.

What did Attlee mean by "community" control and by "economic freedom"? Perhaps nothing more than that government-appointed boards should direct certain important industries. This, after all, is what eventually happened. Taken in conjunction with the statements of other party leaders at the time, however, it was possible to think he had more radical plans. Hugh Dalton, Attlee's future Chancellor of the Exchequer, predicted that under Labour the mines would be "owned by the people and conducted in the interests of the country as a whole, with the miners themselves taking a full share of the responsibility for the control of the industry." Emanuel Shinwell, Attlee's future Minister of Fuel and Power, agreed: "We are working on details of coal legislation so that a Labour Coal Minister should not depend on Civil Servants, but should have the benefit of the ripe experience of those men who know the industry."[19]

Such rhetoric, although vague, must have encouraged less well known Labour candidates likewise to speculate upon the forms which "economic freedom," as Attlee had called it, might take. To cite one example, R. W. G. Mackay, the Labour nominee for North-West Hull, asserted:

> Under common ownership, and working within a broad national plan, the direction and administration of industry will be decentralised into the hands of local communities, and of the workers and technicians within the factories. Only thus can democratic cooperation replace bureaucratic red tape and control.

Other Labour Left candidates were content merely to reiterate basic socialist principles. For example, "What was produced in the country should be distributed fairly among the people . . . and people should work together for one common purpose instead of being forced to compete with one another." Whether detailed or simple, however, such predictions of the cooperative society which a Labour government would build seem as far removed from the supposed Butskellite consensus of 1945 as may be.[20]

With so much apparently at stake, the pitch of electioneering became extreme. "If the nation has to give marching orders to big business," Morrison warned in his 29 June BBC address, "the nation must give them. . . Big business has got to toe the line of public need—and the phrase is—got to." One senses in such rhetoric appeals not merely to class consciousness, which were common on the Labour side during the campaign, but perhaps even to the possibility of overt class conflict. Why else did Morrison choose a semi-military term, "marching orders," and implicitly threaten to use force if "big business" refused "to toe the line"? Listeners on the Labour Left who were hungry, perhaps, for such language can be excused for thinking that the party leadership intended more far-reaching measures than it ever enacted, and that there could never be consensus between Labour and Conservative. Labour Left candidates, at least, drew such conclusions. In Liverpool the redoubtable Bessie Braddock refused to shake hands with the Lord Mayor "or with any of them—none of the Conservatives" and promised, if elected, to represent only the working people of her district and "no business interests." In Chippenham the Labour candidate, Andrew Tomlinson, advised British soldiers in Greece to turn on their Tory officers and mutiny, this being "the only logical action left to them."[21]

Again, one does not wish to exaggerate the militancy of the party leaders, although it appears that some on the Labour Left did so and felt free to express views far beyond anything the leadership could support. At the same time, left-wing Labourites were able to discern, in the speeches of Attlee and the others, a transforming socialist vision of which previously they had claimed custodianship. In this manner were planted the seeds of future alienation.

IV

After the votes had been counted and the full extent of Labour's victory became known, the party's left wing was jubilant. There had been no time for disillusionment. Believing, as Kingsley Martin wrote in the *New Statesman* of 28 July, that "the country has voted for Socialism," they assumed that the party leadership shared this interpretation of its mandate, and would fulfill it. Geoffrey Bing, the victorious Labour Left candidate in Hornchurch who had campaigned on a platform of "straight-out Socialism," assured local supporters that "the policy of the Labour Party would be put into force without delay. There was not going to be any soft pedalling of the programme." Moreover, he declared confidently, "his conscience and Labour Party policies would never come into conflict." Harold Laski, in an interview with American correspondent Edward R. Murrow, predicted that Labour was going "in a straightforward and orderly fashion to socialise the ownership, stage by stage, on a carefully considered plan of priority, of the vital instruments of production upon which the life of this nation depends."[22]

Emrys Hughes concurred: "The things that Keir Hardie stood for have now become practical politics." Hughes, who had to wait six months until a by-election in Ayrshire gave him an opportunity to join others on the Labour Left in Parliament, could only "rub my eyes and wonder whether I am asleep or awake" when he arrived. What pleased him most was "recognizing ever new faces of personalities who were prominent in the old ILP." That party, it will be recalled, had bolted from Labour in 1932, claiming that the larger organization was not sufficiently socialist. Now hoping to stem the flood of members like Hughes who had quit to rejoin Labour, it petitioned unsuccessfully to reaffiliate. Members of Common Wealth were following Hughes's example. Soon after the votes had been counted in July, its founder, Richard Acland, applied to Transport House. As he explained in *Reynolds News* on 23 September, he still believed that "all the great resources of our country . . . and every substantial industry and factory . . . must be owned . . . by the community as a whole." But he added, "I believe that since the election, the effective growing point for one hundred per cent Socialism is inside the Labour Party and not elsewhere."[23]

The Labour Left believed that it had been empowered by the election victory. Historians such as Henry Pelling have argued that Attlee's Cabinet appointments were cautious and conservative. Perhaps so, yet the Labour Left rejoiced when men and women with whom they had identified in the past—Aneurin Bevan, Emanuel Shinwell, Stafford Cripps and Ellen Wilkinson—were invited to join. In *Left News*, Victor Gollancz noted that the new government was composed mainly of former Left Book Club authors (Attlee, Cripps, Wilkinson, Bevan, Strachey, Noel Baker and Lord Addison) and that the back benches too were well populated with men who had written for him during the 1930s (Foot, Edelman, Elwyn Jones, J. P. W. Mallalieu, Swingler, Zilliacus). To many this must have represented a revolution of sorts, at least in the sense that the old establishment had been blasted from power and its former critics elevated instead. In such unprecedented circumstances what was not possible? Laski entertained hopes of being appointed British ambassador in Washington. Sydney Silverman, the veteran ILP-er and Labour Member for Nelson and Colne since 1935, imagined that he might be made a junior minister in the Home Office. He was supported by Shinwell, who mentioned his name to Attlee. Barbara Castle, George Wigg, J. P. W. Mallalieu and Donald Bruce, all of whom had been active on the Left during the prewar popular front agitation, were chosen as parliamentary private secretaries.[24]

Amid the rejoicing on the Labour Left, a few notes of caution, or even of misgiving, might be heard. In Huddersfield the victorious candidate, J. P. W. Mallalieu, held an impromptu rally when the results of the poll were announced: "an open air meeting of 10,000 people. As I spoke the voice of an elderly man kept coming from the crowd, repeating the age old fear of the British working class: 'Don't let us down, lad! Don't let us down!'" Fred Longden, Labour Member for Deritend in Birmingham, voiced the opposite fear, that the party was in advance of the rank and file: "People have not voted for us because they are socialists conscious of what they are doing. I know very well that most people voted Labour from fear of the interwar years being repeated." And in *Reynolds News* on 12 August, Tom Driberg, the former independent Member for Maldon who represented it now for Labour, commented unenthusiastically on Attlee's Cabinet choices, "On the whole it is a Government of the Right rather than the Left of the Labour Movement." Amid the celebrations, however, such voices were barely audible. And even their owners attempted to still these small doubts. Driberg believed the Labour Right dominated Attlee's government, "but it is well balanced politically as well as in other ways, and deserves the staunch support of all socialists."[25]

V

Thus the Labour Left during the summer of 1945, "English Socialism's blissful dawn," as Michael Foot called it many years later. Even its shrewdest and most cautious champions believed that the party's election program had constituted "a direct challenge to . . . capitalist society." Indeed, it had. For better or worse, Labour was in 1945 "a socialist party and proud of it," as its campaign manifesto proclaimed, and as this chapter has attempted to demonstrate. Doubtless left-wing Labourites indulged in wishful thinking when they heard or read the speeches of Attlee, Morrison, Dalton, Shinwell and others. They interpreted the famous Laski incident as not a repudiation of the Labour Left but an endorsement. They thought that a Labour government would maintain the best aspects of coalition foreign policy and reconstruct Europe along socialist lines. On the home front they predicted that it would take control of the "commanding heights of the economy," as Bevan was to call them some years later, and not merely extend state responsibility for the provision of welfare, but also make possible true "economic freedom" as Attlee had called it, by which they meant democratic control of the economy at all levels.[26]

It should be apparent, then, that the compromise of 1945, if one may be said to have existed at all, was not between the Labour and Tory parties. No Butskellite compromise had been conceived yet. The term "Butskellism" had still to be invented. The compromise took place on the left wing of the Labour Party and consisted of an unspoken agreement among Labour leftists to accept a generous interpretation of the leadership's pronouncements and program.

Later the Labour government appeared, to the Labour Left at least, to be practicing policies which did not amount to "socialism." Then left-wing Labourites claimed, with some legitimacy, that the leaders had abandoned the path which they themselves, in concert with the Labour Left, had charted and foretold in June and July 1945. Since that magic summer the Labour Left has regarded it as a talisman of the party's commitment to socialism, and as a model of how a socialist political campaign should be run. What made later disappointments so grievous was that there was more than a grain of truth in this interpretation. Perhaps hidden differences existed during the campaign within the Labour Party itself. But the gulf which separated Bevanites and Gaitskellites only a few years later did not yet exist. In 1945, for once, the party leadership said more than enough to satisfy the Labour Left.

Notes and References

1   It is true that the polls predicted a Labour victory, but few people paid attention to them. Churchill predicted a Conservative majority of more than sixty seats. See Henry Pelling, *The Labour Governments 1945–51* (London, 1984), p. 27. He adds that "most political observers expected . . . the Conservatives and their allies would have a lead in the end." On the Labour side, Dalton foresaw "either a small Tory majority or deadlock." Chuter Ede, Bevin and Bevan thought Churchill would be unbeatable. See Kenneth O. Morgan, *Labour in Power, 1945–51* (Oxford, 1984), p. 39. Strangely enough, it appears that among Labour Party notables only George Strauss and Harold Laski believed Labour would win the election. See Kingsley Martin, *Harold Laski, 1893–1950, A Biographical Memoir* (London, 1953), p. 172.

2   R. B. McCallum and A. Readman, *The British General Election of 1945* (Oxford, 1947); Paul Addison, *The Road to 1945* (London, 1975), p. 280. "Butskellism" was a term coined during the 1950s to suggest the similarity of economic policies followed by Labour Chancellor Hugh Gaitskell and Conservative Chancellor R. A. Butler. Other works

which have treated the 1945 general election from the same perspective include: Morgan, *Labour in Power*; Pelling, *The Labour Governments, 1945–51*; Pelling, "The 1945 general election reconsidered," *Historical Journal*, Vol. 23, no. 2 (June 1980), pp. 399–414; Angus Calder, *The People's War* (London, 1971). Calder criticizes the Labour Party precisely for establishing the new consensus.

3 Calder's account, *The People's War*, comes closest to this perspective.

4 For the split within the Labour Party over the timing of the general election, see Pelling, "The 1945 general election reconsidered." Pelling does not mention Laski. However, *The Times* of 25 June 1945 quotes Randolph Churchill: "It is notorious that at the Blackpool Conference last month Professor Laski was among the most assiduous in forcing Mr Attlee and his colleagues to leave the Government."

5 Wilkinson is quoted in McCallum and Readman, *British General Election*, p. 132.

6 *The Times*, 15 June 1945.

7 Morgan, Pelling and Addison take this view. *The Times*, 16 June 1945.

8 File on Tom Braddock compiled by the editors of the *Dictionary of Labour Biography*. I am grateful to Dr Joyce Bellamy and Professor John Saville for opening the *DLB* to me. *The Times*, 26 June 1945.

9 *The Times*, 5 July 1945. For other statements by Laski, see ibid., 15 June, 16 June, 20 June 1945.

10 Ibid., 16 June 1945.

11 Ibid., 3 July 1945.

12 See, particularly, Kenneth Harris, *Attlee* (London, 1982).

13 For Zilliacus, see Labour Party papers at Walworth Road, 1945 general election file; *Labour Party Annual Conference, 1945*, p. 114.

14 *The Times*, 26 June, 18 June, 2 July 1945. For Bevin's Central Hall speech, I am indebted to John Platts Mills, who sent me a private letter describing it; also to Ernest R. Millington, then the sole Common Wealth MP, who granted me an interview and also described the effect of Bevin's speech.

15 According to Platts Mills and Millington, after Bevin finished his speech he turned his back on the audience and winked hugely to the other party leaders waiting on the platform for their turn to speak. The two backbenchers could see this because they sat close to the front and at an extreme angle from the stage. They concluded that Bevin had been insincere.

16 *New Statesman*, 19 May 1945; Sussex University, Kingsley Martin papers, Box 11, Correspondence, Robert Boothby to Martin, 7 July 1945.

17 For Jeger, see Labour Party 1945 general election file. Bevan is quoted in McCallum and Readman, *British General Election*, p. 113.

18 For Awberry and Monslow, see Labour Party 1945 general election file. For Acland, see *The Times*, 30 June 1945.

19 Attlee, quoted in *The Times*, 22 June 1945; Dalton, *The Times*, 28, June 1945; Shinwell, *The Times*, 1945.

20 For Mackay, see British Library of Political and Economic Science, Mackay papers, 25/6; *Hornchurch, Dagenham and Romford Times*, 13 June 1945.

21 Millie Toole, *Mrs Bessie Braddock* (London, 1957), p. 126. For Tomlinson, see Labour Party, NEC minutes, Vol. 91, p. 71, 28 February 1945. The NEC forced Tomlinson to retract this statement.

22 For Bing, see *Romford, Hornchurch and Upminster Recorder*, 3 August 1945. For Laski, *Daily Herald*, 2 August 1945.

23 For Hughes, see *Glasgow Forward*, 12 January 1946.

24 *Left News*, September 1945. Silverman's aspirations are recorded by Emrys Hughes in *Sydney Silverman, Rebel in Parliament* (London, 1969), p. 89.

25 Mallalieu recorded this incident in *Sunday Pictorial*, 23 March 1947. Longden is quoted in the *Labour Pacifist Fellowship Bulletin*, November 1945.

26 *New Statesman*, 2 June 1945.

2

The Labour Left on Russia and America

IN NO RESPECT was the contradiction between the Labour Left and the rest of the party sharper than with regard to foreign policy, though amid Labour's victory celebrations in July and August 1945 this was not yet apparent. The conflict—which, when it came, was about nothing less than the shape of the postwar world—was eceptionally revealing: first, for the light it cast upon problems faced by all modern democratic socialists; second, for the insights it provides into the history of the Labour Party, both before and after 1945. While much has been written about Labour's postwar foreign policy, however, relatively little attention has been paid to the men and women in the Labour Party who opposed those policies, or to the impact which their failure to change them had upon the British Left or upon the Labour Party itself. Yet, arguably, the defeat of the Labour Left approach to foreign affairs during the half-decade after World War II was among the most important episodes in the history of British Labour. It will be traced in the following two chapters.[1]

The root of the conflict over international affairs between the Labour Left and the government was this: the Labour Left fervently believed that a Labour government's foreign policy would be based upon socialist principles and, therefore, must be qualitatively different from the foreign policies practiced by Conservative governments. A Labour government would work for socialist reconstruction of a world devastated by war. It would aid revolutionary movements in Asia and Africa. Believing that the concept of a popular front of socialists and communists had been vindicated during the war, the Labour Left assumed that a Labour government would undertake these tasks in concert with Russia. Finally, as a result of the Labour Party leadership's handling of the "continuity issue," during the general election campaign, the Labour Left was confident that the Prime Minister and Foreign Secretary shared these views.

Perhaps in July 1945 the party leaders agreed that Labour's foreign policy would be fundamentally different from Churchill's. Against this, however, may be set their experience of wartime inter-party collaboration and their exposure to problems of government which most of them never had faced before, or had faced only briefly. These seem to have suggested to the handful of Labour leaders who belonged to the coalition Cabinet that Britain's long-standing world interests transcended party-political differences, however sharp they might be over domestic matters. Perhaps, in the heat of a general election campaign, Attlee and the others had been unaware of their own conversion or had been unable or even unwilling to articulate this new approach to international affairs. Confronted from the moment they reassumed office with a host of complex problems and flashpoints demanding British action in one form or another, however, they acted upon the new approach—and not upon their campaign rhetoric. In retrospect, the new government appears surprisingly predisposed to view foreign crises in traditional terms; which is to say, usually as threats to long-standing British interests.

No doubt Foreign Secretary Ernest Bevin was feeling his way in 1945. He hoped to reach an accommodation with the Soviets based upon something more than mutual fear. He believed already, however, that Stalin, while not wanting another world war, wanted the fruits of war; and very early on he came to discern the Soviet hand in nearly every challenge to the status quo, whether in Europe, Africa, Asia, the Middle East, or even Britain itself. He was convinced that Russian power would flow into any crack or crevice which the West failed to stop up. In order to maintain a balance of power (and as Bevin's biographer, Alan Bullock, has pointed out, Britain had fought two world wars in thirty years to do so), Bevin intended now to frustrate Russian expansionism, as he perceived it, wherever the United Kingdom possessed sufficient strength. As the limits of British power became increasingly apparent, Bevin sought to persuade America, whose support he craved above any other country's, to fill Britain's traditional role.[2]

In 1945 Labour Left attitudes towards Russia, America and left-wing movements in which Russia might have some influence were different from Bevin's. Of course, the Labour Left never was a homogeneous group. Even at the climactic moment of Britain's common victory with the Russians over Hitler there were some on the Labour Left, like George Orwell, who could not forget the Nazi–Soviet Pact and the conflict in Spain between communists and anarchists. For most Labourites, however, such memories were less vivid in the immediate aftermath of the war than they were in 1951, when cold-war tensions had reduced Russia's outright supporters in the PLP to a tiny, isolated and defensive minority. A sea-change occurred during those years in Labour Left attitudes towards the Soviets. Meanwhile a similar process, in reverse, took place with regard to Labour Left views of the United States. In 1945 most on the Labour Left were extremely suspicious of America; by 1951 a majority probably supported US foreign policies. Historians have never subjected this momentous transformation in the outlook of the Labour Party to detailed scrutiny, no doubt because it seems an inevitable and obvious by-product of the cold war. In fact, the evolution of Labour Left views towards the new superpowers represents a watershed in Labour Party history which deserves examination in its own right. Moreover, it was a more complex and difficult process than has been appreciated. The hesitations, doubts and heart-searchings which the clash between Russia and America prompted on the Labour Left constitute a crucial aspect of the history of the postwar era and continue, even today, to affect Labour Left perceptions and activities. They form the subject of this chapter.[3]

II

In 1945 the Soviet Union found favor in Britain not merely among many on the Labour Left but also among what probably was a majority of the British public. Russian fortitude during the war was widely admired. As one successful left-wing Labour candidate, Geoffrey Bing, put it in a typical election speech, Russia was "a socialist country which had saved itself and the world during the war." In fact, nearly every Labour candidate (and many Liberals and Conservatives) made friendly references to the Soviet Union during the electoral campaign. They were common currency then.[4]

When pressed, however, even the most Russophile Labour Members were prepared to admit that "Communism had assumed very harsh and dictatorial forms in the USSR." Perhaps, therefore, in 1945 it was gratitude for Soviet wartime heroics which induced a certain tolerance for Russian failings. Harold Laski, whose 1942 pamphlet, *The Secret Battalion*, had excoriated British communists and their Soviet masters, now thought that "it would be something akin to a miracle if, after the tortured history of fear and suspicion and Nazi occupation, Russian rulers exhibited the habits which have become almost second nature to members of the House of Commons." Feelings of guilt may also have played a role. Thinking, no doubt, of socialist refusals to join an anti-fascist popular front during the prewar era, *Tribune*'s editors declared on 4 May 1945, "So far the Russians have a contempt for the Socialist Parties of Europe and no one can honestly blame them." Now, *Tribune* maintained, the Labour Left should bend over backwards to conciliate the Soviets. The editor of another influential non-communist left-wing journal concurred; Kingsley Martin, of the *New Statesman*, wrote privately to Victor Gollancz, "The worst service one can do is to add to the uninformed or malignant hatred which is waiting to burst out against the Soviets."[5]

During the summer and autumn of 1945 the Labour Left had no doubt that a popular front with Russian and European communists was the necessary prerequisite to a peaceful and prosperous new world. As Martin put it on 29 September in a front-page article in the *New Statesman*:

> The main hope of the future is for Britain and the Soviet Union to develop with the liberated countries of Europe—all necessarily moving towards Socialism—a common policy of economic welfare with integrated transport and social services for the whole continent.

Such cooperation would also be a powerful lever for political advance. Zilliacus believed that "only through unity of action between Socialists and Communists ... can the workers hold power in Europe." Moreover, as Aneurin Bevan put it in *Tribune* on 3 August 1945, "Friendship with the Soviet Union is the keystone of world peace."[6]

The Labour Left remembered that Russia had been invaded from the West once by the French in the nineteenth century, twice by the Germans in the twentieth and, during 1918–20, by the British, French, Americans, Japanese and Poles combined. Bevin, who had encouraged British dockers to strike in 1920 rather than to load the *Jolly George* with munitions to be used by Poland against Lenin's new regime, did not need reminding of Russian history. He was unsympathetic to Soviet fears of renewed invasion, however, and hostile from the outset to their attempts at creating a protective buffer zone of states, which he viewed as an offensive rather than a defensive strategy. Not so the Labour Left, at least initially. As Bevan had written for *Tribune* on 7 April 1944:

> It is quite natural and inevitable that Russia should influence preponderantly the life of nations immediately on her borders, and that she should seek to prevent them from combinations that may be aimed at her. That is the price we have to pay for the bitter recent past.

It was over the form which that postwar "preponderant interest" began to take, and the methods by which it was established, however, that Labour Left misgivings about Russia, dormant during the war, started to resurface.

There were in the Labour Party unabashed defenders of Soviet moves in Eastern Europe, the Balkans and the Middle East. For example, Leslie Solley concluded in a speech of 6 October 1945, "the actions of the Soviet Union are not motivated by imperialistic designs or the desire to act as a predatory power. She is doing what she is in the interests of the working classes of the world." John Platts Mills, Labour Member for Finsbury, endorsed this judgment even after the communist seizure of power in Czechoslovakia three years later. It had been, he explained to the press, "a working class victory," and "a great defeat for Mr Bevin." In July 1946 Konni Zilliacus neatly reversed Bevin's assessment of the source of turmoil in the world: "The Russians are desperately anxious to be let alone, to be free to concentrate on their terrific internal problems." It was the American and British refusal to cooperate with the Soviets which was producing "economic and social disintegration, sheer starvation and chaos."[7]

The number of Labour MPs who were prepared to echo such statements, however, declined markedly over time. We may leave aside the small group within the parliamentary Labour Left whose positive attitude towards the Soviet Union underwent no significant evolution during 1945–51, since we will treat them in Chapter 5. More significant, both at the time and historically, were the vast majority on the Labour Left who were driven, often reluctantly and a step at a time, to take up anti-Soviet attitudes nearly indistinguishable from those of Ernest Bevin.

In this important but difficult process, four weekly newspapers of the Labour Left played a prominent part. They have been quoted extensively above. One was *Tribune*, which had close ties to the government. Perhaps this helps to explain the line which, eventually, it took. After all, Bevan, Cripps and Strauss, who had helped to found the newspaper in 1937, were now, or soon would be, Cabinet ministers; Jennie Lee, a *Tribune* editor and the Member for Cannock, was Bevan's wife; and Michael Foot, another editor and now the Member for Devonport, was one of Bevan's close friends. Foot, in fact, was close enough to the government at this stage to write a weekly column for Labour's official organ, the *Daily Herald*, in addition to editing *Tribune*. This did not prevent him, or other *Tribune* staffers, from criticizing the government, or from holding it to what they considered to be a strict socialist standard. Perhaps, however, it helped to make the journal quick to defend the government from its foreign, and especially its Soviet, critics.

The second Labour Left newspaper was Kingsley Martin's *New Statesman*. It was not as organically linked to the Labour Party as *Tribune*, though Martin's chief lieutenant at this time was Richard Crossman, the Labour MP for Coventry East, and others connected with the weekly included Labour MPs then associated with the left wing of the party; for example, Stephen Swingler, Woodrow Wyatt and Maurice Edelman. Where *Tribune* was required reading for left-of-center Labour Party activists, however, the *New Statesman* appealed equally to independent leftists associated with Common Wealth, the ILP or even, in 1945, the Communist Party. It was a journal, not a newspaper, more rarefied and intellectual in tone than *Tribune*.

The *Glasgow Forward* was another non-communist left-wing weekly newspaper. Its editor, Emrys Hughes, did not enjoy a high reputation either among the party leaders or even among his colleagues on the left wing of the parliamentary party. Attlee referred to him with some contempt during the South Ayrshire by-election in January 1946, which Hughes won for Labour, and Stephen Swingler once wrote that "everyone likes Hughes but no one takes him seriously." These judgments notwithstanding, one reads Hughes with growing respect. A veteran member of the ILP, he held no brief for communists or the Soviet Union. (He had publicly criticized the Russian prewar show trials.) Nevertheless his columns in the *Glasgow Forward* represent a sustained and intelligent critique of Bevin's approach to the Soviets. If they were repetitive and emotional, they were also honest and, in many ways, prophetic. "If we are going to have this millstone a large army around our necks," he wrote in September 1945, "where are we going to find the money for housing, education, better health services and all the other things that people will expect (and rightly so) from a Labour Government?" That is the question which led, finally, to the climactic Labour Left rebellion in 1951.[8]

Reynolds News, official organ of the Co-op Movement, was a fourth weekly newspaper whose editors and columnists were on the Labour Left, although the Cooperators were not otherwise known for holding left-wing views. Harold Laski (who also wrote a weekly column for the *Glasgow Forward*) and numerous other left-wing Labourites contributed on an occasional basis. Tom Driberg wrote for it regularly.

Far from concerting a "line," these four newspapers competed with each other for readers and influence. It was a rare wind that blew through the Labour Left which did not rustle the pages of at least one of these journals. It is possible, therefore, to trace in their columns, as nowhere else, the evolution of Labour Left attitudes towards the Soviet Union.

Tribune was the first of the Labour Left weeklies to sound an anti-Soviet warning. Initially it had been critical of Bevin's close cooperation with the Americans and of his hostile approach to the Russians. When in January 1946 Soviet delegates at the UN criticized British policies in Greece, however, *Tribune* leaped to Bevin's defense. Previously it had charged that the results of British policy in Greece were "the one-sided disarmament of the left . . . the imprisonment without trial of thousands . . . a government . . . supported by none but the Royalist parties." Now it dismissed the

```
(WX827B) CONSOLIDATED PICK SLIP          02/24/89
*-LOCATION-*
54-803-04

*-QTY-*      *- -  T I T L E - - *        12649067
    1     LABOURS CONSCIENCE TH LABOUR LFT 45 5

*-EDITION-*   *-PUB-*    *-AUTHOR-*   *-PRICE-*
    TXT        UNWIH     SCHNEER,       45.00

B&T NBR.--    746350
TYPE---REG
*- BATCH -*
    014
                              STATION---  54

*- P/L NBR. -*
    52
```

Russian critique, which, it claimed, really had been motivated by fear and jealousy. If British Labour succeeded in bringing about the socialist transformation peacefully, then "the Soviet Union might have to face a competition for international attraction from a country which is neither capitalist and reactionary, nor Bolshevik, but the champion and pathfinder of democratic socialism." It was this sort of visceral response which came to characterize *Tribune* articles during the cold-war period.[9]

If simple loyalty to the Labour government was one factor in the evolution of *Tribune*'s anti-Soviet outlook, abhorrence of Russian practices was another more powerful one. As the victors of World War II commenced to jockey for postwar advantage, Tribunites, and indeed most of the Labour Left, became convinced that Russian policies were more selfish, ruthless and unprincipled than the policies of the other great powers. Of course, this was a dawning conclusion, but it dawned earlier in some quarters than in others. As early as 1 March 1946 Foot was writing in *Tribune* that, because of Russian pressure,

> the agreement on the reconstitution of the Bulgarian Government was never put into force . . . In Poland the Communists have successfully blackmailed the Socialists into agreeing to joint electoral lists . . . In Yugoslavia men like Subasic, who promoted the idea of cooperation with Britain as well as with the Soviet Union, have been dropped . . . In East Germany . . . by a mixture of intimidation, terror, censored propaganda and despicable tricks the Communists have achieved control of all life in the Russian zone.

On what basis could there be collaboration between democratic socialists and the authors of such practices? Foot was rapidly coming to the conclusion that there could be none. Hopes of a postwar popular front with the Russians and various communist parties were naive, dangerous and inappropriate.

Other Labour Left journals were much more hesitant, at first, to take this line, or to accept these conclusions. Martin's friend and a frequent author of *New Statesman* articles, the writer and radio broadcaster J. B. Priestley, returned from Russia in November 1945, "appalled, horrified, terrified to discover the amazingly rapid growth of anti-Soviet feeling here." His editor-in-chief agreed. Although originally Martin had welcomed Bevin's appointment as Foreign Secretary because he thought him to be "one of the few men tough enough to reform the Foreign Office," now he held the former head of the Transport Workers' Union to be primarily responsible for the rapidly changing political climate. "What is to be done about Ernest Bevin?" he asked angrily in March 1946, at almost precisely the moment that Michael Foot, in *Tribune*, was defending the Foreign Secretary from the Russians. Five months later, after consulting with members of a Labour Party delegation who recently had returned from Moscow, Martin concluded, "With patience and generosity of outlook there is no problem between Russia and Britain that is insoluble, though the road may be long and difficult."[10]

In the *Glasgow Forward*, Emrys Hughes, likewise, continued to hope for Anglo-Soviet cooperation. Even in the rosy afterglow of the Allied defeat of Hitler he held no illusions about the Soviets. "What does Russia need," he asked on 6 October 1945, "to cease to become a nightmare to the rest of us and to settle down to the work of reconstruction so urgently necessary after the havoc and devastation of war?" His answer, pressed as urgently at the height of the cold war as in the comparative warmth of 1945, however, was the antithesis of Bevin's or Foot's. In Hughes's opinion Russia needed, above all, "relief from the fear of another attack from the West. . . Until some great gesture comes from Britain and America . . . her fears will continue." Hughes then carefully added, "That is not to say that we should act as stooges for Stalin, or excuse and justify every Russian diplomatic move." Hughes also differed from Foot, Martin and, indeed, most of the Labour Left in trying to imagine how British policy must appear to the Soviets. His conclusions were not flattering. "To the Russians," he wrote in June 1946, "our foreign policy looks very much like a continuation of the old Imperialism."[11]

Hughes's most notable regular columnist was Harold Laski, the author for the *Forward* of a weekly "London Letter." Possibly no one better expressed the Labour Left outlook on foreign affairs than this donnish, owlish figure. Certainly no other individual so clearly reveals how overwhelming the impact of disillusionment with the Soviets could be, especially when it was coupled with a parallel process of growing disenchantment with the Labour government. During the first two or three years of peace, Laski's hopes for socialist reconstruction based upon the unity of socialists and communists were first deferred and then shattered irretrievably. And Laski's experience only encapsulates that of the Labour Left as a whole during the early postwar era.

At first, however, as we have seen, Laski's expectations knew no bounds. Like the rest of the Labour Left, he assumed that the basis for Anglo-Soviet and socialist-communist cooperation had been laid during the war. Like Martin, he greeted Bevin's appointment as Foreign Secretary with enthusiasm. It "opened up exciting vistas," he wrote in the 19 August *Reynolds News*, because, as he noted in the *Forward* some months later, "Mr Bevin realises that Anglo-Russian friendship is an elementary necessity for both countries." During the summer of 1946, while *Tribune* was publicizing "Soviet threats and . . . abuse," Laski was reminding readers that

> Russia has suffered the immense invasion its rulers had always predicted, and its cost has been literally overwhelming. The price of the Russian victory may be fairly put by saying that another generation will not only have to mourn its dead, but also will have to continue to accept the immense sacrifices all Russians have experienced since 1917 . . . the old nightmare of the "anti-Bolshevik crusade" of 1919 casts a shadow over the whole Russian mind.

When later communists accused the Labour Left of undying, unyielding anti-Sovietism, they conveniently ignored such articles as this.[12]

As for *Reynolds News*, it too remained unimpressed with Bevin's increasingly belligerent approach to the Russians or with *Tribune*'s conversion to it. And yet one begins to find in its columns the glimmerings of doubt about Soviet policies and practices which, much heightened, virtually the entire Labour Left eventually came to share. For example, in an article of 17 February 1946, Lyall Wilkes, the Member for Newcastle-upon-Tyne Central, who had parachuted into Greece during the war and fought side by side with the partisans, launched a slashing attack upon the government for betraying the ideals of the Resistance. He believed that Russian criticisms of British policies in the Eastern Mediterranean were mainly justified. On the larger question of Anglo-Soviet relations, however, he thought that they would never be improved

> by concessions on one side alone. The violently anti-British tone of Russian wireless propaganda, the veiled territorial claims on Turkey, the refusal of the British invitation to help supervise the Greek elections . . . have now endangered that good will between us on which depends the world's peace.

This was a specific list of Russian errors, but increasingly the general tone of Wilkes's article was to be found in other Labour Left publications. They resisted Bevin's outlook; but they were growing ever more suspicious of the Soviet Union. The process of disillusionment had begun.

It was most visible in the columns of Harold Laski, perhaps because he most visibly struggled against it. Yet even as early as 17 November 1945 Laski was listing "Questions to Molotov" in *Forward* which the Russian Foreign Secretary cannot have welcomed.

> Are there any more territorial adjustments desired by Russia? If so what are these adjustments and on what grounds are they sought? . . . If Russia is entitled to make a series of treaties economic or political with States which it regards as friendly to itself, why is not Great Britain entitled to make a series of treaties on a similar basis? . . . Why is the formation of an Eastern bloc by Russia unexceptionable while the formation of a Western bloc is to be regarded as a threat to the peace?

An earlier article had underlined the essential dividing line between socialist and communist which the Labour Left, Laski included, increasingly feared to be unbridgable. "Socialists of the Left have no more regard for the virtues of the one party state when Russia imposes it" than when non-interventionist Western governments allow "its continuance in Spain and Portugal," Laski wrote on 16 March 1946. "The deep sympathy of Socialists with the high aims of the Russian Revolution does not mean a blind admiration for whatever Russia does."

Yet before June 1947 it seemed to many on the Labour Left that whatever their distaste for the policies of Russia it was more than counterbalanced by their equal dislike of the policies of America. Later in this chapter we will examine the evolution of Labour Left attitudes towards the United States. Here we may say only that the Labour Left approach to the Soviets was transformed, in part, by an American initiative, Secretary of State General George Marshall's speech at Harvard University raising the possibility of massive US aid to war-torn Europe, not necessarily excluding Russia and other communist countries.

The European Recovery Plan, as it was called originally, has never ceased to be the focus of controversy. Some have seen the plan as an unparalleled example of altruism in international affairs, others as a machiavellian device for assuring that there would be European markets under American control for American exports, still others as the means by which the United States, knowing that the Soviets could never accept such an offer, split the social democratic and communist Lefts in Europe which had seemed to be on the verge of reconciliation, thereby assuring the dominance of the anti-socialists. Ernest Bevin, however, did not hesitate. He wanted to take advantage of Marshall's offer immediately, whatever had motivated him. The ensuing series of events greatly accelerated the process of realignment on the British Labour Left which ended in the isolation of a tiny minority of pro-Soviets and a drastic weakening of those who, while reluctantly anti-Soviet, remained suspicious of the Americans.[13]

Whatever one's opinion of the Marshall Plan, no one doubts that it placed the world in the melting-pot. Future chapters will explore Labour Left views of the economic and political ramifications of Marshall's offer. Here we are concerned only with how it affected Labour Left attitudes towards the Soviets.

In retrospect it is obvious that Moscow could neither participate in the Marshall Plan nor allow the Eastern European countries under its domination to participate, without ceding the political initiative to America. At the time, however, the Labour Left thought otherwise. Foot wrote in Tribune on 20 June:

> Then, into the midst of this world of darkened hopes, tedious wranglings and cut-throat competing strategies, came a new offer: the offer of a fresh start: one which presented the chance to Britain, France, the Soviet Union and the United States of honourable association in the work of bringing sustenance to the hunger-stricken peoples of this tragic postwar epoch. This and nothing less is the meaning of the Marshall Plan.

And he warned, in another article, "If the Russians . . . contract out, then they alone will be the architects of a divided Europe."[14]

Others on the Labour Left took a less strident approach, while agreeing with Tribune that Marshall's speech opened intriguing possibilities. If, however, there were "unstated principles of exclusion in Mr Marshall's mind, the application of which is . . . intended to produce a divided Europe" or a "Western bloc," then British participation should not be taken for granted. The warning was Laski's in the Forward for 21 June. The New Statesman of the same date agreed: "Britain has everything to gain from the Marshall proposal, if it matures, on condition that she does not break her . . . contacts with Eastern Europe." Thus the Russian response to the plan became the crux of the matter for the Labour Left. Would Soviet ministers attend the meeting of European nations convened in Paris on Bevin's initiative to draw up a united response to Marshall's offer? Hoping, perhaps, to exercise such influence in the Kremlin as he may have possessed, Laski wrote:

Russian statesmen owe this cooperation to their friends all over the world . . . If the Marshall plan is no more than a new road to American domination . . . much the best way to expose it is to present the American Government with a reasonable and well articulated plan on which European Governments are united. The test of American good faith then becomes the terms it asks for accepting the plan.

It is known that Laski often exaggerated his influence in the Labour Party and, indeed, on the international scene. We may take his claims with the proverbial grain of salt. He had, however, been part of an official Labour delegation to Moscow the previous year, enjoying a private audience with Stalin. It was this which led him to believe that he had a role to play at this crucial juncture in world history. "I have been busy with Ernest Bevin and Morrison over Marshall's offer," he wrote to his close friend, the American Supreme Court Justice Felix Frankfurter:

> With just that shade of luck it is almost too much to hope for, I may—very much only may—have got Moscow to assign Maisky to the job of the discussions here. If it comes off I shall feel that I ought to be given at least a Congressional medal of honour. But at least I got the Poles and Benes and Tito all to press for this; and the Big Cheese himself actually wrote to me about it.

This last claim, that Laski had received a letter from Stalin, seems exceedingly unlikely. Years later Martin, who was writing a "biographical memoir" of Laski, agreed in correspondence with Frankfurter that there was no evidence to support it. Yet Laski's general approach to the Marshall Plan and his hopes for Soviet acceptance of it, tempered by his suspicion of American motives, were at least as typical on the Labour Left, at this stage, as Tribune's uncritical acceptance of the offer. Certainly Laski's concluding line in his letter to Frankfurter encapsulates the Labour Left outlook of late June 1947. "I feel," he wrote, "like someone hanging onto a cliff's edge by a hair."[15]

His hopes soon were dashed. The Russians attended the discussions in Paris, but sent Molotov as their chief negotiator, and he quickly denounced the Marshall Plan ostensibly because it "violated national sovereignty." More or less reluctantly the East European countries followed suit; perhaps the Russian refusal meant that Stalin would offer them advantageous trade agreements by way of compensation. Now the Labour Left in Britain had come to a fork in the road. For the first time it could not avoid choosing sides in the rapidly polarizing world which was putting paid to all the hopes of 1945. Even the Labour Left, which understood and sympathized with Russian objections to the plan, found it difficult to support the Soviet decision to oppose it.

Not surprisingly, Foot condemned the Soviets most emphatically. Marshall dollars would make possible.

> a centrally organised plan in which the claims of national sovereignty would be abated. That is what Socialists have long prayed and worked for. Does a Soviet veto

and the rigid Soviet insistence on the rights of national sovereignty transform this ideal into an imperialist plot?

Kingsley Martin developed a different critique of the Soviet position. As he explained at a UDC conference on "The Drift towards World War III," the Russians had blundered in pulling out of the plan. Had they stayed in, the US Congress never would have voted funds for it. "Then Russia could have taken the lead in planning Europe's recovery on Socialist lines." Moreover, in refusing to participate, the Russians had "really drawn the line across Europe." Their decision on the Marshall Plan, as much as anything the Americans had done, was responsible for the division of the world into rival power blocs, and thus for the cold war.[16]

The two most influential Labour Left journals had undergone a decisive shift in their attitudes towards the Soviets. Even now, however, there remained important voices on the left wing of the Labour Party which resisted blaming Russia for splitting Europe. Fenner Brockway, for example, was

> quite sure that America never contemplated Russia's participation . . . I am told that in all his London talks with British Ministers, Mr Clayton of the American State Department proceeded on the assumption that Russia would exclude herself from the Plan.

Yet Brockway was certain, too, that "no international Socialist can endorse Molotov's plea at Paris for the retention of national sovereignties in Europe in economic matters." For his part, Laski remained broadly sympathetic to Russian suspicions, if regretful that they had not been suspended, if only to test American sincerity. Still, in his opinion, the "decision to proceed without Eastern Europe" was more responsible for dividing the world into antagonistic blocs than Russia's decision to stay out of the plan. He wrote privately to Frankfurter:

> I wish I could share Bevin's ardent faith in the Marshall offer. But I think it was done in the wrong way, that it was badly timed, and that it has been set in a perspective which opens ugly horizons . . . I know with all the mind I have that Russia cannot make war, does not want to make war, would be broken by war. All that American policy does is give an ever deeper impression of deliberate provocation, of making ideological conflict where there need be none, of self-righteousness which is almost as infantile as the propaganda of Moscow.

Yet this was the position of a minority. The attitudes of Martin and Foot were more important, highlighting a gradual shift taking place among the critics of Bevinism. Richard Crossman, who, as we shall see, played a crucial role on the Labour Left, wrote, "I have often criticised Bevin . . . Now . . . he has seized the initiative . . . He can . . . lay the foundations of a real peace—in spite of Mr Molotov."[17]

Thus, by their reaction to the Marshall Plan, the Russians lost an important round to the Americans in the contest for Labour Party support. Against its wishes and deepest instincts, the Labour Left was being driven into the arms of Ernest Bevin.

III

Events in Czechoslovakia dramatically hastened this process. There were two reasons for this. Firstly, the Labour Left felt a moral obligation to defend Czechoslovakian democracy because in 1938–9 British appeasers had betrayed it. Secondly, the Labour Left believed that postwar Czechoslovakia was one country in which democratic socialism really worked. As Laski reported enthusiastically in the *Forward* on 10 May 1947 after a visit to Prague:

> If ever I saw a really democratic commonwealth I saw it in Czechoslovakia. . . This . . . is a really free people. . . There is the fullest freedom of discussion. . . Religious freedom is complete . . . The mixed Government of Communists, Social Democrats and National Democrats works together surprisingly well.

Consequently, when events threw Czech democratic institutions into jeopardy once again, the Labour Left reacted strongly.

The Czechoslovakian crisis took shape in early 1948. The twelve non-communists in the Cabinet resigned, ostensibly because eight high police officials in Prague had been replaced summarily by communists. In reality this was their last move in a larger campaign they had been waging to avert a general communist takeover, which itself seemed likely as a result of increasing East–West tensions. If the division of Europe did occur, it was obvious that Russia would never permit Czechoslovakia to side with the West. The non-communists who had resigned from the Cabinet hoped that general elections, which they were confident of winning, would now be called. However, the resignations backfired. There being thirteen members of the Cabinet remaining, a quorum still existed, so that Premier Clement Gottwald could continue legally to govern. No elections were necessary. Moreover, with an end to socialist and liberal opposition, Gottwald could proceed with the consolidation of communist power. This was achieved during February.[18]

So far as *Tribune* was concerned, communist activities in Czechoslovakia were ruthless, brutal and without justification. Moreover they confirmed to the hilt *Tribune*'s previous warnings about the Soviet Union. As reports from Prague trickled into London, Foot thought they proved that the Russians were "finally resolved to stamp out all opinions and political activities except those of their own partisans . . . They have shown they are out for complete control wherever they can get it. Czechoslovakia is the latest example of this strategy." Having survived one despotism, Europe now was threatened by another. A popular front was indeed necessary, but in opposition to communists, not with them. They had betrayed the democratic promise of socialism. They falsely argued, according to Foot, that "there is only one road to the goal of a socialist society . . . that Force must be employed; criticism must be banished; democracy must be suppressed; dictatorship enthroned." Confronted with this "fraudulent parody" of Marxism, democratic socialists must seek a common front even with American anti-communists in defense of freedom. Foot was well aware of the irony of this reversal in his outlook. In stark contrast with his buoyantly optimistic

columns of 1945, when he had recalled Wordsworth, now   he   quoted
Heine: "Wild, gloomy times are upon us." But he evinced no doubts. "The threat
of war today comes not from the United States but from the Soviet
Union."[19]

The *New Statesman* was less strident in its reaction to events in Prague, but most of
its conclusions were similar. Martin dispatched Richard Crossman to attend the funeral
at Larney of Jan Masaryk, the Czech Foreign Minister whose recent apparent suicide
was said to have been caused by despair at the communist triumph. Crossman was
accompanied by George Wigg, the left-wing MP for Dudley and PPS to Emanuel
Shinwell at the War Office. According to Tom Driberg, writing on 7 March in
Reynolds News, Foot and Donald Bruce, the MP for Portsmouth and PPS to Aneurin
Bevan, also planned to make the journey. In the event, however, Crossman and Wigg
traveled alone.

"It was on a Sunday morning that we drove out to Larney, a cloudless day with a nip
in the air," Crossman wrote afterwards:

> When we parked the car outside the wall of the little village graveyard which looks
> across to the bleak slagheaps of a coal mine, there was already a long queue shuffling
> down the path to Jan Masaryk's grave . . . We laid our wreaths and went into the
> chapel to sign our names.

Then, astonishingly, the two men managed to interview most of the important
politicians in the country, including Slansky of the communists, Fierlinger and
Lausman of the Social Democrats and Majer of the right-wing opposition.[20]

Their reaction to these conversations was extremely interesting, and much less
rhetorical than Michael Foot's. Wigg maintained a careful objectivity, admirably
demonstrating the classic democratic socialist response to Leninism. As he put it in
Reynolds News on 21 March, "Without doubt there has been a revolution in
Czechoslovakia, backed by the overwhelming majority of the organized working
class. On the other hand, civil liberties for the middle class have gone under."
Crossman, writing at greater length in the *New Statesman* of 20 and 27 March, was also
cautious. He did not accept Foot's conclusion that the event had been masterminded by
the Kremlin. "The Russians were notable by their absence." The majority of Czechs
probably were pro-Russian anyway, because they feared above all else the revival of
Germany, and believed that Russia would protect them from it. Because the Social
Democrats and parties of the Right had favored closer relations with the West, which
wanted to build up Germany again, they were unpopular. And this meant that in so far
as the communist seizure of power could be viewed as reinforcing the Czech
relationship with the anti-German Soviets, it was actually popular with the broad mass
of Czech citizens. On the other hand, communist charges of a well-laid plan of counter-
revolution by the socialists and right-wing parties were absurd: "The aim of the Czech
Socialist Party, which is now accused of leading the conspiracy, was very modest; they
wanted to score a tactical victory by making Gottwald concede on a single minor
issue—the appointment of eight police officials in Prague."

Finally, as a democratic socialist, Crossman, like Wigg, could not but abhor the abrogation of civil liberties which followed the communist victory:

Three weeks ago, Czechoslovakia was a country with civil liberties and Parliamentary institutions. Today that is no longer true. When I said this to a young Communist he replied: "But it's such a small price to pay for a great leap forward to Socialism." Such a small price? . . . Alas! . . . it was much too high.

In this, at least, Foot, Wigg, Crossman and indeed nearly the entire Labour Left joined hands.

The crisis in Czechoslovakia had a profound impact upon the Labour Left. Laski's writings, once again, provide the best access to contemporary left-wing Labour emotions. This was no accident. The coup affected him greatly. Laski had been a leading exponent of the theory that World War II foretold international revolution in which communists and socialists would take the same side. He had seen in Czechoslovakia proof not merely that collaboration between the two wings of the working-class movement was feasible, but that its fruits more than justified the endeavor. The Czech leaders, Masaryk and Benes, were his personal friends. He had been their honored guest when visiting Prague, had entertained them when they came to London. Now he wrote:

A democratic community has been placed under the control of a dictatorship. . . there are purges in the universities and schools, in the army and civil service; newspapers are suppressed; editors are dismissed. . . Even the boy scouts have been ordered to unite with the Communist youth. . . Why has this been done? The fear that reactionaries would attack the regime set up in 1945 is nonsense. . . It is, I fear, impossible to avoid the conclusion that the Czech Communists overthrew the democratic freedom of their country at the order of Moscow.

And he asked bitterly, "What new strength comes to Russia by the change of a friendly and grateful ally into a compulsory and sullen dependant?"

Bitter though he was, Laski eschewed easy explanations of the crisis. Its roots were to be found in history. Jan Masaryk would not have died, Laski asserted on 20 March, "if Mr Neville Chamberlain had not thrown Czechoslovakia to Hitler." He would not have died if Churchill had sought "genuine friendship with the Soviet Union," instead of a temporary wartime alliance, or if, later, the Americans had tried to convince Russia that its fears of renewed conflict with the West were groundless, or if the Attlee government had viewed "the postwar world in Socialist terms and not in the perspective of that Foreign Office tradition which always looks backwards to a dead past." Laski would not, however, absolve the Soviets, whom he considered to be

direct accomplices in Jan's assassination. Blind with the fury of fear, they broke a free democracy to exhibit to those whom they deemed their enemies their power and the ruthlessness with which, should conflict come, they would defend themselves.

The brave new world which Laski and the entire Labour Left had thought to be within their grasp in 1945 was further from realization than ever. Laski took the ruination of his hopes very hard, harder than was typical or even healthy, but he did express, if in heightened tones, the anguish of many on the Labour Left. "If the statesmen will not make an end of this twilight world in which hope is born to be broken, and victory won only to be thrown away," he ended dispiritedly, "it is better to finish the fruitless effort of civilization which lacks the wisdom and the magnanimity without which life is indeed an idiot's tale, for all its fury still signifying nothing."[21]

For the ardent Laski to have despaired of cooperating with communists meant that the idea of a popular front was all but dead. The *New Statesman* spoke, now, for nearly the entire non-communist Left in dismissing the once potent concept. "What should be the Socialist attitude towards Communists and Communism?" Kingsley Martin asked on 8 May in a long and thoughtful article:

> It is impossible to avoid drawing one conclusion from the experience of the last three years. Though it was right and necessary between 1933 and 1945 to accept unity of working class action in resistance to Fascism, collaboration with Communists in government is a risk no Socialist can now accept. The history of Eastern Europe, culminating in the Communist coup in Prague, shows that the Socialist cannot survive in a coalition dominated by the Communists; and if he is the stronger . . . he does not need the Communists in the Cabinet.

In three short years the Labour Left had come full circle from the heady days of 1945, when collaboration with the Russians and other communists had seemed both necessary and desirable. The notion of a popular front with them, once the inspiration and rallying point of the British Left, had been hopelessly discredited. The idea has never recovered. This was a watershed in the history of the Labour Party and the Labour Left, a turning-point in modern British history. For some younger or, perhaps temperamentally more optimistic members of the Labour Left, or for those who had no sentimental attachment to memories of the popular front battles in the 1930s, the new situation may have seemed preferable to what had gone before. Others, like Laski, however, could see little place for themselves in the bifurcated world of the cold war. "I have the feeling," he wrote to Frankfurter, "that I am already a ghost in a play that is over."[22]

IV

Labour Left attitudes towards the United States were likewise transformed during 1945–51, though this reversal was less wrenching psychologically than the change in attitude towards Russia. It was equally significant, however, in reducing Labour Left opposition to the post-election Bevinite interpretation of "continuity in foreign policy."

During the closing stages of the war, and during its immediate aftermath, the Labour Left was nearly unanimous in regarding the United States with suspicion, despite the personal popularity of the American President, Franklin Delano Roosevelt. As Bevan had written in *Tribune* on 7 April 1944:

> There is nothing in the foreign policy of America which should perplex us. It is merely British 19th century foreign policy in the modern medium . . . it obeys the outward thrust of American capitalism just as ours expressed the appetites of British finance and industry.

Bevan and others on the Labour Left, particularly Laski, had regarded Roosevelt as a restraining influence over these appetites. With his death in April 1945, however, they could see little to alleviate the grim picture taking shape in their minds of the most powerful country in the world.

This outlook was compounded of numerous ingredients. Traditionally the British Left regarded the United States as a wild and woolly land, and Americans (in Crossman's words) as "a violent people who live by extremes." They were horrified by US racism and skeptical of American claims to be a great democracy. As Donald Bruce put it, "American political democracy . . . excludes from the polling booths in the Southern States . . . large numbers of coloured US citizens—and is accompanied often by brute force which has sometimes ended in murder." While the Labour Left venerated the memories of Jefferson, Lincoln and Roosevelt among others, it had nothing but contempt for Roosevelt's successor in the Oval Office, Harry Truman, "a decent and honest man," as Driberg put it in October 1946, but "caught up in a whirlwind which he does not know how to ride . . . His inept public vacillations are not due to weakness, but to sheer plumb ignorance, to an appalling lack of the most elementary general knowledge." With this verdict Laski agreed. Truman was

> an amiable man of good intentions who, despite his experience in the Senate, was not born to organise and control the supreme office in the United States. . . His temperament is neither incisive enough nor determined enough, his mind has neither the depth nor the range, to make him capable of the leadership the times require.

Such assessments, it may be said, ring strangely today. After all, Truman became the American President famous, among other things, for firing General MacArthur, for standing up to US Steel and for saying "the buck stops here." Whatever one's political views, in retrospect Truman appears singularly decisive.[23]

Next to Truman, the Labour Left's favorite American bête noire was "Wall Street," which had come to symbolize in its eyes "arrogant, self-confident, merciless capitalism," as Michael Foot wrote in the *Daily Herald* on 14 December 1945. In addition, the power of Wall Street meant, according to the Labour Left, that the American labor movement was necessarily weak, "still fighting battles we fought and won in this country fifteen and twenty-five years ago."

The developing red scare in America also offended the Labour Left. Crossman, who traveled to the US in 1946, reported in disbelief, "this country has swung so far to the right that it is dangerous for an American to call himself a Socialist." Jennie Lee, visiting the United States a year later, was shocked to discover that "every day, morning to night, in almost every newspaper, and over almost every radio station, a roaring hymn of hate towards all things Russian is kept going." The Labour Left smugly congratulated itself on the impossibility of such intolerance gaining sway in its own country.[24]

It was American foreign policy, however, which most deeply worried the Labour Left. By mid-1946 *Tribune* had begun documenting Russian perfidy and ruthlessness. Nevertheless the catalog of American mistakes and brutalities which it and others on the left wing of the Labour Party drew up was proving almost equally extensive. In Greece, Turkey, China, Japan, Iran, Germany and Italy, according to Laski, US foreign policy reflected "a pattern of large scale economic imperialism which shows no interest in the peoples of the countries in which it is now involved." Kingsley Martin agreed. "Roosevelt is dead," he lamented, "the Four Freedoms are submerged. The Atlantic Charter and Freedom from Want are forgotten. . . the present rulers of America realise that nothing less than an Empire is now necessary to make the world safe for American free enterprise." The Labour Left viewed the famous Truman Doctrine from this perspective. "It means that America is willing. . .to back up any regime it approves, wherever it may approve it. America is to become a combination of patron and ruler over any country it may think it should bring within its sphere of influence."[25]

To the Labour Left, Russian imperialism seemed no more threatening than the doctrine proposed by the American President. According to the editors of *Reynolds News*, Truman had made

> clear beyond any shadow of a doubt that the men who rule America are determined to go to any length to stop the development of Socialism, and to open up the world as a vast colonial area for American capitalism. To these able, unscrupulous and basically ignorant men any form of communal enterprise which extends beyond the ownership of the local tramway system is Communism and must be stopped.

"When," the editors asked in some trepidation, "is it to be Britain's turn?" In the *Sunday Pictorial* of 16 March, Crossman summarized in four words the common response to America's agenda as perceived by the Labour Left in early 1947, "No thanks, Mr Truman!"[26]

That atomic weapons should be the exclusive property of such a country with such a foreign policy became the Labour Left's supreme and all-consuming anxiety. "The United States may be regarded as a Rogue Adolescent with a Bomb," Driberg wrote in horror, after journeying to the US in early 1946. The Labour Left unanimously condemned the American decision to keep the mysteries of atomic energy secret. Had the Russians done such a thing, Emrys Hughes speculated, "we would have thought that Joe Stalin was the biggest double crosser that had yet appeared on this earth." On 2 November 1945 *Tribune* agreed: "At the moment, the most important task is to dissuade the United States from their disastrous intention to maintain monopoly control of the atom bomb. This is the key that will open the door to Russian good will." That key, however, never was turned. World tensions grew more severe. A year and a half later Driberg could discern a genuine "war party" in the United States, "Navy chiefs, army chiefs, some of the Roman Catholic hierarchy, some of big business." As he warned Labour's annual conference in the spring of 1947, Britain was in danger of becoming an "atomic aircraft carrier" for the United States, which was planning a world crusade against socialism.[27]

During the first two years of peace, then, the Labour Left could see little to choose from between either of the superpowers. Each, in its own way, seemed to represent an equally grave threat to Labour Left hopes of socialist reconstruction. But the suspicion of American motives, as unanimous at first as the general tolerance accorded to Russia, was gradually eroded. In the final analysis, revulsion at Soviet practices proved to be the dominating emotion of the era. Nor were the Americans passive spectators of this reversal in attitude. Rather, with the Marshall Plan they gave an enormous positive impetus to the reversal of Labour Left attitudes.

Marshall's speech was the perfect antidote to fears raised by the Truman Doctrine. The Secretary of State seemed to be offering Europe salvation from hunger and funds for reconstruction without imperiling British socialism or the independence of socialists elsewhere. The Labour Left did not cast off its suspicions of America's ultimate intentions immediately—but very few thought Marshall's plan was necessarily incompatible with socialist ideals. "The American motive is not humanitarianism or pacifism. It is markets and dollars. . . I understand that," Brockway acknowledged on 12 July in the *Forward*. He believed, however, that Britain should accept Marshall Aid anyway. "Let the government give a lead to the Socialists of Europe by preparing an economic plan which overrides political frontiers and which extends State ownership to Continental ownership." More common was the reaction of Michael Foot. He did not share Brockway's hesitations or suspicions. "There are no onerous conditions . . . no choking political or economic strings." In fact, Foot announced triumphantly, "the rebuilding of Europe" could now take place "with American aid, but along Socialist lines." This was precisely what the Labour Left had been calling for, with ever-diminishing hopefulness, since 1945.[28]

Though the announcement of the Marshall Plan marks a turning-point, the reassessment of American motives which it helped to spark did not take place in an instant. It was a gradual and complex process, one which helped to crystallize a new split on the Labour Left, this time between those who, while sharing a negative view of the Soviet Union, now disagreed about the world role of the United States. This important schism was easily visible in conflicting Labour Left reactions to the American Henry Wallace, who may have inspired Marshall's speech by calling, long before June 1947, for his country to sponsor a "World New Deal."

Wallace had been Vice-President under Roosevelt during 1940–4, when his views on foreign affairs generally coincided with those of his chief. With the advent of Truman in the Oval Office, however, he grew increasingly dissatisfied. Wallace, who had been demoted by Roosevelt to Secretary of Commerce in order to make room for Truman in the vice-presidency, believed it was still possible to avert the division of the world into antagonistic blocs headed by America and the Soviet Union. After Roosevelt's death he openly criticized the anti-Soviet orientation of the new administration. On 20 September 1946 Truman sacked him. Almost immediately, Michael Straight, proprietor of the influential liberal American journal the *New Republic*, offered the former Cabinet member an editorship. From this springboard Wallace eventually launched a presidential bid, not as a Democrat, but as the standard bearer of his own Progressive Party.[29]

No sooner had Wallace been installed in his offices at the *New Republic* than Richard Crossman suggested that the journal of which he was co-editor, the *New Statesman*, arrange for him to visit and tour Britain. Kingsley Martin enthusiastically agreed. He wrote to Wallace proposing the trip. "My idea," he explained to Straight in another letter, "was that if he [Wallace] would pay us a visit in the early spring, we could get up some really big meetings here, and begin that closer union of American and British progressives which you have so long advocated." On 6 January 1947 Wallace wrote back to Martin accepting his invitation.[30]

In addition to being a great editor, Martin was a great organizer and publicist. As he ingenuously explained later, "once the news was out that he [Wallace] was coming there was just no stopping the publicity. We had nothing to do with it, it just happened, and this letter of mine started an event of international importance."[31]

In fact Martin organized the event carefully. He persuaded the BBC to give Wallace airtime for a speech which he had himself drafted. In addition he arranged a series of public meetings for Wallace to address, all of them apparently successful. "There were five thousand people at the Manchester meeting, crowded meetings were held at Liverpool and Stoke and, judging by enquiries from all over the country, similar crowds were anxious to hear Mr Wallace in a score of English and Scottish cities," Martin wrote on 19 April in the *New Statesman*. The London meeting at Central Hall was deemed the greatest triumph. Only three thousand tickets for it were available. These were sold in a few days. "We could have sold out the Albert Hall three times over if it had been obtainable," Martin crowed. "The whole trip was the greatest success from our point of view," he wrote to Straight.[32]

At this relatively early date, the Labour Left unanimously supported Wallace. Even Michael Foot, who later led a section of the Labour Left into Truman's camp, was lauding the former Secretary of Commerce as "the most significant figure in American politics." In Foot's opinion, Labour Left "hopes of a better world depend[ed] partly on the establishment of a real understanding between Labour in Britain and the kind of opinion which Henry Wallace represent[ed] in the United States." Immediately after Wallace's British tour and only two months prior to Marshall's Harvard speech, Foot considered that Truman's former colleague

poses for us the paramount challenge of our foreign policy. Are we to act as a great crusading and liberating power, abjuring exclusive alliance with either the United States or the Soviet Union . . . ? Thanks to Mr Wallace we shall go about our duties with a better will and a braver hope.

By the end of the year, however, Foot was less sanguine.[33]

The interval had enabled him to digest Marshall's proposal, the Russian reaction to it and, above all, events in Czechoslovakia. As a result Foot and *Tribune*, of which he became editor-in-chief in 1948, abandoned Wallace's hope of preventing the division of the world into rival camps. And this meant that the most influential newspaper of the Labour Left threw its support behind Truman's foreign policy. Increasingly, *Tribune* found common ground not with Wallace's supporters (grouped in an organization called the Progressive Citizens of America) but rather with those who backed the President (organized as the Americans for Democratic Action). As Foot noted, the latter excluded communists; therefore the ADA's "is the same crusade as our own." Jennie Lee, returning from a visit to the US, had been struck by a similar point. "Inside America the non-Communist Left is in the ADA; such support as Wallace has comes from the pro-Communist unions and Liberals."[34]

It followed logically that *Tribune* would oppose Wallace's presidential bid. "A vote for Wallace will be a vote taken from Truman," Foot averred. "Meantime the Communists hail Wallace as Roosevelt's successor." Here was the line *Tribune* chose to develop. In opposing Truman from the Left, Wallace had become the tool of communists. His Progressive Party was

a fake and a fraud . . . dangerous. . . Most of the general programme of the new Party was drawn up by a conspicuous fellow traveller of the Communists . . . the dominating groups within the Wallace Party are unshakably Communist. . . He proposes a gigantic appeasement of Soviet demands.

By contrast, Truman was perceived now as being "imaginative" and "bold." His program was one "of which no Socialist would have need to feel ashamed." And his triumph in the 1948 presidential election was "a victory for the common people all over the world."[35]

While the Tribunite reversal became increasingly apparent, the *New Statesman* and those for whom it spoke continued to advance the pro-Wallace line. Martin, Crossman and the others were no less severe than anyone associated with *Tribune* in their condemnation of Soviet policies, but they still maintained that Britain should not ally with the United States in opposing them. As polarization between the superpowers proceeded apace, the editors of the *New Statesman* held out for British independence of both camps. They argued that Britain should take the lead in forming a third force in world affairs, politically democratic like the US, economically socialist like the USSR, capable of mediating between them. This was a program of great significance in Labour Party history, and will be treated in Chapter 3. Suffice it to say here that the *New Statesman*'s greater commitment to the third force helps explain its continuing hostility to Truman. After all, what was the use or the need of a third force in world affairs if the

American President's policies were so generous, disinterested and far-sighted as *Tribune* now claimed?[36]

When Wallace announced his candidacy for President on a third-party ticket, the *New Statesman* was cautious. On 3 January 1948 Martin wrote:

> What is needed in America today is a politically conscious labour movement strong enough to ensure that the Harvard speech remains the inspiration of American policy and that it is not twisted by reactionaries into a variant of the Truman Doctrine. But this is the very opposite of what Wallace's candidature is likely to produce.

Martin shared too, with most Tribunites, the fear that this third-party bid would ensure Republican victory at the polls, by dividing the liberal vote.

Nevertheless the *New Statesman* did not join *Tribune*'s increasingly shrill denunciations of Wallace and his new Progressive Party. Martin glumly conceded a Republican triumph, yet discerned a silver lining. "If there is no war before 1952, it is some consolation to think that Americans will at last have a Third Party to speak for that great mass of the under-privileged whom the Republican and Democratic Parties only consider when they want its votes." He was contemptuous of *Tribune*'s red baiting. "Wallace is too obviously not a Communist for this particular smear to do him much damage." He blasted American laws which kept the Progressive Party from the ballot in Illinois and other states. And, summing up, as the election drew near, he wrote on 30 October, "Reading Wallace's speeches I find once again that he still talks more sense about social problems in general and the proper aims of man, and of Americans in particular, than any other prominent politician."[37]

Nor did the *New Statesman* share *Tribune*'s newly found enthusiasm for Truman. The President remained "a faithful if rather commonplace public servant . . . likeable and friendly, but . . . too little for the job." If the Republicans won, Martin wrote, "at least . . . the contradictions and muddles of the Truman period will be done with." When, on 6 November, Martin had to report Truman's startling victory, he was delighted that the Republicans had been defeated, and he lauded Truman's effective campaigning. However, the credit did not belong entirely to the candidate. "For the fifth time in succession," Martin explained, "the American people . . . have voted for Franklin Delano Roosevelt." And he speculated hopefully that Truman would have to soften America's aggressive foreign policy in order to maintain support among the core of Rooseveltian liberals who had resisted Wallace's embrace, thereby providing the Democratic margin of victory.[38]

V

The disagreement about American aims which divided the editors of *Tribune* and the *New Statesman* extended to left-wing Labourites in general. One section of the Labour Left, because it saw in the Marshall Plan a chance to realize socialist objectives and because it profoundly objected to Russian practices, embraced Russia's most powerful enemy, the United States, and enthusiastically supported the American leader who had launched, in the Truman Doctrine, something approaching an anti-communist crusade. The other section of the Labour Left, although it shared Tribunite objections to Soviet interventionism and communism generally, nevertheless could not support America's counter-strategy, but looked instead to the resurrection of F.D.R.'s more conciliatory approach. This was a division of great significance in the history of the Labour Left, one which has not healed to this day.

In a sense, however, the argument was less about America than it was about Britain's relationship with America. Here we discover a second, equally enduring split within the British Labour Left. It was between those who saw Britain and Europe as part of a Western, democratic sphere in a world irrevocably divided between two hostile blocs, one communist the other free; and those who argued that Britain and Europe should constitute a third bloc, politically democratic like the United States, economically socialist like the Soviet Union, to balance and eventually to reconcile the other two. As Fenner Brockway put it for this group:

> The world has to choose not between two ideologies but three. Russia embodies one . . . America embodies the second . . . Britain, under Labour leadership, is moving toward the third, a planned economy combined with political democracy. . . I want to see this third ideology find international expression. We need a third grouping of the world which will serve first as a barrier to war between Russia and America, and secondly as a bridge to reconcile their differences.

The emergence of this sentiment and the movement it inspired during the postwar era constitutes another vital and revealing chapter in the history of the Labour Party and the Labour Left, and is the subject to which now we must turn.[39]

Notes and References

1   There is an enormous and growing literature on Britain's postwar diplomacy, some of it cited in note 5 to the Introduction to this book. See also Elizabeth Barker, *Britain between the Superpowers* (London, 1983), and Ritchie Ovendale (ed.), *The Foreign Policy of the British Labour Governments, 1945–51* (Leicester, 1984).

2   Alan Bullock, *Ernest Bevin: Foreign Secretary, 1945–51* (London, 1983), traces this process in painstaking detail.

3   Michael Gordon, *Conflict and Consensus in Labour's Foreign Policy 1914–1965* (Stanford, 1969), does treat Labour's internal debate, but strictly from the leadership's point of view.

4   *Romford, Hornchurch, Upminster Recorder*, 3 August 1945.

5   Konni Zilliacus, *Britain, USSR and World Peace* (London, 1946), p. 29; Harold Laski, *Russia and the West*, p. 3, a National Peace Council pamphlet printing an address of 20 November 1947; City University of London, *New Statesman* files, "G," Martin to Gollancz, 25 June 1945.

6   *Daily Worker,* 30 March 1946.

7   *Thurrock Gazette,* 6 October 1945; *Islington Gazette,* 5 February 1948; *Daily Worker,* 1 February 1948; Zilliacus, *Britain, USSR and World Peace,* p. 19.

8   Oxford University, Bodleian Library, Attlee papers, MS Attlee, dep. 30, folio number temporarily mislaid. Andrew Roth, "Parliamentary Profiles," file on Emrys Hughes; I am grateful to Andrew Roth for opening these files to me. *Glasgow Forward,* 15 September 1945.

9   *Tribune,* 24 August 1945, 2 February 1946.

10   Sussex University, Kingsley Martin papers, Correspondence, Priestley to Martin, 19 November 1945; *New Statesman,* 23 March 1946, 28 August 1946.

11   *Glasgow Forward,* 15 June 1946.

12   Ibid., 23 February 1946; *Tribune,* 8 March 1946; *Glasgow Forward,* 29 June 1946.

13   For the generous view of American motives, see, among many, Barker, *Britain between the Superpowers;* Bullock, *Ernest Bevin;* Ovendale, *Foreign Policy.* For the less generous interpretation, see, among others, Walter La Feber, *America, Russia and the Cold War* (New York, 1980), and Gabriel Kolko, *The Limits of Power: The World and the United States Foreign Policy, 1945–54* (New York, 1972). For a review of the literature, see Scott Jackson, "Prologue to the Marshall Plan: the origins of the American commitment for a European recovery program," *Journal of American History,* Vol. LXV (March 1979), pp. 1043–68.

14   *Tribune,* 13 June 1947.

15   *Glasgow Forward,* 28 June 1947; Library of Congress, Felix Frankfurter papers, microfilm reel no. 46, Laski to Frankfurter, 21 June 1947.

16   *Daily Herald,* 4 July 1947; Martin papers, Box 28, file 5; BBC Written Archives, Reading, "London Forum," 25 June 1947.

17   *Glasgow Forward,* 12 July 1947, 26 July 1947; Frankfurter papers, Laski to Frankfurter, 16 July 1947; *Sunday Pictorial,* 6 June 1947.

18   This outline of events leading to the coup is based upon D. F. Fleming, *The Cold War and its Origins, 1917–1960,* Vol. 2 (New York, 1961), pp. 489–94.

19   *Tribune,* 19 February, 27 February, 12 March and 2 April 1948, 5 March 1949.

20   *New Statesman,* 20 March 1948.

21   *Glasgow Forward,* 6 March 1948.

22   Frankfurter papers, Laski to Frankfurter, 27 September 1947.

23   *Sunday Pictorial,* 20 October 1946; *New Statesman,* 11 January 1947; *Reynolds News,* 13 October 1946; *Glasgow Forward,* 2 November 1946.

24   *Sunday Pictorial,* 10 November 1946; *Tribune* 5 December 1947.

25   *Glasgow Forward,* 22 March 1947; *New Statesman,* 19 April 1947.

26   *Reynolds News,* 16 March 1947.

27   Ibid., 13 October 1946; *Glasgow Forward,* 18 August 1945; *Labour Party Annual Conference, 1947,* p. 173.

28   *Tribune,* 16 January 1948, 2 July 1948.

29   Michael Straight, of course, is the man who was approached by the art historian Anthony Blunt, "the fourth man," to become a Soviet agent. Straight declined this invitation but did not report it to British or American authorities.

30   *New Statesman* files, "S," Martin to Straight, 12 December 1946.

31   Martin papers, Box 29, file 1, "K.M. Speeches," 11 April 1947.

32   *New Statesman* files, "S," Martin to Straight, 9 May 1947.

33   *Daily Herald,* 11 October 1946, 15 April 1947.

34   Ibid., 24 January 1947; *Tribune,* 5 December 1947.

35   *Tribune,* 2 January 1948, 30 July 1948, 28 January 1949, 5 November 1948.

36   For an earlier attempt to trace the Labour Left fascination with third force ideas, see Jonathan Schneer, "Hopes deferred or shattered: the British Labour Left and the third

force movement, 1945–49," *Journal of Modern History*, Vol. 56, no. 2 (June 1984), pp. 197–226.

37 *New Statesman*, 10 April 1948, 31 July 1948.
38 Ibid., 23 October 1948, 16 October 1948.
39 BBC, Written Archives, Reading, "I Speak for Myself," 28 July 1951.

3

The Labour Left and the Third Force Movement

THE EVOLUTION OF Labour Left attitudes towards the Soviet Union and United States during the early postwar years marks a crucial shift in British political history. Also, it provides the essential context for understanding the policy which left-wing Labour developed as an alternative to Bevinism. This was the attempt to create a third force in world affairs as outlined above by Fenner Brockway. The origins, efflorescence and ultimate defeat of the Labour Left agitation for this program form the subject of the present chapter.

That Great Britain should retain an independent voice in world affairs naturally appealed to the entire political spectrum. Right-wing Tories, suspicious of Roosevelt's attitudes towards Russia and British colonialism, often were as anti-American as their left-wing counterparts in the Labour Party, at least in the immediate aftermath of World War II. But, of course, they could not accept the basic ideological thrust of left Labour third force advocates.[1]

The third force idea was embedded in Labour's outlook. Its roots may be discovered in the bedrock of nonconformist conscience which W. E. Gladstone, high Anglican though he was, had personified and turned to his own advantage in the nineteenth century: Britain must stand for moral principles. Its more recent forebears were radicals in the British tradition like E. D. Morel and C. P. Trevelyan, leaders of the Union of Democratic Control which had demanded an end to secret diplomacy during and immediately after World War I. In the aftermath of World War II, one catches echoes of the old UDC demands. "Decisions which in my view make permanent peace in Europe almost impossible were taken by the Big Three, and only the vaguest description of them was given by the British Prime Minister to Parliament," Crossman complained at one point. "We have had a bad reversion to secret diplomacy."[2]

The socialist tributary to the third force movement complemented the radical Liberal one. It had two branches: one whose origins were located in the chauvinism of socialist pioneers like Robert Blatchford and Ben Tillett, men who had envisioned British trade unionists leading their benighted foreign comrades to the promised land of English-style socialism; the other in the more genuinely internationalist and egalitarian sentiments of figures like William Morris, Keir Hardie and Tom Mann. During the 1920s and especially during the 1930s it was this branch which attracted men and women who later became prominent advocates of the third force. One of the movement's main tap-roots, then, may be found in the non-communist socialist Left of the interwar period, the Independent Labour Party, the Socialist League and the Left Book Club.[3]

During the war the third force movement began to take shape. Bevan wrote, "If America gives us headaches, Russia gives us heartaches. . . The only solution likely to lay the foundations for peace and prosperity . . . is an organic confederation of the Western European nations." By autumn 1944 William Warbey, a former ILP activist soon to be elected Labour Member for Luton, was predicting socialist victories in French and British postwar elections which could become the basis of an independent force in world affairs. "By creating a Western European Region," he wrote,

> [Socialist] Britain and France could provide the world with a working example of a "supranational" organization. By taking the lead in reviving a vigorous International Labour Movement they could create a bloc of political power which could exert its influence in every sphere of international policy.

Some six weeks later the editors of *Tribune* outlined specifically the third force vision of postwar Europe. "The vital interests of the Labour Movement of Great Britain consist in the creation of friendly socialist Governments in Europe working more and more closely with a Labour Government." These sentiments did not contradict the numerous professions of friendship towards the Soviet Union so common then on the Labour Left. Russia, it was held, would rejoice in the creation of an independent, socialist Europe.[4]

Since Labour Britain never gave the slightest hint of lining up with the Soviets, it was Bevin's pro-American policy which prompted the first calls for Britain to follow a more independent course. The first mutterings of discontent with "Bevinism" appear very early in the postwar period. On 22 August 1945, at what was only the PLP's second weekly meeting since the general election victory, "Major Donald Bruce raised the question of the statement on policy made by Mr Bevin in his speech last Monday, particularly in regard to Spain, Bulgaria and Greece." Minutes of these PLP meetings are tantalizingly cryptic, but it is obvious in this case that Bruce objected to Bevin's having followed the American lead by denouncing communist activities in Bulgaria and Greece, and refusing tangible aid to democratic forces in Spain. Little more than a month later, on 10 October, Barbara Castle broached another Labour Left concern in moving a pointed resolution for the PLP to consider "that in order to preserve the unity of the Party, the Parliamentary Labour Party be consulted before policies are announced by Members of the Government which modify or ignore decisions of the Annual Conference." Here the issue was Palestine, on which Britain and the United States were divided, but Castle's purpose was more general. She was drawing attention to the dawning possibility that Bevin might fail to carry out the "socialist foreign policy" to which, ostensibly, he was bound. Ten days later Laski voiced similar reservations in a private letter to Frankfurter. "I fear," he wrote, that Bevin at the FO may prove a disaster. . . He should have got rid of Halifax, and Leeper and Duff Cooper. He should have agreed to the Russian suggestion of withdrawing recognition from Franco, and he should have insisted on smashing this royalist conspiracy in Greece.

Thus, as the former ILP militant and current Labour Member for Aberavon, W. G. Cove, wrote in the October issue of *Left Forum*, "Within the space of a couple of short weeks the thin mists of disillusionment arose on the benches behind the Government, and the faint murmurings of frustration were heard in the Lobbies."[5]

Bevin's response to early criticism set the tone for later broadsides. On 11 December 1945 PLP secretary Carol Johnson forwarded a note to him from the parliamentary party's External Affairs Group. Like other formally designated PLP area or subject groups, the External Affairs Group was supposed to keep ministers in touch with backbench opinion, but already it had developed an adversarial relationship with the Foreign Secretary. Now Bevin read:

The External Affairs Group of the Parliamentary Party . . . is of the opinion that . . . 1. The British Government should recognize the Governments of Romania and Bulgaria; 2. The USSR should be invited to become one of the sponsors to the proposal that a United Nations Commission on Atomic Energy should be formed; 3. The British Government should support the proposal of the USSR that a 4 Power Council should be established for the control of Japan.

Across this note Bevin scrawled, "This Group is very near Communist." He disregarded its advice.[6]

During the spring of 1946 Labour Left doubts about Bevin gradually increased. Subjects discussed at the weekly PLP meetings may serve as a rough index of the growing uneasiness. On 6 March a motion presented jointly by the former radical Liberal Leslie Hale, now Labour Member for Oldham, and by Christopher Shawcross, Member for Widnes and brother of the Attorney-General, echoed Laski's suspicions of Leeper, Halifax and Duff Cooper. It demanded reform of the Civil Service so that it might "carry out the policy of this and future [Labour] Governments." On 20 March, Ian Mikardo echoed Barbara Castle, demanding that the PLP discuss Bevin's attitude towards Palestine since, in his opinion, it contradicted long-standing Labour policy. On 27 March the External Affairs Group again aired its objections to Bevin's policies in Greece and elsewhere. On 3 April, William Warbey agreed only at the last moment to withdraw a Notice of Motion which condemned Churchill's famous "Iron Curtain" speech in Fulton, Missouri, and sought to put the Labour Party on record against it. More than forty Members had put their names to this motion.

Discontent with the government's foreign policy was, of course, muted at this stage. In no case cited above can the critics have expected a majority of the PLP to back them. Their efforts, however, suggest a critical mass within the party upon which the Labour Left and the third force movement could build later. Moreover, between the springs of 1946 and 1947 Labour Left critics were provided with what seems, in retrospect, to have been their most favorable climate during the postwar period. Earlier dissent had run up against memories of the great general election victory. Criticism then seemed ungenerous, even uncomradely to many. Later the Labour Left faced not merely the resistance of entrenched and powerful party leaders but, with the communist victory in Prague and cold-war tensions at their zenith, all the difficulties which normally confront dissidents during periods of perceived national emergency. Between early 1946 and early 1947, however, there had been a sufficient interval since the election to legitimize some criticism of a Foreign Minister who did not seem to be fulfilling campaign promises which remained fresh in people's minds; while the cold war had not yet frozen the attitudes of many on the Left into uncompromising hostility to the Soviet Union or anything connected (or even seemingly connected) with it. If 1946 was Labour's "*annus mirabilis*," in Hugh Dalton's memorable phrase, the period from June 1946 to June 1947 belonged to the critics of Bevinism on the Labour Left.

The essence of their criticism in its early form was that Bevin privileged the Anglo-American relationship. As Crossman put it on 13 September 1946 in an article for the *Sunday Pictorial*, "Fourteen months ago the Labour Party pledged itself, if it won power, to mediate between Russia and America. Many of us believe that it is still not too late to try." So far, however, there had been no concerted Labour Left pressure on the government to play this role.

That there was much sentiment which favored it but no organization to press for it became apparent only a month later, when a two-day debate in the House on foreign policy took place. Bevin was scheduled to deliver a major speech. Earlier the young James Callaghan had written privately to Kingsley Martin:

> We must stop (in the House) letting Ernie hypnotise us. The curious thing is that most of us are half afraid of him— he is so massive, immovable and apparently impenetrable to any influence he does not wish to acknowledge. . . our foreign policy is on the skids . . . there is every danger that British socialism will find itself bolstering up capitalism abroad. We must deflect Ernie (and half the Cabinet) from the present course.[7]

In the debate, however, Bevin was not deflected. He made no concession to his critics on any of the major issues, simply plowing ahead with the explanation of his program as though there were no objections to it which merited reply. The Labour Left attempted to respond. But "Platts Mills got lost in Rumania," as "Phineas" put it on 26 October in the *New Statesman*; and, according to Driberg the next day in *Reynolds News*, "Zilliacus was, as usual, too long winded." Lyall Wilkes, by common consent, made the best showing. On 1 November *Tribune* allowed him to restate and broaden his charges:

> Mr Bevin's negative approach to the problem presented by the Eastern and Western Mediterranean, his continued refusal to change Foreign Office policy in Spain . . . the double standard of judgement reserved for American and Russian imperialism . . . are only symptoms of the more fundamental disease. We are the victims of a

coalition on foreign affairs . . . which exacts its sacrifice now of Socialism abroad, but which will almost certainly in time exact its sacrifice of Socialism at home.

This was, according to "Phineas," the "first serious and critical comment on the Government's foreign policy" to be delivered by a Labour Member, but it represented a common concern. "Already it is evident," "Phineas" added, "that . . . there will be serious trouble for the Government at the next Session."

The government, however, was determined to nip it in the bud. On 25 October the leading article in the *Daily Herald* threatened Bevin's main critics in the PLP with expulsion. "Some of their criticisms of the Government's foreign policy have lately become so extreme in tone that it is difficult to see how [they] . . . can reconcile their attitude with even nominal adherence to the Labour Government." Given the bitter tenor of later criticisms, this seems an over-reaction. According to the *Evening Standard*, Bevin had insisted on it, "saying that there is no room in the same party for exponents of two different foreign policies. He told the Party he will tolerate no longer sniping and backstabbing from 'comrades'."[8]

The critics, however, were not so easily silenced. On 29 October 1946 twenty-one backbenchers of the Labour Left sent Attlee a "private and confidential" letter of protest against the government's foreign policy. A crucial document in the history of the postwar Labour Left, it deserves to be quoted at length. "Firstly," its authors began,

> we would affirm our belief that British Social Democracy has an historic role to play in proving to the world . . . that democratic Socialism is the only final basis for a world government; and that it can therefore provide a genuine middle way between the extreme alternatives of American "free enterprise" economics and Russian totalitarian socio-political life.

They listed Labour Left criticisms of Bevinism:

> We have answered the power politics of others by pursuing power politics ourselves . . . The Government gives too often the impression of being infected by the anti-Red virus which is cultivated in the United States . . . Gross imperfections in . . . states such as Greece, Spain and even the United States itself tend to evoke but a fraction of the criticism directed Eastwards.

They condemned the division of the world into two hostile blocs and argued that only a socialist Britain could overcome it:

> The democratic pursuit of live socialist policies in this country and abroad will do much to aid those forces in the United States . . . whose hostility to the imperialist policy of the US administration is as great as our own . . . Moreover, the pursuit by ourselves of live socialist policies . . . should do much to encourage the Soviet Union

in extending political and personal liberties once the danger of poverty and the fear of war have been overcome.

Finally they issued a warning. Threats of expulsion would not deter them:

We feel it right and necessary to inform you of these views which we believe to be in accord with the Party's declared Foreign Policy. We must make it clear that, believing that the future of Britain and of humanity is at stake in these matters, we cannot continue to remain silent and inactive.

Signatories included Crossman, Callaghan, Foot, Wilkes, Wyatt and Sydney Silverman. The names of so-called communist fellow-travelers, Zilliacus and Platts Mills, for example, were conspicuous by their absence. This was by design. The Labour Left was asserting that a loyal opposition, not merely a left-wing fringe, opposed the government's foreign policy.[9]

The list of signatories is intriguing for another reason. It included the names of Aneurin Bevan's wife, Jennie Lee, and his PPS, Donald Bruce. The latter was the main author of the letter. Michael Foot has written that, while Bevan was in the Cabinet, "no interchange occurred between him and any left-wing groups in Parliament." On the other hand, in the House of Commons smoking room Bevan sat at the center of a lively group not exactly noted for inhibited conversation, and he was deeply opposed to Bevinism, as Foot and a host of other sources have amply demonstrated. It seems inconceivable that he did not give vent to his feelings before his wife and PPS, and unlikely that they did not discuss the letter to Attlee with him and with their smoking-room companions. Bevan could not have forbidden any course of action to Jennie Lee even had he wished to, and there is no evidence that he did. Could he not, however, have kept his PPS from composing and circulating a letter critical of the Prime Minister and Foreign Secretary, or have disciplined him afterwards? He did neither. It seems safe to conclude, therefore, that the Labour Left had an important sympathizer in the Cabinet. And it is conceivable that Bevan himself played some part in the first organized Labour Left protest against Bevin's foreign policy.[10]

There was more to come. Driberg had noted in his column for *Reynolds News* on 27 October.

the considerable body of opinion which, while desperately anxious not to contribute to disunity within the Party, is equally anxious about . . . the Government's foreign policy. More will be heard from Members next month . . . many who failed to catch the Speaker's eye last week . . . will try to do so in the debate on the Address in reply to the King's Speech at the opening of the new Session.

The private letter to Attlee had warned that Bevin's critics did not intend to "remain silent and inactive." But why confine themselves, as Driberg seemed willing to do, to isolated and uncoordinated interventions during the debate on the Address from the Throne? Here Crossman appears to have taken the initiative, organizing a concerted

Labour Left attack on the government's foreign policy. It would consist of a critical amendment to the Address, expressing

> the urgent hope that His Majesty's Government will so renew and recast its conduct of international affairs as to affirm the utmost encouragement to and collaboration with all nations striving to secure full Socialist planning and control of the world's resources, and thus provide a democratic and constructive Socialist alternative to an otherwise inevitable conflict between American capitalism and Soviet Communism in which all hope of world Government would be destroyed.

Crossman circulated the amendment with the aid of Foot, Benn Levy, the playwright and Member for Eton and Slough, Mark Hewitson, Sydney Silverman and Joe Reeves, all of whom had been signatories to the earlier protest. By 13 November, when the amendment was tabled, forty-three Labour MPs had put their names to it. As with the letter to Attlee, Zilliacus and those associated with him were not asked to sign.[11]

The government treated this development with great seriousness. Bevin was at the United Nations in New York City, so he could not meet his critics. Instead the under secretary for foreign affairs, Hector MacNeil, gave them an audience. It was, he wrote to Attlee afterwards, "an agreeable meeting," but the critics would not withdraw the amendment.[12]

Later in the day the parliamentary party convened. "Well over two hundred" Members attended, an unusually high number. The atmosphere was tense. "So seriously does the Government regard this censure on its foreign policy," wrote the parliamentary correspondent for the *Manchester Guardian*, "that the Prime Minister and Mr Herbert Morrison spent over two hours . . . arguing the case for loyalty and for the foreign policy itself." Attlee asserted that it was improper for Labour Members to offer amendments to the Address from the Throne in the first place and impolitic to publicize their dissent when he was willing to discuss matters with them privately. Morrison warned that standing orders to maintain party discipline, which had been relaxed at an earlier PLP meeting, might now be reimposed. "Challenges of this kind might be misunderstood abroad. They were, in effect, votes of censure on the Government. Those who had put their names to the motion should, in loyalty to the Party, withdraw them." Morrison then moved the following resolution: "That in the opinion of this Party Meeting it is undesirable that facilities should be sought for the moving of Amendments to the Address by Labour Members; and that the Members concerned be requested to consider withdrawing their names." This was passed by 126 votes to 33, but "there were more than sixty abstentions, possibly as many as ninety or one hundred . . . the exact number was not revealed."[13]

The next day forty of the critics met to consider the position. Refusing to withdraw their names from the amendment, they decided instead to seek additional signatures. They could not agree, however, on how far to carry their opposition to the government. Thirteen of the signatories, according to the *Daily Mail*, "a maximum of twenty," according to the *Telegraph*, wanted not merely a debate on the amendment but a division, and expressed the intention of voting against the government when it was called. To this the majority would not consent. As "Phineas Minor," himself a PLP opponent of Bevin one suspects, put it in the *New Statesman* on 23 November, "a Tory amendment seeks to change the Government, a Labour amendment seeks to change its policy."

This meeting took place on Thursday 14 November. The Address from the Throne was to be delivered on the following Monday. The intervening three days saw a hardening of positions. The Labour "rebels," as they now were being called, canvassed additional signatures, raising the number of names attached to the amendment from forty-three to fifty-seven. Donald Bruce announced resolutely in the *Sunday Pictorial*, "My name is down on the Address and is staying there because . . . it is high time our great nation followed a constructive foreign policy of its own and stopped trailing along in the wake of the United States." Meanwhile Attlee was determined to exert maximum pressure on the critics, in order to separate intransigents from those who might be brought back into the fold. He agreed with Bevin, who had cabled angrily from New York, "Am I not entitled to know where Parliament and the Cabinet stand, and is not the world entitled to know by a vote? In addition, the element of treachery . . . ought to be brought to a head . . . It is vital if I am to carry on here." Attlee now announced that he would call a division if no one else did, and treat it as a vote of confidence. And he, rather than Hector MacNeil who had been scheduled to speak, would wind up for the government in the debate. Moreover, a three-line whip had been declared.[14]

With public attention on the 18th riveted on the House, perhaps something of an anticlimax was inevitable. Crossman, reiterating the case made in the original letter to Attlee, was credited generally with an accomplished performance. Attlee's reply for the government was unyielding but good humored. There were few smiles on Labour's front bench, however, when the division was called by the ILP's two remaining Parliamentary Members, John McGovern and Campbell Stephen. According to the chief government whips, of 387 Labour Members, 154 did not vote. This included thirty-four Members who had reported ill or who were out of the country. Who knows which side they would have chosen? As Driberg pointed out in *Reynolds News* on the 24th, "When one considers that there are some seventy Ministers senior and junior, practically bound to vote for the Government, the number of Labour MPs who positively and wholeheartedly support the Government on this issue dwindles considerably." Even the Cabinet included men and women long associated with the Labour Left. Quite probably Bevan was not ill disposed towards the "rebellion." Hugh Dalton was positively sympathetic. On 29 November he confided to his diary, "There is no doubt that there is deep concern in a wide and sensible section of the Party . . . about what E.B. Ernest Bevin seems to be doing and how he is doing it. . . I am not at all unsympathetic to part of their case, but have had to conceal this fact." Were Shinwell, Cripps, Wilkinson and perhaps others concealing similar doubts as well?[15]

Dalton had written, "One hundred is too many to be disciplined." Whatever the reason, no disciplinary action was taken. On 27 November the NEC, with Attlee attending, resolved after "considerable discussion" only to inform the PLP that it was "seriously disturbed by the incident" and did not wish to see "a repetition of a division of this character." The PLP, meeting on the following day, had before it a resolution with forty-four signatures demanding reimposition of standing orders and unspecified disciplinary measures. Yet it too finally was content merely to "deplore" the episode. Standing orders remained suspended. According to one journalist, "Ernest Bevin would like a showdown, but neither Attlee nor Morrison is prepared to pillory a hundred of their brightest backbenchers . . . If you have a list of them, hang onto it. I prophesy you'll be able to tick off more than half the Ministers in the next Labour Government." Callaghan, Crossman and Castle had to wait for the next Labour government but one, Foot for the next but two. Still, this was not a bad prediction.[16]

The amendment to the King's Speech revealed the extent of disaffection among the Labour Left. It revealed its limits as well. Of the hundred Members who abstained from supporting the government's policy, only a handful had been prepared to vote against it. During the debate Sydney Silverman, one of Bevin's most ardent critics, carefully explained that the "rebels" did not wish to divide the House. "They did not want to bring down the Government. They wanted it to succeed." During the aftermath of the incident, Labour Left activists often repeated this point. Foot, indeed, had anticipated it, writing in the *Daily Herald* on 15 November, "this open debate of differences sincerely held will result not in a weakening, but in a strengthening of the Labour Movement." In the *Glasgow Forward* of 30 November, Laski took a similarly reassuring line: "There is neither a split, nor the remotest prospect of a split in the Labour Party."

The Labour Left was in an ironical position. Perhaps one-third of the parliamentary party shared its objections to Bevinism; yet the vast majority of "rebels" also accepted the good faith of the party leadership and would not countenance a split. The curious paradox to which the Labour Left was subject during the Attlee years was revealed. The stronger the Left in the Labour Party, the less likely it was to take decisive action which might damage the government. In November 1946, although it possessed significant strength in the PLP, the Labour Left was unwilling to push matters to extreme conclusions. Later, when some on the Left perhaps wished to do so, they no longer had the backing to make such a gesture effective.

II

The wave of discontent with Bevinism which produced the public letter to Attlee in October and dissent from the King's Speech in November had not yet crested. During December 1946 the Labour Left made no important interventions. But, "one evening in January 1947, when the House of Commons was sitting late, a dozen Members began talking . . . and we all agreed," a participant recalled afterwards, "about the need for a more drastic Socialist policy if we were not to drift into disaster." It seems doubtful that the formation of the "Keep Left" group was quite so informal. Again, there is the shadowy presence of Bevan to consider. After all, he too was accustomed to sit up late in the House smoking room, talking and gossiping with like-minded Members. And his PPS, Donald Bruce, once more played an important role in subsequent events.[17]

Whatever its precise origins, a group of fifteen Labour Members on the Left was soon meeting regularly. Probably the ringleaders were Bruce, Foot, Crossman and

Mikardo, men who had organized the letter to Attlee and the amendment to the King's Speech. Other members of the group may have been invited to join on the following basis: Fred Lee, because, as a trade unionist (AEU), he helped to balance the "middle-class intellectuals" who dominated "Keep Left;" George Wigg, because he was PPS to Emanuel Shinwell, the Minister for Fuel and Power who vied with Bevan for leadership of the Labour Left; Stephen Swingler and Harold Davies, perhaps on the recommendation of Wigg, who shared a flat with them; R. W. G. Mackay, because, as one of Labour's foremost advocates of European federation, he would be useful in the third force movement which "Keep Left" intended to champion; Leslie Hale, on the recommendation perhaps of Mackay, with whom he shared law offices, or possibly of Geoffrey Bing, another close friend, who may have been asked to join "Keep Left" by Foot. Other members were Benn Levy, J. P. W. Mallalieu, Ernest R. Millington and Woodrow Wyatt. At first Maurice Edelman and Sydney Silverman also attended, but they were dropped deliberately. In Edelman's case the reason is not immediately apparent; possibly Silverman's extreme individualism accounted for his exclusion.[18]

The group began meeting during the winter crisis of 1947, when coal supplies ran out, transportation was blocked by record snowstorms and temperatures dropped to all-time lows. Many feared that the government would fall during this difficult period. This did not deter "Keep Left," which held that only a U-turn in government policies could retrieve the situation. The group now produced a 47-page pamphlet, *Keep Left*. Crossman appears to have been the driving force. The chapter on foreign policy, "The Job Abroad," was essentially his, the final draft written at a feverish pace over the Easter weekend at his country home, where Foot and Mikardo labored over other sections: "What We Are Up Against," "The Job at Home" and "Twenty Things to Do." Another chapter, "Demob," was largely the work of Wigg, Wyatt and Mallalieu.

In the "The Job Abroad," Crossman again stressed the equal culpability of Russia and America for the division of the world into two hostile blocs, though dwelling more this time than in the past on the "disastrous diplomatic folly" of Molotov. But he now set out in detail the necessity for socialist Britain not merely to maintain independence from both sides, but to do so as part of a united Europe. "A Socialist Britain cannot prosper so long as Europe is divided." Unfortunately European unity was not an immediate prospect, but "nearly every country in Europe is now planning its economy on Socialist lines. . . These various national plans should be carefully coordinated." Relations with France were particularly important. Crossman wanted not merely economic ties with the French but military ones, and none with the United States. This should demonstrate to Russia that Europe would not join an American-led anti-Soviet bloc. Moreover:

> We should try to expand the Anglo-French Alliance into a European security pact, and announce our readiness, along with other European nations, to renounce the manufacture and use of atomic bombs and to submit our armed forces and armament factories to inspection of UNO, irrespective of whether Russia and America reach agreement on this subject. This involves no sacrifice of security for

us, since our security depends not on winning the next—atomic—war, but on preventing it.

Here was an essential thrust of Labour Left foreign policy. It has run through the history of British politics and the Labour Party ever since.[19]

Keep Left marked yet another demonstration of vigor and ability by the Labour Left. It was well received by the left-wing press, representatives of which had been invited to a cocktail party "to give it a boost," as Hale put it in his diary. Even Gladwyn Jebb, one of Bevin's advisors at the Foreign Office, thought Crossman's chapter "the work of an intelligent, if rather hurried amateur." Moreover, publication of the pamphlet followed hard on the heels of Crossman's most recent triumph in the House, one shared with other "Keep Lefters," which considerably broadened the basis of their support.[20]

The authors of *Keep Left* opposed Bevin's plans for the British army to maintain garrisons around the world. They accepted, however, that some British forces would be necessary for the foreseeable future, and that the men in them might have to be drafted. Conscription was anathema, however, to the sizable pacifist contingent within the Labour Party. And there was still an element in the PLP which so distrusted Bevin that it wanted to deprive him of any army at all. On 1 April 1947 these two Lefts within the Labour Party combined to record the largest demonstration yet of left-wing opposition to the government's foreign policy, seventy votes against the National Service Bill. The "Keep Left" group, however, scored a more practical victory. "We voted for the Government," Crossman wrote on 6 April in the *Sunday Pictorial*. "We made it clear, however, that if the Government did not do so, we should put down an amendment reducing the period of service from eighteen months to a year. And on this issue we won."

This was the first time the government had backed down to satisfy the Labour Left —not an inconsiderable event. Hale confided to his diary on 11 May:

> There is no doubt whatever that this committee "Keep Left" was responsible for the drop in the National Service from eighteen months to twelve, and they are being angrily criticized on one side of the House as a self-constituted caucus endeavouring to influence the Party, facetiously complimented from the other side.

Government attitudes may be imagined. With the open letter to Attlee, the amendment to the Address from the Throne, the popular pamphlet, and now the successful demand for a reduction in the period of National Service, "Keep Left" was emerging rapidly as a real factor in British politics, one capable of causing serious difficulty to the party leadership. Hale predicted that the government would attempt to silence the group by "offering some sort of job to Crossman and Mikardo." In the event, however, it chose to employ harsher methods.

It is a measure of the seriousness with which the government had come to take its Labour Left critics that it now trained its very biggest guns upon them. It chose the battleground shrewdly. Foot, Crossman and Mikardo had written *Keep Left* with an eye to influencing Labour's annual conference, which was to meet at Margate only a few weeks after the pamphlet had been published. But conference, dominated by the trade-union bloc vote, still was very much government territory, as the party leaders realized. Very well, then: the confrontation would take place at Margate.

When it came, the government's counter-attack was three pronged—and devastating. It took the unprecedented step of replying to *Keep Left* with a pamphlet of its own, *Cards on the Table* (for which it denied responsibility, but which Dalton, Phillips and Bevin had asked Labour's International Secretary, Denis Healey, to write) and distributed it to the entire conference. No sooner had assembled delegates digested Healey's forceful prose than Labour Party Chairman Philip Noel-Baker delivered an address which also vigorously combated Labour Left views. If global polarization was in process, Noel-Baker asserted, it was Russia's fault, not Britain's. "Does the Party know all that the Government have done to stop a split?" In order to avoid the division of the world into rival blocs, Britain had made "loans to Czechoslovakia and Hungary; trade agreements with Poland and Czechoslovakia," had sent "food to fight famine in Rumania . . . and so much more." What else, Noel-Baker demanded, could reasonable Labour Members want? Crossman, Harold Davies, Sydney Silverman and, in an effective speech, Tom Driberg, attempted to respond. All things being equal perhaps they could have held their own with Noel-Baker and Healey. None of them, however, were capable of coping with the Foreign Secretary, who, in winding up for the platform, delivered the *coup de grâce* to Labour Left hopes of influencing the conference.[21]

"Under huge arc lamps, and amid the whirl of newsreel cameras a squat figure stands on the high platform at the centre of a long table," Crossman wrote afterwards in what was a remarkably detached, even generous, article given that he had been foremost among the recipients of Bevin's wrath:

> To his right sits the Chairman, Philip Noel-Baker, his handsome face strained and anxious, and beyond him Manny Shinwell, and biting hard on his pipe dapper Harold Laski . . . On his left is Hugh Dalton . . . and beyond him Nye Bevan in sombre mood . . . Bevin stands quite still waiting for the ovation to cease. It surges up from a thousand delegates on the floor, and from the packed galleries to left and right . . . Ernest Bevin wipes the sweat from his forehead. The papers shake in his hand, but the voice is as strong as ever, and soon rises to a hoarse roar of righteous indignation. . . No man alive is so skilful at handling a working-class audience, mixing the brutal hammer blow with sentimental appeal . . . He did not merely smash his critics; he pulverised them into applauding him.

The climax of Bevin's long review and defense of British foreign policy came when he referred to the parliamentary "rebellion" of November 1946. Reminding his audience that he had been in New York at the time serving his country, and therefore unable to defend himself from this "stab in the back," the former leader of the Transport and General Workers declared, "If you are to expect loyalty from Ministers, the Ministers —however much they may make mistakes—have a right to expect loyalty in return. I grew up in the trade union, you see, and I have never been used to this sort of thing."[22]

That brought down the house. After all, the Labour Party, since its inception, had represented an at times uneasy alliance between working-class trade unionists and members of the middle class. It was a common, though often inaccurate, charge that only the solid good sense of organized labor kept the party from following middle-class socialists into the political wilderness. Bevin was attempting to widen a long-standing breach here and, in doing so, to separate his critics from the mass of the party. He entirely succeeded, as Dalton recorded immediately afterwards in his diary. Bevin, Dalton wrote, "scored a very great personal success and swept away all opposition. He has a most astonishing—and a unique—conference personality. There was no comeback . . . Crossman was obliterated, humiliated and deeply offended."[23]

Bevin's "tidal wave of a speech" (to cite Dalton again) was a hammering of the Left almost without precedent in Labour Party history. Once before Labour's annual conference had witnessed a similar brutalizing, in 1935, when George Lansbury the party leader and pacifist was directed to quit "hawking his conscience round the world asking what to do with it." In that instance, too, Bevin had been the hammerer. Then his speech was credited with finally destroying Labour's opposition to rearmament; this time it marked the beginning of the end of Labour Left organized resistance to Bevinite "continuity in foreign policy."

Reeling from its conference defeat, the Labour Left stubbornly refused to surrender. Crossman, in the *Sunday Pictorial* of 1 June, insisted that Bevin "has not answered any of the Labour Left's questions or rebutted their constructive proposals." Mikardo, at a Reading party meeting, "stood by his criticisms of the Government's foreign policy . . . To speak of people stabbing you in the back is moonshine." Zilliacus, in the *Daily Herald* of 3 June, promised that the "fight goes on, in spite of spell binding at Margate." Perhaps so; but these brave words were followed in a matter of weeks by a veritable earthquake—General George Marshall's speech at Harvard, which seemed to offer financial assistance to war-ravaged Europe regardless of each country's political complexion. The ground on which the Labour Left had based its calculations and projections was shifting beneath its feet. If Margate had demonstrated to them the dominance of the party leadership and the insignificance of their own influence, Marshall's speech and Russia's reaction to it seemed to cast a new and redeeming light upon American motives—and upon Bevin's policies. From this the Labour Left in its present form could not recover.[24]

Left-wing Labour broke up into warring factions. A small "hard" Left continued to oppose the Foreign Secretary and Marshall Aid, which, it held, would compromise a democratic socialist third force that the East Europeans still might join. A less "hard" Left continued to press for a democratic socialist third force based at first upon a "Western union" of West European countries. Meanwhile, a "softer" Left accepted Bevinism to this extent: in the wake of the Marshall Plan it agreed with the Foreign Secretary that Russia was responsible for the division of Europe, and that neither Britain nor the western portion of the continent could rebuild without American aid. For this "soft Left" a third force in world affairs was no longer necessary. Western union, funded by the US but not necessarily capitalist, could become an essential bulwark against communist aggression.

In two short years Labour Left backbenchers had demonstrated an impressive critical faculty and the capacity to challenge their party leaders effectively. This was not a sufficient period, however, to do more than indicate potential. And the precondition of success for the Labour Left was unity, which broke down in the wake of two epoch-making speeches, Bevin's at Margate and Marshall's at Harvard. Henceforth Bevin's critics would be on the defensive.

III

The debacle at Margate and General Marshall notwithstanding, many on the Labour Left remained convinced of the need for a democratic socialist third force to balance and mediate between the two superpowers. There was in the Labour Party, and indeed among all the British political parties, long-standing sentiment in favor of world government and a united Europe. Churchill had struck that chord in his Iron Curtain speech, summoning up another grand alliance to confront communism. Could this sentiment be harnessed to the third force movement? Such considerations must have occurred now to Labour Left activists. At any rate, "Keep Left" was superseded for a time by another unofficial parliamentary group, the "Europe Group," which began to agitate for a united Europe as the nucleus of a third force.

Within the Labour Party the leading exponent of a united Europe was the Member for North-West Hull, R. W. G. Mackay. Coincidentally he was a member, though not a prominent one, of "Keep Left." An Australian barrister whom Stafford Cripps had persuaded in 1934 to pursue a political career in Britain, Mackay had resigned from the Labour Party in 1940 to help build what eventually became Common Wealth. In June 1942 he had contested the Welsh seat at Llandaff and Barry for the fledgling party, polling a startling 13,753 to the Conservative's 19,408. From then until January 1945, when he rejoined Labour, Mackay was chairman of the Common Wealth Party. "An organiser of legendary ability," according to the party's historian, in 1947 Mackay already was engaged in attempting to establish an all-party parliamentary group to agitate for a united Europe. During the summer of that year, however, shortly after Bevin's speech at the annual conference, he temporarily changed focus to concentrate instead upon organizing a group within the Labour Party alone.

At this stage Mackay believed a united Europe would help Britain to maintain independence from the superpowers and serve as an obstacle to war. This had been "Keep Left's" position too. Not surprisingly Mackay asked six members of the group —Crossman, Mikardo, Foot, Levy, Wigg and Hale—to participate in preliminary discussions about forming a Labour Party group whose purpose would be to explore the feasibility of the united Europe idea. He also invited several veterans of the prewar Federal Union (of Europe) movement—Gordon Lang, Henry Usborne and Colonel E. King (who later joined the Conservatives)—as well as several interested backbenchers, of whom Christopher Shawcross came to be most important to the project as a whole.[25]

This preliminary group immediately revealed its general political slant in a letter opposing Conservative talk of a "United Europe" which Mackay sent to members of the PLP. European federation was desirable, Mackay wrote, but not if it became a "bloc against the USSR, which of course would lead to war." In a second letter formally inviting Labour members to join a "Europe Group," Mackay stressed the need for Britain to maintain distance from, especially, the superpower to the west. "It has been increasingly recognized," he wrote, "that in the changing circumstances of the present day, and so as to escape from economic dependence on America, it may be in the interests of Great Britain to establish in cooperation with other European States an equally self-supporting area of trade in Europe and the Empire."[26]

Perhaps this approach alienated the old Federal Unionists Lang, Usborne and King, who now disappeared from Mackay's circle, but it faithfully reflected the outlook of "Keep Left." The "Europe Group" was designed originally as much to forward the third force program of the Labour Left as to carry on the long-standing agitation for a supranational authority. For some of its members, at least, it appears to have been a supplement, perhaps even an alternative, to "Keep Left," which had temporarily ceased to meet. It was intended to be more broadly based than the original group, but had a similar object: to push for a foreign policy based upon alliance with the European nations rather than with the USA or the USSR.[27]

Starting on 2 December 1947 the "Europe Group," now composed of more than eighty Labour Members, began to meet regularly. Mackay was elected chairman, John Hynd, who was momentarily also chairman of the beleaguered External Affairs Group, became vice-chairman, Christopher Shawcross was secretary. Among those generally reckoned to be on the Labour Left who also joined were Richard Acland (now MP for Gravesend), Bing, Bruce, Castle, Ronald Chamberlain, Cocks, Crossman, Harold Davies, Norman Dodd, Foot, John Haire, Hale, Fred Lee, Jennie Lee, Mallalieu, Leah Manning, Mikardo, John Rankin, Reeves, Swingler, Wilfred Vernon, Warbey and Wigg, though only a few became active members. All of "Keep Left" had joined. The Labour Left seemed to be in control. As soon became clear, however, European union presented a host of divisive issues, even to Labourites united in their opposition to Bevinism. And there were not only Bevin's critics in the "Europe Group," but his supporters as well, among them Barbara Ayrton-Gould, Aiden Crawley, Hayden Guest, Margaret Herbison, Richard Stokes and Ivor Thomas.[28]

On one general point, however, the group as a whole agreed, at least initially. The agitation for European unity, in which the Conservatives, and especially Churchill, suddenly were exhibiting great interest, must not become the property of Labour's opponents. Perhaps this could be forestalled if the government came out in favor of European union. Could Bevin be induced to support it in the House debate on foreign affairs scheduled for the third week of January 1948?

Mackay and Crossman, who were neighbors in the country, met at Crossman's cottage, "Radnage," over the weekend of 20–22 December, and composed a letter to the Foreign Secretary which began with great circumspection:

A number of Labour Members, some of whom have been your critics in the past and others your supporters, have found themselves in agreement over the future of Western Europe. We are writing this letter in the hope that our views are close enough to your own to have some weight in the next few critical weeks.

This time Crossman had learned discretion. The letter remained unpublicized. Moreover, though it warned against the "anti-Russian colour" of Conservative plans for European union, it took a decidedly anti-communist line, striking confirmation of the evolution of views among many on the Labour Left:

The damage to the French economy caused by communist-led strikes has already mortgaged in advance part of the American aid. We are convinced that the Communists will launch a new offensive in the not too distant future. . . The position in Italy is almost equally precarious.

Appended to the letter were the signatures of Bruce, Crossman, Foot, Fred Lee, Levy, Mackay and Mikardo, all of "Keep Left," as well as the names of eleven other Labour Members. In Mackay's opinion, "about fifty signatures" could have been obtained, "but we thought that numbers were not so important."[29]

In the event, the letter writers could take little heart from Bevin's response. In his speech during the foreign affairs debate he seemed skeptical, though not overtly hostile:

While I do not wish to discourage the work done by voluntary political organisations in advocating ambitious schemes of European Unity . . . I am afraid it will have to be done a step at a time. But surely . . . the free nations of Western Europe must draw more closely together.

This was a lukewarm endorsement at best, but at least there was no mention of a "stab in the back."[30]

Meanwhile the "Europe Group" sought links with continental socialists. In late December the group met with M. Bohy, leader of the Belgian Socialist Party. In early 1948 Walter Paget and Hale held a second meeting with him in Brussels and conferred with socialist leaders in Amsterdam, while Mackay (in Copenhagen and Oslo) and Shawcross and Hynd (in Rome and Paris) were engaged in similar conferences.[31]

Simultaneously the "Europe Group" established contact with the ILP, which had been agitating for what it called the United Socialist States of Europe since World War II. The ILP had better connections with third force advocates on the Continent than did the Labour Left. During the summer of 1947 it had helped to organize a conference in Paris attended by communist and socialist delegates from France, Italy, Spain, Germany, Holland, Luxemburg, Poland and Greece. Now the ILP helped the "Europe Group" to meet European colleagues. John McNair, the ILP general secretary, arranged a meeting in London on 9 December between five members of the French Socialist Party, including two who belonged to its executive committee, and Mackay, Shawcross, Foot, Mikardo and Crossman. A second meeting in Paris took place over the weekend of 27–29 February, the British representatives this time being Mackay, Shawcross, Hynd and Hale. As a result formal links between the "Europe Group" and French socialists were established.[32]

So far so good, Mackay might have told himself; but in the end setbacks were more numerous than these small triumphs. If initially it seemed obvious to the Labour Left that victory in World War II presented it with a golden opportunity to build a democratic socialist third force, subsequent events and additional consideration threw cold water upon its optimism. Where enthusiasts like Mackay and Shawcross welcomed the ILP's agitation for a USSE as late as January 1948, they had become "a bit worried about this business of the United Socialist States of Europe" by the end of February. "Europe Group" members generally shared these anxieties.[33]

The tides were flowing rapidly during late 1947 and 1948, and they were flowing against the Left. Under such circumstances perhaps the most difficult question the "Europe Group" had to consider was whether European union was practical politics at all. Here members like Crossman, who believed in the possibility of economic coordination among the European countries, but not in the merging of their political systems, came into conflict with Mackay, who passionately advocated political federation of Europe as a precondition to effective economic cooperation. Then, given the division of Europe into two blocs, only one of which would be receiving Marshall Aid, there was the question of East European participation, and of Soviet influence. There was also the vexing question of whether a country such as Britain, which was governed by social democrats, would be justified in joining a European federation dominated either by anti-socialists or by coalitions in which socialists were weak. Further complicating matters was the issue of what should be the relationship of European colonies, former colonies, or Commonwealth countries to a united Europe. Before the "Europe Group" could endorse the USSE movement, before it could exert effective pressure simply on behalf of a British foreign policy independent of the superpowers, it would have to reach some form of consensus on these and related issues.

Bravely the group tried to sort them out. At a meeting on 16 December 1947 it agreed that two position papers should be prepared. One, to be written by Crossman, would consider the European-wide economic measures which might be implemented quickly. The other, to be written by Leah Manning, would "examine the political developments and agreements" necessary for a European union. Unfortunately these papers did little to settle matters. Mackay presented a summary of their main points to a meeting of the group on 3 February 1948. Minutes of the "long discussion" that ensued reveal the variety of viewpoints. From the Left, William Warbey and Sydney Silverman objected to European union which excluded East European countries. A merely Western union was likely to become the vehicle of anti-communists. From the Right, Aiden Crawley, who eventually joined the Conservative Party, argued not merely for exclusion of the Eastern bloc but for cooperation with Churchill or anyone else interested in the integration of Western Europe: "Mistake to give impression approaching from narrow Party view." He was supported by Julian Snow, brother-in-law of Geoffrey Bing—who thought it "cowardly" to oppose Western union just because Labour's opponents favored it—and, unexpectedly, by Shawcross, who, as a participant in the parliamentary "rebellion" of November 1946, was thought to be firmly on the Left. Shawcross now believed that "we should promote the unity of Europe as it is, rather than of a socialist Europe which does not exist." Surprisingly, he drew support from another left-winger, Ronald Chamberlain, and from Mackay himself. John Haire, among others, now objected. The group should press for socialist federation rather than Western union in order to help heal the widening division between East and West. Leah Manning intervened: "It depended upon one's definition of socialism."[34]

Could a group so riddled with differences achieve meaningful results? The upshot of this meeting was agreement only to produce three more papers. In Paper A, Hynd, Shawcross and Mackay would explain the "Federal Approach," by which was meant the approach desired by those who believed in political federation. In Paper B, Aiden Crawley and Crossman would elaborate the "Functional Approach," by which was meant the priority of economic federation. Manning and Warbey would produce Document C, eventually entitled "Britain and Europe," but which might have been named the "Fundamental Approach," since it argued from the original third force position, the one held by Brockway and the ILP, for a United Socialist States of Europe, including the East European countries.[35]

By now, however, the communist coup in Czechoslovakia had occurred. Few on the Labour Left thought the Eastern European countries would join a united European third force independent of the USSR. This became clear at the "Europe Group" meeting on 2 March, when the three documents were discussed. Unfortunately no detailed record remains of what was said. There is, however, a summary:

> The meeting was adjourned with the feeling on the part of most members that . . . the best practical chance of getting a European federation would be through the functional approach . . . It was felt that there is now a good prospect of the group agreeing upon one paper—a synthesis of A and B.

Warbey and Leah Manning's Document C had few defenders in the "Europe Group," or on the Labour Left which dominated it. The third force movement, as originally conceived, was in rapid retreat.[36]

Meanwhile pressure from the Right further complicated matters. Churchill had helped to organize a "Movement for a United Europe" in January 1947, as a follow-up to his Iron Curtain speech, and in December 1947 an "International Committee for European Unity," which set into motion plans for a "Congress of Europe" to meet at The Hague during 7–10 May 1948. The proposed conference, which received much publicity, generated intense enthusiasm among the general public and great controversy within the Labour Party.

Mackay confronted a cruel dilemma. He could not but recognize that Churchill's immense prestige had accomplished in a few bold strokes more for the united Europe ideal than all his work over the years. Would not a true believer attempt to take advantage of Churchill's achievement? Should there not be an effort to make use of the Hague conference? On the other hand, as has been demonstrated, Mackay was under no illusion about the nature of Churchill's commitment to a United States of Europe. The proposed Hague conference would be used to generate support for another grand alliance, aimed this time at the Soviet Union.

There was an additional problem. The Labour government did not disagree with Churchill about the need for an anti-Soviet combination. Indeed it was Bevin's great objective to call one into being. It very much opposed the Hague conference, however, since inevitably Churchill would dominate it. Moreover, wishing still to play the part of a world power, albeit on a less grand scale than the USA or USSR, the Labour government had no intention of submerging British identity in a united Europe, socialist or otherwise. It regarded Churchill's pronouncements in favor of some supranational authority, to which even Britain would submit, as so much demagogy. In the government's view no good could come from the Hague conference; and, in the form of a letter from the party's general secretary, Morgan Phillips, it forbade attendance to PLP members.

This prohibition further divided the "Europe Group." It placed "Keep Lefters" in the dangerous position of courting once again the wrath of Ernest Bevin and other party leaders. For a moment Crossman, at least, was willing to do so. Leslie Hale wrote that, when the prohibition was announced,

> Dick Crossman's reaction was of the most violent possible description. He regarded it as an affront to his freedom of thought and freedom of conscience and was not going in any circumstances to allow Morgan Phillips to dictate any course of action to him.

Then the Member for Coventry East must have recalled his last brush with the party establishment at Margate. "The following day," Hale continued, "Dick Crossman arrived and said he had come to the conclusion that none of us ought to go."[37]

The ban drove a wedge between those of the "Europe Group" who were prepared to disobey the NEC and those who were not. To quote Hale again:

> There were six or seven, including Rankin, who just dodged us and never came to the meetings we summoned to consider the matter... Dick Acland, who had agreed to come only on being assured by Mackay that he would be given ample opportunity of exercising his somewhat limited oratorical powers, refused within five minutes of getting the Morgan Phillips letter... Mark Hewitson, a member of the National Executive, promised to turn up and with equal constancy assured the Executive that he had never agreed to go and would not go; whilst Percy Shurmer I overheard assure Alice Bacon that he had never had any intention of going . . . and ten minutes later assure Kim Mackay, with a break in his voice, that he was sorry he could not go because of constituency engagements.

The "Europe Group" was breaking up.[38]

A resolution moved in the House of Commons on 1 April by an all-party group pressing for Western union reveals the divisions which now beset it. The resolution said in part:

> In the opinion of this House, steps should now be taken, in consultation with other members of the British Commonwealth, to create in Western Europe a political union strong enough to save European democracy and the values of Western civilization; and a trading area large enough with the colonial territories to enable its component parts to achieve recovery and stability.

Signatories included Hale and Crossman of "Keep Left" as well as Mackay himself. They believed that a Western union, whatever its economic basis, was desirable in itself and would constitute a bulwark against communism. Benn Levy and J. P. W. Mallalieu, however, proposed an amendment. The political union should eschew military matters and concern itself only with economics. Otherwise it would harden the division of Europe which already was in danger of congealing permanently. And a dozen other Labour Members, including Silverman and Warbey, and Harold Davies of "Keep Left," proposed a second, tougher amendment, taking the fundamentalist third force line. Pending establishment of an effective world government through the United Nations, this group argued,

> the British Government should use its best endeavours to act as a reconciling and mediating force between the USSR and the USA, and to that end should forthwith divest itself of such military entanglements, cooperation or alliances with either USSR or USA as might tend to hinder or embarrass its mediating function.

A "Europe Group" so deeply divided could play no useful role. It now discontinued meeting.[39]

The protagonists went their separate, indeed mutually exclusive, ways. Mackay still worked assiduously for European union but no longer for a democratic socialist third force. His appeals for support, therefore, were couched in non-partisan terms. As he wrote a year later to Chancellor of the Exchequer Hugh Gaitskell:

> What is wanted in this country and in Europe is increased production, high wages and low costs. These can never come about until there is an economic unification in Europe with a large market, mass production and standardisation.

And to the Conservative Sir R. A. Butler:

> After all, Europe is at least 80% private enterprise, but the benefits of private enterprise (i.e. competition) such as they exist in the United States are completely lost in Europe because of the tariff barriers ... Mass production and standardisation, i.e. the lowering of costs and production ... would come about automatically over a few years if the barriers were broken down and if inefficient businesses were forced into bankruptcy by competition, all of which would come naturally by the demand which a free trade area would create.

He would work for this Cobdenite program "with any democratic group." This brought him far from the closed circle of "Keep Left," or even the "Europe Group." He wrote to Arthur Moyle, Attlee's PPS, "I don't want to be embarrassing, I only want to help in the best way possible." He greeted not merely the Marshall Plan, but eventually NATO, as stepping-stones to the unification of Europe, which seems to have become almost an obsession to him. When, in 1949, a meeting of European foreign ministers, including a grudging Bevin, agreed to set up at Strasbourg a consultative committee to discuss establishing a supranational authority with real if limited functions, Mackay obtained a place on the British delegation. "He was inclined to talk a bit too much both in the Assembly and . . . to British Tories and other unsympathetic types," Dalton, who headed the contingent, reported to Attlee. "He caused me some trouble at the end by having himself nominated . . . for the Permanent Committee."[40]

For his part, Mackay confessed to Crossman that he had "put up with a great deal from Dalton and Co." But the former chairman of Common Wealth endured it all willingly. He was operating now in new and more exalted circles than previously. By 1950 he was accepting donations from Sir Alan Anderson of the International Chamber of Commerce. A year later he was closeted with Lieutenant-General Sir Frederick Morgan, whom he hoped would approach General Eisenhower "with the ultimate object of getting from him an impulse towards setting up, for his benefit as Supreme Commander, NATO, some over-all Western European authority." Thus it would appear that Mackay's devotion to the concept of European union led him to abandon first the Labour Left and then the Labour Party altogether, and to champion in the interests of a federated Europe the very "anti-Soviet bloc" which, at first, he had believed would lead to war.[41]

Others in the "Europe Group" followed paths more difficult to chart. Crossman, for example, continued to advocate a third force, but what he meant by the term is unclear. He claimed that Bevin had been won over to Western union. In fact, if a conversion process had taken place, it was all the other way. Formerly the leading opponent of the Anglo-American alliance, Crossman now claimed it could become the cornerstone of a socialist Western union. His definition of democratic socialism, however, was elastic. The Americans "call it a Fair Deal, and we call it Socialism," he explained. Crossman, like Michael Foot, now believed that "The third force policy of 'neutrality' . . . is a fantasy." A "defensive alliance of the Western world" (NATO) was as close to the original third force goal as one could get in an era of cold war.[42]

This change of front by so prominent an advocate of the third force worried Crossman's employer at the *New Statesman*, Kingsley Martin. "The fact is," Martin explained to G. D. H. Cole, "that Dick does not accept, as you and I do, a certain Marxian basis in historical development, and is not in any serious sense a Socialist." To Crossman himself Martin eventually wrote:

> You made a great and deserved reputation early in the Government by standing as the man who opposed the American alliance. Now people—not leftists—say that your recent speeches show that you wholly accept the position of Bevin and Attlee. I know well that you can produce a good argument for each change of emphasis, but

the point is that each time you speak or write you put your position with an impressive force that seems to exclude the change of position that quite soon afterwards you find necessary.

Crossman's response, if there was one, does not appear in Martin's files. Yet an obvious riposte existed. For Martin himself did not remain committed to the original precepts of the third force movement either. As early as 18 March 1948 he too had begun to hedge. "I would have liked Western union to be a balancing factor between America and Russia," he explained on the BBC radio program "London Forum," but "that has now become extremely difficult to pull off... At the moment it must be anti-communist."[43]

Anti-communist, perhaps, but not yet pro-American. Martin was now instrumental in launching a campaign on behalf of this more modest third force which Foot and Crossman refused to endorse. The impetus came from Leah Manning, who had objected passionately, in May 1948 in the House of Commons, to what seemed to her a common assumption that war with Russia was inevitable. A flood of favorable letters followed this outburst, which moved her to approach the Union of Democratic Control, whose chairman happened to be Kingsley Martin. Manning wanted this body to arrange a mass meeting in support of a motion she hoped to bring before the House of Commons, "That the Government should take the initiative in calling into consultation the heads of the three great powers which were allies during the late war, in the hope of removing present misunderstandings." The UDC initially agreed not merely to sponsor the meeting but to supply speakers—Seymour Cocks, Konni Zilliacus, Sir John Boyd Orr and J. B. Priestley. Upon reflection, however, it decided to attempt something bigger.[44]

Priestley, a member of the UDC executive, "roughed out" a draft "Manifesto for a World Truce" which, after much discussion and revision, was released in November 1948. It advocated

A determined effort... to secure a truce between the Western world and the Soviet Union, on the basis of "an agreement to disagree" in the political sphere, combined with positive cooperation on vital problems of food, health, productive, scientific and technical progress.

The underlying theme of this latest project of the Labour Left remained the need for a third force in world affairs: "We in Britain are striving to solve our problems by the method of evolutionary socialism... We cannot be part of the Soviet system, and we refuse to behave as satellites of American capitalism."[45]

A national conference demanding the world truce took place during 12–13 March 1949 at Beaver Hall, Garlick Hill, in London. Martin took the chair for Priestley, who was ill. It was, perhaps, a comment on the relative decline of third force sentiment in the PLP that the two MPs who addressed the meeting were Maurice Edelman and Ashley Bramall, obscure figures in comparison with Foot and Crossman. Nevertheless, third force sentiment remained strong among those who attended. A report issued afterwards by the UDC stressed that

The main themes of the Conference were profound anxiety at the preparations, both material and psychological, which are being made throughout the world for a new war, and the desire to see the British Government pursuing an independent policy based on Socialist principles and directed towards securing a truce in the present cold war.

Yet the conference had no sequel. The World Truce Campaign petered out.[46]

The problem was lack of conviction among the leaders of the campaign. Priestley was rapidly moving to the Right, a course which finally led him out of politics altogether. As for Martin, by 1949 he no longer believed there was room in the world for a bloc of unaligned European nations. "It comes down to this," he said on the BBC on 16 August 1949; "Though the Socialists . . . are afraid of American capitalist influence, and urgently desire agreement with the Soviet Union, they yet agree with Churchill (whom they regard as a dangerous reactionary) when he denounces the 'police state'." The wing of the Labour Left which Martin represented did not embrace Bevinite anti-communism, but it no longer doubted the need for some form of anti-communist alliance with American backing.[47]

A non-communist "hard" Left within the Labour Party still espousing early third force ideals remained, though sadly depleted in numbers. It had kept its distance from the UDC World Truce Campaign, which it thought a pathetic venture. Benn Levy refused an invitation to join in the following terms:

> A call for a world truce is in effect a pious wish for a continuation of the existing situation. In so far as it means agreement to disagree indefinitely, Bevin, I am sure, would now subscribe to every word in the Manifesto. Now it's unusual, to say the least of it, for a pressure group to exert all its resources for the purpose of pressing the Foreign Secretary to do precisely what he is already doing.

Levy, a charming figure, did not intend to remain in politics. Already he had begun to reduce his political commitments. Dismissing the World Truce Campaign for its lack of bite, he nevertheless refused to play a leading part in the "hard" Left agitation for a third force, which continued, in the face of all odds, to voice the original demands.[48]

A new leadership emerged: Silverman and Warbey of the old "Europe Group." During the summer of 1948 they established an unofficial PLP group to replace it, the "Socialist Europe Group." Thirty-five Labour Members belonged. And they produced a pamphlet, *Stop the Coming War: A Plea for European Unity and Recovery*, in which the fundamental third force arguments, adapted somewhat to the reality of the moment, were restated. Signatories included Harold Davies, Ernest Millington and Stephen Swingler of the old "Keep Left" group, Leah Manning and John Haire of Mackay's "Europe Group" and a handful of others.

The "Socialist Europe Group" maintained a busy schedule. It organized a weekend conference in London on 30–1 October 1948 at which Warbey was the main speaker. It produced in 1949 a second pamphlet, *A Socialist Foreign Policy for the Labour Party*. It composed a lengthy memorandum for the British Delegation to the Consultative

Assembly of the Council of Europe at Strasbourg—hoping, no doubt, to influence at least one old ally, Mackay. It maintained contact with Brockway's movement for a USSE, which likewise refused to abandon the essential third force program. With support from the "Socialist Europe Group," USSE conferences were held in Paris during 18–22 June 1948, in London on 22–3 October 1949 and in Paris again on 5–7 November 1949. Like Silverman and Warbey, Brockway (who had rejoined the Labour Party by then) kept up a steady stream of newspaper articles endorsing the third force in *Labour's Northern Voice*, the *Glasgow Forward* and *Reynolds News*. In comparison with earlier Labour Left efforts, however, the impact of this stubborn campaign was negligible.[49]

A good deal of bitterness now divided those on the "hard" Labour Left from their "softer" comrades. Emrys Hughes wrote snidely, if prophetically, of *Tribune*'s editor, "Too much Parliament is bad for him . . . and Michael has already one foot in the Labour Party Executive." Ian Mikardo angrily compared the attitude towards Russia of his old friends Foot and Crossman with Churchill's toward Nazi Germany. "Unconditional surrender" was their only policy. They had "run away" from their principles. Mikardo added sadly:

> It's no use arguing that all our views of 1946–47 have been put out of date by the behaviour of the Russians . . . If the Keep Lefters and others really believed in a Third Force, the behaviour of the Russians should have induced them not to run away from that Third Force, but to work harder for its achievement.

Mikardo, a member of *Tribune*'s board of directors, now resigned his position. Hugh Jenkins, the peppery leader of the National Union of Bank Employees and future Minister of the Arts under Wilson, likewise was disappointed by the disappearance of "Keep Left." "There is a sizeable group of rank-and-file opinion in the Labour Party which has good reason to feel more stabbed than stabbing. One by one, many of the leading left-wingers have melted."[50]

Behind such angry charges there lurked a sense of near despair. The "hard" Labour Left could not but recognize how strongly the tide was flowing against it. "You should be with us," Silverman exhorted Benn Levy. "After all, it is *possible* we are not too late yet. . . The third force is a thin hope, but all there is."[51]

By 1949 there was no hope for the advocates of a democratic socialist third force, whatever Silverman might write. The movement on its behalf was a small fragment of its former self. Its leadership lacked stature and charisma. In the bifurcated cold-war era few on the Labour Left were willing any longer to be identified publicly with a movement demanding that Britain maintain equal distance from both superpowers.

There remained on the Labour Left, however, a pervasive, if unfocused, opposition to the Anglo-American military alliance which Bevin finally cemented in the Atlantic Pact (NATO) of May 1949. Before it was sanctioned in the House, Driberg wrote, "A large NO lobby is improbable, but there may be a good few abstentions." He was right. Even at the height of the cold war 142 Labour Members did not endorse the formation of NATO. Of course, not all who failed to vote opposed it. Some were absent through illness, or otherwise occupied when the division was called. Still the rate of abstention was high, bearing comparison with earlier Labour Left "rebellions." Seven of the fifteen original "Keep Left" members did not vote; only one of the eleven signatories to Warbey and Silverman's pamphlet supported the pact. And five critical amendments to the Bill were tabled by Labour backbenchers, though none was moved.[52]

The NATO vote (which usually is taken as an overwhelming endorsement of Bevinism, since the tally was 333 to 6) reveals that third force sentiment remained a subterranean presence in the Labour Party. Stubbornly resilient, it surfaced yet again after 1951, in the Bevanite movement, which cannot be understood without reference to Labour Left efforts on behalf of the third force movement during 1945–9. And though Bevan himself was eventually to prove a grievous disappointment to his followers, the sentiment favoring a democratic socialist Britain independent of the two superpowers, which he had channelled and revived during the 1950s, survived even his apostasy (as many thought it). Nearly forty years after the NATO vote in the House of Commons, the third force remains a potent if ambiguous rallying-cry on the Labour Left. Its realization, however, seems even more distant than it was when the cold war was new.

The movement for the third force which crystallized under Crossman's leadership in the November 1946 parliamentary "rebellion," and in successive waves of diminishing force and effectiveness attempted to change the government's foreign policy towards the USA and USSR, encapsulates the experience of the Labour Left during a crucial period in postwar history. It highlights the cruel dilemma that faced democratic socialists on the Left of the Labour Party during the early cold-war years. Nearly irresistible pressure was exerted upon them to choose sides among the two superpowers, when the cardinal element of their faith was that salvation lay in refusing to choose sides. The result was a fragmenting of the party's left wing, a wing that was none too stable in the best of times.

At one point the Labour Left critique of Bevinism was capable of rallying a good third of the PLP. Even at the zenith of the government's popularity and effectiveness, an identifiable Left in the Labour Party held that the leadership was failing to strive for the foreign policy which, being socialist, it was obliged to uphold. This seriously worried the government. In Crossman, Foot, Mikardo, Mackay and others the Labour Left possessed a talented cadre of young leaders. The gradual falling away of most of them from the third force movement they had helped to establish represents a significant moment in Labour Party history and an end in Britain to effective opposition to the polarizing process by which the world was divided into hostile blocs. A forgotten chapter in the history of Labour, the third force movement of 1945–9 was perhaps the brightest hope of the Labour Left to be deferred or shattered in the grim postwar world.

Notes and References

1   For Tory suspicions of America, see Terry Anderson, *The United States, Britain and the Cold War, 1944–47*] (Columbia, Mo., 1981).

2   For the origins of the UDC, see Marvin Swartz, *The Union of Democratic Control in British Politics during the First World War* (Oxford, 1971); BBC Written Archives, Reading, "Any Questions?," 28 May 1946.

3   For more on socialist nationalists like Tillett, see Jonathan Schneer, *Ben Tillett, Portrait of a Labour Leader* (London, 1983). For socialist internationalists, see, for example, Edward Thompson, *William Morris* (New York, 1976), and Kenneth O. Morgan, *Keir Hardie* (London, 1975); for the British Left during the interwar era, see especially Ben Pimlott, *Labour and the Left in the 1930s* (Cambridge, 1977, London 1987), and Bernard Crick, *George Orwell: A Life* (London, 1980).

4   *Tribune*, 7 April 1944, 27 October 1944, 8 December 1944.

5   BLPES, microfilm no. 19, minutes of meetings of Parliamentary Labour Party, 22 August 1945, 10 October 1945. Library of Congress, Felix Frankfurter papers, Laski to Frankfurter, 20 October 1945.

6   Public Record Office, FO800/491/77, Johnson to Bevin, 11 December 1945.

7   Sussex University, Martin papers, Box 11, Correspondence, Callaghan to Martin, 28 July 1946.

8   *Evening Standard*, 25 October 1946.

9   Copies of this letter may be found in the House of Lords Record Office, Benn Levy papers, file 57.

10   Michael Foot, *Aneurin Bevan*, Vol. 2 (1973), p. 91.

11   *Daily Herald*, 14 November 1946.

12   Public Record Office, FO800/492/178, MacNeil to Attlee, 13 November 1946.

13   See particularly here *Daily Telegraph* and *Daily Herald*, 14 November 1946. For the resolution itself, see BLPES, microfilm no. 19, PLP meetings, 13 November 1946.

14   Public Record Office, FO800/492/147, Bevin to Attlee, 14 November 1946.

15   *Daily Herald*, 20 November 1946; BLPES, Hugh Dalton papers.

16   Labour Party, NEC minutes, Vol. 96, p. 443; BLPES, microfilm no. 96, minutes of Liaison Committee, 26 November 1946; PLP meetings, 28 November 1946; *Sunday Pictorial*, 24 November 1946.

17   *Keep Left* introduction, "How this book came about."

18   In his diary Lord Hale mentions Edelman and Silverman at the early meetings of the group, but their names do not appear as signatories to *Keep Left*.

19   *Keep Left* (London, 1947), pp. 38, 41.

20   Hale diary, 11 May 1947; Public Record Office FO800/493/113, Jebb to Bevin, 5 May 1947.

21   *Labour Party Annual Conference, 1947*, p. 99.

22   *Sunday Pictorial*, 1 June 1947; *Labour Party Annual Conference, 1947*, p. 179.

23   Dalton Diaries, 24–9 May 1947.

24   *Daily Herald*, 31 May 1947.

25   For a brief resume of Mackay's early career, see Angus Calder, "The Common Wealth Party, 1942–45," D.Phil. thesis, Sussex University, 1968, pp. 93–5; I am indebted to Lord Leslie Hale for additional information. Hale shared law offices with Mackay during the postwar period. See also BLPES, R. W. G. Mackay papers, on which much of the following is based.

26   Mackay papers 13/1, Mackay to "Dear Colleague," 1 September 1947; ibid., 8/3, undated letter by Mackay to "Dear Colleague."

27   Ibid., 13/3, undated, unsigned fragment of a letter.

28   Ibid., "List of Members of the Europe Group."

29   Ibid., 23/2, Mackay to Maurice Webb, 9 January 1948; 8/3, Europe Group to Foreign Secretary, 9 January 1948.
30   Ibid., 12/1, text of Bevin's speech preserved in Mackay's papers.
31   Ibid., 8/3, 16 December 1947, minutes of Europe Group meeting; Leslie Hale, interview with the author.
32   Mackay papers, 14/3, Shawcross to McNair, 11 December 1947; 8/3, British report of meeting with French Socialists. See also *Daily Herald*, 9 December 1947.
33   Mackay papers, 14/3, Shawcross to McNair, 11 December 1947; ibid., Shawcross to Mackay, 26 January 1948; 25/2, Mackay to Brockway, 21 February 1948.
34   Ibid., 8/3, Shawcross to Mackay, 12 December 1947; 8/3, minutes of 3 February 1948, Europe Group meeting; 13/4, notes on 3 February 1948 Europe Group meeting.
35   The three documents are preserved among Mackay's papers.
36   Ibid., 8/3, minutes of Europe Group meeting, 2 March 1948.
37   Private papers of Leslie Hale, "Congress of Europe at the Hague," an unpublished report by Leslie Hale.
38   Ibid.
39   Mackay papers, see materials in 9/8.
40   Ibid., 7/8, Mackay to Gaitskell, 3 March 1950; 12/5, Mackay to Butler, 15 April 1949; 8/1 Mackay to Moyle, 3 May 1948; Dalton papers, 917/45, Dalton to Attlee, 10 September 1949.
41   Mackay papers, 8/1, Mackay to Crossman, 10 September 1949; 9/10, Sir Alan Anderson to Mackay, 8 November 1950; 9/3, Mackay to Morgan, 3 March 1951.
42   For Crossman's views, see *Tribune*, 26 November 1948; *Sunday Pictorial*, 25 October 1949. For Foot, see *Tribune*, 18 March 1949.
43   Martin papers, Box 2, Correspondence, Martin to Cole, 4 October 1948; Martin to Crossman, 1 July 1950.
44   Hull University, UDC papers, 4/33, EC meeting 6 May 1948.
45   *New Statesman* files, Priestley to Martin, 10 July 1948. For the manifesto itself, see UDC collection, materials in 4/33 and 6/1.
46   UDC collection, 4/3, "Report to EC."
47   Martin papers, file on "KM's Radio Broadcasts."
48   Ibid., "Miscellaneous Letters," Levy to Martin, 26 October 1948.
49   Material which helps trace the activities of this group may be found in the Mackay papers, 14/3 and 21/1; and in the House of Lords Record Office, Benn Levy Papers, file 64.
50   *Tribune*, 11 June 1948, 20 May 1949, 19 November 1948.
51   Levy papers, file 64, Silverman to Levy, "Sunday."
52   *Reynolds News*, 8 May 1949; *The Times*, 12 May 1949.

4

The Alternative Economic Program of the Labour Left

DURING THE GENERAL ELECTION CAMPAIGN in 1945, Labour candidates often warned that Conservative victory would lead to repetition of the economic ills that plagued Britain during the interwar era. According to George Wigg, Labour candidate for Dudley, Tories had promised, after 1918, " 'homes for heroes' that never got built . . . 'trade revivals' which produced the biggest mass unemployment we have ever known." These failings, Labourites claimed, were inevitable under capitalism. That Tories now were promising to lift wartime economic controls in the name of freedom meant that they had not learned this elementary lesson. "If uncontrolled capitalism comes back to Tyneside," Zilliacus warned, "unemployment will come back to Gateshead." On the other hand, Labour victory "would mean full employment and security" for all Britons, as Richard Crossman promised in his election address. "What is there . . . in the policy of the Labour Party that is absolute proof against . . . the brutal injustices and sordid poverty" of the interwar years? Fred Lee inquired rhetorically of the voters of Hulme. "There is, to start with, the fundamental faith that the wealth and resources of the country must be owned by the people of the country, and must be developed to meet their common needs."[1]

Victory in the general election provided Labour with an opportunity to meet the expectations raised during its campaign. Attlee's governments maintained full employment over six years, developed a wide range of generous welfare benefits and nationalized nearly 20 percent of the country's industry. The Labour Left applauded these achievements as a first installment on the road to socialism. Many, however, did not consider them to represent the transformation of society which had been promised in 1945.

The Labour Left never criticized the government's economic policies as fiercely as it attacked Bevinism. On the other hand, it grew ever less confident of the government's determination to build socialism in Britain, while becoming more supportive of the leadership's approach to foreign affairs. By 1950–1 issues of social and economic policy had become as divisive within the Labour Party as issues of foreign policy. When these strands of dissent merged, as they did over the charges that Hugh Gaitskell levied on the National Health Service in order to help pay for rearmament, the result was the most important Labour Left rebellion of the postwar era.

The Labour Left critique of the government's economic measures fell into three broad categories. It criticized the government for failing to control the economy with sufficient strictness, for imposing undemocratic forms of such controls as were established and for pursuing a foreign policy which interfered with building socialism at home. Nor did the Labour Left hesitate to suggest other "more socialist" policies for Attlee to consider. The following chapter will examine the growth of Labour Left disillusionment with the government's economic policies, the alternative program which it developed and, finally, the creativity and will to power which it displayed in approaching these issues.

II

In order to win the war, the coalition government had taken unprecedented powers. It could order labor where and when to work, control prices by a variety of means including rationing and cash subsidies, regulate imports and exports and allocate scarce resources to industry. Because Labour took office with the war against Japan in process, it found itself after victory in the Far East still possessing these and other related powers. In 1918, when Lloyd George had come into a similar inheritance, he deliberately pared it down. In 1945 the Labour Left was determined that history would not be repeated. Labour had acquired peacefully prerogatives which otherwise could have been gained, probably, only in the course of revolution. It would use them to direct the economy along socialist paths.[2]

Above all, the Labour Left hoped that key industries which had been controlled by the government during the war would now be brought into public ownership. During the general election campaign, Labour promised to nationalize industries capable of affecting the general well-being. In *Let Us Face the Future*, Labour submitted to the voters a list of industries which it considered ripe for public ownership: the mines, railways, road haulage, gas, electricity, civil aviation and iron and steel; and it promised also to nationalize the Bank of England. Governors of the latter, it was held, had dictated to Ramsay MacDonald in 1931 in order to bring down the second Labour government. Nationalization would protect socialism from another "bankers' ramp."

In the immediate aftermath of the war the public was well disposed to such promises of government activism, as the general election results illustrated. The Labour Left was confident they would be fulfilled. There was little recognition of the profoundly weak economy which the war effort had produced. In fact, if Labour possessed greater interventionist powers and public support for using them than it might have expected, it also confronted economic circumstances of unprecedented severity. Controls and "planning" would not be applied in an auspicious economic climate. Inevitably the harsh postwar reality came to threaten the government's ambitious domestic program.

No sooner had Attlee chosen his Cabinet than the peril was revealed. With the surrender of Japan, President Truman abruptly suspended the Lend Lease program. Forced by his unexpected decision to make a realistic assessment of Britain's economic situation, the government quickly concluded that additional American assistance was vital. Keynes was dispatched to Washington in search of aid, in the form of a gift if possible, or a loan if necessary. Many on the Labour Left, however, were shocked by Truman's attitude and believed that Britain should attempt to get along without American assistance. In speeches to the House of Commons, Attlee and Chancellor of the Exchequer Hugh Dalton attempted to combat this idea. Nevertheless, when the American negotiators disclosed their terms for a loan they seemed sufficiently harsh for Bevan and Shinwell to argue, at a Cabinet meeting of 6 November, that Britain should reject them. The USA, according to the Minister of Fuel and Power, needed Britain as much as Britain needed America. He believed that "the custom of the debtor countries is essential to US prosperity," at a time, as Alec Cairncross notes, when British exports to the USA amounted to a mere 0.5 percent of American GNP! Not surprisingly, Shinwell failed to carry the Cabinet or even a majority of the Labour Left. More persuasive were Dalton's dark ruminations. Without the loan, he wrote,

we would go deeper into the dark valley of austerity than even during the war. Less food—except for bread and potatoes—in particular less meat and sugar; little cotton and therefore less clothes and less exports; and worst of all from the point of view of public morale, practically no smokes since 80% of our tobacco costs dollars. . . . We should be on the downward slope, leading to defeat at the next election.[3]

Subsequent scholarship has tended to confirm Dalton's judgment, not merely that Britain was in desperate need of the loan, but that rejection was never a viable option. At the time, however, serious objections were raised by Conservatives who believed that a government led by Churchill would have received more generous treatment in Washington, and by a minority of the Labour Left who agreed with Shinwell and Bevan that accepting American assistance on harsh terms would raise as many problems as it solved. According to Kingsley Martin, the Americans had forced upon Britain "a disastrous bargain," opening up the sterling area to multilateral trade, and imposing onerous terms of repayment. The young Edward Thompson introduced an equally disturbing consideration. In his opinion, the loan would tie Great Britain "to financial conditions that will leave no time or thought for Socialist reforms." In the 14 December *Daily Herald*, Michael Foot repeated Thompson's charge. "American capitalism is arrogant, self-confident, merciless and convinced of its capacity to dictate the destinies of the world," he warned. "If we are not to become the bondslaves of Wall Street, a terrific, unexampled burst of productive energy must be revealed in this country."[4]

For Labour activist and Oxford historian G. D. H. Cole, too, the loan raised fundamental issues. Without that massive infusion of cash, he argued a year later, Britain's external relations, especially with the Soviet Union, would necessarily have been different. Britain could not have maintained most of its foreign commitments. It would have been forced to dispense with most American imports. As a result the nation would have had, on the home front, to reorganize its metal and engineering industries to meet the demands of industrial re-equipment. Above all, it would have had to plan, "and to plan thoroughly, not merely in patches, but over the entire economic field." When the government rejected this course it had, in effect, postponed embarking on the socialist path to which it was pledged.[5]

Cole, of course, had no vote in the House of Commons. But Foot, Barbara Castle, Jennie Lee, Seymour Cocks, Raymond Blackburn and a dozen other Labour Members entered the lobby to vote against accepting the loan. Ellis Smith, parliamentary secretary to Cripps at the Board of Trade, was not supposed to vote against his masters. As he explained in the *Reynolds News* for 24 February, however, he too opposed accepting the loan, which he believed would interfere with socialist planning. Smith resigned his position in protest.

Most of the Labour Left, however, could see no alternative to the American offer. They remained enthusiastic about the government's approach to economic matters generally. Laski went further. He believed that "certain aspects of the agreement did great honour to the spirit of the American negotiators." Moreover, they had helped make possible Labour's domestic accomplishments, which, as late as 2 June 1946, he thought to be "enough to satisfy the most eager zealot for swift change." In the 15 June *Glasgow Forward* one such zealot confirmed the professor's judgment. "No critic has any reason for complaining that this Labour Government has been slow or timid on the Home Front," Emrys Hughes wrote. "The nationalization of the Bank of England, the Mines, Civil Aviation, Iron and Steel and Transport are all coming . . . and during the next five years the capitalist ownership of our key industries will have ended for ever." Still, debate over the American loan and the government's decision to accept it had been a harbinger of future divisions.

The first serious manifestation of Labour Left disillusionment with the government's approach to economic matters came a year later, as the result of another crisis. Early in 1947 fuel shortages, coinciding with bitter winter weather, threatened the economy and the government again. Scholars have examined carefully the causes of the emergency and the government's response. They have largely ignored the attitude of the Labour Left, however, no doubt because it, like the right wing of the party, rallied in support of the leaders. Yet the 1947 coal crisis marks the beginning of an important shift in Labour Left attitudes towards the government. For some it confirmed a disturbing impression, first perceived during the debate over whether to accept the American loan, that the Cabinet was unable, or even unwilling, to implement the hard socialist measures which the Labour Left firmly believed alone would promote prosperity and economic justice.[6]

The crisis began with production of coal already at dangerously low levels due to insufficiency of labor. In February record snows and frigid temperatures further reduced output, and hampered transportation of supplies. Shinwell, the responsible minister, was unprepared for these difficulties, despite often having received advance warnings that there were too few coal-miners to maintain stocks. In panic, on Friday 6 February, he advised the Cabinet that rationing of coal must begin at once, even though industries which depended on it would lie idle for part of each day, and individual consumers would not be able to heat their homes. This was a grave threat to the government's recovery program, popularity and reputation. The Cabinet had no option, however, but to accept Shinwell's recommendation, though postponing its implementation until Monday 10 February.

That afternoon, Shinwell announced the cuts in the House. Before he rose to speak, Members had no inkling of the crisis facing the nation. Shinwell did not break the news with aplomb. According to Dalton, writing in his diary later in the evening, the minister "made a very poor performance." The effect upon Labour backbenchers was devastating. One wrote afterwards, "I was in the Chamber when the Minister of Fuel made his statement. That was a turning point for me. My unquestioning certainty of the ability of the Government to ride the storms that I knew lay ahead was gone."[7]

Despite the gravity of the situation, the Labour Left thought the crisis offered the government an opportunity. As during the war, people would support sweeping measures to overcome danger and hardship. The government, therefore, could now strengthen its hold on the economy. Foot issued a clarion call on 14 February in the *Daily Herald*: "The great need of the hour is a Socialist offensive, a more deadly assault upon the ramparts of privilege." Six days later Crossman (writing in the *News Chronicle*, because the *New Statesman* could not publish during the fuel shortage) attempted to translate Foot's inspirational exhortation into practical politics. The country needed a Ministry of Production, he explained, to direct "the Regional Production Committees, and armed with full powers to fix priorities and allocate our rare manpower and materials despite the clamour of competing Departments and industries."

Not all Labour Left prescriptions for dealing with the crisis were so specific. All demanded, however, that the government give greater emphasis to planning and control. Ellis Smith, now a backbencher, was quick to concede that "we have carried out the huge programme of social legislation to which we pledged ourselves." But, he added, "in regard to the national planning of productive resources on which everything else depends . . . we have not done enough . . . I do not believe we have a national plan." Laski, on 5 March in the *Daily Herald*, likewise called for more planning and stringent controls. He introduced, as well, a puritanical element to his exhortations which, possibly, Labour politicians, including those on the Labour Left, did not appreciate. "The vital industries must push the luxury industries to the periphery of production," he advised reasonably enough. And then: "we cannot afford to luxuriate either in the expensive escapism of Hollywood films or the pleasant opium of Virginia tobacco. We cannot waste thousands of workers upon pools and dog-racing and midweek football." He added somewhat disarmingly, "Let us face it quite frankly. We cannot have two world wars in one generation and expect not to have a hard time."[8]

The coal crisis came to an end after about five weeks, when the weather improved. It represents an important moment in the postwar history of the Labour Left. They had been relatively quiet in public about individual responsibility for the emergency, possibly because the minister most apparently at fault, Shinwell, had been associated (albeit episodically) with the Left since before World War I. No doubt, they wished also to avoid being branded as destructive critics at a moment when the party's natural inclination was to rally behind the government. Nevertheless, for the Labour Left, the fuel crisis was a turning-point which failed to turn. The Cabinet had not mastered it with new, socialist initiatives, but merely had ridden it out. It was during this period that the "Keep Left" group first began to hold regular meetings. "Round the table were Mallalieu, Foot, Crossman, Mackay, Wigg, Harold Davies, Swingler, Mikardo, Edelman, Benn Levy and Millington, with myself in the chair," Leslie Hale wrote in his diary on 9 February at the height of the crisis, "and we arranged to get out a book before the Labour Conference this year."

The coal crisis had confirmed the Labour Left in the belief, as one member put it, that there was great "need for a more drastic Socialist policy if we were not to drift into disaster." Of what would such a policy consist? The *New Statesman* for 22 March reiterated the need for more government control of the economy. Attlee must "take emergency powers at least as large as those assumed in 1940 and use them far more drastically against the employers' class." In the same journal three weeks later Benn Levy was more specific. The government should implement a "five point plan" which would give it powers to control and direct raw materials in the national interest, tax the rich, prohibit the expansion of "inessential industries," pay high wages in "unattractive industries" and establish a wages policy.[9]

Levy had provided a preview of *Keep Left*, which one month later attempted to lay down the Labour Left economic program in greater detail. According to the pamphlet Britain's economic crisis was rooted in the country's failure "to pay its way." The solution, recognized by all, was to raise exports 65 percent above the prewar level. But exhorting labor to work longer and harder, as the government was doing already, was not enough. Rather exports could be raised to the requisite level only if the government undertook a "more drastic socialist policy." It must establish the "full scale Ministry of Economic Affairs" urged by Crossman and, as Laski had recommended, do "without frills," by generally favoring "essential industries" over inessential ones through a variety of increased controls which *Keep Left* described. It must also "rationalise and standardise production," force efficiency upon management and raise working-class morale by strengthening the joint production committees which had been established during the war to ensure worker input in all decisions affecting the shop-floor. In addition, the pamphlet urged that nationalization be extended to "every industry which has a hold over our national economy, or which cannot be made efficient in private hands." Among the former, *Keep Left* listed heavy chemicals and "some non-banking forms of finance, such as insurance." Among the latter it included iron and steel, motor vehicles and "certain electrical components." Moreover Britain's financial dependence on America could be lessened by "close economic cooperation with Europe" and by trade agreements with the Soviet Union and the Eastern bloc.[10]

Keep Left was inspired by the government's failure to adopt more resolute policies during the coal crisis. Yet a striking aspect of the pamphlet is its authors' assumption that the party leaders generally shared their goals. As with their critique of Bevin's foreign policy, so with the demand for "a more drastic socialist policy" at home, left-wing Labourites did not wish to defeat their leaders but, as Sydney Silverman had said during the debate on the Address from the Throne, to help them carry out the program on which they had been elected. As *Keep Left* warned the government, simultaneously reflecting bravado and solidarity with the leaders, implementing its proposals would cause controversy, but "this is a Socialist Revolution, not a National Savings Week." If this was disillusionment it did not go very far. Paradoxically, a pamphlet sparked by left-wing doubts about the government reveals a fundamental confidence in its socialist commitment.[11]

Within months, however, that confidence had been sorely tried. During the summer of 1947 a third crisis further emphasized Britain's dire economic position while further casting into doubt the government's determination to take the measures which, according to the Labour Left, were necessary for the country's salvation. During this period Bevin finally had succeeded in putting his Labour Left critics on to the defensive. Critics of the government's economic policies, however, stepped up the volume and intensity of their attack.

III

When the original American loan of 1945 had been arranged, Keynes thought it would last for six years. By the summer of 1947, however, the loan was almost gone. One reason for this, which *Keep Left* had recognized and warned against, was that free convertibility of sterling was due to begin on 15 July 1947, a year after the loan had been ratified by the US Congress. The Americans had made convertibility a condition of the loan because they wished to penetrate British-dominated markets in which sterling was the sole currency and bilateralism the primary mode of trade. The British had accepted this stipulation, although they foresaw that it would reduce the attractiveness of the pound, because they underestimated the disruption which convertibility would cause and did not wish to jeopardize the entire agreement. As soon as convertibility went into effect, however, holders of sterling scrambled to convert their pounds into dollars. The British government did not know how to stop this catastrophic process except by suspending convertibility, which it did after five harrowing weeks. Even more than with the fuel emergency, its credibility, popularity and self-confidence had been severely wounded. For Labour, "It was never glad confident morning again."[12]

During this crisis the Labour Left took a highly visible role. The very figures whom Bevin had obliterated at Margate two months earlier reappeared to agitate against the government once more. The Foreign Secretary had hammered them, but Foot, Crossman, Mackay and the others remained articulate and, all things considered, effective critics. As Dalton recorded sourly in his diary on 8 August at the height of the crisis, the "Keep Left" group had "been in a state of perpetual hysteria during these last few days, holding two or three meetings each day or night." It would take the carrot offered by Marshall Aid as well as the stick brandished by Bevin to permanently alter Labour Left perceptions of what the British government could and should do.

What the critics feared was that the government would succumb to Conservative (and American) calls for reductions in public expenditure. No one could be confident that the massive financial aid which Marshall had broached in his speech would be forthcoming. In the meantime, memories of 1931 remained vivid, especially on the Left. "If cuts have to be made because of our import difficulties," Foot warned in the *Daily Herald* on 18 July, "it becomes all the more necessary that the wealth we possess should be shared as fairly as possible. . . That is the only alternative to another 1931." On 26 July the *New Statesman* echoed Foot. "Either the Labour Government redeems the disaster of 1931 by mastering this crisis with Socialist measures and Socialist incentives, or it must sooner or later accept the necessity for deflation and for unemployment as a whip for the working class."

In fact the Cabinet was occupied by frantic meetings at which one solution to the crisis after another was canvassed and discarded. There is no evidence that coalition with the Conservatives received serious consideration. Ministers were tempted, however, to abandon or postpone measures which, perhaps coincidentally, Conservatives and the American government opposed. Among these was nationalization of the iron and steel industries, considered by some a talisman of Labour's commitment to socialism. Inevitably word of the Cabinet's anguished proceedings filtered down to the rest of the party. This did little to assuage Labour Left fears that some form of "another 1931" was being contemplated.

Tension mounted. Citing the "mood of uncertainty . . . growing in the Parliamentary Party," and the "wild talk" to which it was giving rise, "Keep Left" dispatched a private letter to Attlee:

> The Government should wait no longer, and should now undertake and put into force the drastic measures . . . required. . . We all need a revived spirit of comradeship under a leadership which is ready to gamble, not on assistance from outside [Marshall aid], but on the spirit of our people.

The letter went on to reiterate suggestions proposed in *Keep Left*, though stressing, this time, the need to reduce the size of the army so that additional labor would become available. Meanwhile, on 26 July, Kingsley Martin printed "an open letter to the Prime Minister" from "an influential Labour MP who for special reasons must remain anonymous." This communication, probably written by a PPS, called for the dismissal of incompetent ministers, and for socialist measures which would amount to a "national patriotic revolution." One day later, the political correspondent of the *Sunday Pictorial* predicted "very blunt speaking next Wednesday" at the regular PLP meeting. Backbenchers would demand hard information about the rumours of coalition, an early election and the abandonment of iron and steel.[13]

Sadly, no detailed record of the meeting, which took place on 30 July, survives. To judge from newspaper accounts, however, the party leadership did not close the door on radical solutions to the crisis. Driberg wrote for *Reynolds News* on 3 August that "although I must not . . . reveal what took place at last Wednesday's meeting of the PLP, I can say that MPs of all shades of opinion in the Party were immeasurably encouraged and stimulated by it." Driberg himself was "exhilarated by the knowledge that the leadership is adequate to the grave task ahead." Similarly a heartened, if sardonic, Mikardo predicted in the same edition of *Reynolds* that "Attlee will produce next week as the Government's own ideas all the many suggestions which backbenchers have been making for the last six months." He listed a wages policy, a profits policy, better control of raw materials, rationing of labor and cuts in overseas commitments. Not coincidentally these were all measures proposed in "Keep Left's" letter to Attlee, and in the pamphlet itself.

Believing that finally the government had adopted their domestic program, members of the Labour Left looked forward to an economic debate in the House, at which the Prime Minister was scheduled to speak. They thought he would announce the Cabinet's conversion there. Their confidence, however, was misplaced. As Leslie Hale recorded afterwards in his diary, the galleries were packed when Attlee rose. But "the speech was inexpressibly bathetic. It was impossible not to come to the conclusion that the Prime Minister had not even mastered the problem." Perhaps most disappointing to the Left was the inadequacy of the cuts projected for the military. The forces were to be reduced from 1,087,000 to 1,007,000 men. At this, Hale recorded, "there was a gasp of surprise from [Attlee's] most ardent supporters." Other disappointments were nearly as great. The Prime Minister announced economies to the tune of £200 million. As Laski complained in the *Glasgow Forward* for 10 August, however, the sum had been reached by cobbling together "an incoherent chaos of bits and pieces which no one can seriously call planning." Worse still, "there is nothing but an appeal to companies not to pay too large dividends. Almost all the new compulsions will fall upon the workers."[14]

As soon as Attlee had finished speaking, Hale called a meeting of the "Keep Left" group "to consider what action should be taken." Deciding to supplement private exhortation by public advocacy, they composed a letter to the *Daily Herald* which was printed on the following day, 8 August. It began uncompromisingly: "The Prime Minister's statement on the economic situation has dismayed many members of the Parliamentary Labour Party ... We believe no purpose is served in concealing this fact." The letter cited "five major points of policy on which the Government should think again and act more courageously if a worse crisis is not to occur within a few months." These were the by now familiar list of suggestions: that the armed forces be reduced to 750,000 men by March 1948, that the government announce the nationalization of iron and steel "at once," that it end convertibility and establish greater trade with Russia and the East European countries. In addition, "a capital levy, or at least drastic additional taxes on profits," was essential. These represented the bare bones of a "real, Socialist plan." "We fear," the signatories to the letter added, "that no such plan exists."

"Keep Left" hoped to press these recommendations on the Prime Minister in person. Attlee agreed to receive a deputation composed of Crossman, Mikardo, Callaghan and Swingler—an indication of the influence these junior Members were thought to have, and of the government's insecurity at this critical moment. Hale described the deputation's experience in his diary:

They had spent an hour with the Prime Minister and had got no further with him. Every time they came to figures he referred them to the Chancellor [Dalton], and all they got was an impression that the Prime Minister did not really understand the position. They had left him after ten, and had gone to see the Chancellor and reported that the Chancellor had been fortifying himself in the Smoke Room . . . to the extent that he was not in the mood to discuss business at all.[15]

The impression of lack of resolution at the top was widespread, extending even to government whips. One of them, Percy Daines, resigned his position in order "to speak his mind on the crisis," as the editor of *Reynolds News* put it on 10 August. The erstwhile disciplinarian did not mince words. "The British people were keyed up last Wednesday for a mighty lead from the Prime Minister," Daines began:

> The members of the Parliamentary Labour Party were prepared to support measures, however drastic, to meet the crisis and preserve the Socialist advances to which they are pledged. The facts must be stated: the inspiration has not been given us. The measures pronounced by the Government will neither mobilise the people nor ensure our independence from America, without which hopes of progress must be in vain.

Sensing that the country confronted "a revolutionary moment," Daines argued against adopting "coalition policies." They represented "political suicide." Worse still, renewed rumors that iron and steel would be dropped from the nationalization program seemed to confirm "that we are not prepared to attack the main citadel of British capitalism."

Such rumors now were sweeping the party. A memorandum calling for the nationalization of iron and steel during the next session was submitted to the Prime Minister, along with a request for another party meeting to discuss the issue. Duly convened on 11 August, this gathering proved among the most difficult the government ever faced. Hale described the debate which took place as "very forthright." Gaitskell, who did not attend, recorded in his diary that the leaders themselves were divided, Bevan "signalling to Jennie [Lee] and (so said Shinwell to me) applauding the critics of the Government." Morrison explained why nationalizing iron and steel should be postponed, but not abandoned. In Hale's opinion, the Lord Chancellor was less than convincing:

> The motion, had it been put, would have been carried against the Government, but the previous question was in fact moved in view of the fact that the carrying of the motion would have been for all practical purposes a direct vote of censure.

The previous motion was declared carried by 81 votes to 77. Hale doubted these totals. They had been estimated "by a couple of men walking down a very crowded room and purporting to count the hands."[16]

The 11 August meeting of the PLP was as near as the Labour Left came, during 1945–51, to defeating the government. Further agitation might have carried it to victory, although Parliament's summer recess intervened. Certainly, however, other factors now emerged to inhibit what, so far, had been a vigorous and effective campaign mounted by the Labour Left against government policy. As always, simple loyalty acted as a constraint. Even on the day preceding the meeting, Driberg confessed that he doubted the wisdom of pushing the "rebellion" to its logical conclusion. As he wrote in *Reynolds News*, "Ministers have a right to expect some leniency from their supporters. Their burden, indeed, is so onerous that one hesitates to say anything that might hurt them." Probably, however, the Labour Left made another calculation. Victory over the leaders during so critical a moment would have been more dangerous, perhaps, than the ambiguous outcome of the party meeting. If Attlee had been forced to resign by a vote of no confidence, who would have replaced him? Not Morrison, who was held, correctly, to be more responsible than the Prime Minister for the hesitations on steel. Certainly not Bevan, although rumor had it that Donald Bruce was attempting to organize a campaign in his behalf. Possibly Cripps, who was, in fact, conspiring with Dalton to reorganize the Cabinet in their favor almost precisely at that moment. But the most likely candidate would have been Ernest Bevin. And while the Labour Left would have welcomed his removal from the Foreign Office, it could hardly have approved his elevation to the premiership. Moreover, according to another current rumor, if a national government was formed, Bevin would become Prime Minister and Churchill Foreign Secretary. This was a combination the Labour Left would have opposed at all cost.

And so the economic crisis of summer 1947 was allowed to run its course. Aside from its grudging assurance eventually to nationalize iron and steel, the government had done little to comfort Labour Left fears about its commitment to socialism. Nor had it quieted a growing apprehension among Labour Members generally that it might be incompetent to handle the economy. No one could claim that suspension of convertibility represented a victory for the Labour government. The entire episode represented a grave setback, and was understood as such. Moreover, though this was not appreciated at the time, in fact the dollar drain was checked mainly by cutting imports. This was achieved after convertibility was suspended. Thus the sole action which the government took to end the crisis had little to do with its eventual solution.[17]

There was a denouement to the crisis which can have done little to cheer the government's left-wing critics. They had not been alone in condemning vacillation at the top. In the Cabinet itself, Cripps had concluded that a more vigorous lead was necessary. He hoped to provide it by replacing Attlee, and appealed to Dalton for support. The Chancellor had his own reasons, not entirely disinterested, for backing a Cabinet shuffle. He hoped to replace Bevin at the Foreign Office. But the result of his and Cripps's machinations was not what they had hoped. Attlee, refusing to abdicate, took the wind out of Cripps's sails by appointing him to head a new Ministry of Economic Affairs. Dalton and Bevin remained where they were. The young Harold Wilson replaced Cripps at the Board of Trade. And Hugh Gaitskell was promoted to the Ministry of Fuel and Power to replace Shinwell, who had been moved to the War Office without Cabinet rank. Other less important promotions and demotions completed the reorganization which, if anything, strengthened the Labour Right. The new ministry, which Crossman had proposed seven months earlier and which the Labour Left might have regarded as at least a partial response to its agitation, survived for only a short time. In November, Dalton committed a minor indiscretion just before announcing the Budget and resigned. Cripps became Chancellor. The six-weeks-old Ministry of Economic Affairs was abolished.[18]

IV

On 6 June 1947, the very day Marshall delivered his great speech at Harvard and thus forever altered Labour Left perceptions of Britain's economic needs and policies, a *Tribune* editor wrote, "So interdependent have our economic problems and our international policy become that it is hardly possible to discuss one without the other." The intersection of Labour Left agitation for changes in foreign and economic policy produced a synthesis, the call for a third force described in Chapter 3. Whereas earlier we treated the political aims of third force advocates, however, here we will examine their economic goals. The third force never was viewed by the Labour Left as simply a political demand; it was deemed, also, to be an essential component of Labour's economic program.

Immediately after the war the Labour Left wanted not so much a third economic force in the world as a second one: "an Economic Union of Planning Countries which would include the greater part of Europe." Left-wing Labourites believed that democratic socialism would survive in Britain only if the nation coordinated its economic policies with those of other socialist states. The first American loan had required Britain to endorse multilateralism, which some on the Labour Left thought to be "only a euphemism for unrestrained economic competition." According to the Labour Left, Britain could never develop cooperative links with Europe on the basis of "external laissez-faire." Henceforth, then, it must avoid close economic ties with the USA.[19]

At first the Labour Left meant the "Economic Union of Planning Countries"to include Eastern Europe and Russia. During the spring of 1946 Fabian chairman G. D. H. Cole directed the society's International Bureau to begin work on "an alternative approach to the problems of reconstruction in Europe" which would provide blueprints for economic cooperation with the USSR. Based upon the 1942 Anglo-Soviet Treaty, the study would make "clear what concessions should be made to the Soviet authorities on the one hand and the British authorities on the other to achieve this purpose." Cole hoped this would be only one of several economic projects undertaken by the FIB along similar lines. Another would "show in detail how problems in the economic field could usefully be tackled on a European as distinct from a West European basis, irrespective of whether such economic arrangements would carry with them political and military commitments." A third would focus "on the relations between socialised Europe and the US."[20]

The response of the FIB to Cole's suggestions reveals the many difficulties which beset the Labour Left even during the relatively fluid period immediately following the war. The bureau contained men and women with diverse, indeed conflicting, views. Its most active members were the publicists Leonard Woolf, Margaret Cole and Rita Hinden, the journalists Doreen Warriner and Dorothy Woodman, the Labour peer Lord Faringdon and Denis Healey. Less active were several Fabians who sat in

Parliament: Warbey, Zilliacus, Crossman and Patrick Gordon Walker. A group so constituted would have been unlikely to endorse close economic ties with the Soviet Union at the expense of the United States even in the spring of 1946. Yet Woolf, the FIB chairman, initially agreed with Cole that "high priority should be given to the effort to disentangle ourselves from USA economic domination." When he set pen to paper, however, it was discovered that he feared Russian domination in equal measure. As a result, the draft pamphlet which he circulated among bureau members during the summer of 1946 advocated that Britain steer a middle course between the USA and the USSR.[21]

Woolf's draft pamphlet found few supporters. From the far Left of the FIB, Zilliacus and Warriner opposed its publication since they wanted an Anglo-Soviet alliance. From the Right, Denis Healey and former Fabian chairman Bosworth Monk objected because they favored alliance with America. Warbey, an early advocate of close relations with the Soviets, supported publication of the pamphlet—if he could write another one less hostile to Russia. The result was stalemate, and during the discussions which ensued the prospect of close economic collaboration between Britain and the Soviet Union grew increasingly remote. The FIB never performed the service which Cole had requested.[22]

By the time a pamphlet suggesting pan-European economic collaboration had been written, Woolf's outlook rather than Cole's was ascendant on the Labour Left. *Keep Left* was published six months after the FIB rejected Woolf's essay. Crossman, who wrote the chapter dealing with Britain's international economic policy, hoped to balance British dependence on America by increasing trade with Eastern Europe and the Soviets. "Foodstuffs, timber and other products of Poland and the Danubian countries, as well as the Scandinavian States," were available. So was "timber from Russia." But trade agreements with communist nations were necessary to correct Britain's tilt towards America, not to help build a single socialist economic entity which would include the Soviets. "To gradually remove the Iron Curtain" by constructing "an economic union of European states" was desirable but an impossible short-term goal. In the meantime less spectacular forms of "European collaboration" could be realized. Crossman had in mind coordinating the national economic plans of European countries in order "to avoid competition in export markets and to provide long-term agreements for agricultural producers." This could help establish a third economic force independent of the superpowers and capable of acting as an honest broker between them.[23]

In its international as much as its domestic economic prescriptions *Keep Left* was the product of a specific, short-lived moment. Marshall's speech, which came less than a month after publication of the pamphlet, transformed Britain's economic prospects and Labour Left proposals for improving them. In Chapter 2 we examined the political conclusions which the Labour Left drew from the Harvard speech, and from the Russian decision not to participate in the Marshall Plan. The economic conclusions which it drew deserve equal consideration.

Marshall's offer faced the Labour Left with an issue posed originally by the first US loan. Could socialism be built in Britain upon a foundation of American dollars? Some were skeptical. Mikardo, for example, wanted to accept Marshall Aid and yet to "achieve a greater independence of American economics." He suggested welding "the 26 states of Europe into a single free trade economic unit which could do all the Americans can do because it would have material resources, labour, machinery and an integrated market all greater than those of the United States." He believed that "the Customs Union between Belgium, Holland and Luxembourg can be extended outwards and eastwards to embrace the whole of Europe." He added almost wistfully, "an agreement between the USSR and ourselves could have been the keystone of a European Union."[24]

In R. W. G. Mackay's "Europe Group" the "hard" Labour Left attempted to develop Mikardo's line of thought. Warbey and Leah Manning asserted, in their position Paper C, that Marshall Aid posed a separate issue from European unity. Britain should accept American dollars while continuing to strive for the establishment of a socialist European union including the communist nations. This body would develop a "Regional Trading Club" to set prices for all members, guarantee markets, form "Joint Purchasing Commissions" to buy products from countries outside the group and "generally assist each other . . . to maintain full employment." Naively, they argued that Soviet membership in the group would not jeopardise its independence.[25]

More common, however, was Crossman's opposite conclusion. "The Harvard speech, the Marshall Plan and the Russian refusal to cooperate in it . . . completely outdated our proposals for an independent Third Force." Crossman had reversed himself, yet he claimed merely to have adapted to new circumstances. In language reminiscent of *Keep Left* he informed the "Europe Group" that "we must begin at once to pool and plan our resources with countries which are prepared to do the same." Then came his new line. "Where countries are governed by Communists . . . they will not be allowed to cooperate. It is tragic, but we cannot for that reason do nothing." Claiming that it was chimerical to suppose that the Western union he advocated could become socialist in the near future, Crossman argued nevertheless that British socialism depended upon its formation, since without Marshall Aid austerity at home would lead to Labour's defeat in the next general election. He appeared as blind to the possibility that America would undermine socialism within Britain, and the Western union it was supposed to underwrite, as members of the "hard" Left were about Soviet interference in the European union of their heart's desire.[26]

The division between Crossman and Mikardo extended to the Labour Left as a whole, which, massively divided as it now was, proved incapable of producing specific proposals for economic cooperation between European or even West European countries. "Hard" and "soft" Labour Leftists agreed only that the policies of whatever union eventually was established should not be overtly anti-socialist. Cole, who on the non-communist Left continued almost alone to question the wisdom of accepting Marshall Aid, advocated joint purchasing and development planning agencies as a first step. Crossman thought the initial aim should be "to reach constructive agreement with some of our Western European neighbours" on "joint planning of colonial development, and joint planning of domestic heavy industries." As might have been expected, he also advocated "an agreement to set up joint machinery for the allocation, between members of the group, of assistance received under the Marshall Plan." Mackay proposed a common European currency and the abolition of trade barriers between non-communist and non-fascist West European states. Later his "All-Party British Committee of the European Parliamentary Union" offered, in the House of Commons, a motion to establish a West European political union whose

> first and most important task . . . would be to frame concrete proposals for the stabilisation of the currencies of Western Europe; for the development of trade; for the execution of the European Recovery Plan; for a comprehensive production plan, including agriculture and the heavy industries; and for Colonial development.

Mackay did not suggest how such measures might be implemented.[27]

Nevertheless this steady agitation for some form of economic cooperation among European states began to bear fruit. Bevin was willing for the recipient nations of Marshall Aid to concert their requests to America. Late in 1947 Britain helped to establish a Committee of European Economic Coordination. What the British government did not want, however, was to jeopardize its "special relationship" with the Americans. As a UDC position paper observed, the CEEC, with British backing, preferred "orthodox economic measures which will find favour in the USA—balanced budgets, multilateral trade and convertibility of currencies."[28]

More important and ultimately more disappointing from the point of view of the Labour Left was the government's attitude towards the Council of Europe, which met first in Strasbourg in November 1948. Crossman entertained lavish hopes for it. The Council was, he wrote, "something new, unpredictable and vastly exciting." Mikardo agreed. "There's a revolution brewing in Europe," he wrote uncomprehendingly. In reality the Council had no intention of constructing the socialist European union he desired. Nor did it represent, even in embryo, the potentially socialist Western union of Crossman's imaginings. Edelman and Mackay, the two putative left-wing Labourites on the British delegation to Strasbourg, were reduced, essentially, to checking the "economic liberals" of other European nations. Edelman summed up their largely negative role as having been

> not to accept any economic principles which run counter to the policy of full employment; not to accept a coordination of policy with other countries for deflationary purposes which would lower Britain's standard of life; not to forsake Britain's Commonwealth attachments.

Somewhat more positively, according to Edelman, the British delegation had urged "that there should be structural changes in Europe's economy with a view to making the best use of its resources—planning of capital investment, a proper division of labour between countries, specialisation, standardisation, joint agencies of consultation," in short the shopping-list of well-intentioned generalizations advocated by the Labour Left since 1945.[29]

Originally the Labour Left had wanted to reduce dollar dependency by building a European union including the Soviet Union and its allies. As opposition to Russian policies grew, the communist nations were excluded from this plan. Consequently, many on the Labour Left favored economic collaboration within a socialist third force of West European nations, one aim of which would be to maintain balance between the superpowers. Naively, they held that the Marshall Plan would foster this independent Western union, since the Americans wanted economic coordination between recipients of Marshall Aid. Instead, the Americans, with unstinting support from the British government, succeeded in building up Western Europe as part of an anti-Soviet bloc. Few Cabinet members were attracted by the vision of a united socialist Europe, which beguiled so many on the Labour Left. The socialist potential of a united Europe would not be revived as a topic of serious debate within the Labour Party for thirty-five years.

V

After 1947 Labour had to begin thinking about the next general election. The debate which developed then, between advocates of extending socialism and advocates of consolidating the gains achieved already, marks another important chapter in the early postwar history of the Labour Left.

The great champion of "consolidation" was Herbert Morrison, the Lord President. His most determined antagonist within the Cabinet was the Minister of Health, Aneurin Bevan. An early indication of the conflict between them came with the debate over iron and steel. Bevan claimed that early nationalization was essential, both for the achievement of socialism in Britain and for the morale of the party. Morrison argued that it would alienate voters. In the end, a compromise was arranged. Iron and steel were nationalized during the 1945–50 Parliament, but not until almost the last possible moment, and vesting day was postponed until after the next general election.

Another portent of the debate over consolidation came after Labour's poor performance in the municipal elections of 1947. At a post-mortem held by the parliamentary party on 5 November, Benn Levy voiced a common Labour Left complaint. The campaign had been designed to appeal to the "floating voter," which Levy took to mean middle-class voter. "Although none of us wanted to alienate the middle-class," Levy said, "it was hopeless trying to conciliate [them] by using the soft pedal." Instead Labour should try "to collect the maximum working-class support . . . we would do much better to try and rally our friends than conciliate our enemies." In his contribution to the party meeting, Foot concentrated upon the government's alleged failings in public relations. But also he backed up Levy. "Does the Government believe in itself?" he asked bluntly.[30]

Foot's query posed the essential division between consolidators and their opponents. Increasingly during 1945–51 the Labour Left was inclined to think that the party leaders had lost faith in socialism. This seed of doubt had been sown during the coal and convertibility crises. It germinated when Gaitskell imposed charges on the

National Health Service to help pay for rearmament in 1951; and it reaped a bitter harvest in 1959 when he attempted to delete the socialist Clause IV from Labour's constitution. Even during the period before Gaitskell had come to prominence, however, the debate between the two wings of the party was carried on with an intensity which seemed at times like warfare.

Opening salvoes were fired in 1948, when the party began to discuss its next general election program, *Labour Believes in Britain.* In April, Mikardo published *Labour's Second Term,* a pamphlet designed to influence debate against consolidation, and in favor of continued socialist advance.

"The Government's industrial record since 1945 is a good one," Mikardo acknowledged at the outset, "but it isn't Socialism: it isn't, in fact, any more than the very first step in the transition to Socialism." Mikardo had given serious thought to "the transition." He believed the government should employ seven techniques to speed it up. The first, and most important, was nationalization of whole industries. Mikardo believed that during its second term Labour should nationalize joint stock banks, insurance companies, industrial assurance, shipbuilding, shipping, aircraft and aero engines, motor vehicles (excluding luxury and sports cars), margarine, flour, sugar, bricks, shoe-machinery, cement and some specialized chemicals. Second, Mikardo favored "nationalization by function," for example of food wholesaling and export merchandising. Third, "where large scale output of standardised products is required, it is better for the Government to build suitable plants from scratch." Mikardo called this "Direct Enterprise." In addition, where free enterprise was "really free," the government should supply capital, buildings, stocks and "other forms of assistance" to entrepreneurs. He also thought that the government should establish a public tribunal to hear complaints of cartel practices and enforce a "code of reasonable commercial behaviour" and that manufacturers with more than one hundred employees should be compelled to set up joint production committees or strengthen those established earlier, in order to guarantee worker participation in shop-floor decisions. Finally, standards of industrial management should be coordinated by a government-appointed body.

Mikardo readily acknowledged that he was advocating a program more ambitious, even, than *Let Us Face the Future.* However, "1950 and 1945 are not strictly comparable. . . We shall have the benefit and experience of the First Five Years to facilitate the tasks of the Second." His proposals, Mikardo averred in conclusion, would not dismay an "unswervingly Socialist Government."[31]

Perhaps not, but there is no evidence that the party leadership paid them much heed. At Labour's annual conference in May, Herbert Morrison made, perhaps, a veiled reference to Mikardo's recent recommendation. He suggested that the Left was taking things too fast. Labour's program should be "of . . . a somewhat different tempo from the last, for we have to embody in it proposals for the consolidation of existing achievements . . . Let us prepare for a victory of consolidation." With Morrison's pronouncement, the issue between consolidators and fundamentalists had been formally joined.[32]

The Left had representation on the NEC, which now divided over the Morrisonian line. On 28 July it asked the party's Research Department to examine the feasibility of nationalizing "Commercial Insurance, Chemicals, Water, Shipbuilding, Motors, Cotton, Aircraft, Oil Distribution and City Financial Institutions." But in February 1949, when Morrison and Michael Young, secretary of the Research Department, submitted a draft of *Labour Believes in Britain* to the NEC, of the industries originally proposed for nationalization only shipbuilding and water remained, though industrial assurance, sugar, cement, Imperial Chemicals, the meat trade and minerals had been added. Of these, however, industrial assurance was eventually dropped, while shipbuilding and chemicals were reduced to an intermediate status. They would be nationalized only if private enterprise in them was shown to be failing. The majority of industries which Mikardo had considered ripe for nationalization were not mentioned in the document.[33]

In April 1949 a draft of *Labour Believes in Britain* was released for public discussion. The Labour Left reacted to it with dismay. Crossman, in an article for the *Sunday Pictorial* of 17 April, thought its purpose was to "bridge the gap which undoubtedly exists between the idea of Socialism which the Cabinet has after four years practical experience of government, and the very different ideas of the rank and file." The document would be ineffective, however, since it was aimed primarily at a middle-class audience. Echoing Levy's 1947 complaint, Crossman wrote, "The issue is not whether Transport House can by clever publicity convert middle-class voters . . . but whether it can persuade enough Labour supporters to vote Labour. . . Judging by recent history the answer is 'No'."

Perhaps the most detailed criticism of *Labour Believes in Britain* was offered by G. D. H. Cole, in two successive articles for the weekly *Glasgow Forward* (later published as a pamphlet by the Fabian Society). In Cole's opinion:

> The worst thing about the draft programme is that . . . it can[not] have caused any Socialist . . . to feel his heart uplifted or his determination reinvigorated . . . Most of us anticipated that the second five years of Labour Government would be marked by a much more rapid advance towards a Socialist society.

In a remarkable passage, Cole cut through the vague exhortations which often characterized Labour Left agitation, to focus upon the nub of its critique of the government's economic policies. "There is," he wrote,

> a kind of Keynesian Liberalism, sometimes masquerading as Socialism, which does in fact see the solution of the social problem in these terms: a limited sphere of public enterprise, full employment policies to guard against slumps, low rates of interest, budget surpluses and deficits as means of keeping the economy on an even keel, and therewith a retention of the profit motive as the main driving force in industry, and a continued reliance on the old incentives, despite their weakening by full employment and social security, to drive the labourer to do his job. There are suggestions in the new Labour programme that some, at any rate, of those who

drafted it are thinking consciously or half consciously along these lines, and are minded to put off any further advance to Socialism.

The Labour Left case against consolidation was rarely put so succinctly or well.[34]

Cole was not content to let the matter rest. He believed that Labour's 1945 program, *Let Us Face the Future*, had summarized the creative thinking of the labor movement since 1900. A new departure was necessary, but *Labour Believes in Britain* did not represent one. Cole thought that an updated collection of *Fabian Essays* could lay out the socialist agenda for the next half-century, rendering the same service to the movement which the original volume had performed.

Cole convened a series of discussions at which this new project could take shape. Some were held in London, but most took place at Buscot, Lord Faringdon's country home. The first meeting occurred over the weekend of 15–17 July 1949, the last over 14–15 October 1950. They resulted in publication of *New Fabian Essays*. Cole, however, was not its editor. Perhaps the Fabian chairman did not believe that the volume, containing contributions from Labour centrists like Anthony Crosland, Roy Jenkins, Austin Albu and John Strachey, fulfilled the purpose he had intended. The immediate cause of his resignation from the project, however, was a "flaming row" with John Strachey over the British and American positions on the Korean War.[35]

The Buscot conferences were a revealing episode in the history of the Labour Party and the Labour Left. At those meetings, consolidators and fundamentalists came into headlong collision. Detailed minutes of some of their debates survive.[36]

The climax of the first meeting came during a session chaired by Mikardo, who offered for discussion a paper asking, "whether universal nationalization is necessary?" Interestingly, given the tone of his earlier pamphlet in which emphasis had been placed upon nationalization, now Mikardo thought it would be better to "envisage the growth of public enterprise as coming in more little bits spread over a wide area." He had learned to his dismay that "the public as a whole don't care a damn" about nationalization. The general indifference, however, had its compensations: "one has . . . only to consider the reactions of the people directly affected in each case—i.e. the managers and shareholders." From this it followed that nationalization could be "forced" by putting "the squeeze on an industry until it conformed or revolted." But "this sort of behaviour demanded a much more resolute Government."[37]

Predictably, consolidators disagreed. What is unexpected to a historian, however, is the approach to nationalization now favored by the Labour Left. They were almost eager to concede that nationalization, as it had been practiced so far by the government, was problematic. Moreover, they emphasized that it was only one, and not necessarily the best, method of directing an economy. Mikardo himself focused upon techniques developed since 1945; for example, "government bulk purchase . . . or government intervention through Development Councils with greatly increased powers, or the nationalization of a particular function as in the wholesaling of meat." Cole, the old guild socialist, reiterated a familiar warning: "The danger of nationalisation was too much centralisation." This was not, however, the traditional Conservative criticism of big government. Rather, Cole "wanted to create a greater sense of responsibility by decentralisation in all other possible respects, subject to the necessary minimum of central planning control." His wife, Margaret, mentioned yet another drawback of traditional nationalization, "inefficiencies." In fact, Labour Left doubts about nationalization, as the socialist pioneers had conceived it, were to occupy an increasingly prominent place in their overall critique of government policies.[38]

Cole had asked at the outset of the discussion, "What should we want to happen in the next fifty years if we had a free hand?" By the end of the session, Mikardo felt able to answer, posing simultaneously the Labour Left vision of a socialist economy. "The picture with which we finished," Mikardo explained, "was that of the industrial and commercial life of the nation being shaped like a rifle target, with a bull's eye, an 'inner' and a 'magpie'." The "bull's eye" would consist of what Aneurin Bevan later called "the commanding heights of the economy." They must all be under public ownership. The "inner" would be represented by less crucial industries,

> centrally planned and centrally controlled, using all the appropriate tools for that purpose, including government bulk purchase, part state ownership (which could be some part of all the companies in the industry or total ownership of some of the companies in the industry), development councils with a majority of government nominees and wide mandatory powers, reinforced by statutory joint consultation, again with defined and wide powers, and so on.

The "magpie," Mikardo concluded, would consist "of the fringe of non-basic and small-scale enterprises which were under only the general economic controls." Consolidators can hardly have imagined a socialist vision more opposed to theirs, even though they shared some Labour Left doubts about the value of traditional nationalization.[39]

The first Buscot conference took place with its participants aware that the general election (which will be treated in Chapter 7) could not be far off. Voters went to the polls in February 1950. On 31 March the Buscot conferees met again, but in altered circumstances. Labour's majority in the House had been reduced to six (although the party's popular vote had increased). As might have been expected, fundamentalists and consolidators interpreted these results in conflicting ways. The antagonism between them sharpened.

For consolidators, the election results proved the importance of winning the swing voter, someone unlikely to support militant socialist measures. According to Michael Young, "Progressives . . . should say clearly that they do not stand for nationalising everything. They should produce a criterion for laying down what parts of the economy they have no desire to nationalise, and should make this public." Young had drawn a more general conclusion as well. He "had become much less utopian" and now looked upon "the Socialist Commonwealth . . . as an ideal society towards which we sought to advance, rather than as a goal we expected actually to reach."[40]

The Labour Left condemned this approach. Crossman, in a provocative paper, conceded that "the Labour Party had tended to erect nationalisation into an end, which it was not," with the result that "today we had 'nationalised' but not 'socialised'" industries. More nationalisation would not necessarily mean more Socialism". The answer, however, was not to abandon "socialism in our time," as Young advocated, but rather to democratize the nationalized industries, and generally "to divide power, not to keep it concentrated." The greatest danger, in Crossman's opinion, was that "right-wingers" in the party, by which he meant consolidators, were working towards a "corporate" rather than a socialist state.[41]

Cole, who differed violently with Crossman on foreign affairs, nevertheless supported his condemnation of the "right-wingers" and his emphasis on the democratic aspect of socialism. According to Cole, "the Labour Government, side by side with its great and immensely valuable human achievements in the Social Services, showed both a most alarming disregard for Local Government and a regrettably centralising and bureaucratic attitude in its measures of socialisation." This was in part a legacy from the past, when "the Webbs' lack of libertarian impulse" had been fastened on to the labor movement. "Our only chance," Cole argued, "lies in recognising the need for large-scale units, but also creating within them the largest practicable amount of decentralisation and devolution of power."[42]

Too often historians have presented the conflict between consolidators and their opponents as though it pitted pragmatic moderates against old-fashioned socialist dogmatists. It seems worth remarking, therefore, that Morrison himself was closely identified with Labour's traditional approach to nationalization, having applied it first of all to London transport before the war. Consolidators did not so much question its bases as doubt that they were popular with the electors. As the Buscot conferences reveal, it was the fundamentalists who hoped to alter the traditional approach to nationalization, and who had begun to explore alternatives to traditional methods of controlling the economy.

The Labour Left had long been interested in the concept of workers' control. During 1945–51 trade-union interest in this subject became intense, as Chapter 6 will show. Cole, of course, had been an advocate of workers' control and guild socialism since the early years of the century. The parliamentary Labour Left indulged in similar musings.

Buscot was hardly the only, or the first, outlet for their speculations. Among the "Twenty Things to Do Now" listed in *Keep Left* the authors had suggested: "9. *Industrial Democracy.* Pass an Act to make Joint Production Committees compulsory, to define and extend their powers, and to link them with the regional and national production boards." As Crossman wrote in the *Glasgow Forward* for 11 October 1947, "nationalisation is merely the essential thing that you must do first before you start on all the rest. The biggest thing that you have to do is to socialise the nationalised industry."[43]

In the spring of 1948, on the BBC program "London Forum," Driberg argued that "Nationalisation is not an end in itself, it's merely a means, it's merely providing the material framework for the good life and the more egalitarian society." A year later he was reiterating again on the BBC, that "merely taking over an industry into public ownership does not in itself restore all that sense of vocation, partnership, keenness on the job and all the rest of it which is the ideal for every worker." He went on to advocate "much much more and more real joint consultation between worker and management."[44]

Mikardo, who seems to have specialized in concrete proposals rather than loose exhortation, prepared for the "Keep Left" group "A Note on the Need for Legislation on Joint Production Consultation," by which he meant consultation between management and workers in industry. Mikardo thought it would be possible to frame an Act or parliamentary Order which would, "give such a broad general definition that workers' representatives would be able to claim an interest in real things." In addition, the Act (or Order) could "specify the sort of data to which workers' representatives should have access." He thought that the government should make establishment of joint production committees compulsory.[45]

What was missing from such prescriptions was any sense of how democratic control of industry would operate in practice. Cole, of course, had attempted to develop methods of workers' control during his guild socialist days and had seen his theories adopted by Post Office workers and even applied by some builders. Trade unionists were to apply themselves to this issue with intelligence and determination, as Chapter 6 will demonstrate. The calls for workers' control made by Labour Left Members, however, seem formulaic, almost perfunctory. And in comparison with those of trade unionists they lacked urgency.

This lack of urgency was apparent in *Keeping Left*, an updated version by the "Keep Left" group of its original pamphlet. The authors contented themselves in this work to reiterating previous vague demands for compulsory joint production committees. They did not even attempt to suggest how these bodies would work.

On the other hand, *Keeping Left* was intended by its authors to answer the consolidators. It was meant to demonstrate that "our recovery had been made possible by Socialist planning" and that further recovery depended not upon diluting the socialist content of Labour's program, but upon strengthening it. Whereas consolidators emphasized the need to maintain such achievements as the Welfare State and full employment, the "Keep Left" group unabashedly entitled the fourth chapter of their pamphlet "From Full Employment to Socialism." They reiterated the old charge that the government must show "a lot more toughness and imagination" if the great goal was to be fulfilled. And they amplified, as never before, the methods which would make fulfillment possible.[46]

Its authors intended above all, however, that *Keeping Left* should demonstrate the flexibility and adaptability of Labour's left wing. While reiterating the need for nationalization of major industries, therefore, they were at pains to point out the alternatives they had considered. They demanded establishment of "development councils" for important industries, staffed by employers, workers and independent members, subject to parliamentary control and possessing "wide powers of reorganisation." Their aim was to increase the efficiency of each industry, and thus to raise production. They advocated, too, bulk purchasing by government departments, public corporations and other public agencies, as supplements to the traditional mode of controlling the economy by nationalizing it. In the realm of finance, they advocated tighter exchange controls to counteract any future flight from the pound, stronger direct controls over investment and dividend limitation through high taxes. They thought financial controls should be complemented by physical controls on prices and profits and by the allocation of raw materials. Such measures should not be viewed as expedients, they argued, but as necessary and permanent aspects of a socialist economy, though some reform of the control system would be necessary from time to time.[47]

. Redistribution was not exempt from Labour Left prescription either. The most important redistributive measure advocated in the pamphlet was "a capital levy or annual capital tax." "To be effective," wrote the authors, "a capital levy would have to be very large indeed." Taxes in general, and estate duties in particular, had to be raised. In the meantime, food and other subsidies should be maintained.[48]

The economic sections of *Keeping Left* testify, at least, to the resources of the Labour Left. The debate between consolidators and advocates of advance is perennial in the socialist movement. In 1950, after five extremely difficult years, the Labour Left, more even than the government, remained fertile with ideas and plans. One senses in the pages of their pamphlet a will to power greater than that of the party leadership, some of whom were ill and exhausted. Moreover, because *Keeping Left* provided the left-wing riposte to consolidation, it became, after 1951, a primary source for Bevanites in their conflict with the followers of Hugh Gaitskell. In that sense, it is more significant in the history of the Labour Left than the famous pamphlet of nearly the same name which preceded it.

VI

The Labour Left critique of the Attlee government's economic policies was neither static nor simple. It evolved as circumstances changed, and as Labour Left confidence in the party leadership gradually was eroded. There is one aspect of the Labour Left critique, however, which has not been examined in this chapter, namely, its reaction to Gaitskell's 1951 Budget, which introduced charges on the National Health Service in order to help pay for rearmament. The Labour Left response to that was so important, and so complicated, since it involved attitudes towards the government's foreign policy as well, that it deserves separate treatment in a chapter of its own—Chapter 8.

Notes and References

1   Labour Party archives, 1945 general election file.
2   For the economic policies of Attlee's governments, see Sir Norman Chester, *The Nationalisation of British Industry, 1945–51* (London, 1975); Alan Milward, *The Reconstruction of Western Europe, 1945–51* (London, 1984); Sir Andrew Shonfield, *British Economic Policy since the War* (London, 1959); G. D. A. Worswick and P. Ady (eds.), *The British Economy 1945–50* (Oxford, 1952); Ben Pimlott, *Hugh Dalton* (London, 1985); Alec Cairncross, *Years of Recovery, 1945–51* (London, 1985).

3   See Pimlott, *Hugh Dalton*, pp. 429–49, for the negotiations; also Cairncross, *Years of Recovery*, especially p. 108 for the attitudes of Shinwell and Bevan; see also BLPES, Dalton papers, Dalton's diary, 7 December 1945.

4   Cairncross, *Years of Recovery*; *New Statesman*, 15 December 1945.

5   *New Statesman*, 5 April 1947.

6   Cairncross, *Years of Recovery*; Pimlott, *Hugh Dalton*, pp. 476–94.

7   *New Statesman*, 27 July 1947.

8   *Reynolds News*, 9 March 1947.

9   *Keep Left* (London, 1947), introduction; *New Statesman*, 10 April 1947.

10   *Keep Left*, pp. 11–21.

11   Ibid., p. 45.

12   For the convertibility crisis, see especially Cairncross, *Years of Recovery*; Pimlott, *Hugh Dalton*; Kenneth O. Morgan, *Labour in Power, 1945–51* (Oxford, 1984), p. 334.

13   House of Lords Record Office, Benn Levy papers, file 57.

14   Private papers of Leslie Hale, diary entry, 22 August 1947.

15   Ibid.

16   Ibid., Philip Williams (ed.), *The Diary of Hugh Gaitskell, 1945–56* (London, 1983), p. 24 (diary entry, 12 August 1947).

17   Cairncross, *Years of Recovery*, pp. 163–4.

18   For the Cripps–Dalton plot, see especially Pimlott, *Hugh Dalton*, pp. 500–18.

19   *Left News*, December 1946.

20   Nuffield College, Oxford, G. D. H. Cole papers, Fabian International Bureau, J52/4.10.

21   Ibid., For membership lists and attendance, see FIBJ52/5.6; for Woolf's pamphlet, see FIB, J52/5.63–74.

22   Ibid., For Healey and Monk versus Zilliacus and Warriner, see FIB, J52/5.81–92

23   *Keep Left*, pp. 38–9.

24   *Reynolds News*, 3 August 1947.

25   This is Document C, discussed above (see page 70), BLPES, R. W. G. Mackay papers, 13/4.

26   This is Document A, discussed above (page 70), Mackay papers, 13/4.

27   For Cole, see Cole papers, FIB, J67/6.37, Cole to Woolf, 15 March 1948; for Crossman, see *New Statesman*, 22 November 1947; for Mackay, see Mackay papers, 9/1, Mackay to Cripps, 20 August 1948; for the "all-party" resolution, see Mackay papers, 9/8.

28   Hull University, UDC papers, 4/3, "Notes on Foreign Policy," 1 November 1947.

29   For Crossman, see *Sunday Pictorial*, 4 September 1949; for Dalton's role, see Morgan, *Labour in Power*, p. 395; for Mikardo, see the undated excerpt from his article in the Mackay papers, 7/2; for Edelman, see *Europe's First Parliament* (Fabian tract No. 280, 1949), p. 24.

30   NEC minutes, vol. 95, p. 594, "Notes of points made by speakers at discussion at Party meeting on 5 November 1947 on the results of the municipal elections."

31   Ian Mikardo, *Labour's Second Term* (London, 1948), pp. 11–18.

32   *Labour Party Annual Conference, 1948* pp. 121–4.

33   NEC minutes, 28 July 1948.

34   *Glasgow Forward*, 28 May and 4 June 1949.

35   Margaret Cole, *The Life of G. D. H. Cole* (London, 1971), p. 276.

36   Cole papers, B3/5/E.

37   Ibid.

38   Ibid.

39   Ibid.

40   Ibid., "2nd Buscot Conference, March 31–April 2, 1950, Session I, part 2."

41   Ibid.

42   Ibid., "Session IV."

43   *Keep Left*, p. 46.

44   BBC Written Archives, Reading, "London Forum," 3 June 1948, 31 May 1949.

45   A draft of Mikardo's "Note" is preserved in the Benn Levy papers, file 57.

46   *Keeping Left* (London, 1950), p. 29.

47   Ibid., pp. 34–7.

48   Ibid., pp. 41–7.

5

The "Hard" Labour Left

DURING THE GENERAL ELECTION campaign of 1945, Labour's NEC had rejected overtures from the Communist Party, the ILP and Common Wealth for formal "unity on the Left," in part because it recognized that Labour finally had an opportunity to become the single major progressive political party in Britain. Afterwards, successful beyond their dreams, Labour's leaders faced a party bulging with former members of those militant socialist organizations who had abandoned them because they believed, as Fenner Brockway put it, that "the best work for socialism and for peace could be done within the [Labour] Party" and not elsewhere. Was any church broad enough to contain so disparate a membership? In the aftermath of the general election, inner party divisions which had been healed or glossed over during the war reopened. New disagreements emerged. These were not only between the party leadership and its left-wing critics. The various Lefts of the Labour Party, augmented by the new recruits, likewise rediscovered their differences. During the postwar period "Keep Left" was only one, and not the most militant, albeit the most prominent, of the radical pressure groups within the parliamentary party. It is now time to focus upon the others and their members, the "lost sheep," as Labour Party General Secretary Morgan Phillips disarmingly (and misleadingly) termed backbenchers on the extreme Labour Left.[1]

II

"Keep Left" was an exclusive body. Membership appears to have been based upon ties of friendship as well as upon similarity of outlook. Scores of left-wing Labour members never participated in its meetings. As disillusionment with the government's policies gradually increased, these Members, too, agitated for "a more drastic socialist policy," as the introduction to *Keep Left* put it. They too established formal groups to facilitate their aims. In the end, some pushed their agitation farther than "Keep Left" and suffered dire consequences.

This "harder" Left began to attract attention early in 1946. In Parliament, Eden suggested, late in February, that about thirty Labour Members owed allegiance to the Communist Party. On 10 March 1946 "Liberator," in the *Sunday Observer*, claimed that there were three groups in the Parliamentary Labour Party demanding changes in the government's foreign policy. Of these the largest was critical only of Bevin's approach to Spain and "of the delay in carrying through the reform of the foreign services." Its leaders were Foot, Jennie Lee, Benn Levy (each of whom later became a member of "Keep Left"), Francis Noel-Baker, Patrick Gordon Walker and S. N. Evans. According to "Liberator," however, "the most active and vocal" of the groups he had discerned advocated "a policy which is, in its essentials, indistinguishable from that of the Communists." It was led, he thought, by Driberg, Swingler, Leah Manning, Stanley Tiffany and three Members with whom this chapter will be dealing in more detail, Zilliacus, Leslie Solley and John Platts Mills. Moreover, there was a smaller group, almost equally "critical of Mr Bevin's foreign policy particularly in Greece and at UNO, but [which] does not accept the Russian view so wholeheartedly." Its chief members were Wilkes, Warbey, Edelman, John Freeman and "one of the outstanding younger men in this Parliament, Lt L. J. A. Callaghan." "Liberator" reckoned that "on what may be described as straight Communist issues," Bevin faced the opposition of both groups. They contained twenty-two Members. This was a negligible figure, given Labour's massive parliamentary majority. But, "Liberator" added, the "pro-Communist group is pressing hard in the Labour Foreign [*sic*] Affairs Committee."[2]

Some of "Liberator's" conclusions about individuals were questionable (and Driberg immediately disputed them on 17 March in *Reynolds News*). Moreover, "Liberator" had neglected to mention several of Bevin's most formidable and vocal early critics, for example Seymour Cocks, who was the original chairman of the External Affairs Committee, Sydney Silverman and Richard Crossman. But "Liberator's" article, like Eden's charge in the House of Commons, testifies to the existence of a body of opinion in the PLP more extreme than was later represented in "Keep Left."[3]

It was, however, most uncertain of its line and role, as a debate on foreign affairs at the weekly party meeting of 27 March 1946 reveals. At this gathering Cocks, Wilkes, Blackburn, Driberg and Evans voiced unsparing criticisms of Bevin's policies in Greece and elsewhere. But after the Foreign Secretary replied with "a carefully prepared defence of his whole foreign policy, and demanded a vote of confidence," only six Labour Members cast negative ballots. In a characteristic indiscretion Zilliacus revealed at a Gateshead party meeting that the six had been himself, Elizabeth Braddock, Emrys Hughes (only recently elected to Parliament), Julius Silverman, Wilkes and Warbey. Of the "hard" Left Members who had spoken against Bevin only Wilkes was prepared to follow words with action. This suggests that the "hard" Labour Left did not yet know what its relationship to the government should be.[4]

Meanwhile a second party meeting revealed that relations between "hard" and "soft" left-wing Labourites already were in jeopardy. A week earlier, on 20 March, twenty-eight Labour Members had sent a message to the German Social Democratic Party wishing it "success in bringing about the political unity of the German workers on terms fair and just to both Social Democrats and Communists." Attitudes towards "fusion" between communists and socialists were a litmus-test within the Labour

Party, dividing the "hard" from the moderate Left. Over time, opinions of "fusion" varied. Now Michael Foot notified the PLP Liaison Committee that he desired to bring a motion before a meeting of Labour Members on 8 May:

> That this Party Meeting dissents from the message sent by certain Members of the Parliamentary Party to the recent fusion Conference in Berlin, and in order to avoid misunderstanding makes it clear that the message in no way reflects the attitude of the Parliamentary Party.

He was seconded by Jennie Lee, who thought that "when a Group of Members are sending a message to a Political organisation outside Great Britain, all Members of the Party ought to know what is going on and that it should be done through the Secretary's Department."[5]

Prewar divisions, between members of the Independent Labour and Communist parties, and between popular front advocates and Transport House, were reopening. Zilliacus submitted to the Liaison Committee a counter-motion to Foot's. Because he failed to give proper notice, it was not brought to the floor, but it staked out the "hard" Labour Left position. The always prolix Member from Gateshead wanted the meeting to agree that,

> while opposed to any form of intimidation or pressure either against or on behalf of cooperation and unity between Social Democrats and Communists in Germany, [the PLP] endorses the statement by the National Executive Committee to the Annual Conference in 1943 that it would be a tragedy of the first order if the twenty-five years after this war were followed by the same kind of internecine conflict as distinguished the twenty-five years between the two wars, and declares that Labour Members have the right to communicate their views to fellow Socialists in other countries.

Zilliacus was insisting upon the feasibility of a popular front. Yet this concept which had been so potent on the Labour Left only eight months earlier could muster few supporters at a PLP meeting. After a discussion in which Platts Mills and Julius Silverman were the only easily identifiable "hard" Left participants, Morrison summed up in favor of Foot's motion, which then was carried overwhelmingly, only eight Members opposing. This time Driberg may have been one, for he wrote after the meeting that "though Zilliacus is too verbose, no one else on the left has quite his inside knowledge of international affairs."[6]

During the following six months, Labour Left disquiet about Bevin's foreign policy grew. Increasing unease did not, however, bring "hard" and moderate Labour leftists closer together. When, in October and November 1946, Bruce, Foot, Crossman, Jennie Lee and others circulated the open letter to Attlee and then the amendment to the Address from the Throne, they chose to associate only with "Members whose loyalty to the Labour Party could not be questioned." In the aftermath of the "rebellion," disturbed Foreign Office officials could at least take satisfaction in noting that

> the original sponsors of the amendment deliberately excluded the "cryptos" and fellow travellers . . . It is indeed impossible for critics such as Foot and Crossman to cohere with Zilliacus, Platts Mills and others of the extreme left. The two wings are already publicly attacking each other.[7]

The essential thing to remember about the Labour Left during the first half of 1947 is that, while its influence was growing, whatever unity it possessed was fast diminishing. On the one hand, the fuel and convertibility crises as well as opposition to aspects of Bevinism helped spark diverse demands for "a more drastic Socialist policy" and an organization, "Keep Left," to push for it. On the other hand, increasing cold-war tensions produced countervailing tendencies. The men and women who founded "Keep Left" seemed determined to put as much distance as possible between themselves and those whom *Tribune* scathingly referred to as "pro-Communists who gate-crashed into the Labour rebels' ranks."[8]

The rift between the two wings of the Labour Left widened swiftly during 1947–8. Simultaneously, as revulsion against Soviet practices grew, the number advocating co-operation with communists steadily diminished. Nevertheless more Labour Members persisted in demanding some form of partnership with Moscow and the various communist parties than is often realized. The pro-fusion telegram to Germany was the first organized manifestation of this tendency within the Labour Left. Others followed.

In fact, provocatively, given the response to their first effort, the "hard" Left in the Labour Party sent a second pro-fusion telegram to Germany in early December 1947, when the German Socialist Unity Party in the Soviet sector of Berlin convened a "Unity People's Congress." "We are convinced," thirteen Labour Members asserted in this message,

> that it is essential for establishing a lasting peace with Germany that the views of genuine German democrats be heard by the Allied Governments. Therefore we welcome all efforts made in Germany to organise a united representation of all democratic forces . . . We send greetings to your Congress and wish it all success.

Nine of the signatories also had signed the earlier telegram. They were H. L. Austin, Harold Davies, Driberg, Platts Mills, Julius Silverman, Charles Smith, Solley, Tiffany and Zilliacus. According to Driberg, in the *Daily Herald* on 12 December, had the organizers of the telegram "devoted more time to canvassing signatures they could easily have gotten fifty or sixty."

The response of the party leadership and of the "soft" Left was much as it had been after the first pro-fusion telegram. At the regular PLP meeting on 10 December, the Labour Party chairman, Maurice Webb, "gave information to show that the Socialist Unity Party was a Communist-sponsored body." Morrison reminded Members that conference had outlawed Labour Party participation in events organized by communists, and "maintained that the signatories to the telegram had acted contrary to

Labour Party policy." Will Nalley then formally moved that the PLP disassociate itself from the message.

The strategy of the "hard" Left at the PLP meeting, however, had changed. Solley proposed an amendment to Nalley's motion: "This meeting of the Parliamentary Party, without commenting on the merits or otherwise of the message sent by 13 Members of Parliament, places on record that those Members signed the message entirely on their own individual responsibility." This appeal to the right of free speech represented a retreat from Zilliacus's argument after the first fusion telegram when the "hard" Left had hoped to win PLP endorsement of the popular front. Yet even Solley's much more limited claim was declared lost on a show of hands, and the original motion carried.[9]

The "hard" Labour Left was losing ground. If the atmosphere of the party meeting seemed no more tense than usual, outside Parliament a storm was brewing. The *Daily Herald*, for example, condemned the signatories of the telegram as communist dupes. When Driberg protested, Percy Cudlipp, editor-in-chief, replied, "You accuse the *Daily Herald* of purveying what you call 'negative scared, anti-Communism.' If the *Daily Herald* purveyed pro-Communism would that please you? I bet it would."[10]

Red-baiting was not rare in the Labour Party during this period, and it was to become more severe in the coming months. Nevertheless, in February 1948 the "hard" Left attempted to organize a more ambitious protest against Bevinism. Zilliacus, Driberg and several others met in the Wimbledon flat of Tom Braddock, Labour Member for Mitcham (and no relation to Mrs Elizabeth Braddock), "to draft a letter or a motion demanding the withdrawal of our troops from Greece." As Zilliacus recalled, it was decided after some discussion "to take the thing on a broad basis and begin by objecting to the whole drift to war." Driberg was asked to draft a resolution embodying the sense of the meeting.[11]

For once the "hard" Left seemed determined to follow protocol. It had become much more certain of its role and relationship to the party leaders and to the "soft" Labour Left. It was willing to vote against the former; and it hoped to steal the initiative from the latter. This time the resolution was to be circulated widely. After it had been signed by fifty Members, proper notice would be given to the Liaison Committee, and time for discussion at a PLP meeting would be requested. After that, according to Driberg's notes, the signatories would reconvene to "consider further action in the light of the discussion at the Party meeting."

Driberg prepared the draft resolution, a revealing document about the "hard" Labour Left in early 1948. It began:

> That this House, while recognizing the need for American aid . . . regards the association of such aid with undue American economic and political expansion, directed mainly against the Soviet Union and its neighbours, as a threat to the peace of the world; and calls on His Majesty's Government to make it plain to the United States Government that Great Britain will in no circumstances become involved in a war intended to further such expansion or arising out of it.

The resolution went on to demand that Britain establish better relations with the countries of Eastern Europe and "withdraw all British troops, police and military missions from Greece."[12]

In the event, neither the House nor even the parliamentary party discussed Driberg's motion. The Member for Maldon had taken the ill-advised step of first showing it to Seymour Cocks. The latter, who had not attended the meeting at Braddock's flat, amended and shortened the resolution. It still called for Britain to establish better relations with Eastern Europe and to remove its forces from Greece, but it no longer identified American expansionism as the primary threat to world peace. Instead it merely "regretted any suggestion that acceptance of [US] aid implied the adoption of a policy directed against the Soviet Union and its neighbours."[13]

In Driberg's view, the amended resolution "had the merits of being briefer, more positive, and (on America) less provocative" than his own effort. Yet Cocks's revisions had stripped the resolution of its "hard" Left identity. As it stood now, the motion might almost have been written by "Keep Left," which currently was championing the third force. Another meeting at Braddock's flat must have taken place, for a third resolution appeared:

> This Party, while recognizing the need for American aid to Europe and the vital importance of friendship and cooperation with the United States within the framework of the UN, repudiates the policy and strategy of a western defence bloc under Anglo-American leadership directed against the Soviet Union and Eastern Europe, as inconsistent with the Charter of the United Nations; and it urges His Majesty's Government, as a first step towards resolving the present deadlock, to refer the Greek situation to the Security Council, at the same time giving notice of a definite and early date for the withdrawal of British troops, police and military missions from Greece.

This version, which in its references to the UN bore the unmistakable imprint of Zilliacus, soon was circulating within the PLP. Eighteen signatories quickly were found, and there seems little reason to doubt that dozens more could have been garnered. Only two months later the famous "Nenni telegram" supporting the fusionists in the Italian Socialist Party was signed by nearly forty Labour Members. At this point, however, the project was abandoned. A letter from Tom Braddock to Driberg may help explain what happened. Braddock wrote, "I am personally against recognizing the need for American aid, but . . . I should probably stand almost alone in adopting this attitude and it therefore becomes impracticable." Probably so, and yet perhaps anti-Americanism on the "hard" Labour Left still was more widespread than Braddock imagined. Conceivably the resolution in its final form was unacceptable to several of its original sponsors precisely because it welcomed Marshall dollars. And what could Seymour Cocks have thought of it? As we have seen, by March 1948 the vast majority of the Labour Left could see no alternative to accepting not merely US funds but also an Anglo-American alliance to resist communism. The resolution in its final form had the drawback, perhaps, of alienating Bevin's critics on both the right and left wings of the Labour Left.[14]

III

Meanwhile, the object of these criticisms was hardly oblivious to them. Indeed, although Ernest Bevin had grown up in a very hard school, he was, at least while Foreign Secretary, remarkably thin-skinned. Incensed by the open letter to Attlee in October 1946, and by the amendment to the King's Speech one month later, he had demanded the expulsion of his main critics from the Labour Party. Bevin appears to have hated all Labour Members who criticized him, not merely those on the "hard" Left. MPs who participated in investigative trips abroad, to communist countries or to countries in which Bevin's policies were under attack, were particularly at risk. In the spring of 1947 George Thomas, the Member for Cardiff West, who had travelled on such an expedition to Greece, told Leslie Hale that he was being followed by an agent of MI5. Hale discounted the tale:

> The suggestion that a Labour Government would permit this to be done to a Labour Member in breach of all constitutional rights, and that reports should be submitted to the Foreign Office and to the War Office on the people to whom a Labour Member talks in his constituency, struck me as too utterly fantastic to be worthy of credence.

By November, however, Hale had changed his mind. He had witnessed "a most extraordinary incident in the House," Bevin warning Thomas "that he had got him under observation, him and his Communist friends, that he knew him and knew of his plans against the Greek Throne . . . The man is really losing his control and his sense of proportion," Hale concluded. "This is real, utter disaster."[15]

Hale was shocked by Bevin's conduct. Yet many shared the Foreign Secretary's fears. By now the cold war was in full swing. "Hard" Labour Left agitation on behalf of fusion took place against the backdrop of communist victory in Czechoslovakia and communist opposition to the Marshall Plan, which practically everyone thought indispensable. In Britain the political climate had undergone a sea-change since 1945 when almost the entire Labour Party had extolled cooperation with communists. Now rumors that Labour would purge persistent advocates of such collaboration had become common, extending even to the smaller local newspapers. For example: "There is Tom Driberg," mused one hunter of reds under beds in the *Essex and Chelmsford Chronicle* for 5 March 1948:

> He is almost a fellow traveller, but never quite commits himself. Then there is Wing Commander Millington. . . How near is this clever young man to being a Communist? Others who might find a purge rather embarrassing are Captain Charles Smith of Colchester, Mr Geoffrey Bing, Hornchurch, and Mr Leslie Solley, Thurrock.

Three days later, in fact, the Labour Party Liaison Committee convened a special meeting, attended by Attlee, Bevin, Shinwell, Morgan Phillips, Maurice Webb, Lord Shepherd and the Chief Whip, to discuss "the position created in the Party as a result of the activities of a number of Labour Members whose speeches and actions give cause for misunderstanding abroad." No conclusions were reached at this gathering, but it was an ominous portent for the "hard" Labour Left. So was Attlee's announcement in the House of Commons on 15 March that communist civil servants would no longer be permitted to handle sensitive documents. This raised an angry storm on the Labour Left and, indeed, among civil libertarians generally. Forty-one Labour Members signed a resolution protesting that the new order "constitutes a departure from the principles of Democracy and Civil Liberty," and demanded a House debate. The government declined to provide time for one.[16]

By now the general trend had become obvious. The party leadership was preparing to crack down on persistent "hard" Left critics of the government. On Tuesday 13 April at 3:45 in the afternoon, Attlee, Morrison, Dalton, Shinwell and Morgan Phillips met in the Prime Minister's room at the House of Commons to discuss statements by Platts Mills and Zilliacus "that appeared to be subversive of Party policy." With impeccable timing, the Labour Members in question were engaged, literally at that very moment, in circulating a third pro-fusion telegram, addressed this time to Pietro Nenni and his followers in the Italian Socialist Party. Perhaps this intelligence reached the gathering in Attlee's chamber. At any rate, there could be little doubt of their reaction when they learned of the latest "hard" Left effort.[17]

The British government feared an imminent communist insurrection in Italy, where national elections were about to take place. Perhaps this helps explain the vehemence with which Labour Party leaders condemned the signatories of the famous "Nenni telegram." Yet the message did not influence the elections, in which both Nenni socialists and communists were trounced. Its impact upon the candidates also appears to have been negligible. A correspondent of the *Sunday Pictorial* asked one Nenni socialist his opinion of Platts Mills. The Italian was nonplussed. "Are they in Lancashire, perhaps?" he asked. The Nenni telegram is more important in British than in Italian history.[18]

The message itself read simply, "Greetings to our Italian Socialist Comrades and warm hope for your triumph in the election." It may have been drafted by Geoffrey Bing, but the original idea of sending it probably belonged to "some young Italian left-wing journalists in London" with whom Platts Mills was in contact. Zilliacus, Warbey and possibly several other Labour Members also had been thinking about sending the Nenni socialists a message of support. Warbey began to collect signatures but then went abroad, as did Zilliacus. While they were gone, Maurice Orbach took up where Warbey had left off. After gathering about a dozen names he asked Platts Mills to help. The latter now became the moving spirit behind the project. By Friday 16 April he had secured thirty-seven names, probably with the aid of Herschel Austin, Tom Braddock and perhaps Zilliacus, who had returned from the Continent. The Italian elections were due in two days. Platts Mills actually was holding the telephone and preparing to send the message on Friday evening, when Geoffrey Bing burst in to say that "the

Whips knew of our intention and were determined that anybody whose name went on such a telegram would be at once expelled from the Party. He asked whether we really meant to send it, and was deeply worried about what he had learned."[19]

Had Platts Mills taken counsel at this point with other organizers of the telegram they might have concluded that this was not the issue on which the "hard" Left should stake its future. Years later, Platts Mills thought it possible "that if everyone had known what the Whips were saying all would have withdrawn." It was the end of the week, however, the House had long since risen, and no one was about. The Member for Finsbury "retired to [his] room across the road from Parliament and worked a bit and had some supper." Possibly he decided on his own that the leaders could never expell thirty-seven Members. At any rate, "at about 9 o'clock ... [he] drove to what was then the all-night Post Office at King Edward Street in the City" and dispatched the telegram "with every name attached to it." He also gave the story "to every news agency and directly to several main papers, including the *Herald*." One wonders what Bing and the others, who were perhaps still unaware of the risk they now courted, came to make of this unilateral action.[20]

Whatever the signatories may have thought, the government was sure of its position. Months previously it had withdrawn recognition from the Nenni socialists, even though they represented the vast majority of the Italian Socialist Party, and had thrown its official weight behind a smaller, anti-communist breakaway group led by Giuseppe Saragat. The telegram supported the wrong faction, and so contravened Labour Party policy. The government's course, therefore, was clear. Every attempt would be made to separate the sponsors of the telegram from those who had agreed to sign it. Then an example would be made of the isolated few, "hard" Labour Leftists, who persisted in defying them.

On Saturday morning Morrison travelled to Wolverhampton East, where he had been scheduled previously to speak for the sitting Member, John Baird, who happened to have signed the telegram. The Lord President of the Council, who already knew the names of all the signatories, disingenuously expressed the hope that Baird was not mixed up with the message senders. The hapless backbencher confessed that he was but promised to recant publicly. The *Daily Telegraph* of the next day carried his disclaimer, and that of four other Labour Members who already had experienced second thoughts.[21]

Morrison's manner of dealing with Baird was formalized and applied systematically on Monday morning. Morgan Phillips dispatched a letter to each Member whose name had appeared on the fatal document. "I should be glad to know from you," he wrote, "whether you signed the telegram, and if so whether you have any observations to make." Recipients of this communication were given food for thought later in the afternoon at a debate in the House of Commons which had been demanded by Raymond Blackburn. A maverick formerly identified with the Labour Left, Blackburn had turned sharply right and become obsessed by the communist menace. Now he extracted, without difficulty, a promise from Morrison that signatories who did not recant would face disciplinary action. Morrison singled out Platts Mills for particular mention. It was becoming clear that this time the government would exert itself. With the climate of opinion hardening so quickly against them, it is little wonder that in the end fifteen signatories of the telegram disassociated themselves from it by one means or another.[22]

On the previous day, Sunday, Platts Mills must have realized that a storm was about to burst. Belatedly he conferred with Zilliacus, Austin and Tom Braddock. The upshot of this gathering was a letter to all Members whose names had appeared on the telegram. "We feel it would be very helpful for a meeting of the signatories to be held. We feel, too, that such a meeting could usefully consider what steps need to be taken to make clear the reasons why the message was sent." The meeting was held the day after the parliamentary debate, and in the ominous shadow of Phillips's letter. Nine Members attended and penned a joint reply to the party general secretary which established the main lines of the "hard" Left defense. Rather than defend the case for fusion, they denied knowing that Saragat had received Labour's official imprimatur, while reiterating their belief in "the freedom of individual Members of Parliament to express their views." They requested a party meeting to discuss this general principle.[23]

The government now increased the stakes. The meeting in Attlee's room on the 13th had concluded with an agreement that the Prime Minister should arrange for further discussions "as circumstances warranted." Another gathering must have taken place shortly after the telegram had been sent on Friday evening, possibly during the weekend or on Monday morning, when Phillips would have been instructed to draft the first letter. At this meeting the decision must also have been taken to single out Platts Mills for immediate punishment. A second letter was dispatched to him alone, with an invitation to appear at Transport House on Wednesday morning, 21 April. This confrontation duly took place, with Platts Mills facing Attlee, Dalton, Morrison, Phillips, Sam Watson, the miners' leader, and several others. Shinwell, his only possible ally among this intimidating group of NEC subcommittee chairmen, was effectively neutralized, since he chaired the meeting. According to the minutes, "a discussion ensued on [Platts Mills's] declarations over a period of time, which appeared to be subversive to Party policy. Many questions were asked of him." At the end it was decided to give him an opportunity to reply in writing. Then, after he left, the government widened its net. All Labour Members who had not repudiated the telegram would receive another letter from Morgan Phillips warning that they had committed "an open defiance of Labour Party principles and policy." Unless they agreed to withdraw their names from the message and to promise not to engage in similar activities in future, they would face disciplinary action. Platts Mills's fate, ostensibly still in the balance but in reality obvious to all, might serve as a reminder of what defiance could entail.[24]

Twenty-one of the original signatories proved unwilling to recant, despite the possibly grave consequences. There appears to have been little coordination among them at this point. Each must have answered Morgan Phillips in his own way. The "Nenni goats," as they were called by the press to distinguish them from "Attlee's sheep," had to take their stand, however, on the two issues raised by the nine Members in their joint reply to Phillips's first letter. As S. O. Davies, the Welsh miners MP explained in his letter to Phillips, he merely had sent a telegram of support to the official Italian Socialist Party. "Will you, if you can," he demanded, "be good enough to tell me in clear, explicit language" how this subverted party policies and principles? Davies concluded, "Unless I receive from you satisfactory replies . . . I fear that I shall continue to regard your communication as being most offensive and utterly unworthy of our great Movement."[25]

A brave effort, but positions were hardening, stakes increasing. On 19 April the *Daily Telegraph* had predicted that seven Labour Members were due for "disciplinary action," without attempting to define what their punishment might be. On the 21st the *Yorkshire Post* helpfully listed Members who had signed the German People's Congress and the Nenni telegrams: Austin, Tom Braddock, Harold Davies, Mack, Platts Mills, Julius Silverman, Solley and Zilliacus. Presumably these were (with one unidentifiable exception) the Members the *Daily Telegraph* had in mind. On the 22nd, as we have seen, Morgan Phillips had added to the tension by warning in his letter that the signatories indeed faced "disciplinary action."

Moreover, the Labour Left was divided. On the 23rd *Tribune*, while carefully refraining from recommending expulsions, demanded that those who declined to repudiate the telegram depart from the Labour Party. "Their place should be with the Communist Party of Great Britain which has also dedicated itself to the aim of destroying the Labour Government and disrupting the Labour Movement." The *New Statesman* was less crude, but still censorious. Anticipating a tightening of party discipline, its columnist concluded, "there is no doubt that Platts Mills, whatever else he has done, has struck a deadly blow at the freedom of action for the individual Socialist MP." The breach between "hard" and moderate members of the Labour Left, which Michael Foot had underlined early in 1946 in his opposition to the first fusion telegram, had widened perilously. As in the prewar period, the Left would greet a purge in disarray.[26]

On the 26th twenty-one Labour Members who had not recanted met to consider Morgan Phillips's letter of the 22nd. Historians have described them as "mostly . . . contrite," and willing to pledge "their future loyalty to the Government and its policy." While accurate, such descriptions are too simple. The twenty-one were defensive and conciliatory. Their collective reply to Morgan Phillips reiterated that "we were not aware that the NEC had formally withdrawn recognition" from the Nenni socialists. They claimed, disarmingly, that their "action was not intended to be an open defiance or any defiance, either of the Party's principles or policy or of the Executive's authority." There was, however, more to their letter than contrition. They also reminded Phillips that "all of us are old members of the Party. Some of us are foundation members. The Executive may rest assured that we . . . would certainly confine our disagreements, if any, to what is permitted by the Party's constitution." The "hard" Left never had claimed to be doing otherwise. We are back to Leslie Solley's suggestion of the previous year, that the real issue was the NEC's attempt to curtail the right of Labour Members to free speech.[27]

Not surprisingly, the party leaders did not respond sympathetically to this letter. Attlee, Morrison, Dalton, Griffiths, Watson, Phillips and the others convened the next day, in the Prime Minister's room in the House of Commons. Again Shinwell was in the chair. First they disposed of Platts Mills. Phillips read the written answers composed by the Member for Finsbury to the questions put to him in person the previous week. "After a lengthy discussion," the group agreed to recommend to the NEC that he be expelled from the Labour Party. Phillips then read the letter from the twenty-one signatories. "A full discussion ensued," during which it was decided that the collective letter was unsatisfactory. Phillips was directed to reply by the next day.[28]

This time the form of punishment in store for unyielding dissidents was spelled out. "The Executive has noted that a number of Members of Parliament persist in acting as a group in organised opposition to Party policy," Phillips wrote:

> In these circumstances I have been directed to write to each of the Members alleged to have signed the message of good wishes to the Nenni Communist combination . . . and who have neither repudiated their alleged adherence to the message nor withdrawn such adherence, and to inform them that unless they individually undertake by first post Thursday 6 May 1948 to desist in future from such conduct they are excluded from membership of the Labour Party.

The fate of Platts Mills testified that the party leadership possessed the will to carry out such threats.[29]

The twenty-one selected Austin, Barstow, Bing, Braddock, Cove, Harold Davies, S. O. Davies, Dobbie, Lever, Sydney Silverman, Warbey and Zilliacus to prepare a draft reply to Phillips's letter. Zilliacus informed S. O. Davies that he had reached the conclusion

> (derived from information, not guesswork) that a. The NEC know they cannot expel 21 MPs in a body; b. By demanding individual replies they hope the 21 signatories of the collective letter will fall into two pieces, the majority recanting, and a small hard core remaining defiant and taking the rap.

Cannily, Zilliacus recommended that the desired individual replies be sent, but in identical terms, "emphasising our common responsibility, and so drafted as to give full and explicit undertakings on every point raised . . . while safeguarding the right of minorities to express dissent within the limits allowed by our Constitution." A carefully written reply to Phillips was then drafted by the subcommittee. The twenty-one met to consider this message at five o'clock on 4 May in the Scottish Grand Committee Room off Westminster Hall.[30]

There is no record of the meeting of the twenty-one Labour Members. We know only that they reached a rough consensus, agreeing to follow the advice of Zilliacus. Yet there must have been some debate. Among the papers of Major Wilfred Vernon, the Member for Dulwich, there survives a handwritten note which he must have composed while the meeting was in progress, to aid him when he spoke. "I wish to tell the comrades here assembled," Vernon wrote to himself, that if it had been decided to defy the NEC to do its worst I would have agreed. I believe this would have been the gathering point for the widespread opposition in the country to the Government's foreign policy. Perhaps this is not the time or the occasion to make the break, I do not know. But of one thing I am certain, and that is that the crisis is only postponed. Nothing but the declaration of an alternative and the winning of popular support for it will stop the drift to war.

Cooler heads prevailed. The twenty-one agreed to incorporate in their individual replies to Phillips the phrases worked out by the subcommittee under Zilliacus's direction. These were, "I never have belonged, do not belong and will not belong to any group in organised opposition to Party policy," and "I will not in future take part in any such action as that now declared by the NEC to be contrary to the constitution and rules of the Party." Indubitably these satisfied the formal requirements of the NEC. One cannot help thinking them formulaic, however, as indeed the NEC must have concluded. Obvious scope for defiance remained, so long as it took place, as "hard" Labour Left Members claimed it always had done, within the rules. Vernon's letter to Phillips made this caveat clear. "I consider the NEC to be going too far," he wrote, "if it demands no disagreement, but perfectly within its rights in requesting that expression of disagreement be confined within the limits set by the Party constitution and the common sense practice of the Parliamentary Party." Solley made the same argument: "I do not think you would expect me to promise that I shall always agree with whatever the NEC may do, but you may rest assured that if ever I should find myself in the unfortunate position of disagreeing with the NEC I shall certainly confine such disagreement to what is permitted by the Party constitution." Sydney Silverman, in his response to Phillips, made a slightly bolder point: "I cannot undertake that I will always agree with whatever the National Executive Committee may do. The party is entitled to my judgement; that too is a part of loyalty." And S. O. Davies remained entirely unrepentant:

Our Movement embraces millions of men and women, and not merely a few hundred Members of Parliament and a few dozen who may constitute from time to time our National Executive. The Executive must forgive me if I am habitually inclined to give our millions my first thoughts and consideration. In so doing experience has taught me, as a Socialist, that I need entertain no fears of ever betraying our people and their Movement.

Given responses such as this to the NEC, it is difficult to disagree with the *Scotsman* of 30 April which displayed a grudging sympathy for the sole Labour Member to suffer the extreme penalty for his role in the Nenni telegram affair. "It is all rather hard on Mr Platts Mills who has not always been the most prominent of the dissentients and critics on the Socialist backbenches."[31]

The parliamentary party convened on 5 May for its regular weekly meeting to discuss the Nenni affair. There is no official record of proceedings, but Vernon penned a somewhat partisan account on the following day. According to the Member for Dulwich, discussion opened with Shinwell giving the official case and his private opinion that expulsions were undesirable. This is confirmed by Hugh Gaitskell, who confided to his diary on the 7th that "S[hinwell] made a shocking speech about the Nenni business, trying to give the impression that very obviously he had not really agreed with the Executive's decision." Tom Braddock criticized the NEC position "emphatically but with moderation," in Vernon's opinion. E. R. Millington, the former Common Wealth MP, member of "Keep Left" and according to Driberg an "uncompromising, robustly idealistic Socialist," criticized the leaders for undermining confidence in younger Members upon whom the party depended to keep marginal seats in the next general election. Geoffrey Bing "brought the house down," according to Vernon, by arguing that "the people he might disappoint in his constituency would be retained by the knowledge that the Party also contained Ernest Thurtle," a right-wing Labourite who was to stand against Platts Mills in Finsbury at the next general election, while Labour Leftists would be kept from bolting so long as Bing and the other unrepentant signatories likewise remained party members. Attlee and Morrison gave the official point of view. According to Vernon, however, Morrison "was completely bowled over when he read one sentence out of Warbey's letter, which gave Warbey an opportunity of reading the whole letter, which gave quite a different impression." Driberg, who had not signed the telegram, supported the signatories by reading from a letter, written to him by Laski in January 1947, backing Nenni against Saragat.[32]

This meeting of the parliamentary party marked the last phase of the Nenni telegram affair. In a sense the episode ended not with a bang but a whimper. Vernon, who had thought the NEC "wished to expel between three and five of their most outspoken critics," now believed "the extreme Right wing in the NEC and the Government has suffered a severe setback." There were no more expulsions. Nor, when one reads their letters to Morgan Phillips, is it clear that the twenty-one signatories were very much chastened by their experience.[33]

On the other hand, perhaps the government already had achieved its purpose. The episode must be viewed within the context of developing cold war. The government was determined to teach the public, and the Labour Party, that there could be no cooperation (let alone fusion) with communists. The singling out of individual Labour Members who might be fellow-travellers was designed to make such collaboration impossible by banishing its strongest advocates to the political wilderness. Equally, it was meant to demonstrate to the public that socialists were anti-communist. No doubt it was meant, as well, to be a signal to Crossman, Foot and other members of "Keep Left," three of whom had signed the Nenni telegram, of the political price Labour dissidents might be forced to pay. In this sense perhaps the expulsion was meant more as a warning to the moderate Labour Left than to such sea-green incorruptibles as S. O. Davies and Konni Zilliacus.

There remains the question, why Platts Mills? As the Scotsman had pointed out, he was not the most prominent of the government's "hard" Left critics. He was, however, an easy target. He came from New Zealand, not Britain. He had attended

Oxford. He drove an expensive Daimler. Vernon refers to Platts Mills's "unpopularity." He was, according to one Labour Member, "a born victim." Perhaps more importantly, he had little time to develop strong ties and mutual loyalties with his local Labour Party in Finsbury, a constituency which nevertheless could be relied upon to vote Labour. He was, therefore, vulnerable in a way that, say, Emrys Hughes, the son-in-law of Keir Hardie, and S. O. Davies, a Labour fixture in South Wales since the early years of the century, were not. A personal element may have been involved as well. Platts Mills had never gotten along with Morrison. In 1945 Morrison had spoken for him at Finsbury Town Hall. "He seems to be a bright enough young fellow and you may get a bit of useful work out of him," Platts Mills remembers him saying. "If you're not satisfied, however, you can get rid of him at the next general election." According to Platts Mills, "The Nenni telegram was Morrison's big chance."[34]

Finally, perhaps, a precedent had been set. Having expelled one "hard" Left Labour Member it would be easier to expel others. In a year's time Zilliacus, Solley and Lester Hutchinson were to walk the same plank as Platts Mills. Thus if the Nenni telegram affair did not take the heart out of the "hard" Labour Left, as has been maintained, it nevertheless marked a turning-point in their postwar history. Platts Mills's decision that Friday evening to send the telegram after all proved to have wider consequences than he anticipated.

IV

A fundamental division between "hard" Labour leftists and the rest of the Labour Party, including the moderate Labour Left, lay in their opposing assessments of the world communist movement and of Stalinist Russia. As we have seen, most of the leading figures on the Labour Left concluded during 1945–51, with varying degrees of reluctance and at different rates of speed, that there could be no cooperation between democratic socialists and communists. A dwindling number of Labour Members, however, continued to cherish the hope that the world socialist movement, which had been split since World War I and the Russian Revolution, could be reunited in the aftermath of World War II. The most prominent and talented advocate of this line within the Parliamentary Labour Party was Konni Zilliacus.

The career of Zilliacus resembled a roller-coaster. From a cosmopolitan background, he attended Yale University in the United States before World War I. With the outbreak of war he must have returned to England, for in 1917 we find him in British uniform. Already, however, he was a radical, for he also joined the anti-war Union for Democratic Control. After the Russian Revolution he was sent as an intelligence officer with the British military mission to Siberia. He lost a foot there, possibly in action. He also opposed the British policy of intervention against the new Bolshevik regime and, in an early sign of the insubordinate nature which was to become his trademark, he sent information to Josiah Wedgwood, G. Lowes Dickinson, Leonard Woolf and others in the UDC who likewise opposed Britain's anti-revolutionary policy. Returning to England in 1919, he immediately joined the Labour Party.[35]

Zilliacus possessed boundless energy. During the interwar period he was a member of the Information Section of the League of Nations Secretariat in Geneva. He kept in close touch with the Labour Party, partly through his membership in the Fabian Society, which he had also joined. He worked closely with Arthur Henderson, helping him to draft the famous 1924 Geneva Protocol and, when Henderson became President of the Disarmament Conference in 1930, the "War–Peace Memorandum," which was adopted four years later by the annual conferences of the Labour Party and the TUC. He also wrote the foreign policy section of Labour's 1934 policy statement, *For Socialism and Peace.* He never hesitated, however, to express his differences with senior officials in the Labour Party or at the League of Nations. He was the pseudonymous author of innumerable pamphlets which opposed the appeasement policies of the West European governments. As he wrote in 1949, "We of the League Secretariat had been political valets to prime ministers, foreign secretaries, ministers, ambassadors and the great ones of this earth so long that they meant nothing to us." In a foretaste of things to come, at Labour's 1939 annual conference he opposed the foreign policy advocated by party leaders, favoring instead an anti-fascist alliance with the Soviets. At a private session, he had "a tremendous row with Mr Bevin . . . The uproar was so great that the Conference had to close down and resume the next day." He was throughout his life a quintessential "troublemaker," in A. J. P. Taylor's apt phrase.[36]

Zilliacus was adopted as Labour candidate in Gateshead largely, he thought, because of his notoriety after the 1939 contretemps with Bevin. During the general election campaign of 1945 he made no pretense to expertise on domestic matters. His claim upon the electors of Gateshead rested on his knowledge of foreign affairs. "I appeal to you particularly to support me," Zilliacus wrote in his election address, "because I believe I have something real to contribute on the tremendous and overmastering issue of how to make peace secure. I have given all my adult life to that task, both as an international civil servant and as a student of world affairs. I want a chance to finish the job—or, at least, to go on trying."

Like many candidates in 1945, Zilliacus believed that "Europe can be reconstructed, pacified and united, and democracy can be revived, only on the basis of a new social order. To that policy the Soviet Union are already committed." Britain too, Zilliacus argued, would be committed to a new social order if Labour won the general election. Britain and Russia together could help to build a new European society. Anglo-Soviet cooperation, important as it was, however, would not be sufficient. Zilliacus was one of many Labourites who believed that the essential meaning of 1945 lay in the defeat of fascism at the hands of resistance movements which "derive[d] their main strength from the workers and their allies . . . largely under Socialist and Communist leadership." The indigenous anti-fascist movements could build a new society with British and Russian aid.[37]

This was the core of Zilliacus's postwar vision. It was the yardstick against which he measured the grim reality of power politics and diplomacy. "Conditions have now been created in which the capitalist bottlenecks that prevented democracy operating for the purpose of social change have been shattered, "Zilliacus" observed hopefully.

"The old civil service, the old army and police commands . . . the big landowners and the big businessmen have gone." Under such circumstances Britain, Russia and the various European socialists and communists could remake Europe. It seemed, at times, to drive Zilliacus literally to frenzy to think that such golden opportunities were being squandered.[38]

Certain as he was that reconstruction depended upon cooperation between socialists and communists, Zilliacus did not hesitate to draw the logical conclusion for his own country. He supported the communist application for affiliation to Labour. His party must be prepared, he argued, "to regard Communists as friends and allies." Popular in 1945, this line found less and less favor in the Labour Party as time went by. From 1946 Zilliacus found himself frequently castigated as a "crypto," or secret, member of the Communist Party. By May of that year he found it necessary to deny the charge. "Whatever faults I may have, and they are many, no one has ever accused me of making a secret of my opinions or taking orders when I ought not to do so."[39]

Zilliacus entered the House of Commons with a high reputation on the Left. Kingsley Martin had fallen under his spell during the 1930s. In 1945 Driberg singled him out for special mention as a welcome addition to the Parliamentary Labour Party and praised his maiden speech. Zilliacus's views, however, did not evolve in the same manner as Martin's or even Driberg's. He continued to advocate an Anglo-Soviet alliance and "sweeping concessions to Communists." As the split between "hard" and moderate members of the Labour Left widened during 1946–7, Zilliacus found himself in frequent disagreement with old friends. They, in turn, disapproved of the company he now kept. As "Phineas" put it in the *New Statesman* on 10 August 1946, "Zilliacus, despite his remarkable knowledge of international organisation and the steady improvement of his debating technique, has alienated the House by associating with the small and unimportant group of crypto-Communists."[40]

For his part, Zilliacus grew increasingly disillusioned with the new government. As early as 20 October 1945 he was complaining that it showed few "signs of attempting to apply the Party's declared policies." At first he was willing to counsel patience. "All this is complicated and very hard going," he acknowledged in March 1946. "The Labour Government needs all the support and understanding it can get from the rank and file to get on top of its problems." Soon afterwards, however, Zilliacus's patience had worn thin. He was one of the six to vote against Bevin at the PLP debate on foreign policy on 27 March. As he explained:

> It is reasonable to give the Government time and the benefit of the doubt before deciding. There will always be extenuating circumstances. And in politics you can never achieve absolute certainty . . . But at some point it becomes necessary to balance the probabilities and make a stand. So far as I am concerned I have lost hope of the Government changing its dangerous and disastrous Tory foreign policy unless it is either pulled up short by a revolt of the rank and file or comes a cropper in world affairs.[41]

For the next five years Zilliacus threw himself into the struggle to "pull the

Government up short." No fusionist telegram, critical letter, or protest rally was complete without him. He wrote books while less driven Members were composing pamphlets, pamphlets while they were writing articles, articles while they were resting. He conducted goodwill tours of many East European countries, including one to Russia, during which he and six other Labour Members enjoyed a private audience with Stalin. Withal, he retained a sense of humor. "I regard our policy in Greece as morally abominable, intellectually idiotic and politically disastrous. Apart from that it is all right," he once announced on the BBC.[42]

Some called him "Silly Zilly," and he was capable of statements which today seem ludicrous. "The Soviet Union has not made the slightest attempt to introduce the Soviet system or establish a Communist dictatorship even in the countries that are its neighbours, that it liberated and that it occupied for a longer or shorter period after the cessation of hostilities," he wrote in July 1946. Yet if he cherished certain illusions long after many had abandoned them, he punctured others the party leaders would have liked to maintain. "It's quite absurd, of course, to contend that any of these countries in Eastern Europe are in the state of advanced parliamentary democracy," he admitted on one occasion. "But I say there was more democracy in the Polish general elections than there was in the elections in South Carolina, or . . . in Ulster . . . let alone what happens in the British Colonial Empire. Don't let's be such humbugs about this business of democracy."[43]

Moderates on the Labour Left affected an attitude of amused toleration towards Zilliacus. Mallalieu wrote of him:

> If you merely read about him, you would imagine that he is a wild man who would slit your throat as soon as look at you. Yet . . . any mother . . . would tell him to mind the baby while she was shopping. . . Zilly almost certainly would put the nappies on the wrong end. . . To be a secret agent, Zilly is too clumsy and much too honest.

Yet, eventually, there was a sharp break between Zilliacus and the moderate Labour Left. The times were much too fraught for good relations to survive between politicians holding diametrically opposed views on the most important matters of the day.[44]

Zilliacus had been excluded from the "Keep Left" group, but he welcomed publication of its pamphlet. "It should do a lot to clear people's minds," he wrote. In fact, he opposed its central foreign policy premise. For Zilliacus, a united Europe based upon an Anglo-French alliance must inevitably become "a western bloc served up in pink Social Democratic sauce." He thought that "the only possible framework for a United Europe policy is the triangle of alliances between the three European Great Powers, France, Great Britain and the Soviet Union."[45]

As Zilliacus wrote later, he had hoped that "the march of events" would make this clear to Crossman and others in "Keep Left." The Marshall Plan, however, interfered with the process of education Zilliacus had in mind. He viewed General Marshall's offer as an American bid to finance an anti-Soviet bloc of West European nations. To the advocate of fusion with communists it mattered little that social democrats like Attlee and Bevin would administer the funds. After the Marshall Plan, "Western union" meant to Zilliacus "a bridgehead for the American holy war against the European working class, trying to make Europe safe for Wall Street in the guise of rescuing it from Communism." He believed that "Keep Lefters" and others who advocated accepting US dollars had gone over to the enemy. They "offered no true alternative to the Government's policy of subservience to the United States, which means ultimately capitulation to American capitalism and support of near-Fascism in Western Europe as we are doing already in Greece."[46]

Zilliacus keenly felt his isolation from former friends and allies. "For God's sake," he wrote at one point to Kingsley Martin, "let's meet and thrash this out, for I know you and I at bottom want the same thing, however maddening each of us seems to the other at times." *Tribune* had long since been closed to him. By November 1948 he reluctantly concluded that even Martin's *New Statesman* had "joined the Western Union–Third Force–Anti-Soviet and anti-Communist camp. Not only do you refuse to take my articles giving the opposite point of view," Zilliacus complained to Martin, "but I also find it more and more difficult to get in a letter."[47]

Party leaders determined to establish the parameters of dissent for Labour Members, were bound to clash with a man of Zilliacus's views, energy and temperament. He was a more visible critic than Platts Mills even during the episode of the Nenni telegram, when in fact he was considered, along with Platts Mills, for expulsion. Possibly he was not singled out for punishment then because of his long-standing association with the party and his reputation for knowledge of international affairs. Perhaps the party leaders thought he would learn to moderate his views, or at least his language. Platts Mills's fate, however, did nothing to chasten the Member for Gateshead, who persisted, also, in drawing from his study of foreign politics what Labour Party leaders could only consider to be the wrong conclusions. Less than a month after circulating the Nenni telegram for signatures, Zilliacus attended a conference of international socialists in Warsaw to say "a few words about the fight of the British working class for peace." He had gone to Poland despite a warning from the new NEC chairman, James Griffiths, that "your attendance, even as an observer . . . will give cause for misgiving."[48]

Zilliacus recognized that his continuing defiance of the party executive made him a marked man. Moreover, as he wrote later, "I was now sufficiently isolated in Parliament" to present the NEC with an easy target. By November 1948 Dalton was writing to Phillips, "I feel we cannot, much longer, avoid dealing with [Zilliacus] as we did with Platts Mills. What do you think? Have we got a dossier on him?" In December the NEC, which did indeed have a file on its most troublesome backbencher, considered whether he should be reselected as a parliamentary candidate for Gateshead in the next general election. In the absence of a record of its proceedings, the historian may assume only that it reached a negative verdict but decided to await a decision from the election subcommittee, under whose jurisdiction a refusal to endorse would have to be made. That body met with Zilliacus in January 1949 and voted 9 to 0 that his candidature *should* be endorsed. Once the party leaders had determined upon a course of action, however, they rarely were diverted. "I was warned," Zilliacus wrote afterwards, "that the fight would be in the NEC itself, where my enemies were Mr Attlee, Mr Morrison and the trade union bloc led by Mr Sam Watson." Not surprisingly, the election subcommittee bowed to this formidable triumvirate. Zilliacus had committed the further indiscretion of attending a communist-supported World Peace Conference in Paris. "Are you not afraid," he was asked at a second meeting of the election subcommittee, "that if you sit in a Committee where there are many Communists you will be absorbed?" Zilliacus replied, "I consider that I am difficult to absorb," but this cut little ice with his interrogators. Zilliacus wrote afterwards, "five of the nine heroes on the Election Sub-Committee [who, previously, had supported his reselection as a parliamentary candidate] promptly changed their view." His informant may have miscounted. Leslie Hale learned from Harold Laski that six members of the committee voted against Zilliacus. Only Laski himself, Emanuel Shinwell and Michael Foot held firm. At any rate, Zilliacus was expelled from the Labour Party. If he stood as a candidate in the next general election, he would face a Labour opponent.[49]

For a moment it seemed that the NEC had gone too far. George Bernard Shaw's encomium of 1946 was recalled in more than one newspaper. "Mr Zilliacus is not a man to be ignored," Shaw had written. "He is the only internationally minded Member of any note in the House of Commons . . . He is a man who must be attended to, and his questions answered if another fiasco like that of Versailles and its sequel in 1939–45 is to be averted." Labour Party headquarters were deluged with protest resolutions from CLPs and trade unions, testimony to the depth of support Zilliacus retained among the rank and file despite his "hard" Left views. According to Driberg, he was popular in the PLP as well. Driberg wrote, "Many Labour MPs, not only of the Left, regret the expulsion of Zilly." Jennie Lee informed Leslie Hale that she "could not understand how any sane person could vote for expelling Zilly" (although her husband had). Richard Crossman, with whom Zilliacus had crossed swords on more than one occasion, warned that "Zilliacus has been expelled because he has become the symbol of anti-Bevinism." Crossman maintained that "every party should be big enough to tolerate an unpopular minority of critics. After all, the party disciplinarians are not always right. Think of Churchill, Stafford Cripps and Bevan in the 1930s."[50]

Zilliacus retained the right to appeal to Labour's annual conference to reverse the expulsion decree. The procedure was not simple. Delegates would have to vote first that he be allowed to speak at all. Then he would have to persuade conference that he deserved to remain in the Labour Party. One year earlier, Platts Mills, who had faced the same problem, had failed to obtain a hearing. Zilliacus, however, arranged for Sydney Silverman and Geoffrey Bing to speak in his behalf. More potent still, apparently Harold Laski agreed to open the debate for him. Despite his many public differences with the party leadership, Laski retained a following among rank-and-file Labourites. He was in a position to provide a critical measure of support to Zilliacus. "There was [therefore] something like consternation," Hale wrote in his diary afterwards, "when the news came through that Laski had been persuaded by the Executive that he could not properly do this. It is said that there was a painful scene . . . and fairly high words." The case of the executive was that its individual members were bound by majority decisions. According to Hale, "Mannie Shinwell even supported this view, while Laski said that Michael Foot who had promised to support him did not say a word." Laski then proposed to speak merely as a delegate from his local Labour Party, "but was told he could not because the duly accredited delegate . . . had the vote."[51]

In the lead-up to the conference, maneuvering was intense. Supporters of Zilliacus appear to have thought that Laski was crucial to their cause. "We tried to get hold of Laski alone," Hale recorded, "but he was sitting with Hugh Dalton and others; so finally Dick Crossman and I and Geoffrey Bing went in to raise the issue. Dick Crossman's point was that the whole thing was part of a definite design to stifle criticism of any kind by the backbenchers . . . Dalton was very unconvincing and we were all fairly rude to him." In the end Laski did not speak, but Bing and Silverman made "very able appeals" according to Hale. When it came to the vote, nearly every constituency Labour party supported Zilliacus's appeal to be heard. The trade unions, however, voted almost as a bloc against him, and he was not allowed to speak. Afterwards, a depressed Hale thought he perceived "a very real sense of disquiet and unease among the delegates." He told Morgan Phillips, with some bitterness, that "a number of us were really preparing to mount the scaffold, the only interest being the order of extermination." Phillips replied that Hale flattered himself:

> So far as he knew I was not in the next twenty for the tumbril. I suggested that he might have a look at Herbert Morrison's eye and then reread the history of the French revolution, when he might find with some trepidation that the most brutal and painful death was reserved for [Robespierre] himself. Morgan seemed inclined to be a little less matey after this observation.[52]

A second Labour Member, Leslie Solley of Thurrock, shared Zilliacus's fate at the conference. Much less popular and politically experienced than the Member for Gateshead, Solley proved less difficult for the NEC to isolate. Afterwards he, Platts Mills, D. N. Pritt and Lester Hutchinson, who was denied reselection by the election subcommittee in July 1949, formed a "Labour Independent Group" which continued to voice the original "hard" Labour Left views. At first Zilliacus lent the group his support. "The trouble was," Platts Mills recalled later, "if two of us were to be the tellers on a division, it left only three to vote. We usually managed so to arrange things that the Tories were united with Labour, so the votes, I suppose, were of the order of 500 to 3." A less effective Left is hard to imagine. In the 1950 general election the Labour Independent Group paid the price. All its members were trounced. Hutchinson and Solley lost their deposits.[53]

Zilliacus, however, was far from finished. We will examine his relationship with the Gateshead Labour Party in Chapter 7. For the moment, suffice it to say that he possessed a substantial local following. He was able, therefore, to base his claim to readmittance to Labour's ranks partly on the issue of "Democracy in the Labour Party, that is the right of Divisional Labour Parties to select their candidates without having their choice dictated to them by Transport House abusing the right to endorse candidates." In contrast to the Militant Tendency of the 1970s and 1980s, which argued that Labour Members are primarily the delegates of their local Labour parties, Zilliacus maintained that Labour Members must not become "mere stooges, rubber stamps, party hacks and political cannon fodder that do what they are told and never mind election pledges, conscience and judgment."[54]

Zilliacus claimed to be fighting for more than readmittance to the party. He wanted a complete revision of Labour's attitude towards communism. Despite his blind spots, in some ways Zilliacus was a more perceptive student of the world communist movement than anyone in the PLP. He was a living refutation of the canard that communist sympathizers were always dupes or agents of a foreign power. Where members of the Labour Independent Group identified the Soviet Union as the fountainhead of the world socialist revolution, and insisted that opposition to Soviet policies was opposition to socialism itself, Zilliacus demonstrated his independence by arguing against the notion—accepted by the Labour Party hierarchy, moderate Labour Left and Labour Independent Group alike—that communism was a monolithic movement. "You say I 'beg the question about the nature of Communist Parties," he wrote to Martin in July 1948. "I say that the Communist Parties vary considerably according to their national backgrounds, and would vary even more if the West ceased to treat them as enemies, and thereby force them into positions of intransigence." Zilliacus was an early, perhaps the first, postwar advocate of Eurocommunism.[55]

Unlike most Labour Members, Zilliacus viewed the 1949 rupture between Yugoslavia and the Soviet Union as confirmation not that Russia was a threat to world peace, but that diversity among communists was possible. On one of his innumerable trips to Eastern Europe he had met Tito, who convinced him, as he wrote later, that "the present regime in Yugoslavia has the support of the overwhelming majority of the people, is building Socialism according to Marxist-Leninist principles . . . and wants peace." When Russia attempted to lead Yugoslavia out of the world communist movement, Zilliacus wrote:

> I stand by everything I have ever said about Anglo-American postwar policy . . . The main responsibility for the drift to war . . . still rests with the diehard defenders of Capitalism in the West . . . the Labour Government has a heavy share of that responsibility . . . The Soviet Government and people want and need peace.

Yet his support for Tito's insubordinate attitude proved too much for many former allies. The *Daily Worker*, which previously had praised him as one of the few "independent minded Labour Members," now reviled him as a "war monger and deserter from the peace front" and refused to print his reply. Even his allies in the Independent Labour Group were suspicious. Platts Mills wrote afterwards, "Zilliacus made a deep genuflection by leaving one Yugoslavia friendship society and joining or setting up another which then became an anti-Soviet one."[56]

For his part, Zilliacus kept his head. He must have known that the communist quarrel presented him with a golden opportunity to re-enter the good graces of the Labour hierarchy. By siding with Tito, he could easily launch a few broadsides against Russia. Instead he argued for Eurocommunism. "It is important to realise," he wrote in the *Sunday Pictorial* for 4 December 1949,

> that the other great Communist Parties differ in degree rather than in kind from that of Yugoslavia. There is no chance of a Communist Party becoming nationwide and firmly established in the political and trade union leadership of the workers of its country unless it is patriotic.

Six months later he had further developed this interpretation. The cold war had frozen the world into two hostile blocs, but Tito pointed a way out. "Yugoslavia is a challenge to both sides: to the Russians to repudiate the claims to direct Communist parties in other countries; to the West to say what they mean by defending democracy against Communism."[57]

In February 1950 Zilliacus lost his seat in Parliament. But he did not lose his voice or relinquish his distinctive viewpoint:

> I do not believe the leaders of the Soviet Union have any enthusiasm for world revolution, for who could guarantee that the revolutionary regimes would be loyal Stalinists . . . ? I think their aim is to [do a] deal with the USA which would divide the world into capitalist and communist spheres of influence, leaving them a free hand to impose Stalinism in eastern Europe and their part of Asia, and the US a free hand to put Communist Parties and their allies out of business in the rest of the world.

Zilliacus, in 1952, had arrived nearly at the "Keep Left" position of 1947.[58]

This seems less a genuflection, as Platts Mills would have it, than the genuine evolution of an idiosyncratic and original mind. Yet in so far as Zilliacus had moved from nearly total identification with the Soviets to a much more critical stance, he had become acceptable to most Labour leaders. Early in 1952 he was readmitted to the party. By 1955 he was back in Parliament, as much a thorn in the side of the NEC as ever. In 1961 he was temporarily suspended and nearly expelled again, this time for writing in the *World Marxist Review* an article which was critical of right-wing Labourites. The communists, whose common membership in the labor movement he continued to advocate, however, had no hesitation in reading him from theirs. Not content merely to excoriate his politics, they claimed to have discovered during the Slansky trials in Czechoslovakia that he had been a secret agent of Anglo-American imperialism all along. Zilliacus made the only possible reply to this absurd accusation: "I didn't do it really, you know."[59]

V

Meanwhile, it had become apparent that a political space existed on the Left of the Labour Party between the moderates in "Keep Left," most of whom were rapidly moving towards the center, and the fellow-travelling Left represented by the Independent Labour Group. On 22 May 1949 Ellis Smith reported in *Reynolds News* that "I, and a number of other members of the Labour Party whose devotion to the movement cannot be challenged, have come to the conclusion that something must be done." His answer was "a new ginger group." "We will bring Socialists together in every locality, and from these local groups we will form a national association of Socialists," Smith predicted hopefully. "We base ourselves on the conviction that the Labour Party is the only working-class party with sufficient backing to carry us on the road to Socialism, but that the speed at which it travels depends upon the measure of Socialist dynamic within the rank and file." This was the beginning of the Socialist Fellowship.

Smith's search for members brought him into contact with another circle of "hard" Left Labourites clustered around a monthly newspaper called *Socialist Outlook*. This publication, first printed in December 1948, was edited by John Lawrence, whose experience finally was to encompass membership of the Labour, Trotskyist and official communist movements. Tom Braddock wrote a regular column for the paper. Herschel Austin, Harold Davies, Bessie Braddock, Ronald Chamberlain and Stephen Swingler were other Labour Members who contributed articles during 1948–50. At Labour's 1949 annual conference in June, the newspaper sponsored a meeting at which Smith formally announced the formation of the new group. Lawrence, Chamberlain and Tom Braddock also addressed the gathering of approximately 160 delegates.[60]

The Socialist Fellowship was never as rich in talent as "Keep Left." Tom Braddock was at least as mercurial as Zilliacus, but without his knowledge. Bessie Braddock, rapidly moving to the Right of the Labour Party, soon passed beyond the ambit of the new ginger group altogether. Chamberlain and Austin left little mark upon the political scene. Yet Smith succeeded in recruiting Fenner Brockway, who possessed a national reputation. Moreover, Swingler and Harold Davies, both of whom also belonged to "Keep Left," were already influential figures on Labour's left wing. In short, Socialist Fellowship was not inevitably fated to the ignominious and obscure end which, in fact, it achieved.

At first it appeared that the organization would avoid the mistakes of earlier left-wing ginger groups. Brockway wrote on 17 December 1949 in the *Glasgow Forward*:

> Once establish special groups within the Party which devote themselves to policy problems, and the danger arises that we shall create a minority movement which will deteriorate into divisive manoeuvres and distrusts. . . We are not a new Party. We are a fellowship to serve the Labour Party and Socialism.

This was a crucial distinction. It had been possible for the party leaders to attack earlier Labour Left critics for representing, or having the potential to represent, a "party within a party." Socialist Fellowship was determined to deflect such charges in advance.

Socialist Fellowship was equally circumspect about the Soviet Union and communism. Harold Davies wrote in the October 1949 issue of *Socialist Outlook*, "Labour must work for understanding with the East and the Soviets," whom he included among the "progressive nations of the world." This was a far cry, however, from the old call for "unity on the Left." And it was balanced by Braddock's pointed questions to Zilliacus. "Can he take a group of free Socialists . . . into Czechoslovakia, Hungary, Bulgaria, Rumania or Russia . . . [to ask] where are your political prisoners, they belong to our class and we want to speak to them?"[61]

As they began to emerge, the main goals of Socialist Fellowship went slightly beyond those of "Keep Left" in its most militant phase. The new group's manifesto advocated, in general terms, "socialisation, workers' control, ending the gross inequalities of income, a Socialist Europe and freedom for the colonies." More specifically, at its first annual conference, members resolved that the government should

1) Subsidise food and clothing further in order to meet price increases . . . 2) Maintain the building programme and social services, 3) Link pensions and benefits with a cost of living scale, 4) Drop the wage freeze and aim at more output by better technique and organisation rather than longer hours.

To pay for this defense of living standards, the Fellowship proposed "increased taxation of the rich, higher death duties, and capital gains, [as well as] drastic reduction of arms expenditure and manpower in the Forces."[62]

These were the traditional Labour Left demands as we have seen them since 1945. What placed the Socialist Fellowship on the "hard" Labour Left was its attitude towards the cold war and British foreign policy. Suspicious of the Soviet Union as it was, it remained equally doubtful about the United States at a time when most Labour leftists had reluctantly concluded that some form of Anglo-American alliance was necessary to resist communism. For example, Ronald Chamberlain argued against British membership in NATO, though he did not vote against it in Parliament. "I have always adhered to the view that a country must take reasonable defence measures," he admitted.

But will any fair minded person deny that "reasonable" has been left far behind when we tie ourselves in an Atlantic Pact with the United States of America, when we fit ourselves into her military conceptions, provide her with air bases and give her far reaching rights of "stockpiling" and of acquisition of raw materials in British colonies?

Tom Braddock, idiosyncratic though he undoubtedly was, voiced the "hard" Labour Left perception of the role his party had come to play under Attlee: "Saving American

1.   "One of the outstanding brains of the Party" according to Leslie Hale.
Ian Mikardo in 1949.

2. Richard Crossman in pensive mood in 1945; But see Attlee's verdict on him: "Bad judgement, why, he has no judgement at all".

3. "A lean, tall, shy youth whose conspicuous personal qualities are seriousness, sincerity and devotion." Michael Foot in 1954.

4.   Tom Driberg in 1955.

5.   Geoffrey Bing in 1957.

6.   Sydney Silverman in 1949. Woodrow Wyatt wrote of him: "Whatever the Government, he would oppose it without fear on a variety of issues."

7.   Labour's most arden advocate of a united Europe, R.W.G. Mackay, in 1948.

8. John Platts Mills, the victor of Finsbury, 11 August 1945.

9. Konni Zilliacus. Many years later Michael Foot termed him a political saint.

10.   Kingsley Martin interprets the General Election of 1950.

11. Harold Laski in 1946.

12. Bob Edwards, leader of the Chemical Workers' Union.

13.   Walter Padley makes a point at the TUC of 1950.

14.   A young man in a hurry, Harold Wilson in 1949.

capitalism from Russian Communism. That is, in fact, what we are being called upon to do."[63]

It might have been possible for Socialist Fellowship to move into the space which "Keep Left" had abandoned while steering clear of the pro-Soviet Labour Independent Group. Instead it was overtaken by events. This was the common plight of the Labour Left during 1945–51. The tides moved very quickly during those crucial years, and the Labour Left was always just missing the boat. For Socialist Fellowship, the Korean War proved to be the disruptive factor. Before the Fellowship had managed to recruit additional "Keep Lefters" or any other relatively big fish, its members found themselves divided bitterly as a result of events on the far side of China.

The left wing of Socialist Fellowship appears to have been dominated by John Lawrence, who was passing through a Trotskyist phase, and by Tom Braddock, who defies labels. They both viewed the war in Korea as part of a wider pattern of imperialist aggression emanating from the United States. Although deeply suspicious of the Soviet Union, they argued that socialists must not participate in a capitalist crusade against communism. When the Labour government supported UN action against the North Koreans and Chinese, they ceased to be its critical supporters and went into outright opposition. Braddock now claimed that it would be an electoral asset for Labour if Attlee, Bevin, Cripps and Morrison retired from politics. He also seemed to think that Labour's experience since 1945 had discredited the parliamentary road to socialism altogether. "After five years' trial by a democratically elected Labour Government, the attempt to carry out successfully the declared objects of the Labour Party . . . has failed."[64]

This placed Labour Members like Brockway, Smith, Swingler and Chamberlain in a difficult position. They were hardly uncritical admirers of the government's war policy, but neither were they prepared to condemn entirely Labour's hopes for achieving socialism through the parliamentary process. A struggle for control of Socialist Fellowship took place, in which they were the losers. In September 1950 Smith and Brockway resigned.

Socialist Fellowship now entered the political wilderness. In 1950 Braddock lost his seat in Parliament, and though he never was expelled formally from the Labour Party he never succeeded in re-entering the House of Commons. Likewise Chamberlain, who only reluctantly distanced himself from the group, managed to retain his party membership but not his seat. There was little opposition when the Labour Party proscribed Socialist Fellowship in April 1951.

Conversely, Ellis Smith, Swingler and Brockway found their way back to what might be called the mainstream of the "hard" Labour Left, if such a description is not almost too precise. They joined an organization called Victory for Socialism, a group which dated back to June 1934, when Fred Messer, a former French-polisher who had become Labour Member for Tottenham, helped to produce the *VfS Campaigner*, "organ of the Labour Party's Victory for Socialism Campaign." During World War II, VfS merged with a "Committee against Race Hatred," which opposed Lord Vansittart's view that the entire German people were responsible for Nazi atrocities. Yet it retained a distinctive identity. By 1943 VfS had a formal chairman, the Labour

Member for Penistone, Harry McGhee, and had won support for its campaign to readmit the ILP to Labour from a hundred MPs. In 1945 VfS issued "A Call to Socialists" which locates it firmly in the non-communist "hard" Labour Left tradition. "There is a danger that Socialists will be frustrated and Socialism delayed if the Labour Party allows itself to be bribed into accepting a policy of reforms which in themselves are not a challenge to capitalism," Messer wrote. "Just as in the old days the ILP devoted itself to 'crusading for Socialism,' so today is there need for a similar body inside the Labour Party."[65]

Despite this ambitious announcement, VfS remained inactive during the first Attlee government. With the disintegration of Socialist Fellowship, however, it proved a magnet for Labour leftists like Brockway and Ellis Smith. Augmented by new recruits of this caliber, VfS could attempt to fill the role for which Socialist Fellowship originally had cast itself. On 30 January 1951 it decided that "the government need the support of an emphatic expression of opinion from the organised Labour Movement, to strengthen them in resisting strong reactionary pressures from abroad." Accordingly it would organize "a series of conferences . . . to consider what action should be taken to stop the present drift to war." Labour Members were invited to endorse these demonstrations. In addition to Brockway, Santo Jeger of Socialist Fellowship, Acland, Bing, W. Thomas Williams and Marcus Lipton of the recently expanded "Keep Left" group and Edward Moeran and Maurice Orbach quickly did so. Warbey, Mikardo and Sydney Silverman likewise joined, though somewhat later.[66]

Significantly, the new group sought ties with less "hard" members of the Labour Left. Many Labourites who originally had supported the government's position on the Korean War, because they thought Attlee could restrain the anti-communists in Washington, now feared that the Americans were unduly influencing Attlee. Where Socialist Fellowship had scorned such less than wholehearted opponents of the war, VfS members like Brockway, Mikardo, Harold Davies and Sydney Silverman worked with them. In the House of Commons they joined nine other Labour Members in putting down a motion which regretted that China had been branded as an aggressor, opposed sanctions against China and urged "immediate further efforts" to "secure a Cease Fire in Korea and a permanent settlement by the withdrawal of all armed forces."[67]

VfS looked for support from the moderate Labour Left outside the House as well. Its first anti-war demonstration took place on 10 March 1951 and was addressed by Brockway and the leader of the Chemical Workers, Bob Edwards. Simultaneously the group supported the efforts of a "Peace with China" council whose president was Kingsley Martin. On 8 January this organization had attracted 2,500 people to Kingsway Hall to hear Michael Foot, Martin himself and a former member of the government, Lord Stansgate, condemn Attlee's policies. In this way, the non-communist "hard" Labour Left re- established contact with the *New Statesman*, with Tribunites and with "Keep Left." And it, as much as those "softer" Left groups, provided a crucial element of support when Bevan finally launched his rebellion in 1951.[68]

The very willingness of VfS to associate with Martin's group testifies, however, to the utter defeat of the "hard" Labour Left as it had appeared in 1945. Its *raison d'être* then had been fusion between socialists and communists. This goal now was discredited utterly. The "hard" Labour Left no longer existed as an effective political force. The precondition to its re-emergence was a more timely reason for being.

VI

The "hard" Labour Left was ineffective during 1945–51. One may reasonably ask, therefore, whether the Labour Party either needed to expell intransigent members of that faction or was right to do so.

Surely a political party has the right to expell members who secretly belong to another, rival organization. Were the four expelled Members fellow-travellers? In the case of Zilliacus, it seems doubtful. As for the others, it is impossible to tell. Supposing Platts Mills, Solley and Hutchinson to have been "crypto-communists," if only for the sake of argument, however, it does not follow that the Labour Party helped itself by expelling them. In fact, the opposite seems more likely.

The notion of fusion was not discredited in the PLP by such disciplinary measures as the Attlee government took against the "hard" Labour Left. Rather cooperation with communists was discredited by the communists themselves. In continuing to press not merely for a British foreign policy that was more independent of the United States, but also for alignment with the Soviets and their allies, "hard" Labour leftists quite effectively isolated themselves. Banishing them to the political wilderness was redundant.

The real aim of the expulsions, then, was not so much to silence four troublesome backbenchers as to intimidate others who were more influential. The rigid adherence to protocol of Labour Members like Foot, Crossman and the rest of the "Keep Left" group after 1947 provides indirect evidence for this conclusion. Partly as a result of the expulsions the Labour Left became inhibited in its criticism of the government. Unfortunately it lost enthusiasm and elan as well. Was ridding the PLP of such figures as Leslie Solley and Lester Hutchinson worth that? Given the narrow margin of Conservative victory in 1951, perhaps not.

Or were the expulsions meant to be observed outside the PLP? If sympathy for the communists was waning fast in the House, it had greater staying-power outside, especially in the trade unions. The government depended upon their loyalty above all. It could not, however, demand purges in the unions without having provided an example itself. It is to the trade unions and their Labour Left component that we now turn.

Notes and References

1   Fenner Brockway, *Outside the Right* (London, 1963), p. 75. Phillips kept a file on left-wing Labour Members; its title was "Lost Sheep."

2   *New Statesman*, 2 March 1946.
3   According to Driberg, "Liberator" was Jon Kimche, a journalist of Swiss origins with Trotskyist inclinations; *Reynolds News*, 17 March 1946.
4   Descriptions of the meeting in *New Statesman*, 30 March 1946; Gateshead Public Library, Konni Zilliacus papers, *Socialist Review* (undated clipping).
5   *Daily Herald*, 20 March 1946; Liaison Committee minutes, 2 May 1946, 20 May 1946.
6   Liaison Committee minutes, 7 May 1946; *Reynolds News*, 9 June 1946.
7   "Jack Wilkes" in *Tribune*, 22 November 1946; Public Record Office, Ernest Bevin papers, FO800/176, Orme Sargent and Christopher Mayhew to Lord Inverchapel, 22 November 1946.
8   *Tribune*, 3 January 1947.
9   BLPES, microfilm no. 199, PLP minutes, 10 December 1947.
10   *Daily Herald*, 12 December 1947.
11   Christ Church College Library, Tom Driberg papers, L/2, Zilliacus to Driberg, 8 March 1948.
12   Christ Church College Library, Tom Driberg papers, L/2, Miscellaneous notes.
13   Ibid.
14   Ibid.; ibid, Braddock to Driberg, 5 March 1948.
15   Lord Hale papers, diary entry, 28 June 1947; ibid., 18 November 1947.
16   Liaison Committee minutes, 8 March 1948; for the purge of communists in the Civil Service, see Chapter 7.
17   Labour Party, NEC minutes, vol. 95, p. 248, 13 April 1948.
18   See especially Public Record Office, FO800/471, for Bevin's fears about Italy; quoted by Emrys Hughes in *Glasgow Forward*, 1 May 1948.
19   On Bing's possible authorship of the telegram, see Robert Jackson, *Rebels and Whips* (London, 1968), p. 68. I am much indebted to Mr Platts Mills for sending me a letter of September 1983, and portions of his unpublished autobiography, which describe the Nenni telegram episode.
20   Platts Mills, unpublished autobiography, p. 3.
21   Ibid.
22   BLPES, Wilfred Vernon papers, Phillips to Vernon, 19 April 1948.
23   Ibid., Austin, Braddock, Platts Mills and Zilliacus to "Dear Colleague," 18 April 1948; ibid., J. Silverman, Lever, Bing, Swingler, H. Davies, Mack, Platts Mills and Orbach to Phillips, 20 April 1948.
24   Labour Party, NEC minutes, vol. 95, pp. 256–7, 13 April 1948.
25   University College, Swansea, S. O. Davies papers, Davies to Phillips, 22 April 1948.
26   *New Statesman*, 24 April 1948.
27   Kenneth O. Morgan, *Labour in Power, 1945–51* (Oxford, 1984), p. 66; Henry Pelling, *The Labour Governments, 1945–51* (London, 1984), p. 220.
28   Labour Party, NEC minutes, 28 April 1948.
29   S. O. Davies papers, Phillips to Davies, 27 April 1948.
30   Ibid., Zilliacus to Davies, 29 April 1948.
31   S. O. Davies papers, Zilliacus to Davies, 3 May 1948; Vernon papers, Vernon to Phillips, 2 May 1948; Labour Party, Morgan Phillips papers, "Lost Sheep" file, Solley to Phillips, 5 May 1948; *The Times*, 6 May 1948; Davies papers, Davies to Phillips, 5 May 1948.
32   Phillip Williams (ed.), *The Diary of Hugh Gaitskell, 1945–56* (London, 1983), p. 65; *Reynolds News*, 5 May 1946; Vernon entitled his description of the meeting "Nenni Telegram and European Union."
33   *Reynolds News*, 5 May 1946.
34   Information on Platts Mills and on his relationship with Morrison from the unpublished autobiography, pp. 4–5, and from private information.
35   There is no biography of Zilliacus, although he deserves one. His background and early

career may be gleaned from the vast quantity of his own writings, including *Why I Was Expelled* (London, 1949).

36   Ibid., p. 9.
37   Labour Party, 1945 general election file, Zilliacus election address.
38   BBC Written Archives, Broadcasting House, "Britain's Relations with Russia," 20 May 1947.
39   *Daily Worker*, 30 March 1946; *Gateshead Herald*, May 1946.
40   *Reynolds News*, 5 August 1945, 26 August 1945.
41   *New Statesman*, 20 October 1945; *Gateshead Herald*, March 1946, May 1946.
42   BBC Written Archives, Reading, "Foreign Affairs," 1 September 1947.
43   Konni Zilliacus, *Britain, USSR and World Peace* (London, 1946), p. 27; BBC Written Archives, Broadcasting House, "Britain's Relations with Russia," 20 May 1947.
44   *New Statesman*, 30 January 1948.
45   Ibid., 10 May 1947.
46   Ibid., 6 December 1948.
47   Sussex University, Kingsley Martin papers, Zilliacus to Martin, 24 June 1948; ibid., Zilliacus to Martin, 4 November 1948.
48   For Zilliacus's running battle with Labour Party disciplinarians, see Morgan Phillips's "Lost Sheep" file. Phillips drew up a seventeen-page indictment of Zilliacus; see pp. 9–12 for the Warsaw Conference.
49   Zilliacus, *Why I Was Expelled*, p. 21; Phillips's "Lost Sheep" file, Dalton to Phillips, 1 November 1948; Zilliacus, *Why I Was Expelled*, p. 50; Leslie Hale diary entry, "Labour Party Conference" (n.d.).
50   *Reynolds News*, 22 May 1949; Shaw's tribute appeared first in the *New Statesman*, 16 November 1946; Hale diary, "Labour Party Conference" (n.d.); *Sunday Pictorial*, 22 May 1949.
51   Hale diary, "Labour Party Conference" (n.d.).
52   Ibid.
53   Platts Mills, unpublished autobiography, p. 9.
54   *Glasgow Forward*, 20 August 1949.
55   Martin papers, Zilliacus to Martin, 14 July 1948.
56   *Glasgow Forward*, 3 June 1950; Platts Mills, letter to the author, September 1983.
57   *Glasgow Forward*, 3 June 1950.
58   BBC, Written Archives, Reading, "As I See It," 1 October 1951.
59   BBC, Written Archives, Reading, "London Forum," 8 December 1952.
60   Mark Jenkins, *Bevanism: Labour's High Tide* (London, 1979), p. 92.
61   *Socialist Outlook*, July 1949.
62   Ibid., January 1950, December 1949.
63   Ibid., December 1949.
64   Ibid., October 1950, April 1950, October 1950.
65   For origins of VfS, see Joyce Bellamy and John Saville (eds.), *Dictionary of Labour Biography* (University of Hull), Vol. II, p. 262; Labour Party, file on "Pacifist Organizations," VfS, "A Call to Socialists," August 1945.
66   Labour Party, file on "Pacifist Organizations," W. C. Elliott to Bob Mellish, 31 January 1951; ibid., VfS circular inviting Labour Members to 3 March 1951 demonstration.
67   *Glasgow Forward*, 17 February 1951.
68   *Glasgow Forward*, 10 March 1951; ibid., 13 January 1951.

6

The Labour Left and the Trade Unions

TRADE UNIONS FORM the basis of the Labour Party. They were the rock on which it was founded in 1900. Their loyalty saved it in 1931 during the crisis provoked by the infamous MacDonaldite "betrayal," as many termed it. During 1945–51 the majority of trade unions gave the Attlee governments massive, unswerving and crucial backing.

The trade-union movement, however, never has been monolithic in political outlook or anything else. Although for the most part its members sustained the Attlee governments with overwhelming loyalty, a left wing within the TUC offered a much more critical assessment. The activities and outlook of the non-communist element within the trade-union Left will be examined in this chapter.

The trade-union Left was composed mainly of left Labourites (including members of the ILP) and communists. In the immediate aftermath of World War II, the latter overshadowed the former. Communists numbered among the leaders of several unions including the Miners, Electricians, Firemen and Builders. At the local level and on the shop-floor communists were represented disproportionately among the lower echelon of trade-union officials and rank-and-file militants. Part and parcel of the organized labor movement, they lobbied openly for "unity on the Left," including their entry as an organized group into the Labour Party. Here is an indication of their strength and credibility; when the "Progressive Unity" plank was defeated at Labour's annual conference in 1945, at least 1,030,000 of the 1,314,000 votes it received came from trade unions. The Miners, Engineers, Railwaymen, Foundry Workers, Firemen, Distributive and Allied Workers and Building Trade Workers all supported the motion. The Left in the unions was thus qualitatively different from the Left inside the Labour Party. The latter, by definition, excluded members of the Communist Party; the former was partially defined by them.[1]

Communist predominance within the trade-union Left makes it difficult to trace and analyze the activities and ideology of left-wing Labourites during the early postwar era. Nevertheless there existed among trade unionists an identifiable non-communist left-wing tendency which was particularly strong inside the NUR, AEU, USDAW and Chemical Workers' Union, but which was not limited to them. This tendency proved capable, at times, of influencing labour movement policy. Even when the trade-union Labour Left was less than influential, it often was imaginative and resourceful. However, the Left in the TUC, like the Left everywhere else during 1945–51, cannot be understood outside the context of developing cold war. The main thrust of the age was the steady diminution of left-wing strength and self-confidence. It was not only the communists who suffered from anti-communism. The cold war devastated the entire trade-union Left. It is against that backdrop, which is developed in the next section of this chapter, that one must approach the role and evolution of the Labour Left in the trade unions during 1945–51.

II

In the immediate postwar era, Labour Left and communist trade unionists often could look back upon years of combined effort. They had cooperated in prewar industrial struggles and in the agitations for a popular front and against unemployment. During the war they had worked together to defeat Hitler. The anti-communist purges posed a cruel dilemma to Labour Left trade unionists, forcing them to choose between their party, in which all hopes for a better future were invested, or their communist allies, whose claims to their comradeship and solidarity had been forged over years of common struggle.

　　While the alliance between the two left-wing components of the trade-union movement held, it proved a potent combination, indeed a key to the power of the Left which marked the first few years of peace. It was demonstrated at the TUC in 1946, which demanded that the government alter its policy in Greece and turned back a motion condemning Bevin's foreign policy as a whole by only 3,951,000 to 2,984,000. It was manifested in individual unions as well. The Amalgamated Engineers, for example, strongly favored communist affiliation to the Labour Party. They regularly adopted left-wing resolutions at their early postwar annual conferences. In 1946 they carried a typical resolution by 30 votes to 22:

> This National Committee views with alarm and apprehension the foreign policy of the Labour Government in relation to the British Armed Forces in Greece and Indonesia [and] . . . the maintenance of diplomatic and trading relationships with the Fascist dictatorships of Spain and Portugal. It therefore calls upon the Government to formulate its foreign policy more in keeping with the aims and aspirations of the Labour Movement.

But communist influence was not predominant in the AEU. The same annual conference which supported "progressive unity" and the critical resolution on foreign policy declined, by 27 votes to 25, to purchase shares in the communist People's Press Printing Society. When the popular front of communists and Labour leftists broke down, then, the Left failed to carry the union.[2]

　　Or consider the Distributive and Allied Workers. They consistently took left-wing positions during the early postwar years. They demanded at their annual conference in

1946 that Bevin break off diplomatic and economic relations with fascist Spain, that conscription be abolished, that the USA give up monopoly control of atomic energy, that the Anglo-Russian friendship pact be broadened and extended. They passed a motion condemning the general thrust of Labour's foreign policy by 391 votes to 3, despite the warning of Evelyn Walkden, an MP for Doncaster sponsored by the union, that the resolution possessed "a Communist sting in the tail." Yet on card votes NUDAW, as it still was, opposed communist affiliation to the Labour Party by 144,798 to 31,700, and declined to purchase stock in the People's Press by 111,435 to 50,575. The union's left-wing position on most issues manifestly was due not to communist domination, but to cooperation among NUDAW leftists regardless of their political affiliation.[3]

This combination represented a potential danger to a Labour government whose policies after 1947 often disappointed its own left wing and whose existence in the last analysis depended upon trade-union support. We have seen how the government isolated and intimidated its left-wing critics in the PLP. The Left in the TUC posed a somewhat more difficult problem since it contained communists as well as Left Labourites. In the end, however, similar methods produced similar results. Choosing its targets with care, the government employed anti-communist purges to split the left-wing popular front and discredit its trade-unionist critics.

The target of the first purge was the Civil Service Clerical Association, hardly a bastion of the trade-union movement. Possibly this was one reason for focusing on it first. On 15 March 1948, Attlee announced in the House of Commons that civil servants who were known to be members of the Communist Party would not be allowed to engage in work which was vital to state security. Ideally they would be transferred to less sensitive posts. If suitable Civil Service work could not be found for them, however, they would be sacked. Possibly Attlee had been waiting a full year to deliver this speech. The previous spring, six communist civil servants had lost their jobs after an investigation by MI5. Now, perhaps, the communist victory in Prague, whose groundwork had been laid according to some by Czechoslovakian communist civil servants, provided him with an opportunity to declare policy. Even so, the Prime Minister's statement raised an immediate storm of protest among civil libertarians of all parties. It also split the Civil Service Clerical Association wide open.

Over the course of 1945–51 each British trade union confronted anti-communism in its own way. It is useful to examine the CSCA response to this first "red purge," however, because it presaged and encapsulated in one union and during a relatively brief period the general trade-union reaction to attempts by the government and TUC General Council to curb communist influence, and because in general terms the final impact of the purge on the Left in the union was typical. All sides were represented in the CSCA. Its president, William Hicks, was a communist, and its general secretary, L. C. White, was a member of the *Daily Worker* editorial board, though possibly not a formal member of the Communist Party. A non-denominational Left dominated the CSCA executive. On the other hand, the CSCA contained numerous, indeed as it transpired nearly a majority of, Labour Party loyalists willing to sanction an anti-communist purge. Finally, the CSCA's parliamentary spokesman, W. J. Brown, the

Member for Rugby, was a former independent socialist who had become a crusading anti-communist. He was also extremely clever.

Even before Attlee's speech there had been rumblings of discontent in the CSCA over what was perceived, correctly, as a pending purge of its communist members from the Civil Service. At the union's annual conference in 1947, a motion condemning political discrimination among civil servants passed unanimously. This seems remarkable given the divisions which wracked the CSCA only one year later, grim testimony to the divisive power of the cold war. There also existed strong opposition to Brown's attitude. On 4 March 1948 he asked in the House of Commons, "How many members of the Communist Party are there serving in the headquarters of the Air Ministry today? . . . I know at least one Communist who is serving there because he is the head of my union." This provoked Stanley Mayne, chairman of the CSCA's W. J. Brown Parliamentary Fund, to resign his position and, in a public letter to Brown, to term political discrimination in the Civil Service a "shocking proposal . . . one that would once have been as much anathema to you as it still is to me."[4]

In 1948, however, with the Prague coup and other cold-war developments fresh in the mind of CSCA members, Brown's outlook found supporters. A Conference Campaign Committee was organized to "bring together members of the Association who were determined that this Union should not be a tool in the hands of Communists." According to one of its members this committee, in its single year of existence, gained the support of 125 branches of the CSCA. During July 1948 the union's annual conference was held. "If you will look at the agenda," a Conference Campaign Committee member boasted, "you will find that there are 182 resolutions in our favour, resolutions on matters that we have brought forward, as against 60 against."[5]

So much had the unanimous opposition to a "red purge" been eroded that CSCA members now divided almost evenly over it and over Brown's enthusiasm for it. A resolution recording conference's "belief in the fundamental right of all Civil Servants to enjoy full democratic liberty and freedom of expression and opinion" and renewing the association's membership in the National Council for Civil Liberties (which had taken an active role in defending the right of communists to free speech) was endorsed on a card vote by the narrow margin of 2,776 to 2,626. A slightly larger majority disapproved of Brown's activities. A motion put forward by members of the Conference Campaign Committee, recommending that the union retain Brown's parliamentary services so long as he kept his seat in the House, was defeated by 2,990 votes to 2,486.

Bravely CSCA members attempted to grapple with the difficult questions posed by the cold war. Debate over Brown's conduct, the purge and the rights of unpopular minorities was searching. Brown, in particular, presented the case for a purge with verve and sophistication. He thought there were three accepted premises of democracy: that the will of the people, expressed in secret ballot, should prevail in choosing a government; that the defeated party in an election should enjoy full rights of opposition; and that there should be freedom of speech and press to criticize the government of the day. "It is only when these premises are rejected that any case for political discrimination arises, and they are explicitly rejected by the Communist Party and its fellow travellers," Brown asserted cleverly. This was more convincing than the crude formulation suggested by Mr Charles, a founder of the Conference Campaign Committee. "I do not regard the purge of Communists as being political discrimination," Charles declared. And by way of explanation: "You just cannot trust the Communists."

By the narrowest of margins Brown's opponents carried the day. Their victory depended upon a common front of civil libertarians, communists and the Labour Left. Each had its spokesman. CSCA General Secretary L. C. White denied that membership in the Communist Party could be taken to suggest unreliability or lack of patriotism, or even divided loyalties. "I want to ask Conference whether there is any evidence at all of the betrayal or indeed of the indiscretions on the part of Civil Service Communists in relation to official secrets that come their way." An Admiralty delegate took the classic liberal line. Declaring that he loved "liberty more than anything else in life, for without liberty life is not worth living," he exhorted conference, "not only to defend our liberty, but the liberty of our political opponents." And a Mr Weddel provided what may be considered the model Labour Left response to the purgers: "I do not think that the right way to deal with Communists is to discriminate against them, but to strengthen the internal ties of the Labour Party and show by words and deeds that the British conception of Socialism is best left in the hands of the Labour Party and not in the hands of the Communists."

This popular front of CSCA left-wingers apparently was victorious. After listening to its arguments, a narrow majority condemned the purge and Brown's behavior, and forced Brown to resign his position as CSCA parliamentary general secretary. In fact, however, the Left in the union had been seriously weakened by the struggle. In the annual elections for the union Executive Council the working alliance between communists and Left Labourites must have broken down, for Brown's allies won a majority of seats. Brown crowed, "The Communist-controlled, fellow-traveller domination has been destroyed." The following year the new executive voted him a generous retirement settlement.[6]

These events underscored the fragility of the left-wing popular front in the trade unions. In the CSCA it rallied a bare majority against the purge. It is striking, however, that no non-communist disputed Attlee's main justification for the removal of suspect civil servants from sensitive posts, that communists inevitably were subject to a dual loyalty and, therefore, were poor security risks. Once bow even fractionally to that argument, however, and continued collaboration between communists (potential traitors) and non-communist leftists was problematic. Accept it, and the need for purging communists not merely from the Civil Service, but from sensitive posts in every field, seems apparent.

Thus the purge posed problems only marginally less difficult for Labour leftists than for communists. Communist and Labour Left collaboration was a precondition of left-wing strength in the CSCA, as in other unions. If communists were driven beyond the pale, the trade-union Left as a whole would suffer. By 1948, however, communists were problematical allies. Communist practices abroad and British communist support for them were profoundly worrisome to the Labour Left. Was it fair to blame local communists for the activities of Russians or other East Europeans? The Labour Left did not address this question. It argued instead that purges were an infringement of civil liberties and an ineffective method of defeating Labour's opponents. At the time this may have been the only politically viable line to take. It did little, however, to sustain the popular front with communists upon which all success depended. Over the long run, the Labour Left response to the purges contributed to the defeat of the trade-union Left as a whole.

The Civil Service purge presented in microcosm the issues and problems which nearly all trade unionists had to face within a year. In November 1948 the TUC General Council released a document charging communists with attempting to sabotage the Marshall Plan and economic recovery in general on orders from Moscow. It urged all affiliated societies to take "energetic steps to . . . stop these evil machinations." An obvious measure, and one adopted by several unions, was to prohibit communists from occupying official union posts. Of course there was opposition to this. The arguments deployed by CSCA members in 1948 echoed in trade-union halls throughout Britain during 1949. By then, however, the cold war was even more intense. The communist triumph in Czechoslovakia had not faded from memory, but there was now the Berlin crisis to consider. Non-communist left-wing trade unionists were caught in a whipsaw between a crusading, triumphant Right and a communist Left now not merely profoundly unpopular, but more than ever difficult to defend. As a result, the alliance between communist and Labour Left trade unionists shattered irretrievably, and left-wing strength in the trade-union movement was broken.[7]

Consider again both the Amalgamated Engineers and the Union of Shop, Distributive and Allied Workers (as, with the addition of the Butchers' Federation, NUDAW became in 1946), in which the left-wing popular front had been strong. Like the CSCA, both successfully resisted purges within their own ranks. Nevertheless neither union saved the popular front. By 1949 USDAW General Secretary Walter Padley was attempting to convince his members that only communists and their dupes opposed the government wage freeze. Unsuccessful in this, he did manage to persuade the union to "welcome the TUC General Council's statements" on the communist threat. In the AEU, the former Left majority had been transformed into a minority unable by a four-vote margin (24 to 28) even to pass a resolution condemning the Civil Service purge or attempts by public and private employers to extend it. Jack Tanner, the charismatic AEU president, had gone from being perhaps the most effective non-communist advocate of "progressive unity" to arguing that because communists opposed Marshall Aid they must "look forward to, and work for, the breaking down of the nation's economy, the weakening of the Labour Movement and the Government." This was not an untypical evolution.[8]

Although it survived in a few mining areas, the popular front among the trade-union Left was gone, and with it much left-wing strength and influence. In 1951 Bob Edwards of the Chemical Workers' Union proposed that the TUC endorse a resolution which, while placing "on record its appreciation of the efforts of the Labour

Government in seeking to make possible a cease fire in Korea," nevertheless urged additional consultations and negotiations to bring the conflict to an end. The resolution went on to "register its concern" over intensified competition in rearmament, predicting that many evil consequences would flow from it. Supporters of this innocuous resolution did everything in their power to make clear their disapproval of communists. Harold Smith of the Association of Engineering and Shipbuilding Draughtsmen, seconding the motion, prefaced his remarks with the following disclaimer: "First of all I want to assure all the members of this Congress that I have never been tagged with the title Communist or fellow traveller." The delegate for the London Society of Compositors agreed with opponents of the motion that "sincere advocates of peace are being used as stooges for the aggressive intentions of the USSR," but insisted that he was not a communist dupe although he supported the resolution. A member of the Amalgamated Union of Foundry Workers likewise issued a disclaimer before speaking: "I am not on this rostrum with political allegiance to the Kremlin; I am no stooge of the Kremlin. I stand here with a convinced desire for peace." And the delegate for the National Union of Vehicle Builders made sure to identify himself during his remarks on behalf of the resolution as "a member of the Labour Party, a Labour County Councillor . . . I cannot be associated with the Communist Party."[9]

It would have been hard to underline further the distance which now separated communist and Labour Left trade unionists. Yet "I know you come here as Pollitt's puppets," Arthur Deakin charged in his speech opposing Edwards's resolution. Deakin ran the Transport and General Workers' Union as though it was his personal fiefdom and along lines that were most agreeable to his mentor and former patron, the original general secretary of the "T and G," Ernest Bevin. In this manner the resolution was defeated overwhelmingly. So was every other Left-sponsored motion at the 1951 TUC. "It is perfectly clear what is the origin from which this resolution springs," Deakin asserted when confronted with a proposal for "equal exchange of products among nations, East, West and Commonwealth." In a sense, the Labour Left were victimized almost as much by the purges as were the communists. In their aftermath, all left-wing activity could be tarred with the anti-communist brush.[10]

The anti-communist purges and the cruel dilemma they posed to the Labour Left in the trade unions form the essential backdrop to this chapter. Labour Left credibility and influence in the trade unions were increasingly circumscribed during those years. In spite of this, however, the non-communist trade-union Left remained active, creative and surprisingly ambitious. It is time now to examine the causes it adopted and the agitations it mounted on their behalf, during this crucial period in trade-union and Labour Party history.

III

The campaign for a third force mounted by the parliamentary Labour Left had its counterpart among trade unionists, whose journals and conference reports are studded with criticisms of the Labour government's pro-American policies. As in Parliament, so in the trade-union world third force advocates divided along "hard" and "soft" lines as the cold war grew increasingly intense. We can trace this dividing process by focusing upon Walter Padley of USDAW and Bob Edwards of the Chemical Workers, two prominent trade-union leaders both of whom, interestingly enough, had long-standing connections with the ILP.

Padley's career was an unbroken ascent. A Ruskin College graduate, he joined NUDAW in 1933, rising through the ranks to become its president fifteen years later. He joined the ILP as a rank-and-file member and rose to serve upon its National Administrative Council from 1940 to 1946. He was elected to Parliament in 1950 and kept his seat for twenty-nine years, serving on the NEC from 1956 until 1979. Harold Wilson appointed him Minister of State for Foreign Affairs in 1964. During the postwar period Padley was a prominent, albeit increasingly "soft," advocate of the third force.

Padley's conception of the third force evolved in typical fashion. In October 1945 he penned a "study guide" for the Co-op movement, *Problems of the Peace*, in which he argued explicitly for a United Socialist States of Europe along ILP lines. Soviet support for the project was assumed. A year later, however, his attitude towards the Soviets had changed. A USSE would offer an alternative not merely to capitalism but to communism as well. As he instructed his union's annual conference, "we must neither ally ourselves with the economic anarchy of the United States [nor] the single party dictatorship of the USSR. We can pursue the alternative way of democratic socialism." By 1947 he had further modified his original position. He still believed that global polarization represented the "catechism of doom." In his jumbled, didactic but knowledgable small book, *Britain: Pawn or Power?*, he wrote, "If British Labour boldly proclaims its belief in economic planning without political tyranny, in political democracy without economic anarchy, and acts accordingly, it will find countless allies among the common people of every land." Yet now he believed that Labour could only build a Western union of states in which democratic socialism already was established strongly. The "monstrous inhumanities" of which communists had shown themselves to be capable meant that Russia's "satellite states" could not participate in a third force.[11]

At USDAW's annual conference in 1948 Padley gave striking evidence of his transformed world view. He supported a foreign policy resolution offered by the branch from Chipping Norton which, while claiming to demand a third force, really backed the government. In Padley's opinion, and as the resolution stated, Attlee and Bevin "by encouraging the democratic states of Europe to form a Socialist Union" were "giving a lead to the world." This was the "soft" Left version of the third force as a bulwark against communism. It was far from being the USSE which the ILP continued gamely to advocate and originally Padley had endorsed. The former ILP-er found his Labour Party allies not among former colleagues like Brockway and Warbey, but rather among those relative moderates who looked to Foot and Crossman.[12]

By the end of 1948 Padley could hardly be termed a left-wing critic of the government's foreign policy. Yet even his "soft" Left outlook was tarred with the anti-communist brush. At the TUC in 1950 Padley moved a resolution which rather timidly requested the government to reopen discussions with other nuclear powers on the banning of atomic weapons. Although the resolution paid tribute to previous British efforts in this regard and blamed only the Russians for the present impasse, assembled delegates defeated it decisively for being communist inspired.[13]

Padley did much better in his own union, USDAW, which remained highly critical of many government policies. Indeed, rank-and-file delegates to union meetings and conferences, and members who wrote to the letters column of *New Dawn*, appear to have been more militant than their president. "Remember your Socialist principles before you got power, and your stand against war, especially you Mr Morrison," one typical *New Dawn* correspondent warned members of the government on 13 November 1948. Perhaps this helps to explain why Padley, and USDAW as a whole, supported the rebel ministers who resigned in 1951. Yet the third force movement as such made little headway in USDAW once its president ceased to speak for it. After 1948 no third force resolutions were even brought up for the union's annual conference to consider.

The counterpoint to Padley's career and evolving view of the third force is provided by Bob Edwards. Like the president of USDAW, the future leader of the Chemical Workers' Union joined the ILP early on. His commitment to it and its ideals, however, seems deeper than Padley's. He chaired two ILP delegations to Russia, risked his life as leader of its volunteer force in Spain during the civil war and stood for Parliament on its behalf in 1935, 1939 and 1945, long after it was clear that such candidacies held no hope of success. In 1943 he became national chairman of the party, a post he kept until 1948. Perhaps most significant in his continuing advocacy of the third force, he was the founder president of the British contingent of the USSE campaign.

Edwards advocated the third force at every opportunity, sounding like a combination of Zilliacus and Laski, if that were possible. As he told the ILP in 1946:

> the foundations of a Socialist economy for Europe have been firmly laid. The leaders of monopoly capitalism, with very few exceptions, cooperated with Hitler's New Order and are hopelessly discredited... [In addition] the atomic bomb...has made meaningless all frontiers and made obsolete the sovereign state. Consequently Europe must be Socialist.

Yet Edwards, like Padley and nearly the entire Labour Left, eventually concluded that socialist Europe would have to be built without Russian assistance. His ILP pamphlet of 1948, *Socialist Policy for Today*, ridiculed the view that "this nation's future must be tied up with one or the other of the dominant powers."[14]

In Edwards's case, however, suspicion of the Soviets did not lead to support for Western union. For the president of Britain's USSE campaign, the third force must embrace the entire European continent or it would be meaningless. He opposed the formation of a Western bloc even under socialist auspices long after Padley, Crossman, Foot and the others had endorsed it. In September 1948 he wrote in the *Chemical Worker*, "the Trade Union Movement must not allow itself to be manoeuvred for political purposes into a policy of hostility either to the United States or Soviet Russia."

This was the message he continued to reiterate even at the height of the cold war. In April 1949 he wrote a pamphlet, *War Is Not Inevitable*, in which fundamentalist third force arguments were presented with the pristine clarity and optimism of 1945. "This great continent could give leadership to the world by its Socialist example," Edwards wrote. It "could serve as a base for the great neutral Third Force which is necessary to serve as a bridge for peace between Russia in the East and America in the West." Although Edwards believed that Britain could not afford to reject Marshall Aid, he concluded not that the third force was outdated, but that it was more necessary than ever if Britain was to achieve economic independence from the United States. This was his argument in pamphlets and articles and at the TUC in 1950, when he spoke for a third force resolution which was not merely defeated but crushed by Deakin and other right-wing loyalists.

It is impossible to tell how Edwards's members reacted to his campaign, though there is no evidence that they opposed it. Yet Edwards and his supporters failed to create a mass movement for the third force. There are occasional references to USSE meetings which he addressed. They had little impact. For every non-communist left-wing trade-union leader who persisted in advocating the USSE, or something like it, there were five Walter Padleys. In any event Edwards was a relatively small fish in the labor movement, especially when compared with Bevin, who though now Britain's Foreign Secretary could "talk like a Dutch uncle" to trade unionists. With his long-standing ties to labor, the founder of the "T and G" was even more effective in dismissing and discrediting his critics in the unions than in the PLP—whose left-wing Members thought him quite effective enough already. Perhaps, too, trade-union members took pride in the elevation of one of their own to head the Foreign Office, while doubting the credentials of other workers, even their own union officers, who questioned his policies.

In any event, trade unionists could not claim a "natural" expertise in foreign affairs. When the Labour Left in the trade unions really did provide the spearhead of dissent from government policies it was over an issue closer to home and, perhaps, to the hearts of British workers.

IV

During the postwar period trade unionists were deeply concerned with "workers' control," although often it has been assumed that agitation on behalf of this concept underwent a forty-year hiatus with the defeat of the guild socialists in the mid-1920s. In fact, the demand for increased workplace democracy was broadened during 1945–51 to become also a criticism of the government's nationalization program, since the Labour Left often complained that relations between workers and management in the nationalized industries were as problematic as ever. Moreover, criticism of the government's approach to nationalization was connected to Labour Left criticism of the failure to control the economy more completely. In tracing and analyzing the postwar agitation for industrial democracy, then, it is possible to gain insight into the general critique which the trade-union Labour Left developed of the government's economic program as a whole.[15]

Before 1914 syndicalists had argued that trade unions should control industry. In the aftermath of World War I guild socialists had made workers' control the central premise of their philosophy. The concept won many adherents among miners, engineers, builders and Post Office workers. It intruded, even, into Labour Party programs during the 1920s and early 1930s. During that period, Labourites maintained that nationalization would lead to workers' control. When a Labour government took an industry into public ownership, they argued, its management would become the responsibility of its workers, and its general policy would be decided by boards representing laborers, consumers and the community.

By about 1935, however, the Labour Party had changed its official approach to nationalization. Herbert Morrison played a crucial role in this process, arguing that industrial democracy was utopian because there could be no guarantee that workers in a given industry possessed the necessary expertise to run it. Thus the demand for industrial democracy was divorced from official Labour thinking about nationalization. Under Morrison's guidance "public corporations" modelled on the BBC, for example, superseded "public ownership" in Labour Party documents. Labour now envisioned nationalized industries placed under the direction of boards of governors appointed by a Cabinet minister. The boards would report to the minister, but otherwise could run the industry as they wished. Labour might be represented on the board by trade-union officials. The minister, however, would not be obliged to appoint any. This approach to nationalization also commended itself to a majority of the TUC General Council, which believed that trade-union representatives on the governing boards of nationalized industries would face a conflict of interest during wage negotiations. These members opposed anything that might interfere with free collective bargaining.

The original concept of workers' control, however, remained the *sine qua non* of socialism for many Labourites. The euphoria with which most trade unionists greeted the results of the general election in 1945 was tempered, on the Labour Left, by suspicion of the official approach to nationalization. As *Post*, journal of the Post Office Workers' Union, put it on 15 September 1945:

> We are frankly alarmed at [TUC] worship of the managerial and administrative class, and the lack of faith in the capacity of our fellow workers . . . Unless we achieve industrial as well as political power, we shall find that we have merely changed our masters.

It is not surprising to find Post Office workers voicing such reservations. As one of their delegates to the TUC put it in 1947, "We can speak from the experience of a century of nationalization . . . [In the Post Office] all the abuses of private enterprise are centralized, and those in control can perpetuate them on a unified scale." Arguments stressing the inadequacy of simple nationalization were not limited, however, to Post Office workers. Here is one of many warnings that might be cited, this from an unnamed contributor to the NUR newspaper, the *Railway Review*, of 7 December 1945, who thought that the form of nationalization favored by the new government "must on no account be confused with Socialisation . . . [it] is only a necessary step towards that better way of life."[16]

Over the course of 1945–51 the argument for democratic control of the workplace differed from union to union according to political conditions within them and the structure of the industry concerned. Within industries not scheduled for early nationalization, advocates of workers' control aimed to strengthen the joint committees of workers, managers and employers established during the war. The powers of these committees, and their effectiveness and popularity, varied widely. They seemed, however, a likely basis for increasing labor's participation in deciding industry policies. This possibility, it will be recalled, had occurred to Ian Mikardo of "Keep Left" as well. Mikardo had proposed a draft Bill making joint committees compulsory and widening their powers. Trade unionists made many similar proposals in their journals and at their annual conferences throughout the period.[17]

Consider USDAW, for example. It was conceptually difficult to conceive of industrial democracy among shop and distributive workers along the same lines as, say, among railwaymen, for whom the old belief in "public ownership" suggested a likely model of democratic control. It was easy, however, to think in terms of strengthening the joint committees and the union's role on the shop-floor. As early as 12 January 1946 Harry Binstock, of the London Optical Branch, was demanding that trade unions have access to the accounts of firms whose workers they represented, and control over firing procedures. "If the time is ripe for large scale schemes of nationalisation it is ripe for these things also."[18]

The sentiment which animated Binstock reappears time and again in *New Dawn* and at USDAW meetings. Usually it was couched in vague or sentimental language. No USDAW member ever indicated precisely how the strengthened joint committees would operate, or posed an alternative model of shop-floor democracy. Most common was the simple reiteration of belief in the concept, the demand that the union's "Executive Council advance on all occasions the principle of industrial democracy, i.e. workers' control at all levels from the workshop upwards," as one branch resolution put it in 1947. USDAW's most detailed resolution on the subject also proposed in 1947, by the 211 Portsmouth Branch, suggested that the government and the TUC draw up a plan "for the selection and training of workers in the administrative and managerial functions of industry." This was a good beginning, although it seems to represent a tacit admission that the union itself was unable to develop such a scheme. In any event, however, no concrete suggestions followed.[19]

USDAW's failure to develop a carefully conceived plan for democratizing distribution probably was due, in part, to the structure of the industry itself. The union represented myriads of different kinds of laborers in the transportation and distributive trades as well as shopworkers of all descriptions. No plans yet existed for nationalizing so far-flung an industry, and during Labour's tenure in office even the fertile Walter Padley could not produce one. By contrast, in industries where much previous thought had been given to nationalization, detailed plans for workers' control were often abundant.

Within the NUR, for example, advocates of workers' control were numerous and determined not to be caught unprepared when their industry was taken into public ownership. Nationalization of the railways had been part of Labour's program since 1918. The original Amalgamated Society of Railway Servants had advocated it as early as 1894. Almost immediately after the election of the Labour government in 1945 "Historian," a regular columnist for the NUR weekly newspaper, advised railwaymen "without delay [to] take counsel among themselves as how best to ensure that the change from private ownership to public ownership will be at the same time at least the beginning of a real and substantial change for them." This good advice was not ignored. The pages of the *Railway Review* became a forum in which proposals for workers' control were sifted and debated. It is hard to find an issue of the journal in which the subject does not appear. Workers' control was discussed, also, at NUR branch meetings and at the union's annual conferences. Railwaymen cannot be accused of having neglected this issue.[20]

Advocates of workers' control on the railways agreed that nationalization as conceived by the government would not lead to industrial democracy. Some railwaymen accepted that nationalized industries would be directed by boards of governors, as the Labour Party proposed. However, labor's representatives on these boards should be nominated by the workers "through their trade unions," and their obligation would be "to democratise the industry from top to bottom," as James Seaman put it in the *Railway Review* for 31 May 1946. Other railwaymen disagreed. As an anonymous contributor to the debate put it, "Workers' control does not and should not mean placing a trade-union official upon a Board." For this correspondent, and for "Historian," who contributed countless articles on the subject, the first place to implement workers' control was "at the bottom . . . in the local units, the depots, yards and stations . . . The men who take orders should have an effective voice in deciding the appointments of those immediately above them."[21]

Dissatisfaction with the government's approach was nearly universal, but agreement was difficult to reach on practically anything else. F. V. Pickstock advocated emulating Soviet methods for democratizing the workplace. "If Russia is politically authoritarian it has gone further than we have towards industrial democracy, and we should not be too proud to learn from her." Another working railwayman, T. E. Nixon, produced a pamphlet, *First Stages of Workers' Control on the Railways*, which eschewed the Soviet model. Nixon argued that industrial democracy depended upon the development of regional councils composed of workers and managers. "Transport services are largely localised, and efficiency demands that men in the locality shall have some measure of control and say in order that the service can be most efficiently run." W. J. Jones, a fireman from Shrewsbury, had anticipated Nixon's suggestion at the union's annual conference in 1946. "The whole of the country should be divided into a thousand geographical areas . . . there shall be a hundred divisional areas which cover ten local geographical areas and . . . the workers' representatives on the regional boards shall be drawn from ten divisional areas." This mechanical formulation gained few converts. By contrast, "James Jary," the *nom de plume* of a manager at King's Cross in London, developed a scheme which proved popular. "Jary" produced a pamphlet, *Nationalisation of Railways: Workers' Control*, in which he argued that works councils rather than regional councils could become the basis of a vigorous shop-floor democracy. It was, he thought, "relatively simple" to introduce them into single factories or railway yards employing a few hundred workers. This drew an enthusiastic response from W. P. Dwyer, a railwayman at Paddington Station, who with "a number of other active NUR members" was inspired

> to devise ways and means of constituting all grades committees in the West London area. Old Oak Common [NUR] representatives have already drawn up a constitution for this purpose. And now Paddington railwaymen are hoping to follow their example. On 24th March a conference was held at the Labour Hall, Southall, called by the Paddington No. 3 Branch, with this object.[22]

After coal, the railways were second in line for nationalization. Railwaymen proved close observers of the government scheme for the mines. Many did not like what they saw. "You have a tendency on the part of even the Labour Government to install people in palatial buildings who have little or no knowledge of the mining industry, and little or no sympathy for it, with the result that there is more trouble in the mining industry at present than there was under private ownership," one delegate to the NUR annual conference observed in 1947. "We do not want, as is the case in the Mines Bill, to be divorced from the control of the industry," another railwayman had warned the previous year. W. Bannard, a driver from Woodford, prescribed an alternative:

> the establishment of national, local and area Boards of Management with representatives of His Majesty's Government and Transport Workers constituting the personnel. Merely having representatives to make suggestions . . . will not be good enough.

Bannard argued, "We want to take into our hands a large share in the actual administration of the railways." Conference unanimously endorsed the resolution embodying these demands.[23]

In the end, however, vigilance, warnings, even carefully worked out alternatives to the government plan, proved insufficient. The government tipped its hand in November 1946. "Until there has been more experience by the workers of the managerial side of industry," Stafford Cripps asserted, "I think it would be almost impossible to have worker controlled industry in Britain, even if it were on the whole desirable." In a speech which also created great ill will among trade unionists, Morrison supported Cripps. The government would appoint to the boards of nationalized industries "the best brains," regardless of politics or class background. Inevitably, therefore, the Transport Bill was based upon the familiar model of the public corporation.[24]

This may have satisfied the TUC General Council, but it dismayed many railwaymen. At the NUR annual conference in 1947, when the proposed Bill for nationalizing transport was considered, a signalman from Solihull voiced a common complaint. Transport Minister George Barnes "has said, without giving any reason, that he cannot agree to Trade Unions' direct representation" on the national, area and local boards due to govern the railways:

> I think we should plainly say to him in reply that... it is essential from the point of view of the workers coming into control that they have representation and relationships from the top to the bottom. That is the theory and, I believe, the spirit of nationalisation as the rank and file understand it.

By a vote of 47 to 16 the conference "regretted" the undemocratic aspect of the nationalization scheme and reiterated its belief that "the full benefits of a Nationalised Transport System will not be conveyed to the community without the cultivation of the knowledge, goodwill, and experience of the workers in the industry being sought, and the opportunity given for them to obtain a voice in the highest managerial offices." Nor was this an end to the union's reservations about the Bill. By 42 votes to 30 the NUR recorded its opposition to the "too generous terms" which the government offered former shareholders.[25]

The government, however, turned a deaf ear to these complaints, with the result that when nationalization occurred few railwaymen thought it an unalloyed blessing. "I think I am voicing the opinion of railwaymen in saying that the first five months have proved utterly disappointing," an NUR correspondent wrote. One immediate problem was that despite mounting inflation the government opposed wage hikes. "Since nationalisation has taken effect we have not seen a great deal of change," J. Martin, a relief signalman from Manningtree, complained at the annual conference in 1948. "I can see only one difference at the moment so far as negotiating machinery is concerned. Instead of the Minute reading 'That the company's side decline the application,' we get a Minute 'The employer's representatives [board of governors] decline the application.' "By a unanimous vote the conference reiterated its opposition to nationalization without "workers' participation in the control of the industry at all levels," and demanded

> that it be an indisputable right for wages grades to progress to all supervisory and administrative positions, and that the workers' representatives on the Local Departmental Committees, Sectional Councils, Works Committees and Departmental Line Committees shall have equal rights with the Management in determining all matters appertaining to the industry.

The resolution went on to demand that there be "increased representation at the higher levels from persons experienced both in transport and the organisation of workers, in order that a proper evaluation and consideration of the suggestions emanating from other levels can be assured."[26]

The experience of railwaymen was repeated in all the industries which Labour nationalized during 1945–51. Initial support for nationalization, tempered by suspicion of the corporate model, gave way to growing disillusionment and irritation. Complaints about the composition of the national boards, about the rate of compensation paid to former shareholders, about the bureaucracy created to run the industries under government ownership and about the undemocratic relationship which still divided managers from laborers were widespread. Labour's right wing was prompted by such criticisms and by conservative opposition to any form of public enterprise to question the value or necessity of further nationalization. This produced the well-known debate between Morrisonian "consolidators" and advocates of further socialist advance. The creativity with which the Labour Left in the trade unions no less than in the PLP developed the more militant line of thought has rarely been appreciated. They did not fall back upon traditional calls for workers' control. As we have seen, railway workers attempted actually to think through how industrial democracy would function for them. So did engineers, Post Office workers, miners and chemical workers.

The latter were, perhaps, most ambitious and creative. They were willing to concede not merely that nationalization had proved disappointing, but that workers' control had failed in the one country which had attempted to implement it. According to Bob Edwards, in one of a series of articles on industrial democracy which the Chemical Workers' Union later collected and printed as a pamphlet, the Soviet Union had sought to establish workers' control by following the old syndicalist model. This had posited that rank-and-file trade unionists elected by their fellow workers would take over and manage their own industries. The process had led, Edwards thought, to the development of "a bureaucracy of officials, commissars and executives, who have become even more remote than the previous owners and directors from the life, interests and problems of the industrial worker."[27]

Edwards was equally critical of domestic suggestions for how industrial democracy might function. He dismissed "worker control in the sense of an elected or Trade-Union appointed action committee to function as the Board of Management," because board members "who depend for their position on popular votes will be influenced more by popular opinion than by what is technically, financially and operationally essential in the short- and long-term interests of the industry." On the other hand, Edwards disapproved of "ex-leaders of the Unions, appointed at high salaries to the National Boards. It savours too closely of the corporate state."[28]

In searching for a structure that would not degenerate as it had done in Russia, and which would avoid the pitfalls he had discerned in other models of workers' control, Edwards fell back upon the political traditions of his own country. He thought "the system of control (but not the party politics) of our local government organisations" could provide a model for industrial democracy. Edwards told the TUC in 1950, "We want industrial parliaments based on the voluntary efforts that you have in local government, attached to our nationalised industries, where the workers, the consumers, the technicians and interested elements in our community can participate in these great economic investments." In the union journal he attempted to visualize how the new system would operate. There would have to be a government minister working with a small national council to oversee a nationalized industry, meeting in public and subject to democratic control which could be ensured by "a clear chain of responsibility from the top policy-making board of the Corporation, decentralised to the boards of control at each decentralised unit and down through departmental managers, shop foremen, supervisors, chargehands, to the operative workers." The system as a whole would be based upon "two inseparable principles ... centralisation of policy making and decentralisation of executive responsibility."[29]

Unlike the agitation for a third force in foreign affairs, the campaign for industrial democracy received substantial support from rank-and-file trade unionists. At the annual conferences of their organizations members carried resolutions demanding workers' control time and again. In 1947 the TUC unanimously passed a resolution calling for increased "Workers' Parti ipation in Control of Nationalised Industries." In 1949 with the cold war in full swing and left-wing initiatives under suspicion, the TUC defeated by only 3,566,000 to 2,761,000 a measure demanding that "from the bottom to the top ... the Union should have a fifty per cent share in administration and management." Eventually advocates of workers' control were marginalized. At the TUC in 1950 Edwards was accused of being a syndicalist, and his resolution demanding democratization of the workplace was defeated overwhelmingly. This chapter has attempted to demonstrate, however, that he and his allies had touched a responsive chord among working-class militants.[30]

The right wing of the TUC General Council strongly opposed the campaign for workers' control. Where the trade-union Left believed, as G. Douglas of the Post Office Workers told the TUC in 1948, "that the function of a trade union is the transformation of a capitalist society into a Socialist society," the General Council conceived of trade unionism in more modest terms. Trade unions existed to exert pressure on behalf of their members. The role of a trade unionist, even in an industry taken into public ownership, was to fight for better working conditions and higher pay. Nothing could be allowed to interfere with this, his essential function. On this basis the General Council opposed not merely the plans offered by advocates of workers' control for regional or works councils, but even statutory representation on the boards of nationalized industries.[31]

The government was, if anything, even more opposed to the concept of workers' control than the trade-union Right. The war had confirmed Labour's leaders in the belief that a controlled economy was more efficient and just than unfettered capitalism. But workers' control was not the kind of control they wished to impose. Cripps had objected to the concept not merely because he doubted the capacity of workers to manage their industries, but because industrial democracy would interfere with the national plans the government needed to set.

Nationalization proved among the least popular of Labour's innovations. Nationalized industries were held to be inefficient. They were bureaucratic. Labor relations within them were disappointing, especially given the high hopes which had been entertained at the start. To all this the champions of workers' control offered an alternative, but official Labour paid them little heed.

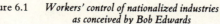

Figure 6.1   *Workers' control of nationalized industries*
                as conceived by Bob Edwards

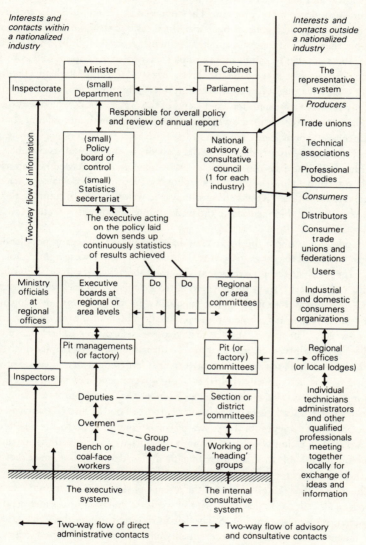

Source: Chemical Worker, September, 1949.

V

The political and industrial non-communist Lefts shared a common critique of the government and a common program. They opposed Bevinism for similar reasons and were equally insistent upon stronger socialist measures at home. Differences there were, but they were of tone and emphasis rather than content. Still, it is necessary to explore them in order to paint a more complete picture of the Labour Left as a whole.

The differences stemmed from social class. Many Members of Parliament were not rich, or even what might be called "comfortable." Moreover most trade-union MPs faithfully reflected the aspirations and views of the organizations which sent them to Parliament. Nevertheless, on the whole, there was often something academic about the parliamentary Labour Left's criticisms of the government's economic policies, and possibly this can be ascribed to the social class of the majority of its members. For example, during the disastrous winter of 1947 when Labour Left Members concluded that the government must be pushed into following "more drastic socialist policies" the natural response of the "Keep Left" group was to write a book. In contrast, there is a sense of urgency and immediacy to the trade-union Labour Left agitation for strong socialist measures.

Consider, for example, the slogan "fair shares for all" which became popular during the war. It seemed to express part of what the British people were fighting for, even though (or perhaps because) it represented almost a shortened version of the traditional socialist rallying cry "from each according to his ability, to each according to his needs." An obvious protest against inequality in all its forms, the slogan was appropriated by men and women from every walk of life. For the trade-union Labour Left, however, "fair shares" appears to have possessed a power and relevance which middle-class socialists could only imagine. To the latter it was a principle which simple justice required them to support; to the former it represented an immediate program which they were determined to help the Labour government implement. For example, early in 1946 the NUR London Branch (Number One) sent a protest resolution to union headquarters, asking that it be forwarded to the Food Minister. Branch members had noticed that it was possible for passengers on commuter trains to purchase food for cash rather than ration vouchers. The railway workers complained that in this way businessmen were able to obtain more than their "fair share" of food, since they could save their vouchers for other meals.[32]

The slogan "fair shares" captured the essence of the Labour Left outlook. It was implicit in all calls for higher taxes on the wealthy, limits on prices and profits and additional economic controls. Such demands rested upon the sense that the government's duty was to enforce equality of opportunity and of sacrifice. The industrial wing of the Labour Left was sharper than the political wing in articulating this sense. When the government called for increased production in order to bolster exports and cut back on dollar imports, Labour Left Members generally accepted the government's logic. Michael Foot, for example, exhorted the workers to "a terrific, unexampled burst of productive energy" so that Britons could avoid becoming the "bondslaves of Wall Street." The workers' response was all that he or the government could have wished. Yet trade unionists resented such demands. "It would be a pity if we had no working class," a correspondent of the *Railway Review* observed on 23 January 1948, "because there would then be no one to bear the nation's burdens, and no one to whom Governments could appeal for more work and less spending." "Certainly never in my lifetime has the working class been so much preached at," wrote another railwayman. Such trade unionists pointedly demanded a quid pro quo in return for their own extraordinary efforts. "We are told that our job now is to recapture the spirit which was displayed after Dunkirk; work harder and produce more so that we might expand our export trade especially to America," a tobacco worker wrote, adding that "if sacrifices [were] really necessary" he would make them —provided that "the increased profits which will obviously accrue from increased production will be shared by the workers whose efforts make them possible, or will be taken . . . to relieve the increased cost of living." Such declarations were typical of the trade-union Left. "If production is to be increased, is it merely to pay for an increase in the standard of living of the non-producers?" an engineer inquired rhetorically. He too was determined to receive a "fair share" of the fruits of his intensified labor.[33]

The concomitant to the government's call for increased production was its call for wage restraint. Here also the trade-union Labour Left response was more pointed than that of Labour Members. The latter demanded that the Government limit prices, profits and dividends as well as wages, but again they accepted the government's basic line. As Crossman argued in the *Sunday Pictorial* of 23 April 1950, wage restraint was preferable to "the 'free enterprise' of old fashioned collective bargaining," which would produce inflation. With a few notable exceptions, Labour Left trade unionists disagreed. Figgins of the Railwaymen, for example, argued at a special conference of trade-union executives that "Profits can rise considerably and dividends still be restrained while the residue goes into reserves and is still taken for the enrichment of the capitalist class." He was determined to make wage claims for his members unless the government limited profits in its war against inflation. So, it turned out, were a majority of trade-union leaders. It is striking that the only time the Left and Right in the trade unions cooperated, and the sole example of TUC opposition to the government on a major matter, came over the issue of wage restraint. It took two years of agitation by the trade-union Left, but finally, in 1950, TUC delegates voted

that until such time as there is a reasonable limitation of profits, a positive planning of our British economy, and prices are subject to such control as will maintain the purchasing power of wages at a level affording to every worker a reasonable standard of living, there can be no basis for restraint on wage applications.

Significantly, communists campaigned visibly for this resolution. On this issue only the old popular front was recreated. It was L. C. White, communist leader of the CSCA, who seconded the motion. He said, "There is still a slogan, 'Fair Shares For All,' and we suggest that the slogan should be made a reality."[34]

Perhaps no issue more clearly illustrates the divergence of experience and approach between trade unionists and parliamentarians than the battle against inflation. The matter held an immediate importance for many trade-union left-wing Labourites which their parliamentary allies could only imagine. A delegate to USDAW's 1949 annual conference spoke of the budget endured by a shopworker's family of three. From a net weekly wage of £4.18s.3d., £2.10s. went for food, £1.1s. for rent, 7s. for coal and light, 2s.3d. for insurance, 4s. for travelling, 10s. for clothing and shoe repairs, 2s. for newspapers, "leaving the magnificent sum of 2s. to enjoy all the necessary vices that make life worth living." Few parliamentarians possessed such detailed knowledge of working-class budgets. One doubts if any faced the dilemma of R. W. Hards, a relief signalman who told the NUR annual conference in 1951 that there was "no bigger supporter of the Labour Party in the room" than he, but "every time I take my wage packet home my wife says, 'I don't know what we are going to do.' "[35]

This divergence of experience produced friction between the two components of the Labour Left. It could be expressed indirectly by trade unionists as simple class consciousness. A discomfited railway worker, for example, thought that

if the House of Commons and House of Lords restaurants were closed and food could not be served in the West End clubs, the Inns of Court, the Incorporated Law Society and the innumerable other places where organized systems exist of supplying food to the better-off of the nation, there would soon be a revolutionary change in the handling of the food supplies of the country.

Such sentiments may have been shared by some on the parliamentary Labour Left, but they rarely were expressed so openly or pungently. The majority of Labour Left Members probably were made uncomfortable by them.[36]

More directly, Labour Left trade unionists claimed to discern a widening gap between their own working-class values and those of the party leaders. "One of our greatest dangers just now is that our leadership can move too far away from the body of our movement," a railwayman warned readers of his union journal on 21 June 1946. Or, as still another railwayman mournfully observed, "The Labour Party is now so 'respectable' that it attracts people into it who would not have been seen dead there a decade ago." In the long run such murmurings were as likely to be directed against figures like Crossman and Foot as against their right-wing colleagues Gaitskell or Crosland. "Bring in the trade-union officers and turn out the university professors," "Observitum" demanded on 26 August 1949 in the *Railway Review*. "It is very pitiful," an engineer observed in the March 1948 issue of the AEU monthly journal. "For trade unionists to believe that high income people will favour a just distribution of the nation's yearly income is really childish."[37]

Explicit tensions based upon class are difficult to pinpoint among members of the Labour Left, but they must have been present. One senses in the writings of Cole and Laski a positive enthusiasm for "doing without frills," as Laski had put it during the convertibility crisis, an almost martyr-like zeal for "fac[ing] whatever unpopularity may be involved" in telling the workers that they must dispense with most American products—"beginning, of course, with tobacco and films," Cole specified with something approaching relish in the *New Statesman* for 5 April 1947. But the workers might wish to define frills and necessities for themselves. At any rate, as Fred Lee, the sole trade-union MP in "Keep Left," was moved to observe, "the ability to obtain academic degrees is a very desirable asset, but it never has, and never can be, a sufficient substitute for years of hard sincere work in the working-class movement."[38]

In any event the position of a trade-union MP was ambiguous. To whom did he owe allegiance? Percy Barstow, of the NUR, followed the logic of his criticisms of the government out of the Labour Party and into the Communist Party which he joined in 1952. Fred Lee moved from "Keep Left" to the respectable center of the party, much like the leadership of his union, and never strayed from it. Alf Robens, the Member for Wansbeck who was sponsored by USDAW, began as a critic of Bevin but wound up as Gaitskell's shadow Foreign Secretary. Tom Cook (Dundee), the Electricians' parliamentary representative, admonished delegates to his union's 1947 "policy conference" to bring pressure "to bear upon the Government to go forward in a Socialist direction. I want you to criticise this Government because it is the one thing it needs." Cook was PPS to Stafford Cripps, who doubted the ability of workers to control industry. Was this in Cook's mind as he stood before the assembled delegates who had entrusted him with their political aspirations?[39]

And yet "they are of us, of our movement," retiring USDAW President Percy Cottrell reminded his union's annual conference in 1947, when it seemed disposed to become, perhaps, too critical of certain Cabinet ministers. Trade unionists revealed this widely shared sense of identification in diverse fashions. "We who return to active political and trade-union life will give the Labour Government every opportunity and every help to reach the peak of the mountain, so that it can gaze onto the plain where 'Utopia' and 'Arcadia' stand," one returning soldier promised in *New Dawn*. "But if our Government slips or stumbles then our voices will be heard, loud and distinct in opposition." Even more revealing are the musings of Emanuel Shinwell at the ETU 1947 conference. As Minister of Fuel and Power, he often received resolutions from ETU branches. "They tell me quite plainly, just like that—as if I were just a Comrade and not a Minister—how I should run this industry, and who should come into it, almost down to minute detail."[40]

Ironically it was this visceral sense of identification, evidence of democratic assumptions which Labour ministers might find threatening, that in the end helped to save them from their left-wing trade-union critics. Shinwell knew how to turn it to his advantage. He emphasized that the Labour Government was a government of the workers. "We know that you, the organised workers of the country, are our friends . . . As for the rest, they do not matter a tinker's curse." It was this sense that Ernest Bevin exploited shamelessly at the Margate conference, when he obliterated the Labour Left by accusing its members of having stabbed him in the back. He explained first that he was not used to such treachery. "I grew up in the trade union."[41]

There was cooperation between the industrial and political arms of the Labour Left, but not enough to offset the instinctive solidarity with the government upon which party leaders relied. Trade-union MPs like Tom Scollan and Percy Barstow signed various fusion telegrams. They and others swelled the ranks of the foreign policy "rebels" in the House of Commons, especially when the issue was conscription. Similarly, Left Labourites in the House could be counted on to support the agitation of the trade-union Labour Left for more, and stricter, controls on the economy and for redistributive measures like higher taxes on the wealthy. Yet "Keep Left" remained almost exclusively middle class. It never sought to become more than a pressure group composed of Members of Parliament. Socialist Fellowship, whose local branches sought to enroll trade-union activists, was founded, not coincidentally, by Ellis Smith, president of the United Pattern-Workers' Union. It is a measure of Labour Left weakness in the trade unions that no more effective vehicle than the Socialist Fellowship could be established for expressing the great and growing discontent whose existence it has been the burden of this chapter to demonstrate. In the final analysis, trade unionists and politicians on the Labour Left interacted only sporadically, aware of each other's activities, but not deeply involved in them. Their common cause suffered as a result of this failing.

Notes and References

1   Martin Harrison, *Trade Unions and the Labour Party since 1945* (London, 1960), p. 215.
2   *AEU Annual Conference, 1946*, pp. 247, 242.
3   *New Dawn*, 18 May 1946.
4   Brown's statement and Mayne's letter both appear in the CSCA journal, *Red Tape*, April 1948.
5   Ibid., July 1948. All further quotations from the 1948 CSCA annual conference are taken from this issue of the journal.
6   For the storm raised by the retirement settlement, see *Red Tape*, July 1949.
7   The TUC statement was reprinted in many trade-union journals. See, for example, the Post Office workers' journal, *Post*, 20 November 1948.
8   For USDAW, see *New Dawn*, 11 June 1949; for AEU, see its *Annual Conference, 1949*, p. 247.
9   *TUC Annual Conference, 1951*, pp. 437–8, 440, 443, 444, 450.
10   Ibid., pp. 453, 429.
11   Walter Padley, *Problems of the Peace* (Leicester, 1945), p. 19; Padley, *Britain: Pawn or Power?* (London, 1947), pp. 8, 10; *New Dawn*, 18 May 1946, 19 April 1947.
12   *New Dawn*, 17 April 1948.
13   *TUC Annual Conference, 1950*, pp. 397–425.
14   Bob Edwards, *The Only Hope Socialism*, ILP national chairman's speech, delivered 20 April 1946, and later printed as an ILP pamphlet; Edwards, *Socialist Policy for Today* (London, 1948), p. 14.
15   For histories of the workers' control movement in Britain, see especially Ken Coates and A. Thopham, *Workers' Control* (London, 1970); A. W. Wright, *G. D. H. Cole and Socialist Democracy* (Oxford, 1979).
16   *TUC Annual Conference, 1947*, p. 521.
17   See above, page 100.
18   *New Dawn*, 12 January 1946.
19   See, for example, ibid., 18 September 1948, 16 October 1948.
20   *Railway Review*, 31 August 1945.

21   Ibid., 11 January 1946, 12 April 1946.
22   Ibid., 5 March 1948, 1 March 1947; *NUR Annual Conference, 1946*, Day 1, p. 90; *Railway Review*, 5 March 1947, 2 April 1947.
23   *NUR Annual Conference, 1947*, 2/29–30; *NUR Annual Conference, 1946*, 1/83, 1/87.
24   Cripps, quoted in the *Railway Review*, 24 January 1947.
25   *NUR Annual Conference, 1947*, 1/70, 3/2, 3/45.
26   *Railway Review*, 11 June 1948; *NUR Annual Conference, 1948*, 2/6, 2/5–27.
27   *Chemical Worker*, July 1949.
28   Ibid., August 1949, September 1949.
29   *TUC Annual Conference, 1950*, p. 513; *Chemical Worker*, August 1949.
30   *TUC Annual Conference, 1948*, p. 371; *TUC Annual Conference, 1949*, p. 409; *TUC Annual Conference, 1950*, p. 513.
31   *TUC Annual Conference, 1948*, pp. 379–80.
32   This revealing incident was discussed at the *NUR Annual Conference 1946*, 1/7. *New Dawn*, 16 September 1950.
33   *Daily Herald*, 14 December 1945; *Railway Review*, 21 November 1947; *Tobacco Worker*, November 1949; *AEU Monthly Journal*, June 1949.
34   *Railway Review*, 20 January 1950; *TUC Annual Conference, 1950*, pp.467, 468.
35   *USDAW Annual Conference, 1949*, page citation missing; *NUR Annual Conference, 1951* 3/26.
36   *Railway Review*, 21 November 1947.
37   Ibid., 10 November 1950.
38   *AEU Monthly Journal*, November 1948.
39   *ETU Annual Conference, 1947*, p. 111.
40   *New Dawn*, 29 December 1945; *ETU Annual Conference, 1947*, p. 134.
41   *ETU Annual Conference, 1947*, p. 130.

7

The Labour Left in the Constituencies

THE YEARS 1945–51 were a crucible for the Labour Left. In the trade unions, and in the parliamentary party, it suffered both disillusionment and a diminution of influence. In stark contrast, however, the Left in the constituency Labour parties gained confidence and strength during this period. When the Labour government fell in 1951, the constituency parties had become the backbone of the Labour Left. Thirty-five years later, they remain so.

The constituency parties never have been monolithic in social composition or political outlook, nor were they during the early postwar period. As will become evident, it is extremely difficult to discern a common pattern in their evolution during those years, except in the broadest sense. Resistant to easy generalization as their experience was, however, it was formative in the history of the postwar Labour Left and the Labour Party as a whole. Moreover, it underlines one of the central arguments of this book: that during what is generally considered to have been the apogee of Labour Party history, many party members not only believed that the pace of the government's reform program was too slow and limited, but said so in emphatic terms and pushed hard for changes. This chapter will attempt to assess the strength of the left-wing critics in the constituencies and to analyze their critique of the government. I hope, as well, to suggest how and why the constituencies became a driving force in the modern Labour Left.

II

During its early years Labour was poorly organized in the constituencies. The party made little provision for individual membership. Local activists almost always worked for Labour through one or another of the affiliated organizations, often a trade union, or one of the socialist societies, usually the ILP. There were no constituency parties, although local Labour representation committees, of which there were fewer than 150 at the end of World War I, were constituency parties in embryo.

In 1918 the party structure was reformed, and the representation committees became constituency Labour parties. Individual membership was encouraged. Now socialists could work, as Labour Party members, for socialism. There remained, however, a significant impediment to their doing so with any effectiveness. Labour's rewritten constitution did not allow constituency parties to help shape party policy. At Labour's annual conferences, where policy was ostensibly determined, the CLPs were hopelessly outnumbered by the trade unions, whose representatives tended to vote as a bloc. On the NEC, which was supposed to implement policy decisions made at conference but in practice formulated policy more than conference did, the constituency parties had little impact. A constituencies section existed, but it was composed of only five members (out of twenty-three on the NEC), and they were elected by conference as a whole, in which the trade unions were decisive.

So long as this situation continued, the constituency parties remained less attractive to rank-and-file activists hoping to influence the Labour Party in a socialist direction than the ILP until 1932 or, after that year, the Socialist League. In 1937, however, conference voted to permit constituency delegates to elect the constituency section of the NEC and increased their representation on that body from five to seven members. These reforms finally induced local socialist activists to focus on the CLPs. Ironically, centrist party leaders and conservative trade unionists had been persuaded to support the changes largely by Hugh Dalton and Ernest Bevin, who believed they would weaken the Left.[1]

Before 1945 Dalton and Bevin's calculation appeared justified. Partly as a result of the 1937 constitutional reform, the ILP entered an era of precipitous decline, and the Socialist League ceased to be a factor in Labour politics. Yet the constituency parties elected only four obvious left-wingers to the NEC: the leader of the Jarrow hunger marchers, Ellen Wilkinson, Cripps, Laski and the lawyer D. N. Pritt. The latter, who was expelled in 1940 as noted previously, had little impact. Cripps too was expelled before the war for agitating on behalf of a popular front. He was readmitted to the party in 1945, but not to the NEC. And Laski, who replaced Ellen Wilkinson as party chairman in 1945, could hardly sway an NEC dominated by the Right, although he tried to do so mightily. Elections to the constituency section of the NEC, however, do not alone reflect political sentiments among CLPs. By the end of the war it was already apparent that the Left exercised significant influence among them.

Scholarship has shown that the constituencies adapted to the wartime political truce with great difficulty and reluctance. The emergence and startling success of Common Wealth would have been impossible but for the covert, and after about 1943 often overt, sympathy and aid of constituency Labourites wishing to oppose local Tories. It is well known, too, that the CLPs generally opposed continuation of the coalition government, while Labour's leadership wanted to maintain it at least until Japan had been defeated. Perhaps the constituency parties were not so much left-wing, as rather more deeply imbued with party feeling than their politically sophisticated national leaders. The most famous resolution submitted to Labour's wartime annual conferences, however—the one introduced by Ian Mikardo in 1944 which demanded that the party commit itself to extensive nationalization and workers' control—was carried overwhelmingly by the rank and file against the wishes of the NEC. This does suggest something more than mere party feeling in the constituencies. And, as the party files reveal, by the end of the war a diverse and representative assortment of CLPs were routinely, if ineffectively, expressing left-wing sentiments. To cite only one, a piquant insistence on the concept of fair shares, on 19 July 1945 the West Cornwall Labour Women's annual rally sent to Morgan Phillips a unanimous protest "against the unnecessary luxury and extravagance of the arrangements for the Potsdam Conference . . . and, in particular, [against] the provision of 5,000 white linen sheets."[2]

In fact, Phillips's files fairly bulge with CLP resolutions, forwarded to central office during 1945–51. The vast majority condemn the government for its allegedly pusillanimous failure to apply socialist principles to affairs of state, both foreign and domestic. Strangely, historians of Labour during this period have made little use of them. To my knowledge, only Kenneth Morgan has done so. In his widely acclaimed study, *Labour in Power*, Morgan acknowledges that "it is clear from the party archives that Phillips brushed aside a good deal of grass-roots disaffection in the unions and in the constituency parties. A torrent of protest . . . was simply smothered." More generally, however, he agrees with all other significant scholars of the period and subject. The Attlee governments, Morgan concludes, enjoyed "to a degree unique" in Labour's history "a background of consensus" for their program. With respect, I believe that examination of the "torrent of protest" may suggest a different conclusion.[3]

There are more than twenty boxes of files containing correspondence between Phillips and the constituency parties. They cover his period as general secretary from 1945 to 1964. From further research it is clear that the files are incomplete. Some local parties appear to have dispatched resolutions to central office almost routinely. At least one earned a rebuke for doing so. "This party spent too much time passing resolutions," a London Labour organizer, Jim Cattermole, informed the Holborn and St Pancras South CLP. According to the minutes of that party's General Management Committee, during 1948–51 it sent twelve resolutions to party headquarters. Only five survive in Phillips's papers. One must assume that many other CLP protest resolutions likewise were lost, or filed elsewhere. Thus, enormous as the Phillips collection is, it undoubtedly understates the scope of constituency dissatisfaction with government policy.[4]

It may be argued that dissent, however broadly based, did not express the essence of the rank-and-file attitude towards the government. Perhaps not: and yet there was nothing perfunctory or superficial about the majority of messages which Phillips was receiving almost daily. One has only to read them to sense the strength and seriousness of purpose, the anger and even, towards the end, the bitterness which animated many of his correspondents. Why not take them seriously?

CLP letters to party headquarters bristled with independence. "In a democratic organization such as ours," Bristol North-East informed Phillips, "no opportunity should be neglected to give every member of our party a full and adequate opportunity to discuss, and amend if necessary, any NEC pronouncement." More pointedly, Stretford CLP (Manchester) regretted "the tendency which is creeping into the Labour Party policy of instructing its members how to think, and hope[d] in the future that not instructions but instructing literature will be issued." Phillips received many letters expressing a similar view. It seems inconceivable that they did not reflect a real, heartfelt sentiment.[5]

Independence was not, however, the only goal of CLP activists. Phillips and the party hierarchy dismissed, at their peril, rank-and-file warnings such as the following, from Epping:

That this [CLP] wishes to remind the leaders of our Party that Socialism was adopted as the official policy of the Party in 1918. We deplore the present day attempts to deviate from this policy and reaffirm our belief in the principles involved.

From Newbury: "Only Socialism can solve national and international problems." And from Saffron Walden: "The present economic crisis can only be solved in a Socialist manner." "We are called Communists or Fellow Travellers," one message from Birmingham (Aston) concluded; "But [underlined in red ink] we sincerely believe in Socialism." Because party leaders chose to disregard these and many similar resolutions, Aneurin Bevan was assured of a substantial following when he quit the government, in 1951, to uphold socialist principles. Massive disillusionment among rank-and-file Labourites was the prerequisite for Bevanism.[6]

It is possible to trace in Phillips's correspondence the gradual growth of this disenchantment. The curve of disappointment follows roughly the same parabola as that experienced by the parliamentary Labour Left. At first, the government's domestic program, generally, was exempt from criticism. From the outset, however, there appear to have been doubts about foreign policy, though to begin with CLPs mainly encouraged the government to live up to what they understood to be its convictions. For example, on 30 August 1945 the New Forest and Christchurch Divisional Labour Party "reaffirm[ed] its conviction that only by Socialism can world peace be permanently maintained, and assure[d] the Government of its wholehearted support for a strong Socialist line in Foreign Policy in amity with the USSR." The assumption here was that the government would endorse the sentiments contained in this communication. Other constituency parties shared this rosy view. Only ten days after receiving the New Forest and Christchurch resolution, Phillips was reminded by the Chelsea Labour Party that it would be "essential to make substantial changes in the higher personnel of the Foreign Office . . . before the Labour Government can carry out an effective Progressive Foreign Policy."[7]

Such relatively friendly encouragement gave way swiftly to more urgent exhortation. As early as 23 September 1945 the Spelthorne Labour Party was demanding that "Mr Bevin be instructed to prepare a policy more in keeping with Labour policy and traditions." Even this rather pointed communication assumed that the Foreign Secretary was out of step with a government which would desire to bring him to heel. A year later, however, the government itself was being urged by the Aireborough Labour Party "to adopt a policy that is more in accordance with past Conference decisions and which reflects the Socialist principles of the Movement." These, it often was asserted, had been embodied in the party manifesto of 1945. On 30 November 1946 the Bridgwater Labour Party discussed Britain's foreign policy "past and present" and agreed unanimously to warn the government that "the policy on which the election was fought and won is not being carried out." Bridgwater, like Aireborough, demanded that the government "abandon the present unsatisfactory policy."[8]

Like the parliamentary Labour Left, the Left in the constituencies began with the assumption that socialist Britain and communist Russia would be natural allies. A typical expression of this view came in November 1946 from the Epsom and Ewell Borough Labour Party. It demanded "a better and closer understanding . . . between Britain, the Soviet Union and other Socialist countries." Gradually this aspiration was eroded among CLPs, which insisted, nevertheless, upon their socialist convictions. As the secretary of the Southport Trades Council and Labour Party informed Phillips in 1950, "my party wholeheartedly supports the Government in its stand against Communist Russia." He had been instructed "by unanimous decision of the General Council," however, "to write to the National Executive protesting strongly against the anti-Socialist trend of the Government," in both its domestic and foreign policies.[9]

Meanwhile suspicion of the United States remained constant. In 1946 the Cowes and District Labour Party condemned "American Imperialism." On 4 December 1948 Rushcliffe Labour Party,

> believing that the presence of US Super-fortresses and military personnel in this country is prejudicial to our independence as well as to the preservation of peace, call[ed] upon the Government to end the agreement authorizing the establishment of US bases in the United Kingdom.

A year later the Wycombe DLP was informing Phillips (and Ernest Bevin) "that this party distrusts the aims of American capitalism." No doubt Marshall Aid did much to soften CLP suspicions of America. During the Korean War, however, anti-Americanism scaled new heights. There were widespread fears that Truman was planning a preventive war against Mao's new regime. In a typical resolution, Holborn and St Pancras CLP urged the government "to publicly declare that it will immediately withdraw its support from the operations in Korea in the event of any further action by the United Nations commander [General MacArthur] tending to promote a full scale clash with China." In the early summer of 1950 the Forth Labour Party urged the government "to order the withdrawal of all land, sea and air forces of the United States of America from British territory and territorial waters."[10]

Like the parliamentary Labour Left, the Left in the constituency parties came to favor British participation in a third force which, it was held, would be powerful enough to mediate between Russia and the United States, thereby preserving world peace as well as offering an alternative to capitalism and communism. Phillips received many CLP resolutions demanding that the Labour government take the lead in building such a force. Here is one, a resolution circulated among all CLPs in early 1951 by North Lewisham. "It is the opinion of this party," the resolution began,

> that the present foreign policy of His Majesty's Government is not assisting the

progress of Socialism throughout the world. It considers that a Socialist Government should free itself from the influence of capitalist countries and yet not ally itself to the Soviet Union. It therefore calls upon His Majesty's Government to take the initiative in creating a true Socialist force in the world.

This, as we have seen, mirrored demands to which trade unionists and Labour Members also were giving voice. Third force sentiment was a critical concept for the non-communist Left in early postwar Britain and has occupied an important space in the Labour Left mental universe ever since. An important tributary to the "torrent of protest" pouring into central office, it represented, too, a crucial element in the world view of Labour's constituency activists during the early postwar period.[11]

CLP activists and left-wing Labour Members travelled a similar route of disenchantment with regard to the government's domestic policies. Satisfied, at first, that Attlee's administration was determined to oversee a genuine socialist transformation, many CLPs began to express doubts when they learned about the dollar gap. West Wickham (Kent), for example, demanded that "military considerations . . . not be allowed to affect in any way the production drive" and called "upon the Government to cut all sections of the Forces to the lowest possible level, and thereby release tens of thousands of personnel to aid production and drastically reduce the present enormous 'Service' Expenditure." A year later, Coventry Borough Labour Party was warning Phillips that "in the minds of many, the situation is the same as it was [in 1931] and there is a feeling that Sir Stafford Cripps is going the way of Ramsay MacDonald, and in the Budget has shown more patriotism than Socialism." Left-wing constituency parties charged, after 1947, that the pace of reform had slackened, that the tough measures which alone could lead to socialism were not being implemented, indeed, that "consolidationism" jeopardized the entire socialist project. One typical, if toughly worded, resolution from Kingston Borough Labour Party took great pains to "repudiate the new definition of Socialism outlined by Mr Herbert Morrison. . . To apply the name 'Socialism' to a policy which includes the assisting and stimulating of private enterprise is a negation in terms." Numerous resolutions protested against the wage freeze, the imprisonment of unofficial strikers, the first proposal, in 1949, to impose charges on the National Health Service, the lack of working-class representation on the boards of nationalized industries and the high compensation paid to the former owners of industries taken from private enterprise. Others demanded further measures of nationalization, the maintenance of economic controls, democratization of the workplace and additional taxation of the wealthy. This must represent a significant level of protest and alienation, an essential aspect of the history of the labor movement during 1945–51.[12]

Many constituency Labour parties wanted "more socialism" at home and a more independent foreign policy. The question remains: how many? One study has calculated that eighty-eight CLPs submitted at least two left-wing conference resolutions or amendments during 1945–51. The extent of left-wing sentiment among CLPs may be measured another way. In the spring of 1951 a core of former Socialist Fellowship members, headed by Tom Braddock and Karl Westwood, the prospective

Labour candidate for Richmond (Surrey), established a committee to demand a special conference of rank-and-file Labourites. By this time Bevan, Wilson and Freeman had resigned from the Cabinet with results for the Labour Left which will be examined in Chapter 8. Westwood's letter of invitation, circulated to all CLPs, was mild:

> It is URGENT that the Party should formulate a policy of peace and higher living standards to carry us to victory. Whatever your own contributions to such a policy we feel sure you will agree that we need an Emergency National Conference without further delay to call a halt to the present fatal drift.

It was clear, however, that such a conference could become a Bevanite demonstration of strength. At the very least it would publicize Labour's deep divisions. There was no chance that the NEC would permit such a conference to take place. How many constituencies declined to participate in the emergency conference campaign on the grounds that it was naive to ask the leadership to summon a meeting whose implicit purpose was to condemn their policies? Nevertheless there remain in Phillips's files requests from 105 CLPs that the gathering be convened.[13]

If anything, these two indices underestimate the number of left-wing constituency parties. Phillips's files contain critical resolutions from local parties which neither demanded the emergency conference nor submitted two or more left-wing motions for debate at Labour's annual meetings. Moreover, dozens of constituencies which had chosen parliamentary representatives on the Labour Left never sent critical messages to Phillips. Undoubtedly, however, most of these were left-wing CLPs. It seems safe to conclude, therefore, that the Left had a significant presence in well over one hundred CLPs.

It is exceedingly difficult, however, to generalize about them, though a few tentative conclusions may be drawn. Incongruously, perhaps, for the most part they were not located in urban, industrial settings. The study previously cited has shown that the local parties in Labour's electoral strongholds were likely to be dominated by former trade-union men and minor party *apparatchiks*, devotees of machine politics. In such areas it proved difficult to persuade Labour supporters even to join the party. The most active CLPs, those which tended to attract enthusiastic, often left-wing rank-and-file members, were frequently in Labour's marginal, or even hopeless, constituencies. They tended, too, to be centered geographically in London and the surrounding Home Counties. Yet it would be absurd to conclude that the Labour Left had little presence in Glasgow, former heartland of the ILP, or in the Welsh mining towns, or half a dozen industrial Midland towns whose local parties sent few critical resolutions to the annual conference and, for the most part, ignored the campaign for an emergency conference in 1951.

Perhaps the most that can be safely said about the Left in the constituencies is that it was stronger and more deeply opposed to a broad range of government policies than usually has been thought, and it expressed its dissatisfaction in unmistakable terms. Rather than attempt to draw further conclusions from this survey of left-wing CLPs, therefore, it would seem more illuminating to focus on a select few constituency parties. Since there was no such thing as a typical Labour Left constituency I have chosen to examine four which were represented by left-wing Labour Members but otherwise had little in common: Hornchurch, a London suburb with a mixed social base; Coventry East, a Midlands proletarian constituency; Gateshead, a north-eastern proletarian constituency; and Finsbury, a working-class district of London.

III

In 1939 the municipality of Hornchurch was a growing, popular suburb of London. Fourteen miles east of London Bridge, it was bounded on the south by the Thames, on the north by the main road from London to Colchester, on the west by the river Rom and on the east by the districts of Brentwood and Thurrock. Before the war, according to the town's *Official Guide*, there were "still to be seen [in High Street] several quaint old world houses with protruding gables and carved façades." Indeed, the *Guide* boasted proudly, the town had been "very much off the beaten track in days gone by." Even after the war it still contained twenty miles of unpaved roads, though it took no more than a half-hour to reach central London by commuter train (today the District tube line).[14]

By the late 1930s, however, Hornchurch was "off the beaten track" no longer. Its population had climbed to nearly one hundred thousand. And if in Rainham towards the north-east of the municipality there were still working farms, there was in the town of Hornchurch itself a Ford Motor Company factory and a Roneo factory which employed more than 1,500 workers. The local trades council contained members of the Electricians' Union, the Amalgamated Engineers, the General and Municipal Workers, the Painters, the National Union of Railwaymen, the Transport and General Workers' Union and the Life Assurance Workers. Many local residents commuted to work in London.

The war dealt harshly with Hornchurch. German bombers killed 139 citizens, seriously injured 370 and hurt 1,119 less severely. They destroyed or badly damaged many buildings, roadways and public spaces. Even a year after the end of hostilities, a local newspaper reported, "horrible memories of the war years stand stark and ugly. Apart from the debris, the roads and footpaths are a public disgrace—craters not yet filled in are producing rats and gnats."[15]

Not surprisingly, the most pressing local political questions in 1945 concerned public health, transport and housing. These were issues which the local Labour party might justifiably have thought likely to work to its advantage. Yet there was little precedent for Labour success in Hornchurch. The constituency itself had been carved with Barking and Dagenham from the older and much larger constituency of Romford in 1944. Over seven general elections since 1918, Hornchurch socialists had helped Romford to elect a Labour MP only twice. They had never won a Labour majority on the Hornchurch Urban District Council or among the Hornchurch delegates to the Essex County Council. And, bleak prospect for the future, the redistricting of 1944 had been carried out in such fashion that the constituency of Hornchurch now contained the village of Upminster, a Tory stronghold.

Despite its history, however, the new divisional party was well organized. Its Executive Committee and General Management Committee, whose members previously had functioned as the Hornchurch representatives on the EC and GMC of Romford Labour Party, continued to meet on a monthly basis. Seventy-five members were entitled to attend GMC meetings, 45 from eight ward parties, 7 from the women's sections, 13 from affiliated trade unions, 1 from the Co-op Party and 9 councillors and aldermen. Typically attendance ranged between 50 and 70 members. The EC meetings, of course, were much smaller. Ward Committees, which met every two weeks, varied in size. The Town Ward, whose minutes of executive committee meetings survive, had five officers, a chairman, vice-chairman, secretary, treasurer and organizing secretary.[16]

Broadly speaking, the three levels of party organization were supposed to deal with distinct types of issues. Ward parties considered strictly local affairs. At a typical meeting of the executive committee of the Town Ward, for example,

> Mr Knight raised question re lack of letter boxes and telephone kiosks in Derby Avenue... Notice was brought before members that no more children were to be admitted to Ayloffs School until May next year... Re horses straying. Secretary to take up matter with police.

The executive committee dealt with issues affecting the constituency as a whole, for example local elections, and it screened the issues which the General Management Committee would be asked to consider. These often concerned the national Labour Party or government policies. Full minutes of the meetings of both the EC and GMC survive.[17]

The inaugural meeting of the new Hornchurch Labour Party took place on 15 March 1945. One of the first items of business was to confirm the appointment of an election agent, a "live-wire" local businessman, Bruce Leonard Wallace. He began immediately to interview prospective parliamentary candidates. Before Churchill announced the end of the coalition government, Hornchurch Labour Party had decided upon a short list of five, including Hector Hughes (who became MP for Aberdeen North), Austin Albu (later a prominent Fabian who became MP for Edmonton), Geoffrey Bing (the eventual nominee) and a local man, Councillor A. J. Twigger, deputy chief clerk to the Engineer at King's Cross Station in London and leader of the Labour group on the Hornchurch Urban District Council. Twigger appears to have been a forceful personality. "He practises what he preaches," a local reporter wrote, "and if that offends any man's susceptibilities, says Mr Twigger, then that man is at liberty to say so." Near the end of 1945 the agent, Wallace, took Twigger at his word. He called him a "semi-fascist"—and lost his position.[18]

Domineering though Twigger appears to have been, he failed by three votes to secure the parliamentary nomination, which went instead to a different sort, equally forceful in his own way. Geoffrey Bing was the grandson of "a famous Orange clergyman" and the son of a "liberal minded Conservative" schoolmaster. He had attended the Tonbridge School, Lincoln College, Oxford, and Princeton University.

Called to the bar in 1935, he employed his legal expertise from the outset on behalf of a variety of left-wing causes. No sooner had he qualified to practice law than he was helping to organize the legal defense of locked-out miners from the Harworth Colliery in Nottinghamshire. They had been charged under the Trades Dispute Act. During the same year he assisted in the defense of the communist leader Mathias Rakosi, who had been charged by the fascist Hungarian government with treason. A delegate at the Penal and Penitential Congress in Berlin, also in 1935, Bing had made a public speech condemning the Nazi penal system and anti-Semitism and had organized a group of delegates to visit working-class leaders in concentration camps. During the Spanish civil war he was active in opposition to Franco's forces as a member of the Spanish Medical Aid Committee and the National Joint Committee on Spain, and with D. N. Pritt, KC, as a lawyer for the Spanish loyalists in the famous Gibraltar cases of 1938. He had been in Bilbao when it was besieged by the fascists.[19]

During the war Bing became an active and successful soldier. Called up in 1941, he served in the ranks for two years. After an OCTU course, he volunteered for parachute duty. He served in the North African campaign and was wounded. He was promoted to the rank of captain.

People who knew Bing believe that he belonged to the Communist Party during the prewar period. He joined the Labour Party in 1935, however, and the Oxford University Labour Club shortly thereafter. He belonged, too, to the Fabian Society, the Haldane Society and the executive committee of the National Council for Civil Liberties. Whatever his past political commitments, Bing typified a significant element in the postwar Labour Left. He was unlike his major rival for the nomination, Councillor Twigger, in that he was only thirty-five years old at the war's end, and his political memory did not reach back to Labour's pioneering days or even to the great unrest of the pre- and post-World-War-I era. Rather, like many others who became prominent on the left of the PLP during 1945–51, Bing had been radicalized during the 1930s. For him a formative political struggle had been that against the Labour leadership who refused to form a popular front with the communists. Perhaps there was something anachronistic, in Britain in 1945, about Twigger, who held "that a Christian should live and talk Christianity" and had once been accused of "flaunting his religion with a self-righteous air." Twigger recalls the crusading Christian socialist and pacifist George Lansbury. Bing was a different type. Secular, tough-minded, upper-middle-class, he presents a vivid contrast to the runner-up for the local party's imprimatur.[20]

When Bing received the Labour nomination in late May or early June, the political situation in Hornchurch was fluid. There were four other parliamentary candidates: a Conservative, Colonel John Vaizy; a Liberal, Norman Clarke Jones; an "Independent," Mrs V. van der Elst, who was "opposed to Socialism and Communism;" and a "Progressive Independent," Corporal Charles Deller, who belonged to the Fabian Society and the Anglo-Soviet Friendship Alliance. Local newspapers carefully avoided predictions, perhaps because since World War I the constituency to which Hornchurch previously had belonged, Romford, had been represented by all three major parties in the House of Commons. On one aspect of the contest, however, the *Hornchurch, Dagenham and Romford Times* for 6 June was clear: "There is no doubt that the Conservative, Liberal and Independent contestants will find Mr Bing a very powerful opponent."

From the outset, Bing took the common Labour line in presenting the election as a potential watershed in British history. "The future of ourselves and of our children depended on the elections," he warned at one early meeting. In Hornchurch this seems to have resulted in a narrowing and a polarizing of the race. Corporal Deller, the "Progressive Independent," withdrew in order, one supposes, to keep from dividing the anti-Conservative vote. There was no other left-wing candidate in Hornchurch, Common Wealth having forsworn all but the most hopelessly anti-Labour constituencies as a matter of principle, the Communists likewise offering candidates in only a handful of contests. On the Right, Mrs van der Elst also withdrew from the campaign, probably in order to avoid splitting the anti-socialist vote, though she claimed to be suffering from laryngitis. The Liberal continued, gamely, to campaign. By 13 July, however, the *Romford, Hornchurch, Upminster Recorder* had read him out of the race: "It is considered . . . that it will prove to have been a close fight between Captain Geoffrey Bing and Colonel John Vaizy."[21]

Perhaps the Conservative candidate's most natural strategy was to picture Bing as a left-wing extremist, recalling his opposition to Labour's prewar policy on Spain, his agitation for a popular front with communists in Britain and the Soviet Union, for which Cripps, Bevan and Strachey had been expelled from the Parliamentary Labour Party, and his association with D. N. Pritt, who also had been expelled. Bing maintained, however, that his outlook no longer conflicted with that of the party leaders. When asked at one meeting whether, if returned to Parliament, he would vote according to his conscience or the party whip, he "replied that he was confident his conscience and the Labour Party policy would always agree."[22]

Yet Bing had not moderated his views during the war years, as his subsequent career and 1945 electoral campaign make clear. He predicted that Labour Britain would naturally befriend foreign socialist and communist movements. He extolled the Soviet Union, a country "which had saved not only itself but the world in the present war." Simultaneously, he campaigned unambiguously for socialism and "fair shares" at home. As he explained at one of his first election rallies, "what was produced in this country should be distributed fairly among the people . . . and people should work together for one common purpose instead of being forced to compete with each other." "It was necessary," he told another gathering, "to send a party to power which would eradicate past evils of unemployment, malnutrition, bad education, etc. To execute this, control and nationalization were inevitable." Harking back to prewar fears on the Labour Left of counter-revolution against a socialist government, he warned that the House of Lords would be abolished if it interfered with Labour's program. He condemned Britain's class-based education system. And he promised that 1945 would be different from 1924 and 1929, when Labour had taken office but had failed to embark upon the socialist transformation it had promised. "The policy of the Labour Party would be put into force without delay," he vowed. "There was not going to be any soft pedalling of the programme." In short, his campaign reflected at once the general radicalism of Labour in 1945 and the Labour Left illusion that it was permanent, that the party as a whole now shared its own commitment to building "socialism in our time."[23]

On the night of 26 July, as crowds began to gather in the Billett Lane cricket field in Hornchurch to hear the results of the election, Labour hopes were high. A lorry draped with flags stood at the edge of the field, and it was around this that people congregated. They expected the votes to be counted before 8 p.m. and to learn who was the victor in the dusk. In fact, the results were not proclaimed until after ten, and by then the crowd had swollen to more than three thousand. Small boys had climbed to perilous vantage-points in the high trees surrounding the grounds, from which they could make out in the fading light red banners and flags waved by Labour supporters. Finally it was announced that Captain Bing had trounced his Conservative opponent by more than 11,000 votes, and the Liberal by 10,000 over that. Jubilantly the crowd lifted Bing to their shoulders and surged down the High Street, past the bus garage where four hundred transport workers "cheered wildly," to Park Lane British Restaurant where the celebrations were to be continued. In acknowledging the intense enthusiasm of his supporters Bing was at pains to identify his own left-wing views with those of Labour as a whole. "You have chosen me not as a person, but as the representative of a party." Hornchurch Labour activists could have little inkling of the great divide which would come to separate Bing's views from those of the party leadership.[24]

They were there from the outset, but did not surface immediately for odd reasons. Bing's maiden speech in the House, scheduled for 26 August, would have identified him as an early critic. He had put down an amendment to Bevin's motion for ratification of the UN Charter, intending to argue that the Charter's security provisions were inadequate because they did not provide for international control of the atomic bomb. Bing was opposed to the "development of atomic power for purely national purposes." In the event, however, the speech was not delivered. "Some of the party members and the Whips discussed the matter with him, and as a result it was decided not to move the amendment." Before he had another chance to speak, Bing was called into Attlee's office. The Prime Minister did not appear to recognize him— perhaps, Bing later told his friend Leslie Hale, because there were so many new Members. Now the Member for Hornchurch learned to his surprise that the Prime Minister wished to promote him to junior whip! The appointment would prevent him asking questions or making speeches in the House. Bing accepted, in some befuddlement. Within days it became known that Attlee had supposed he was promoting someone else, Joe Binns, the Member for Rochester, Gillingham. It was impossible, however, to admit the mistake, and Bing remained—absurdly given his views—a government whip until late 1946, when he resigned voluntarily.[25]

Thus the inevitable clash between the left-wing Member for Hornchurch and the Labour leadership was postponed. In the meantime, his local party gave Bing much to think about. Immediately after being elected he had suggested the appointment of a full-time paid official. He would contribute £100 annually towards the £265 salary the agent would receive. In fact, the party was plagued by financial difficulties, despite the generosity of its parliamentary representative. To make matters worse, the agent,

Wallace, was fired after the difference of opinion with Twigger referred to above, and the man who replaced him, Ben Fieldhouse, turned out to be dishonest. On one occasion he travelled by taxi from London to Manchester, and charged the bill to the Hornchurch DLP election fund. In the end, he admitted liability "for at least £300," and promised to pay it back in £5 monthly installments beginning in September 1947. Four months later he had not begun to repay the money he owed, "and it was the view of the EC that none was likely to be received."[26]

Research suggests that nearly all local Labour parties were chronically short of funds. Hornchurch was fortunate in possessing an enthusiastic rank and file who responded resourcefully and, all things considered, enthusiastically to the perennial appeals for money issued by their GMC. For example, on 24 June 1948 the Ways and Means Committee of Hornchurch DLP agreed

> to organise a Divisional Christmas Bazaar . . . a New Year's Eve Dance . . . a St Leger Prize Draw . . . To urge all wards to consider the possibility of organising Loan Clubs on the lines of the one organised by North West Ward, and also to explore the possibility of running regular Whist Drives on behalf of the Divisional funds. . . Rainsford Way Section of North West Ward are putting on a variety concert.

Other examples of rank-and-file activity are abundant. By July 1947 the North-West, Cranham and Thameside wards were producing a joint newsletter. The party as a whole ran a "Citizens' Advice Bureau," and a "Poor Man's Lawyer Service." With the National Council of Labour Colleges, it co-sponsored numerous lectures, including four by Bing himself. Recruiting drives paid additional dividends. By 1950 Hornchurch DLP had become one of the ten largest local Labour parties in the country.[27]

Throughout, Bing worked assiduously to cement good relations with his local party and as an MP at Westminster. He set a gruelling pace:

> After spending part of Monday morning here in his constituency [wrote a local reporter], he dashed off to London to show some visitors around the House. The evening saw him back when he spoke to the Hornchurch and Romford agricultural workers at Romford. Tuesday . . . he was at Westminster early and before the Commons began work at 2:30 p.m. he had to approach some 200 MPs to get their signatures for his motion on Tied Houses—apart from replying to some 20 or 30 letters. Wednesday . . . he attended a Labour Party meeting at Westminster early in the morning, then was present in the House for the Finance Bill until 3 a.m. He arrived home an hour later. After just over three hours' sleep he was back in the House at 9 a.m., ready to show the Palace of Westminster to a party from Rainham Secondary School. At 11 o'clock children from Bush Elm School were waiting to take a similar tour. A quick lunch and then into the Commons again for the Finance Bill. Mr Bing was voting in the Division lobby at 7:30 that evening, but at 8:30 was in Hornchurch giving his account of the Blackpool Conference to the General

Management Committee of the Hornchurch Labour Party. He spoke to them until 9:15, and a friend then rushed him back by car to the House where they arrived at 10 p.m. He remained until the House rose at 2 a.m. Friday he was in the Commons again early, and after the adjournment went on to Uxbridge, where he spoke on the Irish question. Half an hour after midnight he arrived in Hornchurch to be ready to deal with constituent problems first thing Saturday morning.

Small wonder, with such a schedule, that Bing gave up his position as government whip towards the end of 1946. One suspects, however, that there was more to it than simple fatigue. Bing was prohibited, as a junior member of the government, from signing Richard Crossman's amendment to the King's Speech in November 1946. It cannot be coincidental that he gave up the post almost immediately after that episode, and from then on found his closest parliamentary associates among the circle which established the "Keep Left" group. If anything, he took a harder line than many in the group did. Early in 1947 he argued, in the House, that there was more democracy in Poland than in Northern Ireland. He seems almost always to have supported the various protest resolutions moved by Labour Left backbenchers, most importantly the famous Nenni telegram. He was active in the Victory for Socialism group, and in the Peace with China campaign. When the Bevanite rebellion finally occurred, Bing was a prominent supporter.[28]

The Hornchurch Labour Party loyally backed its left-wing MP throughout the period. During the storm over the Nenni telegram Bing was one of the intransigents who refused to disavow the message. The Executive Committee of his local party supported him unanimously. An expanded meeting of the General Management Committee delivered him a vote of confidence by 92 to 4. A year later he was reselected as parliamentary candidate for the party by 52 votes to 1. During the general election of 1950 Bing "made no apology" for his various rebellions and promised that he would continue to vote his conscience in the House. As he put it in his election address, "The Labour Party is not a party of rubber stamps." Despite a massive swing to the Conservatives, Hornchurch voters rewarded him by returning him to Parliament. They did so again in 1951, when Labour lost the general election.[29]

Hornchurch Labour Party supported Bing not merely from loyalty but because, usually, it agreed with him. It carried a string of resolutions demanding stricter control of the economy, for example, "price controls on foodstuffs," "the immediate reimposition of controls on the price of fish" and, for Labour's annual conference in 1950, that "the Government ... implement a policy of profit control with its attempts at wages control." In October 1948 it "carried by a large majority" a resolution condemning "the rationing of electricity by means of price manipulation." This, it asserted, was "contrary to Socialist principles." Like its parliamentary representative, Hornchurch Labour Party wanted more socialism than the government delivered. This seems to contradict the common impression that it was mainly the government's foreign policy which inspired rank-and-file dissatisfaction and dissent.[30]

Hornchurch Labour Party did not accord to Bing's participation in the various foreign policy "rebellions" the same unanimous support which it gave his demands for more socialism at home. There appear to have been two right-wing wards, Upminster and Town. At the September 1950 GMC meeting, Upminster Ward moved

> That this Party, whilst recognizing the setbacks caused to the Nation's Economic Recovery and to the improvement in the general standard of living occasioned by rearmament, nevertheless regards the measures taken by the Government as inevitable and necessary in the present world situation, and pledges its support for the Government's policy.

The minutes record that "some considerable and at times heated discussion ensued," at the end of which the resolution was defeated by a vote of 33 to 14. This was a fair indication of right-wing strength in the party. When Town Ward moved a resolution supporting UN action in Korea, it was defeated by 23 votes to 16. At the same meeting another right-wing resolution lost by 30 votes to 17.[31]

The Labour Left in Hornchurch had greater, but not decisive, representation in the party. Bing found consistent allies in three wards, North-West, Thameside and Harold Wood, and in the Hornchurch Trades Council. In November 1946 North-West Ward condemned the conscription Bill for being "contrary to Socialist principles" and urged that it be amended in the House. Three months later it urged the government "to reduce the size of the Armed Forces drastically . . . hand over control of Gibraltar and Suez to the UN . . . and withdraw support for reactionary Governments as in Greece." In September 1947 Thameside Ward moved

> that the present actions of the Government do not represent the views of the rank and file of the Labour Party, and therefore demands that the Divisional Party calls on the National Executive to organise a Special Party Conference so that these views can be expressed.

In March 1951 the Harold Wood Ward "deplore[d] the tendency of Her Majesty's Government to proceed with the policy of rearmament at the expense of economic stability." Significantly, none of these resolutions carried. The situation in Hornchurch Labour Party was this: united in demanding further measures of socialization at home, it was divided on foreign policy issues, the Left being able to block right-wing initiatives and vice versa.[32]

These circumstances produced frustration and flaring tempers at GMC meetings. A resolution of 26 October 1950 attempted to smooth matters over:

> this Hornchurch Constituency Labour Party regrets and rejects the ideological clash which has arisen within its ranks; . . . it recognizes and sees within the Socialist thesis adequate scope for variance of views on the method of carrying out the ideals of Socialism, and accordingly supports a policy within this Party of agreement to disagree.

One doubts whether such exhortations would have been effective. Unexpectedly, however, the deadlock finally was broken, in favor of the Left, as a result of a bizarre incident. In November 1950 the secretary of the Executive Committee, F. G. Cullen, learned that Councillor H. F. Newman, a conspicuous member of the Labour Right in Hornchurch and a dominant figure in the Town Ward Labour Party, secretly had contacted Raymond Blackburn, MP. The latter, it may be recalled, was the Labour Member who had demanded a parliamentary debate about the Nenni telegram. He had been under the impression that most of its signatories were fellow-travellers of the Communist Party. More recently he had resigned from the Labour Party in order "to fight communism." Councillor Newman proposed to aid Blackburn in this crusade by providing him with information about Geoffrey Bing. He requested, in turn, that Blackburn make available to him any information concerning Bing that he might discover.

Matters came to a head at the GMC of 23 November. Charged with disloyalty and more, Newman responded defiantly. "He had taken this course of action because he had for some time been troubled by the words and actions of Mr Geoffrey Bing whom he felt to be of Communist tendencies." The most he would admit was that his course of action "had been possibly indiscreet." This did not satisfy a majority of the GMC, which voted by 28 votes to 21 that he should be expelled.

Newman's anti-communist zeal appears to have helped discredit the Labour Right in general in the local party. The evidence is mixed. Newman, who appealed to the NEC at Transport House as was his right, was reinstated in the party after being made to apologize both to it and to Bing himself. His ward party later elected him to the GMC. Clearly he had supporters there. On the other hand, where previously the Right had been sufficiently powerful to block resolutions which criticized the government's foreign policy, it could no longer do so. In August 1951 the GMC agreed, at Bing's urging, to move a Bevanite amendment to the foreign policy section of Labour's report to the annual conference. And it adopted an outright Bevanite resolution of its own,

> That this Party . . . wholeheartedly supports the three ex-Ministers, Messrs A. Bevan, H. Wilson and J. Freeman, in the action that they have taken, and draws the attention of the National Executive Committee to the general feeling of support which is manifested in the Labour Movement.

Town Ward, which had been dominated by the Labour Right since 1945, even mandated its delegates, Newman among them, to support this resolution. Ward parties, like CLPs, like the Labour Party as a whole, cannot be treated as homogeneous units![33]

Even now, however, the hegemony of the Labour Left in Hornchurch CLP was not total. When it proposed, on 23 August 1951, "That this Party strongly deplores the action of Her Majesty's Government in allowing the establishment of American fighter bases in this country," the Right amended the motion, by 16 votes to 12, to read:

> That this Party strongly deplores the action of Her Majesty's Government in allowing the establishment of American Military Bases in this country, in

maintaining military bases in North Africa and elsewhere, and deplores the action of the Soviet Union in maintaining similar bases in the satellite countries.

This was carried by 18 votes to 5, a tally reflecting Labour Left doubts about the Soviet Union as well as right-wing and center Labour opinion.

Hornchurch Labour Party was not a leading left-wing CLP. It did not send two critical resolutions for Labour's annual conferences to debate.Morgan Phillips's files contain no resolutions, critical or otherwise, from Hornchurch DLP, although we know from the Hornchurch GMC minute books that several were sent. There is no record that the party endorsed the campaign for an emergency conference. But the party had as its parliamentary representative a leading member of the Labour Left whom, for the most part, it supported loyally. As we have seen, it took a militant socialist position on domestic matters and, eventually, on foreign policy. It was a left-wing CLP.

What was the essence of such a party's attitude towards the Attlee governments? There is no simple answer. Hornchurch CLP's attitude could not be unambiguous. It approved of much that the government did. It never thought in terms of bringing the government down. This need not mean, however, that essentially it supported Attlee's policies. It would be more accurate to say that Hornchurch Labour supported the efforts of its MP to move the government along more radical paths than it wished to follow, while attempting, on its own, to exert pressure of a similar nature. What else could a left-wing CLP do without entering the political wilderness? It contributed to the "torrent of protest" which flooded Phillips's office in the only feasible way. It would be condescending to denigrate such efforts, which represent an integral aspect of Labour's experience during 1945–51.

IV

Hornchurch was a London suburb, containing a Tory enclave in Upminster and many middle-class residents who commuted to work in London. By way of contrast now we shall examine a provincial constituency of pronounced proletarian character.

Coventry had been an industrial center since the early nineteenth century. During Victorian times it became "a city of tenements and slums," according to a local historian. Like the Manchester described by Engels, Coventry was plagued in Victorian times by public health problems. Open cesspools and sewers were common. Its workers labored in oppressive conditions at the manufacture of ribbons, silk and watches. In the twentieth century, however, Coventry workers engaged in heavy industry at automobile and aircraft factories, and electrical and engineering works, and received high wages. They prospered even during the interwar years. And the city continued to grow. By 1940 its population had reached 252,000.[34]

Not surprisingly, the labor movement was strong in Coventry. In 1937 it gained control of the City Council. The movement was also left-wing, containing a strong communist contingent whose roots were located among the engineers and automobile workers, and an active branch of the ILP which provided the core of postwar Coventry

Labour Party leaders. Yet, like Hornchurch Labour Party, Coventry DLP did not experience much success during pre-1945 general elections. Between 1918 and 1945 it was represented in Parliament by a member of the Labour Party for only three years, 1923–4, and 1929–31 when Philip Noel-Baker was MP.

No British city suffered more during the war than Coventry. During one night in November 1940 German bombers killed 554 people, seriously wounded 865 and made nearly a third of the city's homes uninhabitable. Bombs destroyed the beautiful Coventry cathedral. The Germans coined a new word, *Coventrieren*, which meant to destroy physically and psychologically an entire city. Yet "Coventration" did not destroy the city's labor movement. In a weird and unintended way it made Labour's most far-reaching plans more feasible than previously. Since Coventry had to be rebuilt, Labourites argued, let it be reconstructed along socialist lines.

In 1944 the same Redistricting Act which created the constituency of Hornchurch split Coventry into two parliamentary districts, Coventry East and Coventry North. In 1950 a third division was added. Of the three, Coventry East was socially the most homogeneous, inhabited almost exclusively by a working-class population. During the general election of 1945 its polling-booths were strangely quiet until "after the workers left the factories." From seven o'clock on, however, polling was heavy and overwhelmingly in favor of Labour. The man elected has figured prominently in these pages. He was Richard Crossman.[35]

Crossman's national role and his position within the parliamentary Labour Left have been treated in previous chapters. The son of a High Court judge, he was born in 1907, attended Winchester and New College, Oxford, where he earned a double first. An academic career lay before him; he was elected to a fellowship at New College, where he lectured in philosophy, apparently with great success. Like so many, however, he proved responsive to the radical temper of the times. He joined the Workers' Educational Association, and he became involved in the hurly-burly of Oxford city politics. Elected to the Oxford City Council, he was leader of its Labour group from 1934 to 1940. In 1938 he became an assistant editor of Kingsley Martin's *New Statesman.* As with Geoffrey Bing, then, and many others who gravitated towards the Labour Left during the postwar period, Crossman was radicalized during the 1930s by the threat of fascism and by the struggle to build a popular front. Later he became a scourge of the communists. In 1945, however, he retained the prewar outlook. "It is well known that the Coventry Labour Movement both on the political and on the industrial side has always been a champion of Labour unity and has stood for Communist affiliation to the Labour Party," he asserted during the campaign. "I share that view."[36]

Unlike Geoffrey Bing, Crossman did not see action during the war. Instead he became deputy director of Britain's Psychological Warfare Department. Later he joined Eisenhower's propaganda team in North Africa. His experiences during the war permanently colored his attitude towards politics. His famous diaries, begun (sadly for this history) in 1951, reveal a man who was acutely sensitive to the psychological dimension of political struggle and determined to exploit his perceptions to his own advantage. He was a master at persuasively expressing complicated arguments in simple fashion. One senses, however, a certain self-consciousness in his popular writings and speeches, a disguised condescension towards the audience in need of his instruction. Immensely capable, and aware of it, he was a bully. "When he leaves the room after a discussion of politics," wrote Martin, who knew him well, "there is an audible sigh of relief."[37]

Given Labour's majority on the Coventry City Council, the nearly exclusive working-class character of the constituency, the general mood of the country and his own formidable powers, Crossman's victory in the 1945 general election seems preordained. Local Conservatives, however, remained unimpressed, perhaps even unaware of the threat they confronted. On 23 June the editors of the *Coventry Evening Telegraph* insisted that "Labour is on the defensive," and the *Coventry Standard* agreed. Crossman's opponent, a local businessman called Harry Weston, would emerge victorious, "simply because he is Harry Weston."

Weston himself appears to have shared this view. Short on concrete proposals, his campaign was long on praise for Winston Churchill, "the most worthy statesman and leader the world has ever known." On the eve of polling day Weston summed up his qualifications for a parliamentary career: "Churchill is the man, and I am his representative in this constituency."[38]

Weston relied upon Churchill. Crossman and the Labour candidate for Coventry North, Maurice Edelman, likewise were able to call upon their party's big guns for support. Stafford Cripps spoke on their behalf on 8 June, Attlee on the 20th. In the end, however, the contest probably was determined not by national figures, popular or unpopular as they may have been, but by the contrasting approach of the two main parties to specific issues. It is hard to see how Coventry Conservatives could have hoped to win on the program they advanced.[39]

In 1945 a liberal, pragmatic wing of the Conservative party endorsed many of the social reforms carried out during the war or proposed in the famous Beveridge Plan. Not so Harry Weston. Where some Conservatives advocated the retention of at least a few of the wartime economic controls, in order to maintain "fair shares for all," Weston demanded their total abolition. "I support private enterprise," he explained. Where England's class-based educational system had moved the Conservative R. A. Butler to advocate and begin implementing a far-reaching reform of the educational system, Weston thought "every child could not be a Bachelor of Arts. To try to raise it to that standard of educational achievement would be calculated to make many children nervous wrecks." In Harry Weston, Coventry Labourites were fortunate to confront a Tory of the old school.[40]

Crossman was much less out of touch with the temper of the times. "I am a Socialist," he wrote in an essay for the 30 June *Coventry Evening Telegraph*; "I believe that whenever private profit conflicts with the good of the community, private profit must give way." Weston had spoken vaguely about free enterprise satisfying the postwar demand for housing. Crossman wrote, "Our first priority now is working-class houses of which a large number must be for rent not greater than 25 shillings." Weston's tepid response to the Butler education reforms provided Crossman with an opening he could not fail to exploit. And where Weston had sought, through his endorsement of free enterprise, to appeal to the voters' libertarian instincts, Crossman wrote, "We must make an end of direction of Labour," adding, "but extend direction of Business and Finance . . . I believe," he finished with an almost Marxian flourish, "that workmen and employers have conflicting interests."

Subsequently, Crossman was to make his reputation as a leader of Labour Left rebels demanding a more independent foreign policy. Already he discerned "signs of the formation of two blocs—the Anglo-American bloc and the Russian bloc;" and he warned "that way lies deadly danger." Britain's role as leader of a third force was clear in his mind. His country's job, he explained at an election rally on 18 June, was "to act as a bridge and a mediator between America and Russia." On 20 June he predicted that, if Labour formed the next government, Ernest Bevin would become Foreign Minister. Somewhat less presciently, he thought the former general secretary of the Transport and General Workers would make Britain the leader of the third force.[41]

Little as the election taxed him, even Crossman could not have predicted that his margin of victory would be so overwhelming. On a poll of 71 percent, he received 34,379 votes to 15,630 for Weston. A communist finished third with 3,986, and the Liberal came last, garnering a mere 2,820. In Coventry North, Maurice Edelman also romped to victory, defeating his Conservative opponent by 38,249 to 23,236. The new era of Labour predominance in Coventry had begun.

Despite its impressive victory, however, the Coventry East CLP does not emerge from the minutes of its meetings as a particularly well-organized or well-run party. There were, first of all, the usual financial problems. The party had no money for a central office. Crossman donated £30 to establish one. Six months later he was offering money so that two local members could attend a Labour summer school. Three months went by. Crossman offered £10 towards a "furniture fund." In March 1947 the party began plans for a huge "Field Day Party," the EC secretary recording hopefully that "The chance of placing the Division on a sound financial footing was at hand." There would be "darts, rings, rolling, skittles, coco-nut shies, throwing into pails, treasure hunt, fishing by magnet and Hoop La." Other attractions would include "Donkies or ponies, boxing, dancing, clowns, Punch and Judy, Marquees for refreshments, Unity Theatre." A Novelties Committee met to consider "Fancy dress, ankle shows and nobbly knees." Tickets would cost sixpence for adults, threepence for children. As it happened, this was the only social event of the year to be organized by Coventry East CLP, which may be itself a sign of the party's low morale. Perhaps the charge of admission was insufficient. The profit amounted to only £67.13s.11d. Meeting afterwards to review the situation, the EC concluded, "It was not a healthy position. Money was all going out, none was coming in." One suspects that Crossman continued paying for many of the local party's expenses.[42]

Recruitment proved to be an equally vexing problem. Despite Labour's massive electoral majorities, there were not enough party members to carry out the CLP's activities. The EC rarely attained a quorum of its members. It routinely had to suspend standing orders so that business could be conducted at all. On 12 June 1947, "as several members of the EC had failed to attend three consecutive meetings Secretary was asked to write to the comrades concerned." On 8 August, "Comrade Smythe then proposed that all affiliated bodies and trade union branches who have delegates to this division be circulated and informed that the delegates were generally not attending." On 18 September, "Comrade Rodmell gave a warning of the few willing workers doing too much, and said that a little work done thoroughly was more effective than a lot of work badly done." Four months later there still were no signs of improvement. "Comrade Ritchie [observed] that the same few faces were there to do the job whatever the business was." The malaise extended down to the wards, some of whose meetings attracted only six or seven people.[43]

The small core who carried on the mundane functions of Coventry East CLP thought that streamlined organization might facilitate their task. Normally an EC was divided into subcommittees, each with a separate responsibility, for example, finance, social activities, recruitment, or publicity. There were too few active members, however, for this system to work. Therefore, in March 1947 the EC decided to abolish subcommittees and itself address all problems. One year later it judged that "the experiment . . . had proved a failure." The old structure was reinstated. The same problems remained.[44]

The obvious solution to these difficulties was to increase membership of the party and share out the tasks among a larger group of people. It proved impossible, however, to conduct successful membership drives. In May 1946 a target of 2,000 members was set. It was not reached during the lifetime of the Attlee governments. In March 1948 only 763 men and 370 women belonged to Coventry East CLP. This compared "very poorly with the membership of other towns." The party launched another membership drive. It too accomplished little.[45]

Party members offered varying explanations for the lack of willing workers. "Comrade Mrs Wilcock" of the EC blamed "the smallness of the finance and the dull delegate meetings held." Comrade Brown, the secretary of a particularly weak ward party, All Saints, made a more telling point. "The ward . . . worked well enough at election time. Members [simply] were not keen on the usual meetings." The observation seems apt. Despite its numerous failures and difficulties, Coventry East continued to return Crossman to Parliament until his death in 1974. He never faced a significant Conservative challenge. Local Labourites may well have wondered why, given their party's massive electoral majority, it was necessary to become involved in the drudgery of local political work.[46]

In terms of membership, organization and elan Coventry East and Hornchurch Labour parties provide a striking contrast. In political terms, however, they were cut from similar cloth. Coventry, like Hornchurch, peppered the government with resolutions demanding the implementation of more far-reaching socialist reforms at home. As early as 18 December 1946 Coventry was calling for the development and articulation of "a national plan . . . which will present a cohesive view of all that the Government is aiming at in this period of office." During the convertibility crisis, when workers were exhorted to labor harder and longer than usual so that exports could balance imports, Coventry East GMC demanded the establishment of joint production committees with compulsory powers in all industries. Unless these were created "Government calls for increased production . . . are useless and would [*sic*] be ineffective." In 1949 local party leader George Hodgkinson was directed to inform Morgan Phillips that "in the minds of many the situation today is the same as it was [in 1931] and there is a feeling that Sir Stafford Cripps is going the way of Ramsay MacDonald." "The rank and file of the party are highly critical of the decisions taken," Hodgkinson warned again two years later when Gaitskell imposed the famous charges on the Health Service. And two weeks after that, "our people here want to see more 'Socialism in our time,' and any deviation from, or hesitation to pursue, a line which does not stand up to the test of Socialist accomplishment, is bound to be under suspicion." By 13 September 1951 the local man felt obliged to inform Phillips that "there is a feeling here that the spirit of the [national] Party will deteriorate unless we are pushing forward with our plan for socialism."[47]

Coventry East CLP grew increasingly disenchanted with the government's foreign policy too. The evolution of its outlook roughly paralleled that of Hornchurch DLP. It gave loyal support to the "rebellious" activities of its parliamentary representative (so long as they continued), unanimously endorsing, for example, Crossman's role in moving the amendment to the King's Speech in November 1946. With the League of Greek Democracy, it sponsored a demonstration on 2 May 1948 protesting the government's policies in Greece. It maintained friendly relations with the British–Soviet Society. Its opposition to Bevinism may even have outstripped Crossman's. By 1949, despite cold-war tensions, it believed the Foreign Minister had become so estranged from Labour's traditional outlook that he "should be advised by a council of five from the elected representatives of the people."[48]

Like Hornchurch, too, Coventry East Labour Party contained right-wing and centrist elements which often managed to block the Left. Thus, at an EC meeting of 8 January 1948 which had been called to discuss an anti-communist circular from head office, "Comrade Roberts . . . denounced the members who used the wide term 'fellow travellers,' explaining that many who were on 'left' of the Movement do not accept Communism." In answer, "Comrade Smythe" reminded members that communist leader Harry Pollitt advocated "organized sabotage of the Government's work," on the orders of the Cominform. Faced with this conflict, the meeting decided to postpone any decision on the controversial circular.[49]

Coventry East and West Labour parties published a weekly newspaper, the *Coventry Tribune* (named perhaps in honor of the left-wing journal founded by Bevan, Cripps and Strauss before the war), which also provides access to the views of the local rank and file. The newspaper's official line was slightly critical of the government and adamantly opposed to the "hard" Labour Left. Contributions from local activists, however, expressed a variety of attitudes. Their columns suggest that while many were proud of the Labour government, they held it to a strict socialist standard of their own measure and often found it lacking.

Some in the Coventry Labour Party conceived of their project in the most exalted terms. "S.E.H." thought, on 12 October 1946, that "the greatest task which confronts us is . . . to make ourselves worthy to live in a world of free men and women." Labour must abolish "undue acquisitiveness," which he likened to "a fever which feeds on itself and makes its victim miserable." Alderman W. E. Halliwell expressed similar sentiments in more prosaic terms. "We have a Labour Government pledged to a 100% Socialist policy," he wrote on 26 October 1946. Its task was to "organis[e] the country as a single class for the purpose of owning and controlling all the sources of production." But Labour's aim also was world peace. Here local Labourites could play a special role. "What an opportunity there is for citizens who first suffered 'Coventration' to be foremost in the demand for the destruction of all existing atomic weapons," wrote the vicar of St Thomas's church on 18 January 1947. He was planning a meeting which would demonstrate that on this issue there was "unity on the Left." "Cooperation has been promised from the Trades Council, the Labour Party, the Communist Party, the Society of Friends, the Fellowship of Reconciliation, the Christian Social Action Group and a number of individual persons as well." When the Coventry Labour Left opposed the communists, it eschewed the crude terms of Councillor Newman of Hornchurch. "I have never been in favour of excluding the Communists from the Labour Party. In fact, I have worked with them in Glasgow and in Dundee," another alderman and man of the cloth, the Reverend R. Lee, recalled in an article printed during the storm over the Nenni telegram. But he objected to the failure of his "Communist friends" to subject their own party and the policies of Russia to the same critical scrutiny they reserved for Labour and Great Britain. "Stalin and Molotov are not plastercast saints."[50]

Perhaps above all, one senses in the writings of these left-wing CLP activists a certain suspicion of the "men at the top" and an insistence upon democratic practices everywhere. As the local AEU leader Ernie Roberts put it, in an exhortation to Coventry Labourites cited in the Introduction to this volume, "it is our joint responsibility to see that this Government of ours succeeds. Let us give it drive and boldness through resolutions urging that the things we at the bottom know to be necessary should be done." These egalitarian and democratic sentiments were carried over into attitudes towards foreign affairs. "We [sh]ould no longer be living on the cheap at the expense of some exploited community," another activist wrote. "We [sh]ould voluntarily give up being a Great Power." And he added, "I do not think this would worry a genuine Socialist; it would mean revolution. But perhaps this is what the Labour Party is trying to avoid."[51]

From these writings in the *Coventry Tribune*, and from the minutes of meetings of Coventry East and Hornchurch CLPs as well as from the protest resolutions they sent to Morgan Phillips, it appears that left-wing constituency activists shared a general outlook. Although they were proud of the government's accomplishments, they were deeply disturbed by its failure to implement more drastic socialist measures at home or to develop a foreign policy less dependent upon the United States. Local conditions were not decisive factors in the shaping of their general political attitudes.

Local conditions, however, could be crucial in other respects, and could have wide repercussions. Hornchurch was a marginal seat for Labour. Therefore, perhaps, local Labourites felt the need for continual political activity. They attended ward meetings and vied for the honor of membership on the EC and GMC. Recruitment drives were successful, because prospective members might be made to feel that their participation in the party could make a difference, not merely on the local but even on the national scene. In Hornchurch, success at the general election must have seemed to depend directly upon the strength of the local party. This was not the case in Coventry East.

There is another striking disparity between the two constituencies. Because of his relatively weak position, Bing felt obliged to attend Hornchurch functions and generally to maintain a high profile in the constituency. Because he had continually to keep an eye on his home base, he was prevented from gaining wider recognition. Crossman, however, could always count upon an enormous parliamentary majority. Possibly this explains why he practically ignored demands placed upon him by his local party while carving out a national reputation through his journalistic and parliamentary activities. The minutes of meetings of Coventry East CLP reveal almost constant tension between it and the MP. On 27 March 1946 "Much discussion took place on the need for R. H. Crossman to hold meetings within the Division. Some discontent was expressed." On 5 June 1946 "It was decided that the MP make a special point of a mid-week meeting as soon as possible with a full delegate attendance." Even two years later the tension had not been resolved. On 8 April 1948 the EC "deplore[d] the attitude of the MP, Dick Crossman," because he had failed to participate in their membership drive.

Such complaints weighed little in the scheme of things. Crossman remained with Coventry East CLP until his death. Despite the isolated machinations of Councillor Newman, Bing remained with Hornchurch until 1955, when he was defeated in the general election. There were, however, constituencies which wound up repudiating their left-wing MPs, and we must turn now to examine them.

V

The evidence so far suggests that left-wing CLPs strove earnestly and seriously to alter government policies. They loyally supported their MPs, who, likewise, sought to push the government in a more socialist direction. The fate of the ILP, the Socialist League and Common Wealth, however, was a grim reminder of what secession from Labour was likely to mean. Knowledge of history imposed strict limits upon the activities of dissident CLPs and parliamentary Members alike.

A handful of MPs proved willing to defy these boundaries, courting expulsion. Not surprisingly, however, their constituency parties did not relish the political wilderness. It is one thing for an individual MP to take grave political risks, another for a party, composed of disparate members, to do so. Even the most celebrated of the expelled MPs, Konni Zilliacus, was unable to bring his party with him, despite having many defenders in his constituency, the PLP and elsewhere, and despite his formidable powers as a propagandist.

In Gateshead (Gateshead East after October 1948) Zilliacus represented a safe Labour seat, much like Coventry East. Unlike that constituency's CLP, however, the local party experienced little difficulty in attracting rank-and-file activists to share mundane political tasks. The party "maintained a full-time agent, carried on extensive publicity and ... finished with a favourable balance." It helped to subsidize a "People's Theatre" where the "Progressive Players" performed. It produced a lively, attractive newspaper, the *Gateshead Herald*. Here is an index of the strength of the local party. Even its newspaper was a financial success. At the 1946 annual meeting of the local party it reported a financial surplus of £31.12s.8d.[52]

Zilliacus's main interest was foreign affairs. He appears, however, to have been an assiduous and effective constituency MP. In February 1946 he claimed, already, to have "dealt with about 500 cases of local people seeking advice or assistance." A year later the secretary of the Gateshead CLP, R. G. Purcell, reported that Zilliacus had "received constituents on no fewer than 23 days in the course of the year, a very high average." In April 1949 the president, two vice-presidents and secretary of the local party testified that Zilliacus had "held more meetings in Gateshead since 1945 than all the previous MPs who ever sat for the Borough." Perhaps to his surprise, Zilliacus discovered that he enjoyed this aspect of his work as much as any other. "There is something satisfying and real about helping those in trouble—that is the direct, human, personal side of an MP's job."[53]

Unfortunately, however, Zilliacus was a stormy petrel, a very different personality from Crossman or Bing. He was less a politician than they, more an egocentric crusader. Given his views and his penchant for expressing them with maximum publicity and minimum tact, perhaps it was inevitable that he would create dissension within his CLP, well organized and financed though it was. No doubt, discontent bubbled beneath the surface for some time. In January 1948 the Ravensworth Miners' Lodge, which was affiliated to the Gateshead Labour Party, gave it public voice. "The members desire Mr Zilliacus to note that they loyally support the policy of the Labour Government, and are dissatisfied with the constant attacks he is making against the Government's policy." On 13 February the Gateshead Labour Party and Trades Council met to debate an anti-Zilliacus resolution submitted by the miners. The vote was 45 to 5 against it. "This proves," said Mr J. J. Irvine, party vice-chairman, "that the Gateshead Labour Party and Trades Council has the utmost confidence in Mr Zilliacus and in the course he is pursuing."[54]

Did it really? Sam Watson, the NUM representative on the trade-union section of the NEC, retained a strong connection with north-eastern coalworkers, still living among them in Durham. Watson took a particular interest in Gateshead affairs, possibly because of the "personal hostility" that Zilliacus believed Watson bore him. Watson wrote to Morgan Phillips:

> It is true that Mr Zilliacus receives the support of the majority of the members who attend Gateshead Trades and Labour Council, but these are small in number and in my opinion by no means reflect the feelings of the majority of people in Gateshead.

Against this we may set the recollections of several veteran Gateshead Labourites, who claim that Zilliacus was the sole local MP ever consistently to attract standing-room-only crowds to his "reports-back" from Westminster. In a public letter circulated at the time, the officers of Gateshead East CLP asserted that "at each of such meetings he has almost invariably received a unanimous Vote of Confidence from the constituents."[55]

In Chapter 5 we traced the series of events which culminated in the February 1949 decision of the NEC to deny Zilliacus renomination in Gateshead, despite the unanimous recommendation of the elections subcommittee that he receive it. Gateshead East CLP mirrored this division of opinion. Interviewed by a local reporter, one Alderman McCretton reminded local readers that he had "always said that Mr Zilliacus did not represent the Party either in Gateshead or in the House of Commons. I think his views are much too 'left' for the people of Gateshead." Another councillor, however, assured readers that Zilliacus would be reselected.[56]

At this point a majority of the local party supported their embattled MP. It fired off angry protests to Morgan Phillips. In a circular letter it apprised all CLPs of the situation, arguing that "the action of the National Executive is dictatorial and un-British, and unworthy of this great Labour Movement," and warning that "the Gateshead East Division could justly and easily have been your division." The aim was to rally support for Zilliacus at Labour's annual conference, which was scheduled for June. On the eve of the conference it approved, by a three-to-one margin, a resolution "unhesitatingly reaffirming wholehearted confidence" in its parliamentary representative.[57]

As we have seen, the conference proved a grievous disappointment to Zilliacus and his supporters. Far from overturning the NEC decision against him, it refused even to let him speak in his own defense. If Zilliacus wished to continue his parliamentary career, he would have to win re-election without official Labour support in the next general election.

Zilliacus accepted the challenge. His local party could not back him, but perhaps it would not oppose him either. "It would be impertinent of me . . . to suggest what you should do," Zilliacus wrote, ingenuously, to the leader of the Gateshead Labour group, Alderman Christopher Esther, in a letter which he asked to be read aloud to the next full party meeting:

I, for my part, will do nothing to split the Party and would regard it as a calamity if it did split. That is why I do not ask any of you to come and help me. That is why, too, I hope some of you will not try to put up a candidate against me.

This appeal did not fall upon deaf ears. When the NEC instructed Gateshead East CLP to prepare to nominate another parliamentary candidate, the party's GMC offered passive resistance, refusing to convene the required meeting. "Finally, the local Secretary convened the special meeting when [national agent] R. T. Windle made it clear that the Regional Organiser would be instructed to convene [one] if it was not convened by the Secretary." Esther, a strong Zilliacus supporter, presided at this gathering and voted with twenty-two other delegates who objected to putting up anyone against their former Labour Member. As Esther put it afterwards:

If I am to be put in a position that means that the lifetime I have devoted to the Labour movement has to be thrown to one side merely to satisfy the National

Executive Committee of the Labour Party which, irrespective of the consequences, will bitterly oppose Mr Zilliacus, then I am not playing their game.

On Tuesday 23 August he resigned as party chairman, in order to devote himself to Zilliacus's campaign for re-election. A wider split seemed likely. "At least three other members of the council will quit to join Mr Zilliacus—maybe more," an alderman predicted: "People don't want to show just now what's in their mind, but when the East Division Labour candidate has been selected, then the Labour group will divide. There is a strong pro-Zilly feeling, you can't get away from that." The Ravensworth miners notwithstanding, trade-union delegates shared this sentiment. "Several" were reported to have joined Zilliacus's campaign.[58]

Zilliacus launched his crusade to the enthusiastic applause of an estimated seven hundred supporters in Gateshead Town Hall on 15 September. Councillor Esther was in the chair. Afterwards he released a statement to the press. It brimmed with confidence:

> We received a substantial number of written promises of support for the Zilliacus campaign from well known local members of the Labour Party . . . and we do not now anticipate any difficulty whatsoever in establishing within the East Division not only a firm but a very live and virile organisation that will actively support Mr Zilliacus in all the five wards.

Already Councillors McConway and Canham had joined Esther in support of the former Labour Member. Two prominent Gateshead Labourites quickly followed, Edward Bunyan, secretary of a local NUR branch and its delegate on the Trades Council for twenty-eight years, and W. Stuart Blacklock, a member of the CLP executive committee.[59]

Thus Zilliacus managed to retain the support of important local Labourites. He had natural advantages which other Labour dissidents were unlikely to possess, an international reputation (Paul Robeson sang at one of his election rallies), great rhetorical gifts and boundless energy. Moreover, in Arthur S. Moody, the eventual official Labour candidate to oppose him, he did not face a particularly formidable foe. Yet now the perils of pushing opposition to government policies to their extreme if logical conclusion became evident. Once a majority of the local party had made the difficult decision to side with Transport House, Zilliacus's enemies took it over entirely. They were prepared to do whatever was necessary to defeat him. Previously, Zilliacus had been given the Town Hall without charge when he wished to address local electors. Now he would have to pay a fee. This was petty, if effective, against a candidate without great financial resources. More ominous, perhaps, was the punishment meted out to Zilliacus's vulnerable local supporters. For example, Esther's daughter had volunteered her home as campaign headquarters for Zilliacus. She lived in council housing. The town council, now dominated by Labourites hostile to Zilliacus, voted to evict her. Esther himself was was denied readmission to the Labour Party when he applied for it after the general election. Even the NEC was not so vindictive to Zilliacus.

The greatest obstacle which Zilliacus faced, however, was the massive, unswerving loyalty which local Labourites felt towards the national party. Perhaps no backbench Labour MP had a local following great enough to carry an independent campaign against an official Labour candidate. Zilliacus won the support of several important local activists. These were the kind of men and women who imparted a radical flavor to many a CLP. They were the ones who sought to pressure the national party to implement more far-reaching socialist measures. Some were willing to follow a "hard" Left MP out of the party. In the end, however, most were not. What such people were best able to do, one suspects, is get out the vote for Labour. Without their enthusiastic services, Zilliacus's Labour opponent, Moody, barely beat the Conservative (by 1,719 votes). They could not, however, elect a left-wing candidate against Labour opposition. In the 1950 general election Zilliacus garnered a mere 5,001 votes.

VI

A similar series of events, with a similar conclusion, occurred in Finsbury, where the Labour Member was John Platts Mills. As we have seen, Platts Mills was expelled from the Labour Party in April 1948, after his highly visible role in the affair of the Nenni telegram. Platts Mills was not so well known as Zilliacus, and he had nothing like the same claim upon the affections of the PLP. If anything, however, his constituency supporters were more numerous and better ensconced in Finsbury CLP than were the local supporters of Zilliacus. Yet this was not enough to save him.

Finsbury CLP was unlike any of the constituency parties we have examined. It was located in a predominantly working-class London district. It was considered to be a safe Labour seat. The party itself, however, appears to have been run by middle-class members, including the wife of the Marxist economist and open communist Maurice Dobb. "She is a very active and enthusiastic person," the London Labour Party organizer J. W. Raisin reported. "But there is, in my opinion, an element of doubt regarding her political alignment."[60]

In the event, when the NEC moved against Platts Mills, his GMC "approved the decision without dissent." Twenty-seven local councillors, however, signed a letter of protest printed in local newspapers. In short, as in Gateshead, the local party was deeply divided over the expulsion of its parliamentary member. The existence of a split was confirmed at a special meeting of Finsbury Labour Party's EC on 10 May. The twenty-seven were asked "to undertake to refrain from supporting John Platts Mills at any meeting or in any other way," and they were warned that if this undertaking was not given they too might be expelled. The president of the local party, a Mr Cliffe, replied on behalf of the rebel councillors. Then, on a roll-call vote, "only one of [the twenty-seven] was willing to give the undertaking, and even in that instance it was not clearly given." At this point Raisin, who also was present, intervened. He suggested that "Those who supported Platts Mills should confine themselves to doing so within the Party . . . and the EC should modify its demands by substituting the words 'in public' for the words 'at any meeting or in any other way.' " This formula proved more acceptable. After promising, also, to consider seriously whether he might recommend to the NEC that Platts Mills should be allowed to address Labour's annual conference, another roll-call vote was taken. It resulted "on the first count as follows:— To accept the EC's requirement (answer 'Yes') . . . 12; Not to accept (answer 'No') . . . 10. Before the incident closed, two of those voting 'No' asked leave to alter their vote." At this point, "Mr Cliffe . . . addressed the Executive, conveying the terms of a letter of resignation from the office of president (but not as a member) as a protest against the foreign and domestic policy of the Government. He then left the meeting." Raisin then added a personal note in his report to the NEC:

> The Party in Finsbury has been very badly shaken . . . there is a great deal of unhappiness over the Platts Mills affair. He is generally well liked as an individual, and there is reluctance to proceed against him even on the part of some who dislike his political views.

Raisin therefore recommended that Platts Mills be given an opportunity to speak at the annual conference. No matter how persuasive the speech, he reasoned, it was unlikely to convince a majority of delegates to reinstate him in the PLP, and it would help smooth matters over in Finsbury.[61]

Platts Mills was not allowed to speak, however, and the division remained. Eight councillors had been defiant at the 10 May meeting. They continued to support the former Labour Member afterwards. Asked to desist, at another party meeting on 15 July, each refused, whereupon all were expelled. Immediately they applied for readmission to the party. On 16 September, Raisin and assistant national agent A. L. Williams attended the meeting called to consider this application. "I formed the impression," Raisin reported, "that several of the expelled people were fairly innocent but that one, a member of the ETU, was almost certainly a Communist." Williams's report was more detailed. He thought five of the eight "were aware that they could not continue associating with Mr Platts Mills . . . and expect to remain members of the Labour Party." He recommended that they should be readmitted to the party after 1 November "on giving an undertaking in writing to dissociate [themselves] from Mr John Platts Mills's activities."[62]

Meanwhile a by-election for the Finsbury Borough Council proved decisive for Platts Mills's relationship with the CLP and his rebel supporters. Zilliacus, had he been confronted with such a situation, would have campaigned hard for the Labour candidate. During the 1950 general election he consistently urged voters to cast their ballots for Labour in every constituency but his own. Platts Mills, however, supported a communist. "This action seems to have at last convinced some of his former supporters exactly where he stands politically," the Labour agent who conducted the campaign reported back to headquarters. The five noted by Williams agreed to sign the paragraph repudiating Platts Mills. The by-election, however, had weakened their position. When the ballots were counted, it was found that the Labour candidate received 442, the Tory 218, the Communist 96. The Labour loyalists must have taken these results as a vindication of their own tough anti-Platts-Mills stance. Moreover, as in Gateshead, they probably did not relish the return of the rebel Member's supporters to the local council, which they now completely dominated. According to the assistant London organizer, Jim Cattermole, many loyalists "said that they were not prepared to have [the rebels] back in the Party" under any circumstances. At a meeting of 3 November, Finsbury Labour Party declined to readmit them. It took the intervention of R. T. Windle, Labour's national organizer, to bring the local party around.[63]

Like Zilliacus, Platts Mills campaigned during the 1950 general election as a Labour (Independent) candidate. But he had squandered the considerable sympathy which his expulsion had originally generated on his behalf. Of the twenty-seven councillors who had signed the public letter protesting the action of the NEC, only three refused to repudiate him in the end. No matter the political weight they carried, it could never swing a majority of electors behind him. Moreover, in the general redistricting which took place nationwide during 1948–9, Finsbury had been combined in a new division with Shoreditch. The sitting Labour Member for the latter, E. Thurtle, possessed a massive majority. He received the nomination and in the general election increased his majority, receiving not only the usual tally from Shoreditch, but many Labour votes from Finsbury as well. Testimony to the energy of Platts Mills's supporters, their candidate received 7,602 votes in what was, after all, a hopeless struggle. The Conservative, who finished second, secured a total of only 7,879.

VII

This survey of the Labour Left in the constituencies during the Attlee years underlines both the extent and the limits of their disillusionment with the government. On the one hand, it was deeper than usually has been thought and deserves to be taken more seriously. On the other, it was not so profound that it led CLPs to reconsider their affiliation to the national Labour Party.

The evidence may also suggest a possible explanation for the upsurge of Labour Left strength in the constituencies during this period. Party membership increased enormously during these years, as is well known:

Year	Individual membership
1945	487,047
1946	643,345
1947	608,487
1948	629,025
1949	729,624
1950	908,161
1951	876,275

A plausible interpretation of these figures is that men and women, radicalized by the war, joined Labour, believing it to be the left-wing party most likely to achieve

"Socialism in our time." Prewar constitutional reforms made socialist agitation feasible within the CLPs. And the fate of the ILP warned rank-and-file activists against leaving Labour, no matter how disillusioned they became with the compromises pursued by the leaders.[64]

The Labour Left had become strong in the CLPs well before the famous 1952 annual conference, when it astonished Britain by electing six out of seven Bevanites to the constituencies section of the NEC. In fact, it should now be clear that the left-wing movement of the 1950s, which was called Bevanism, had its roots in the preceding era and, indeed, is inexplicable without reference to it. Hugh Gaitskell's 1951 decision to place charges on dentures and spectacles previously provided *gratis* by the National Health Service, so that Britain could afford the larger role in Korea envisioned for it by the Americans, galvanized activists in the CLPs, already primed for action by what they considered to be the government's near betrayal of socialist promises made in 1945. Previous chapters have shown why the CLPs were likely to discover allies among trade unionists and prominent intellectuals as well, and among Labour Left MPs. When Bevan resigned from the Cabinet, he helped to focus the energies of a broad-based left-wing protest movement which had been developing, in fits and starts, since 1945. The events surrounding what was, perhaps, the most momentous resignation in Labour history represent the climax of a process which had been unfolding for more than half a decade. We turn, now, to that resignation.

Notes and References

1   For the agitation to strengthen CLP influence, see Ben Pimlott, *Labour and the Left in the 1930s* (Cambridge, 1977), pp. 111–40, and Jonathan Wood, "The Labour Left in the constituencies," D.Phil. thesis, Warwick University, 1982.

2   For more detailed discussion of Common Wealth, Mikardo's 1944 resolution and the general growth of radical sentiment during the war, see especially Angus Calder, *The People's War* (London, 1971), and his 1968 Sussex University D.Phil. thesis, "The Common Wealth Party, 1942–45;" Labour Party, Morgan Phillips papers, CLP files, Cornwall West Labour Party, Winifred Berry to Morgan Phillips, 19 July 1945.

3   Kenneth O. Morgan, *Labour in Power, 1945–51* (Oxford, 1984), pp. 70, 93.

4   Labour Party, Holborn and St Pancras South Labour Party, minutes of GMC meetings, 25 January 1951.

5   Phillips papers, CLP files, Bristol North-East, J. K. Browne to Phillips, 26 September 1950; ibid., Manchester (Stretford), J. E. Parkinson to Phillips, 6 July 1950.

6   Ibid., Epping, Tom West to Phillips, 20 June 1950; ibid., Newbury, Aileen Spiller to Phillips, 4 February 1952; ibid., Saffron Walden, W. F. Quinn to Phillips, 18 October 1949; ibid., Birmingham (Aston), F. E. York to Phillips, March 1952.

7   Ibid., New Forest and Christchurch, Mrs K. Watson to Phillips, 30 August 1945; ibid., Chelsea, P. R. D. Shufeldt to Phillips, 17 September 1945.

8   Ibid., Spelthorne, Mrs F. R. Niyogi to Phillips, 23 September 1945; ibid., Aireborough, N. C. Wilby to Phillips, 8 October 1946; ibid., Bridgwater, E. A. Milton to Phillips, 3 December 1946.

9   Ibid., Epsom and Ewell, V. Ullman to Phillips, 9 November 1946; ibid., Southport, P. Cameron to Phillips, 12 June 1950.

10 Ibid., Cowes, L. Tilbury to Phillips, 12 December 1946; ibid., Rushcliffe, G. Beeby to Phillips, 9 December 1948; ibid., Wycombe, C. J. Bloomfield to Phillips and Bevin, 8 November 1949; ibid., Holborn and St Pancras, W. Halford to Phillips, 30 November 1950; ibid., Forth, S. Fraser to Phillips, 3 July 1950. This resolution was later withdrawn.

11 Ibid., North Lewisham resolution quoted by secretary of Sunderland Labour Party, G. Foster to Phillips, 15 January 1951.

12 Ibid., Wickham West, W. D. Garnett to Phillips, 2 February 1948; ibid., Coventry, George Hodgkinson to Phillips, 11 April 1949; ibid., Kingston, date and author of this message to Phillips unavailable.

13 Wood, "The Labour Left in the constituencies," p. 325; Phillips papers, Uxbridge Labour Party file.

14 *Hornchurch Official Guide* (1939), pages not numbered.

15 *Illustrated Hornchurch Chronicle*, 6 June 1946, 2 May 1946.

16 The Greater London Record Office holds minute books of meetings of Hornchurch Divisional Labour Party's EC and GMC and of Hornchurch Town Ward Labour Party EC.

17 Ibid., Town Ward EC, 5 June 1946.

18 *Hornchurch and Upminster News*, 8 May 1947; *Hornchurch, Dagenham and Romford Times*, 5 December 1945.

19 Information on Bing gleaned from Hornchurch newspapers cited above.

20 Information on Twigger gleaned from *Hornchurch and Upminster News*, 8 May 1947.

21 *The Times*, 3 July 1945.

22 *Hornchurch, Dagenham and Romford Times*, 13 June 1945.

23 Ibid., 13 and 20 June 1945.

24 Ibid., 1 August 1945; *Romford, Hornchurch, Upminster Recorder*, 3 August 1945.

25 *Hornchurch, Dagenham and Romford Times*, 29 August 1945; Hale diary, 9 January 1950.

26 Hornchurch Labour Party, GMC, 2 August 1945; EC, 19 December 1946; GMC 29 January 1948.

27 Ibid., GMC 24 June 1948; EC, 16 July 1947.

28 *Hornchurch and Upminster News*, 1 July 1949.

29 Hornchurch Labour Party, EC, 24 April 1948; GMC 29 April 1948, 24 March 1949.

30 Ibid., GMC 24 April 1947, 22 March 1951; Annual General Meeting, 29 June 1950; GMC, 23 October 1948.

31 Ibid., GMC, 28 September 1950, 23 November 1950.

32 Ibid., GMC, November 1946; AGM, 3 March 1947; GMC 25 September 1947, 22 March 1951.

33 Ibid., GMC, 8 February 1951, 29 November 1951; Town Ward EC, 13 September 1951.

34 See Fred Smith, *Coventry: Six Hundred Years of Municipal Life* (Coventry, 1945), and B. Lancaster and A. Mason (eds.), *Life and Labour in a Twentieth Century City: The Experience of Coventry* (Coventry, 1986).

35 *Coventry Evening Telegraph*, 4 July 1945.

36 Ibid., 9 June 1945.

37 Sussex University, Kingsley Martin papers, Box 25, file 5.

38 *Coventry Standard*, 9 June 1945; *Coventry Evening Telegraph*, 4 July 1945.

39 See the local newspapers for those dates for their speeches.

40 Ibid., 27 June 1945; *Coventry Evening Telegraph*, 27 June 1945.

41 *Coventry Evening Telegraph*, 9 June, 18 June, 20 June 1945.

42 Modern Records Centre, Warwick University, minute books of Coventry East CLP: EC, June 1946; GMC, 15 January 1947; EC, 8 May 1947, 23 March 1947, 13 November 1947.

43 Ibid., EC, 12 June 1947, 8 August 1947; GMC, 18 September 1947; special meeting of Coventry East and West Labour parties, 8 January 1948; EC, 28 May 1947.

44 Ibid., second annual meeting of Coventry East CLP, 29 February 1948.

45   Ibid.

46   Ibid., first annual meeting of East Coventry Divisional Labour Party, 9 March 1947; EC, 28 May 1947.

47   Phillips papers, CLP files, Coventry, George Hodgkinson to Phillips, 11 April 1949, 22 June 1951, 6 July 1951.

48   Coventry East CLP, GMC 18 February 1948; EC, 11 December 1947; GMC 10 March 1949.

49   Coventry East CLP, GMC, 20 November 1946.

50   *Coventry Tribune*, 15 May 1948.

51   Ibid., 20 September 1947, 1 November 1947, 17 May 1947.

52   *Gateshead Herald*, March 1946.

53   Ibid., February 1946, April 1947; Gateshead Public Library, Konni Zilliacus papers, Gateshead Central Labour Party and Trades Council to "Secretaries of all Divisional Labour Parties," 25 April 1949; *Gateshead Herald*, May 1946.

54   *Gateshead Post*, 23 January 1948, 13 February 1948.

55   See Konni Zilliacus, *Why I Was Expelled* (Gateshead, 1949), p. 40; Phillips papers, "Lost Sheep" file, Sam Watson to Phillips, 22 February 1949; private information; Zilliacus papers, Gateshead Central Labour Party and Trades Council to "Secretaries," 25 April 1949.

56   *Gateshead Post*, 25 February 1949.

57   Zilliacus papers, Gateshead Central Labour Party and Trades Council to "Secretaries," 25 April 1949; *Gateshead Post*, 27 May 1949.

58   Both the letter and report of the meeting are filed in unsorted boxes, part of the Phillips papers, NEC, 28 May 1952, "Enquiry on the appeal of Alderman G. C. Esther against the refusal of the Gateshead Central Labour Party and Trades Council to accept him into membership;" *Gateshead Post*, 16 September 1949, 26 August 1948.

59   *Gateshead Post*, 16 September 1949.

60   Labour Party, J. W. Raisin papers, J.W.R./Org. 47/56, Finsbury, 21 April 1947.

61   Ibid., J.W.R./Org. 48/31, Finsbury, 10 May 1948.

62   Ibid., J.W.R./Org. 48/71, Finsbury, 16 September 1948; Labour Party unsorted files, Phillips papers, Finsbury Labour Party, 5 October 1948.

63   Modern Records Centre, Warwick University, Jim Cattermole papers, MSS9/3/12/91, 26–7 October 1948; Labour Party, unsorted files, Phillips papers, Windle to Helen Stubbs, 16 November 1948.

64   Figures from Wood, "The Labour Left in the constituencies."

8

The Climax of the Labour Left

DURING THE LAST year and a half of Labour government (from March 1950 until October 1951), Labour Left disenchantment with administration policies was as profound, and as broadly based, as ever before. The dangers of open rebellion were more grave, however. The general election of February 1950 left Labour with a wafer-thin majority of six in the House. In order to carry legislation, the government usually needed every Member to enter the lobby on its behalf. Cabinet ministers and backbenchers alike had to turn up and vote, no matter what their health and regardless of constituency or other obligations, or they had to make sure ahead of time that their presence was not crucial. Under such circumstances, any serious defection of Labour votes would lead, almost inevitably, to the defeat of the government. Thus this period poses the dilemma of the parliamentary Labour Left more clearly, perhaps, than any other.[1]

Outside Parliament, left-wing Labourites confronted equally delicate calculations. Trade unionists of the Left, for example, felt deeply about the wage freeze, inflation, and the undemocratic aspects of Labour's nationalization program. They feared, however, that mass trade-union agitation to abolish them might result in the replacement of the Labour government by a Conservative one even less sympathetic to their outlook. CLP activists were inhibited by similar fears, except perhaps in constituencies where there was no sitting Labour Member and where local Labourites may have thought they had little to lose. In general, however, constraints upon the Labour Left were more powerful during the second Attlee government than they had been during the first.

For this reason it is all the more notable that the period saw the gravest Labour Left rebellion of the postwar era, one which reached, finally, into the Cabinet itself. In late April 1951 the Minister of Labour and former Minister of Health, Aneurin Bevan, the President of the Board of Trade, Harold Wilson, and a junior Minister in Supply, John Freeman, resigned from the government because they could not agree to charging the National Health Service in order to help pay for the rearmament demanded by the USA. Their position, which they claimed to be in defense of socialist principles at home and a foreign policy less dependent upon the alliance with America, essentially recapitulated the critique of the government which the Labour Left had been developing since at least November 1946. The resignations mark the climax of a process of disenchantment which it has been the burden of this book to trace.

At the same time the resignations represented a new beginning for the Labour Left, and not merely because in Aneurin Bevan Labour's left wing finally obtained a charismatic leader of international stature. Lines were drawn in the great clash between Bevan and Chancellor of the Exchequer Hugh Gaitskell (who took the lead in demanding the new health charges) which have divided the Labour Party ever since and are visible even today. This chapter is intended to show why 1950–1 were watershed years for the Labour Left and for the Labour Party as a whole.

II

The general election of 1950 was not as dramatic as that of 1945, and historians have not lavished as much attention upon it. During the campaign Labour stood proudly on its record. Attlee's government, its supporters often claimed, was nearly unique for having carried out the promises made in 1945. If returned again it would continue to advance sober, responsible reforms. If the Conservatives won, however, they would abandon the attempt to guide the economy and instead give market forces free reign. The entire Labour Party, including left-wing CLPs and trade unions, agreed that Conservative victory would be a disaster. This meant, as Dick Beech put it in the *Chemical Worker* for February 1950, that "although we have from time to time criticised the government . . . nevertheless we urge every member to vote LABOUR."

Labour Left candidates generally accepted the party's election strategy. All, even the most critical, proudly endorsed the government's social legislation. "There has been more genuine freedom and real opportunity under a Labour Government than ever before," Warbey informed the voters of Luton. "By full employment, by food subsidies, by better pensions, family allowances and social security measures, wealth is more evenly shared and millions of families enjoy a security that they have never known before," Ashley Bramall explained in Bexley. But this was, after all, only what Labour had promised. "Our 1945 programme has been fully implemented," boasted Ronald Chamberlain in Norwood. "I can truly say I have been a member of a Government who in its first term of office with power carried out the whole of the pledges made to the electorate," Wilfred Vernon reported in Dulwich.[2]

Occasionally Labour Left frustrations and aspirations for a more far-reaching program surfaced. The embittered Laski, who died only a month after the February election, considered the party manifesto "too vague, it has little dignity in utterance, it has not a single memorable phrase." Cole, at the fourth Buscot conference, thought that the "Labour Party has no programme that is worth a straw, except defence of the Welfare State." Equally worrisome to the Labour Left was the threat of a conflict with the Soviet Union which the government was doing too little to avert. "Nothing could be more disastrous for this country than . . . another war," Bing warned the voters of Hornchurch. "I am utterly opposed to war-mongering from whatever quarter it may come." Or, as James Hudson put it in Ealing North, "The making of new and better economic arrangements . . . is a better way to understanding than threats of military power."[3]

Crossman thought that "the leading tacticians of both sides" had blurred deliberately the "sharp choice between Socialism and a return to private enterprise" which voters desired. Consequently the Labour Left, which emphasized differences between the two main parties, would fare relatively well. It did. Among the "Keep Left" group, Millington, Bruce and Swingler were not returned, but they had played relatively minor roles. The rest were successful, including Foot, who had faced a real challenge at Devonport from Churchill's son, Randolph. Bing, on a remarkable poll of 84 percent, squeaked past his Conservative opponent by less than 2,000 votes out of a total of more than 55,000 cast. Driberg and Emrys Hughes won their bids for re-election. But the persistent "hard" Labour Left critics were devastated. None of the Labour Independent Group were returned; Hutchinson, Platts Mills and Solley lost their deposits. Tom Braddock and Ronald Chamberlain, "hard" Labour Members of Socialist Fellowship, likewise were defeated. This was to have an effect later. When the government's approach to the Korean War roused the Labour Left to renewed protest, the original "hard" Labour Left had no representation in Westminster.[4]

III

Labour renewed its tenuous hold on power on 23 February 1950. The inhibiting effects of its slim majority were immediately apparent. Crossman acknowledged in the *Sunday Pictorial* on 5 March that "in such a dangerous passage there can be only one pilot," and predicted that the Labour Left would be "far too shrewd to rock the boat." On the BBC he seemed to rule out extra-parliamentary agitation. Effective political work was best performed "behind the scenes, in committee rooms upstairs, or even over a glass of beer." For a moment it seemed that the Labour Left in the trade unions would be equally circumspect. In *New Dawn* the USDAW-sponsored MP for Jarrow, Ernest Fernyhough, wrote that "we expect our members to back the Government for all they are worth, and we in USDAW must play our part." The new attitude did not go unnoticed or unappreciated. From Labour's right wing Tony Crosland paid tribute to the "morally unassailable position" of those on the Labour Left who had "consider[ed] *all* the consequences" of opposing the government and then had fallen into line.[5]

In the PLP there were Labour Left elements which seemed more anxious to preserve the government than the government itself, if that were possible. In March the "Keep Left" group considered a proposal from Barbara Castle that, in light of Labour's tiny majority, the group should

provide the spearhead of Government support in the House. Members agreed, however, that the questions on which they had been pressing last session could not be dropped, though they would have to be pursued within the confines of the party and not publicly.

In May, Leslie Hale, himself a former Liberal, wrote to Morrison broaching the possibility of a Lib–Lab pact. In November, Hale, Michael Foot and J. P. W. Mallalieu (all of the "Keep Left" group, and all former Liberals) met with three Liberal MPs, Lloyd George's daughter Megan, Foot's brother Dingle and Edgar Granville. If agreement could be reached, Hale reported, the former party of Gladstone

> could guarantee to the Labour Whips that Liberals did not vote against the Government on any vital issue without previous ample notice of their intention, so that they would not thereby imperil the existence of the Government. In other words the Government's majority could be increased from 6 to 24.

Unfortunately, from Hale's point of view, there is no evidence that Morrison, or anyone else in the government, took these negotiations seriously. The Lib–Lab pact, which if arranged could conceivably have extended Attlee's hold on power, was stillborn.[6]

The Labour Left itself was far from unanimous on the virtues of such an alliance. In the *Glasgow Forward* of 4 March 1950, Emrys Hughes wrote, "I sat near that bunch of Liberals in the last Parliament and know how incalculable they are. They are not a party with any clearly defined sort of principles, however much they may proclaim it."

Labour's situation was delicate, and for the most part the party's left wing in Parliament acted accordingly. If they wished to preserve the government, however, they continued to wish also that it would follow a more socialist path. The old debate between the Left and center-Right of the party was muted, but it was far from having been resolved.

In fact, because its field of action was so severely limited, Labour Left rhetoric grew more basic, more philosophical, during this difficult period. "We won [the general election]," Driberg mused in March 1950; "why didn't we win more decisively?" Because, he answered himself, "we have failed to explain to people in this country what Socialism really is." He called for Labour to mount a campaign which would emphasize the "ethical . . . case for Socialism" as well as the economic one. Ian Mikardo added a gloss to this appeal. "We really need," he told Maurice Edelman, "to go back to the sort of propaganda—I'm not afraid of that word—which the pioneers of the Labour Party used." Or, as Michael Foot put it at Beatrice Webb House, Dorking, where the NEC met to consider the lessons of the general election and begin drawing up plans for the next one, "We should spell out . . . our whole case."[7]

In a sense, this "back to basics" approach was simply a continuation of the old debate between Morrisonian consolidators and advocates of further socialist advance. The results of the 1950 general election, far from settling the debate, had given fuel to both camps. Consolidators held that Labour had almost lost the election because it had neglected to woo the middle-class vote; the Left argued that Labour had failed because its moderate program did not attract apathetic or dispirited working-class voters. It was at this point, as we have seen, that Mikardo, Crossman and others attempted to work out the theoretical reply to Morrison at the Buscot conferences. There were, however, no demonstrations in the House, no letters to the press, or private letters to Attlee, demanding that the government follow a different course.

In the House the Labour Left was filing through the voting lobbies. Outside, things were stirring. "Are we going to adopt a namby-pamby brand of socialism?" Rhondda Borough CLP secretary Ray Dallimore demanded of Morgan Phillips; "Or are we going forward to real Socialism?" His members, he added, thought that they "could see Ramsay MacDonald smiling over your shoulder." A veritable torrent of CLP resolutions, less pungent in their language but nearly unanimous in their opposition to consolidation, now descended upon Transport House. Trade unionists, too, scorned the relative propriety momentarily displayed by the parliamentary Labour Left. A member of the NUR asked bitterly:

> What is wrong with us? Have we no guts? Are we going to let the reactionaries beat us, ridicule our humanitarian principles, scorn our efforts to make a decent life for people? . . . Socialism is a receding principle . . . not because less people believe in it, but because [the government] have let their dynamic run down.[8]

Many railwaymen were earning only 95 shillings a week, but the wage freeze and Order 1305 meant that they could not strike to better their position. "How far," asked H. W. Franklin, president elect of the NUR,

> must one's loyalty to the Labour Government cause such an organisation as ours to remain silent when the interests of the general membership are so seriously affected? . . . We must publicly avow our opposition no matter if the Government of the day takes exception to our policy.

It was not only the railwaymen who were preparing to act. "This National Committee declares its opposition to any conception of the 'wage freeze,' and considers it our right to present wage claims when and how we think fit," the AEU annual conference resolved unanimously in June. A series of labor disputes now ensued in which dockers, London busmen and Smithfield lorry drivers were prominent. During the strike of the latter, the government employed several thousand troops "to maintain services." When the London gasworkers came out, the government arrested ten of their leaders under Order 1305 which had prohibited strikes during the war. This galvanized both CLPs and trade unions. Once again Morgan Phillips was deluged with protest resolutions. More effectively, in September the TUC overturned the policy of wage restraint. Under such circumstances Order 1305 was a dead letter. The government might have to apply it to dozens of striking unions. Concluding in this case that discretion was the better part of valor, it abolished the unpopular Order in January 1951.[9]

Meanwhile the threads which would draw the Labour Left in the PLP back together with the more active elements in the trade unions and constituency parties already were being pulled. "US statesmen are always proclaiming their policy is one of seeking peace," noted a contributor to the *Railway Review* on 19 May 1950. "But one must ask, does one seek peace best by displaying the pistol, the dagger and the bomb in every pocket of the suit?" In this case the writer objected to American pressure on behalf of rearming West Germany. Many in Parliament shared these doubts. "Dr Goebbels must be laughing in hell," Crossman wrote bitterly after Churchill came out in support of the Americans on this issue. In the event, however, it was American pressure on the government to rearm Britain, in order for it to play a larger role in the Korean conflict, which revitalized the energies of the parliamentary Labour Left, Crossman among them.[10]

The Labour Left believed that social democracy was more effective than rearmament as a bulwark against the spread of communism. For this reason, its members, in trade unions, CLPs and Parliament alike, scrutinized Stafford Cripps's 1950 Budget with even more care than usual. Already there was fear that defense requirements were beginning to cut into money previously reserved by the Labour government for its domestic program. "We are spending nearly £750,000,000 per annum on war preparations," Dick Beech wrote almost disbelievingly in the *Chemical Worker* for May 1950. Such profligacy would impede production while raising taxes and the cost of living. Emrys Hughes wrote prophetically, "This year Sir Stafford is to find the enormous sum of £780,000,000 [for defense]. But what is he or his successor to ask from us next year?" Hughes really did seem to gaze into a crystal ball. Would the labor movement twelve months hence be "prepared to argue that we must have more cuts in housing and the social services," in order to pay for rearmament?[11]

On 25 June war broke out in the Far East when North Korean troops rolled across the 38th parallel to attack positions in the South. In New York the UN voted to oppose the communists. Soviet delegates were not present when this vote was taken. UN forces, mainly American, were immediately dispatched to the embattled country, under the command of General Douglas MacArthur. Quickly, British land and sea forces were sent to Korea. And now began the American pressure for Britain to increase defense spending which led, ineluctably, to the great split in the Cabinet, the fall of the Labour government and the revitalization of the Labour Left.

Almost without exception, the Labour Left condemned the North Korean army's move south, and therefore supported the UN "police action" to drive it back over the 38th parallel. It was dead set against any widening of the conflict, however, for example into a "preventive war" against mainland China. It demanded negotiations to end the war, opposed General MacArthur's invasion of North Korea, which came in November, and nearly panicked when President Truman acknowledged that his government was considering the use of atomic weapons. The Labour Left supported what it took to be Attlee's more cautious policy and joined in the general rejoicing when the Prime Minister flew to Washington in early December, ostensibly to dissuade Truman from dropping the bomb.

In the end, however, the issues raised by the Korean War and the government's attitude towards it could not but deeply disturb the Labour Left. Few among its members could endorse the American view of the conflict as one pitting Soviet-backed totalitarians against Western-supported freedom fighters. Fewer still believed that the South was blameless or deserved uncritical support. Above all, the Labour Left came to fear that irresponsible Americans would turn the limited conflict into all-out war against China, which, in turn, would lead to nuclear exchanges with the Soviet Union. Driberg wrote in *Reynolds News* on 24 December 1950 that "the Korean War . . . wears less and less the aspect of a crusade." And a month later: "Whatever Soviet intentions or ambitions may be, the Russians will certainly not blunder into war uncalculatingly: therefore, in the immediate future, they are less of a threat to peace than . . . America."[12]

The parliamentary Labour Left, which had been relatively quiet during the months following the general election, rediscovered its voice. The Socialist Fellowship pushed opposition to government policy beyond even what "hard" non-communist leftists like Ellis Smith and Fenner Brockway were willing to tolerate. They resigned from the group, which was already beginning to break up. Into this breach stepped a revived Victory for Socialism group, which helped to renew ties between constituency, trade-union and parliamentary Labour Lefts. On 10 March 1951 Geoffrey Bing, Fenner Brockway, Marcus Lipton and Sir Richard Acland, all of "Keep Left," and Bob Edwards of the Chemical Workers' Union, spoke at a VfS meeting attended by "nearly four hundred party and trade-union delegates." Further VfS anti-war "schools" and demonstrations were organized. They complemented the efforts of a "Peace with China" Council organized and led by Kingsley Martin. Driberg and Maurice Orbach were among the Labour Members who spoke for it. Meanwhile, the National Peace Council also was opposing government policy in the Far East. On 8 January, Martin, Michael Foot and Lord Stansgate, a former member of the government, were the main speakers at one of its demonstrations. On this occasion an audience of 2,500 had attended.[13]

Labour's 1950 annual conference was held during 2–6 October, before anti-war sentiment had crystallized. Even at that relatively early date, however, twenty-five CLPs and two trade unions had formulated resolutions for conference to consider, each of which criticized government foreign policy. In December 1950 Horsham CLP circulated a resolution demanding the dismissal of General MacArthur, immediate negotiations for a ceasefire on the 38th parallel, peaceful relations with the People's Republic of China and other traditional Labour Left foreign policy goals. By the beginning of March 1951 the Horsham resolutions had been endorsed by sixty-three CLPs, twenty-one of which were represented in Parliament by Labour Members. Other CLP resolutions critical of the government's war policy flooded into Transport House. To cite one of many:

> The Holborn and St Pancras Constituency Labour Party urges that the Government should publicly declare that it will immediately withdraw its support from the operations in Korea in the event of any further action by the United Nations Commander tending to promote a full scale clash with China . . . and it should act now to secure the removal of Dr Syngman Rhee from his present position, and the holding of elections throughout Korea under United Nations auspices.

The international department of the NEC was sufficiently worried to begin tabulating CLP resolutions as they poured into Morgan Phillips's offices. During February 12 to

March 5 1951 it received ninety-five such messages. Of these, only six supported government policy. During March 8 to April 9 it received seventy additional resolutions. Of these, eight supported the government. From 4 April to 5 June, Transport House received a further seventy-two resolutions. Four supported the government.[14]

Despite the flap over the possible use of atomic weapons, the British government supported the main thrust of American policy. This meant that it was in no position to refuse when word came from Washington, in late August 1950, that the Truman administration believed Britain should make a greater contribution to the common effort in Korea. Britain's defense budget for 1950–1 had been set, finally, at £700 million, or 7.5 percent of the national income. The government now agreed to raise the figure—to £1,800 million for the year, and to £3,600 million over the next three years. This, according to Attlee, was "the maximum we can do by expanding and using to the full our industrial capacity without resorting to the drastic expedients of a war economy." In fact it was not. In December the Americans requested that the three-year figure be raised from £3,600 million to £6,000 million. Finally they settled for £4,700, which would raise defense expenditure to 14 percent of the national income. Thus the budget for defense had been doubled.[15]

The Labour Left raised an immediate storm of protest. "If this country is irrevocably committed to a vast programme of rearmament, the full effects upon the working class can hardly be imagined," R. T. San warned in the *Railway Review* on 8 December. These effects had been obvious, however, to "Economist," writing in the same journal two months earlier:

> The effort required for war production is accompanied by the necessity for the consumer to abstain from satisfying what would normally be considered as economically legitimate needs. In addition, increased taxation is calculated to reduce all existing levels of consumption ... One could further enlarge upon this by mentioning the danger of inflation.

"The choice, it seems, is now clear," wrote the editors of the *Electron*, monthly journal of the Electrical Trades Union. "It is between the Welfare State and the Warfare State." Emrys Hughes wrote in the *Glasgow Forward* of 9 September 1950, "We will be asked to consider cutting the social services. There will be no more for old age pensioners, and the axe is waiting for housing, education and capital investment in everything except military expenditure." In January and early February 1951, Michael Foot echoed these warnings in the *Daily Herald*. On the Labour Left, only Crossman, idiosyncratic as ever, took a different line. "Faced with problems of fairly distributing rearmament costs and preventing inflation, the Government will be forced to adopt far more Socialist measures than it would have dreamt of if peace had broken out." For once, however, the Member for Coventry East overestimated his political opponents.[16]

Hugh Gaitskell had replaced Cripps as Chancellor of the Exchequer in October 1950. From the outset, he believed that the only way to pay for rearmament would be to place caps on domestic spending and to stick to them. The escalation of American demands strengthened his resolve. At a Cabinet committee meeting on 15 March he proposed, among other economies, that the National Health Service should hold its next year's expenditure to the present level, and that it should institute charges of £1 per pair of glasses (for adults) and of a shilling on prescriptions. The crisis finally had come.[17]

For the Labour Left, almost everything that had gone before pointed towards this moment. From 1945 onwards it had argued for less dependency upon the Americans, for a more nuanced approach to communism and the Soviet Union, for a "socialist foreign policy." Equally it had demanded more socialism at home. In a sense it had been warning against something like Gaitskell's proposal ever since Labour had been in office. For that reason, the Chancellor's plan could not have affronted left-wing Labourites more fundamentally. It went to the heart of the debate about consolidation, and foreign policy. Ultimately, it raised questions about Labour's identity and essential aims.

In 1950 the Labour Left regarded the National Health Service as one of Labour's greatest domestic achievements. It was a rare Labour Left election address which did not call attention to "the finest health service in the world," as Warbey had termed it, and to the benefits it had brought to Britain. With the establishment of the service "the infant mortality rate has fallen to a new low level," Bramall pointed out. In 1949, when Cripps had proposed prescription fees, the Left had been quick to defend what the Lancaster CLP described as "the Socialist principle of a free service, available to all, irrespective of income." Such charges would be "a retrograde step, a retreat in the face of pressure by the forces of reaction in this country." Nothing had happened, during the ensuing period, to change Labour Left views.[18]

Moreover, the creator of the Health Service was a hero to the Left, as Foot's biography has amply shown. At Westminster, Leslie Hale recorded in his diary that there were some doubts. "I think [Bevan] is moving very fast to the right," Hale wrote in January 1950; and again in March: "for the last two years he has been moving steadily to the Right and certainly . . . has been very much *persona grata* with Stafford Cripps and Ernest Bevin." Hale feared "that he might jockey for position instead of adhering to fundamental principle." Yet Hale, like almost everyone else on the Labour Left, had "no doubt whatsoever that he is, excepting the Prime Minister, the outstanding personality of the Movement." The prestige of the Health Service and the stature of its creator served to heighten Labour Left opposition to Gaitskell's plans.[19]

Historians have examined with great care the battle which now developed within the Cabinet. They have discounted personal rivalry between the main protagonists as its primary cause. They dismiss claims, made at the time, that Bevan had given no previous notice that he would oppose the charges. Kenneth Morgan has shown that Bevan went on record in April 1950 against charging the National Health, and "had made major pronouncements in Cabinet from 1 August 1950 to 25 January 1951, warning against the implications of the rearmament programme for the economy." Michael Foot traces Bevan's opposition to earlier dates. He had fought successfully Cripps's suggestions for charging the National Health in December 1949; he had thought the much lower defense budget in October 1949 already "gorged and swollen." Indeed, Foot shows that Bevan was generally critical of Bevinism and, of course, of Morrisonian consolidationism throughout his tenure as a Cabinet minister.[20]

For our purposes the clash is most noteworthy because it marked a decisive stage in the evolution of the postwar Labour Left. In threatening resignation over this issue, the rebel Cabinet ministers finally had decided it was worth jeopardizing the existence of a Labour government in order to protect the socialist and internationalist vision which they believed to be the animating spirit of the labor movement as a whole.

During the crisis, and especially during the middle two weeks of April, a series of meetings took place among Labour ministers, some of whom were anxious to find a compromise, others of whom were seeking to bring matters to a head. A steady stream of visitors shuttled to and from Attlee's hospital room, where the Prime Minister was being treated for ulcers (and no wonder!). These conferences with Attlee have been chronicled by historians. Simultaneously the Labour Left, and especially the old "Keep Left" group, was in conference, attempting to work out its strategy during the crisis. These meetings never have been examined before. What they show is that the Labour Left, even at this penultimate moment, was deeply split over the wisdom of resignation. When Bevan and his main ally in the Cabinet, Harold Wilson, took soundings among possible backbench supporters, they received conflicting advice.[21]

As we have seen, the Labour Left had been galvanized by the Korean War and the escalating US requests for rearmament. During the fall of 1950 at least three government members shared the Labour Left's concern. In December, according to Leslie Hale, Bevan, John Strachey (who was now in the War Office) and John Freeman threatened to resign if the defense budget was raised. It was, to £4,700 million, despite their protests. At this, the "Keep Left" group arranged a meeting at Crossman's house in Vincent Square. The three government members were scheduled to attend, but did not. It is well known that Bevan had been on the point of resigning more than once. This is the first intimation we have, however, that he was in touch with the Labour Left about tactics and strategies before he actually left the Cabinet.[22]

Among members of "Keep Left," Leslie Hale, Ian Mikardo, Fenner Brockway and Richard Acland were prepared to vote against the government, or to abstain, when the defense budget came up in the House. Their resolve was undercut, however, by Bevan's acceptance of a new position, Minister of Labour, precisely at this juncture. One can imagine the anguished proceedings at "Keep Left" and other Labour Left meetings. "Why has Bevan, who was on the point of resigning ... agreed to accept this position?" Crossman asked in his 21 January article for the *Sunday Pictorial*. "By joining the inner Cabinet at this moment, he hopes to strengthen the forces in the Government who ... believe a peaceful settlement with Russia is still possible."

Bevan's move notwithstanding, there remained, in Leslie Hale's opinion, "at least 50 and probably 70 or 80 Labour Members" willing to make a decisive protest. Moreover, the government itself was more deeply split than often is realized. There were ministers and junior ministers who had not made public their objections to helping pay for rearmament by cutting the social services—yet. "The first man to tell me that he was contemplating resigning over the arms issue was [Attorney-General]

Hartley Shawcross," Hale confided to his diary. Junior ministers whom Hale believed also were considering resignation included Frank Beswick, "I think Geoffrey de Freitas, though he never told me so," Kenneth Younger and Arthur Henderson. Another junior minister sometimes mentioned in this context was Tom Cook. These were all in addition, of course, to Strachey, who ultimately reconsidered, and to Bevan, Wilson and Freeman, who did resign in the end. Dalton wrote to Attlee two months later that he had done his best "to stop Nye from leading a stampede. As you know, we were once or twice very close to the precipice." They were closer, in fact, than those who discount the Labour Left care to acknowledge.[23]

Perhaps one reason why the rebellion did not become a "stampede" was that the Labour Left was split over proper tactics. Ten "Keep Left" members composed a letter to Attlee requesting an interview, "saying it would be difficult if not impossible for them to support the Government on this issue." The reply was "a quite contemptuous refusal to see us," which presaged Gaitskell's hard line in the Cabinet and appears to have intimidated at least half a dozen of the group. Crossman, W. T. Williams, Lipton, Castle, Mikardo and Foot now drew up a letter, printed in the *Daily Herald* on 10 February, which rehearsed Labour Left objections to rearmament and government policies in Korea, but also extolled "the invaluable part played by the Government in restraining the dangerous tendencies of American policy." Had the Conservatives been in power, the letter continued, "Britain would have abandoned any attempt to exercise an independent and restraining influence in UNO." For these reasons, the six signatories concluded, they would sustain the Labour government with their votes.[24]

At least four "Keep Left" members did not accept this argument. Leslie Hale, recorded in his diary that

I dissented very strongly from this [letter] because . . . that announcement at once crippled everybody else who was working to get the policy altered; it removed at once from the fray ten [*sic*] of the most prominent figures and left the others helpless.

Hale felt so deeply that he now resigned from "Keep Left." So did George Wigg. Harold Davies and Fenner Brockway maintained their membership, but now made another group the focus of their activities. This was the "Peace Aims" group, founded by none other than Hale to press the government to distinguish its goals in the Korean War from those of the Americans. "Thirty to forty Members" regularly attended its meetings. Fissiparous as any other Labour Left group, however, this one too now divided. Hale himself wanted the government simply to declare publicly that it would confine its actions in Korea to positions south of the 38th parallel. This would remove the danger of war with China. Emrys Hughes, however, circulated a motion he wished to put down in the House which regretted the UN branding of China as an aggressor, opposed any sanctions against China, called for an immediate negotiated ceasefire, opposed the arms race generally and called upon the government to fashion a new peace policy for the world. At a tense meeting of the "Peace Aims" group on the night of 9 February, Hale and Hughes argued their respective positions. The latter was victorious, and Hale "gave up the struggle, I think perhaps a little tactlessly and a little annoyed, but it was the end of a fairly active period." Brockway and Davies signed Hughes's document, which was printed in the 10 February *Daily Herald*. So did Sydney and Julius Silverman, Victor Yates, Wilfrid Vernon and a handful of other MPs. "Sydney swore that he would vote against the Government in any circumstances and of course didn't," Hale recorded in his diary, with more than a hint of contempt.[25]

Why did so many among the parliamentary Labour Left still hesitate to vote their conscience? The answer is that they desperately feared the consequences. The consensus was that if the government was defeated upon an important measure in the House, or if the ministers resigned on a matter of principle, it would precipitate a general election which a disunited Labour Party would surely lose. As Hugh Dalton cleverly wrote to Bevan, whom he wished to dissuade from resigning:

> a Parliamentary Labour Party reduced to its safe seats would be a poor thing indeed, an ugly skeleton. Most of our best young men would have been massacred and the Tories firmly fixed in power, perhaps for a generation, perhaps through a war which would finish us and all our hopes.

For many on the Labour Left, this was a crucial consideration.[26]

If it had been important in February, how much more so in March and April, with MacArthur threatening to support Chiang Kai-shek in a war with China, and the Tories supporting General MacArthur? This was when the battle over health costs reached a climax. The Labour Left feared a split in the party more than ever. Driberg, for example, "was one of those who . . . hoped the Ministers would not resign and did what little I could to help find a compromise formula." Barbara Castle—who, when Gaitskell's Budget finally was introduced, complimented him for "putting the housewife first"—probably was another. Uncharacteristically, so may have been Geoffrey Bing, who argued in the House that "the charges for teeth and spectacles were necessary because there must be some ceiling to the Health Service." And then there was Crossman. He told Dalton, "if it comes to a break, I shall go with Nye." But he told the "Keep Left" group, "If nothing is done to end the cold war between Hugh Gaitskell and Nye Bevan the latter will resign . . . This will benefit no one except the Tories." He wrote on 15 April in the *Sunday Pictorial* that Gaitskell had "made a brilliant political success of his first Budget." A week later he extolled Bevan's "crusader's zeal to kindle a left-wing fire in the constituencies and challenge the present leadership." Crossman had a reputation for inconsistency. His waffling is comprehensible here. Bevan's prospective resignation marked a turning-point in the history of the Labour Party and the Labour Left; and the Member for Coventry East knew it.[27]

IV

Bevan dispatched his letter of resignation on Sunday 22 April. Wilson's followed on the 23rd. On that day, too, Bevan made a personal statement in the House. It was, by almost all accounts, a disastrous performance, "the worst of his career," according to Kenneth Morgan. It was followed by another, however, almost equally counter-productive, at a meeting of the PLP on the 24th, where, again according to Morgan, "Bevan raged almost uncontrollably at Gaitskell's attacks on 'my Health Service.'" By contrast, Wilson's farewell speeches gained him sympathy and respect. Freeman, the sole junior minister to resign, was distinctly overshadowed by his more famous colleagues.[28]

Expressing popular judgment, Crossman wrote, "Aneurin Bevan badly mishandled his resignation." Still, the Labour Left as a whole swept aside previous doubts and hesitations. Driberg, in *Reynolds News* on 29 April, stressed the government's "abandonment of principle . . . [which] provides a precedent for further departures from principle." Hughes, who had been the sole Labour Member to shake Bevan's hand after his disastrous speech to the PLP on the 24th, wrote, "There was no other course [Bevan] could take." Even Crossman made the politically difficult decision to support the rebel ministers. "Bevan's . . . political instinct and the economic reasoning of Harold Wilson and John Freeman were absolutely right."[29]

For the first time since 1945 "hard" and "soft" left-wing Labour Members were on the same side of a major issue. On the 26th Leslie Hale was reconciled with "Keep Left." He met with Acland, Castle, Crossman, Foot and Mikardo, its core members. Harold Davies, who had sided with Emrys Hughes in the debate about peace aims, was also present. So was Kim Mackay of the old "Europe" group, by this time as "soft" a Labour leftist as could be. Driberg, Jennie Lee, Hugh Delargy and Will Griffiths were the other backbenchers in attendance. Most importantly, however, the three former government members were present too. Mikardo's secretary, Jo Richardson, was deputed to take minutes. The "Bevanites" had made their formal entrance upon the historical stage.

The Labour Left in the constituencies had never come so close to losing its voice as had the Labour Left in the PLP. The resignations led left-wing CLPs to redouble their efforts. The constituency party in Basingstoke circulated a resolution, eventually signed by 105 CLPs and trade councils, demanding an emergency conference "to thrash things out," as Wolverhampton North-East explained to Transport House. Blandly, Morgan Phillips assured all petitioners that it would take as much time to summon an emergency conference as simply to get ready for the one already scheduled. This was to take place at Scarborough in October. The CLPs then registered their political wishes in unmistakable fashion. They submitted to the annual conference hundreds of resolutions critical of government policy. There were 37 opposing its rearmament program, 27 opposing the charges on the National Health Service, 37 more demanding changes in its approach to foreign affairs. Most spectacularly, there were 134 calling for socialist measures to control prices and profits or to allow for wage hikes. Many of these were explicitly Bevanite. For example, Hornsey CLP attempted to commit conference to refusing "a lowering standard of living as a consequence of rearmament" and demanded as a first step the restoration of "cuts in the Health Service." Moreover, when the elections for the constituency section of the NEC took place, Bevan scored top of the poll, Barbara Castle came second and, to quote Michael Foot,

Two other Bevanite supporters, Ian Mikardo and Tom Driberg, increased their vote substantially. Three ex-Ministers and anti-Bevanites, Herbert Morrison, Hugh Dalton and Jim Griffiths, saw their votes drop and . . . Shinwell . . . was removed altogether and stormed out of the Conference in a rage.

In 1951 the Left was probably stronger in the constituencies than it ever had been before.[30]

In the trade unions, too, the Labour Left rallied to Bevan, and found new inspiration in his resignation from the government. A front-page leader of 27 April aligned the *Railway Review* with the former Minister of Health. "This journal has always fought for the idea of working-class power, and when a man shows by his actions and informs by his utterances that working-class progress is his prime concern, we will back him." A week later, General Secretary Figgins took the entire front page of the journal to reiterate that support. "Bevan, Wilson and Freeman . . . are pursuing the right course." In letters and columns NUR members supported the rebels. One thought the health charges were "cheating the people." Another warned that "a further extension of the present policy of Right-wing Labour leadership can only lead to the majority of six in Parliament being replaced by a Tory majority." A third claimed, "So afraid are [the Labour leadership] to 'face the future,' that they have turned their backs on it. Could anyone blame me for musing: 'shades of 1931'?" On 1 June, C. C. Peat, who since the recent municipal elections had become

an ex-Councillor . . . tried to find the reason for the apathy of the people which resulted in my defeat. The people seem bewildered and stunned by the trend of events, and many seem to think that the Government have departed from the policy of Socialism.

Each week the letters flooded in, supporting the Bevanites, criticizing the government. The journal printed only two which bucked the trend. One was from an NUR-sponsored Labour Member, W. T. Proctor, and he criticized Bevan's tactic, not the substance of his grievance: "I do not think that by abandoning office we should be serving the interests of the working class of this country."[31]

USDAW, too, was forthright in backing the rebels, though more concerned than the NUR to support the right of dissent than the specific criticisms Bevan, Wilson and Freeman had made of government policy. "Let us get clear in our minds in the first place," General Secretary J. A. Birch exhorted readers of the *New Dawn* on 12 May, "that the resignation of the Ministers . . . is not a question of disloyalty." The AEU was also Bevanite. Competent as always, Jack Tanner outlined the Bevanite case in his presidential address to the union's annual conference in 1951:

We must maintain economic stability and continue the great social advance which has been going on in Britain since 1945. Our capacity to do this will be impaired by a

Defence Programme costing £1,300 millions this year, and a total of £4,700 millions over the next three years. Already this has led to cuts in the Health Service provisions, and a charge is now being made for dentures and spectacles . . . The amount the treasury will save this year as a result is £13 millions. In a Budget amounting to £4,000 millions it should have been possible to find other ways of raising this sum.

The ETU agreed, in dramatic language:

If their resignations serve only to warn the Labour Movement of the grave consequences that are in store for it, should it continue silently to acquiesce in the present policy or blindly support it, they may yet mark a return to the principles upon which the Labour Movement was founded.

So did the Chemical Workers, the Tobacco Workers and the Fire Brigades' Union. Mark Jenkins has shown in his study, *Bevanism: Labour's High Tide*, that the Bevanites enjoyed strong support from the trade unions as well as the constituencies. This brief examination of trade-union journals and conference reports suggests that there was support among trade unionists for Bevan and his followers even before they had cohered in a formal group.[32]

Yet the Labour Left in 1951 was different from the Labour Left in 1945. It had undergone a decisive evolution over the half-decade of Labour government. It had assumed its modern form.

The three ex-ministers and the group of "Keep Lefters" who met with them on the 26th produced a pamphlet, *One Way Only*, to justify their position. Ironic title: there was one way only in which the Labour Left had not changed. In 1951, as in 1945, it was incapable of hewing to a single line. In 1951, however, the "hard" Left was weaker, the "soft" Left incomparably stronger and more influential within the Labour Left as a whole than previously.

Consider the main issue. In the immediate aftermath of World War II, few on the Labour Left would have agreed that the Soviet Union threatened the peace, let alone that it was necessary to rearm against the USSR. By 1951, however, Soviet sympathizers on the Labour Left were silent or gone. Few were willing to question the need for some degree of rearmament. Only Emrys Hughes, in a pamphlet, *Arms and Mr Bevan*, and in his weekly columns for the *Glasgow Forward*, stout-heartedly argued against the entire rationale for a weapons drive. It represented, in his opinion, "the very negation of the hopes of Socialism." Even Hughes, however, did not dispute the existence of the Soviet threat, only the means advanced by the government for meeting it. His was a "hard" Left argument only in the sense that it would not countenance any increase in military spending.

Other Labourites who opposed any degree of rearmament were even less obviously on the "hard" Labour Left than Hughes. G. D. H. Cole objected to the charges from a utilitarian perspective. "If armies march on their bellies, so do whole peoples," he concluded in his pamphlet, *Weakness through Strength*. "A weakened economy [which he was certain rearmament would entail], rent by internal dissensions, can be in no good case either for preventing a war or for fighting one." The Labour Pacifist Fellowship added a moral dimension to the case against any degree of rearmament. "It is not only the size of the arms budget that is mistaken, but the continued belief in powerful armaments and conscripted youth as a basis for foreign policy."[33]

Once such arguments would have commanded broad support among the Labour Left. Now, however, most of the Labour Left objected not so much to rearmament *per se* as to the scope of rearmament envisioned by the government. As John Freeman explained to the 1951 Fabian Summer School:

> I criticize the programme because I believe it [£4,700 million] to have been nothing more than a guess, hastily made to square the Americans. I am not able—I admit it —to say what the figure ought to be. . . £3,600 millions . . . was, perhaps, about right.

Benn Levy wrote to George Strauss, apparently after an argument at a dinner party, "I base my [opposition] not only on the current and prospective evidence of rising prices and inflation, but also on Gaitskell's unequivocal assertion in November [1950] that our economy could not carry more than a rearmament programme of £3,600 million."[34]

Some concluded, as Strauss wrote to Levy, that "there is really very little between us. . . It all boils down to a judgment as to whether £4,700 million is or is not more than the economy can bear." This was seriously to underestimate the nature of the chasm which was opening rapidly between the government and its Labour Left critics. The Soviet threat was no longer an issue on the Labour Left. The best way to confront communism, however, remained very much a matter of contention. Even Fenner Brockway, for example, accepted "the reasons which have led to the present alliance between socialists and non-socialists against Communism. . . Communists have done to death many associates of mine in the International Socialist movement." Brockway, however, also "believe[d] that democratic socialists must regain their independence as soon as possible, not only for the sake of socialism but also, in the long run, for the sake of peace." Bevanites wanted more independence from the US than Labour centrists and right-wingers did. This meant the resurrection of third force agitation with Bevan as an important advocate. In fact, demands for a Western union of democratic socialist states underlay much Bevanite agitation during the 1950s.[35]

At the most basic level, moreover, the charges proposed by the government signified that its commitment to socialism was now dangerously weak. There could be no graver issue than this. From a "soft" Left position, John Freeman argued that the rearmament program would make it impossible for Labour "to pursue enlightened economic policies towards the underdeveloped parts of the world." It would also "strike a severe blow at our own Social Services and our general policy of redistributing income between the rich and the poor." Similarly Hughes claimed that "this rearmament programme . . . finds the money for the tank and the bomber and in so doing starves the schools and perpetuates the slums." Making due allowance for differences in temperament, style and language, "hard" and "soft" Labour leftists discerned a similar threat in the government's determination to levy the charges. Bevanites from all sections of the Labour Left believed they were engaged in a struggle to preserve the soul of the Labour Party.[36]

They would be able to wage it more effectively than at any previous time since the war. In the constituencies, left-wing CLPs now were routinely circularizing each other. There had been the Horsham resolutions calling for a more independent foreign policy and peace in the far East. There had been the Basingstoke resolution demanding an emergency conference of the labour movement. A third resolution, composed and circulated by Dudley CLP, warned the leadership against participating in coalition government with the Conservatives. Moreover, the CLPs were determined to continue this practice of concerting opinion with each other in order to maximize their impact. Morgan Phillips, in a circular of his own, warned against it. The response was immediate and very nearly unanimous:

> When your letter re Constituency Parties circulating other Constituency parties with resolutions asking for their support was discussed at the [Birmingham, Northfield] Divisional Party's Management Committee Meeting, it was felt that it was not a bad thing for this practice to continue, as it gave an opportunity to hear views of other constituencies regarding Policy, etc.

This was, perhaps, among the mildest of the replies which Phillips received. Most demanded that his own letter be withdrawn, while reaffirming their own intention, as Cheltenham CLP asserted defiantly, "to use every constitutional means to bring pressure to bear on the National Executive."[37]

In the parliamentary party, too, Labour Left organization was better than before. The Bevanites arranged for "brains trusts" of left-wing Labourites to speak in the constituencies. These were formidable little groups. On 3 August, Foot, Crossman, Mikardo and Harold Davies journeyed to Hornchurch, where Geoffrey Bing acted as "question-master," and the audience was invited to raise any issue that it wished to discuss with these prominent supporters of the rebel Cabinet ministers. If this meeting was typical of its kind, the government had good reason to worry. Asked whether Attlee's administration had benefited the working class, Mikardo replied that while the government had done much to narrow the gap between rich and poor, "there are too many underprivileged persons that need help and many overprivileged persons that need a lot more taken from them." So much for consolidation! Crossman added:

> Since this heavy and excessive rearmament programme had been thrust upon us the tendency had been recently to go the other way, "the rich growing richer and the poor poorer" . . . This is only the beginning. The bill for rearmament this year is £1,300 million and by 1953 it will be £1,900 million. No! The only way to prevent wages chasing prices in a vicious circle is to provide adequate subsidies and controls.

Driberg wrote later, "the primary function of these brains trusts was not to do Bevanite propaganda, but to do general Socialist propaganda and to get recruits for the Labour Party." In the minds of many Bevanites, there appears to have been no great distinction between these aims.[38]

Meanwhile, further proof of enhanced organization, the Bevanites were meeting weekly in the House of Commons. They now had an elected rotating chairmanship. Until December it was filled by Mikardo. He was followed by Wilson. The Bevanites also developed ten "specialist groups," to educate them and, indeed, the parliamentary party, as issues arose, and they continued the "Keep Left" practice of inviting sympathetic speakers from outside, like the economists Dudley Seers and Thomas Balogh. Under the guidance of Mikardo, they began preparations to help each other in the general election they knew to be coming. These, apparently, were effective. Labour lost, but Driberg wrote happily, under the circumstances, "Quite a few people will be flummoxed by the fact that these terrible Bevanites, including several whose seats were acutely marginal, Freeman, Wilson, Mikardo, Foot, Bing, myself, got in again."[39]

V

In any reckoning of the historical significance for Labour and the Labour Left of the 1951 resignations, there is finally the matter of what did not happen. The resignations did not produce a split. Nor was a split ever likely.

This was one of the greatest lessons the Left had learned during 1945–51. Previously, splits from the Labour Party had not been common, but they had occurred. In 1901 the Marxist SDF had broken away from the Labour Representation Committee (forerunner of the Labour Party) to carry on more militant class politics. During 1920–1 the British Communist Party was founded to compete against Labour for the allegiance of the British working class. In 1931 Oswald Mosley broke from Labour to establish the New Party as a radical alternative to it. A year later the ILP split from the Labour Party, thinking to attract socialists repelled by the communist connection with Moscow, Mosley's developing connection with international fascism and Labour's lingering affinity for "MacDonaldism." During the war, the Common Wealth Party was established, not so much to compete with Labour as to pressure it to greater militancy, if only by the power of its example.

By 1945 it was evident to most socialists that none of the alternatives to Labour could compete successfully. In the general election of that year the communists elected two Members of Parliament, the ILP four, Common Wealth one. Labour elected 393, on a platform which its left wing embraced with pride. There was a stampede afterwards, *towards* Labour, as we have seen.

Attlee then proved that Labour was "fit to govern" in a way that MacDonald might have envied. Under Attlee's leadership the party demonstrated to the political Right that it was "safe," while demonstrating to the Left the real perils of outright opposition. To give an example, in the run-up to the general election of 1950, Walter Stevens, the communist general secretary of the ETU, did not endorse Labour. He knew better,

however, than to advise his members to vote communist. "See that you give your vote
to progress," he exhorted them. And, in the course of an article on the choice
confronting them, he wrote:

> The Labour Government may not have come up to all our expectations. . . But it
> cannot be denied that it has advanced the social security of the people of this
> country, maintained full employment and prevented the industrial strife that
> followed'the ending of the First World War.

Emrys Hughes made the point which Stevens could not bring himself to express. "If
you are critical of Labour Party leadership, take an active part in your own local
Labour Party and become a live wire." This was what the Labour Left was all about. It
was, essentially, what Bevan advised his followers to do, rather than splitting from the
party.[40]

The cold war had helped to drive this lesson home. What politician would wish to
be associated with the international movement which justified. say, the supression of
democracy in Czechoslovakia? The British Communist Party squandered an immense
reservoir of good will during the immediate postwar period by applauding every move
and decision originating in Moscow, while attacking with equal consistency nearly
every act of the British Labour government. The CPGB committed political suicide
during 1945–51, and so would have any member of the Labour Left who joined it—no
matter the strength or validity of their opposition to Attlee, Zilliacus, Platts Mills and
the others formed a "Labour Independent Group" rather than enter the CPGB; the ex-
Cabinet ministers and their followers established the Bevanites. The 1951 Labour Left
rebellion marked a new phase in the history of the labor movement precisely because it
did not break the Labour Party itself.

Notes and References

1 The results were: Labour, 315; Conservatives and their allies, 298; Liberals, 9; and there
were, according to Kenneth Morgan, 3 additional Members unlikely to turn up very
often.
2 Labour Party, 1950 general election file; BLPES, Strauss papers, miscellaneous election
leaflets.
3 *Glasgow Forward,* 28 January 1950; Strauss papers.
4 *Sunday Pictorial,* 26 February 1950.
5 BBC Written Archives, Broadcasting House, "Inside Parliament," 31 October 1950;
New Dawn, 18 March 1950; BBC Written Archives, Broadcasting House, "This Week in
Parliament," 10 March 1950.
6 Modern Records Centre, Warwick University, Richard Crossman papers, MSS 154/3/
KL/5; Lord Hale papers, Hale to Morrison, 8 May 1950; ibid., "Notes of a meeting held
on Tuesday, November 21st, 1950."
7 *Reynolds News,* 19 March 1950; BBC Written Archives, Reading, "Labour Party: Where
Do We Go from Here?" 4 May 1950; Labour Party, Morgan Phillips papers, Dorking
Conference file.
8 Phillips papers, constituency files, Rhondda, Dallimore to Phillips, 17 July 1950; *Railway
Review,* 13 April 1951.
9 *Railway Review,* 21 April 1950; *AEU Annual Conference,* 1950, p. 257.

10   *Sunday Pictorial*, 19 March 1950.

11   *Glasgow Forward*, 22 March 1950.

12   *Reynolds News*, 28 January 1951.

13   *Glasgow Forward*, 10 March 1951, 13 January 1951.

14   Conference resolutions for Labour Party annual conference, 1950, pp. 25–8; Phillips papers, constituency files, Horsham, Roy Ashdown to Phillips, 12 December 1950; Jonathan Wood, "The Labour Left in the constituencies," D. Phil. thesis, Warwick University, 1982, p. 325 Phillips papers, constituency files, Holborn and St Pancras, Will Halford to Phillips, 30 November 1950; Labour Party, NEC minutes, vol. 102, pp. 111, 483 and illegible.

15   Michael Foot, *Aneurin Bevan*, Vol. 2 (1973), p. 305.

16   *Railway Review*, 6 October 1950; *Electron*, January 1951; *Sunday Pictorial*, 27 August 1950.

17   For Gaitskell, see Philip Williams (ed.), *The Diary of Hugh Gaitskell, 1945–56* (London, 1983), and Philip Williams, *Hugh Gaitskell: A Political Biography* (London, 1979).

18   Labour Party, 1950 general election file; Phillips papers, J.D.V. Scott (Lanark CLP) to Phillips, 18 November 1950.

19   Hale diary, 9 January 1950, 1 March 1950.

20   Williams, *Hugh Gaitskell*, pp. 250–270; also Kenneth O. Morgan, *Labour in Power, 1945–51* (Oxford, 1984), p. 443; Foot, *Aneurin Bevan*, Vol. 2 (1973), pp. 290, 274.

21   See, especially, Morgan, *Labour in Power*, pp. 448–52.

22   Hale diary, 29 April 1951.

23   Ibid.; BLPES, Hugh Dalton papers, 9/18/20, Dalton to Attlee, 15 April 1951.

24   Hale Diary, 29 April 1951.

25   Ibid.

26   Dalton papers, 9/18/36, Dalton to Bevan, 7 April 1951.

27   *Reynolds News*, 29 April 1951; *Daily Herald*, 13 April 1951; *Hornchurch and Upminster News*, 11 May 1951; Dalton papers, 9/18/20, Dalton to Attlee, 15 April 1951; Crossman papers, MSS 154/3/KL, "Keep Left group papers, no. 1, Pensions and the Health Service, by Richard Crossman," 19 April 1951; *Sunday Pictorial*, 22 April 1951.

28   Morgan, *Labour in Power*, p. 454.

29   *Sunday Pictorial*, 29 April 1951; *Railway Review*, 29 April 1951; *Glasgow Forward*, 28 April 1951.

30   Phillips papers, constituency files, Wolverhampton, R.F. Ilsey to Phillips, 22 May 1951; Conference resolutions for 1951 Labour Party annual conference; Foot, *Aneurin Bevan*, Vol. 2 (1973), p. 349.

31   See *Railway Review*, 4 May through 11 June 1951.

32   *Electron*, June 1951; Mark Jenkins, *Bevanism: Labour's High Tide* (London, 1979), pp. 113–45.

33   Emrys Hughes, *Arms and Mr Bevan* (London, 1951), p. 32; G.D.H. Cole, *Weakness through Strength* (London, 1951), p. 14; *London Pacifist Fellowship Bulletin*, March/April 1952.

34   House of Lords Record Office, Benn Levy papers, "Armaments" file, John Freeman, "Rearmament—how far?" address delivered to 1951 Fabian Summer School; ibid., Levy to Strauss, 11 September 1951.

35   Ibid., Strauss to Levy, 17 September 1951; BBC Written Archives, Reading, "I Speak for Myself," 28 July 1951.

36   Levy papers, Freeman, "Rearmament—how far?"; Hughes, *Arms and Mr Bevan*, p. 32.

37   Phillips papers, constituency files, Birmingham (Northfield, Perry Bar), Lily Howell to Phillips, 1 June 1951; ibid., Cheltenham, Frank Green to Phillips, 11 September 1951.

38   *Hornchurch and Upminster News*, 3 August 1951; *Reynolds News*, 19 October 1952.

39   Andrew Roth, "Parliamentary Profile" files, "Bevanites, special groups, 1951;" *Reynolds News*, 4 October 1951.

40   *Electron*, February 1950; *Glasgow Forward*, 14 October 1950.

Conclusion

THE LABOUR GOVERNMENTS of 1945–51 could boast proudly of many great achievements. By way of contrast, any assessment of the Labour Left during this period must acknowledge that its positive accomplishments and victories were few. It has been my main purpose to argue, however, that the experience of Labour's left wing during the early postwar era constitutes a chapter of great importance in the history of the larger party to which it belonged, and in the history of the British Left generally.[1]

In broad terms the Labour Left wanted the government to pursue "a more drastic Socialist policy," as the introduction to *Keep Left* expressed it. This meant "more Socialism" at home, and a "Socialist foreign policy" abroad. The trend, however, was all the other way. The Foreign Secretary, Ernest Bevin, either ignored his Labour Left critics or smote them hip and thigh, depending upon circumstances. On the home front, especially after 1947, Labour abandoned many of the economic controls it had inherited from the wartime coalition government, opting for "consolidation" rather than further nationalization or other methods of regulating the economy. Attlee's preferment of Gaitskell over Bevan in 1950 at once summarized Labour's direction since the war and prefigured the front-bench attempt, ten years later, to jettison the socialist fourth clause of the party constitution.

That famous struggle for the soul of the Labour Party which began formally in 1959 had been anticipated during the years of Attlee's premiership. At bottom the Labour Left critique of the 1945–51 governments hinged upon the prescient charge, not often made openly or explicitly except by the "hard" Labour Left, that the leadership was insufficiently committed to, or actually was preparing to abandon, socialism as Labour understood the term. Yet the Labour Left itself rarely attempted to define what it meant by socialism, even as it demanded more of it in the government's foreign and domestic policies. The first task of this concluding chapter, therefore, will be to examine the Labour Left conception of the great goal.

II

The Labour Left was monolithic in nothing, least of all in its understanding of so imprecise a term as socialism. It is possible nevertheless to discern at least the broad outlines of consensus on the meaning of the word, although it was compounded of Fabian, Marxist, libertarian and Christian elements.

For the Labour Party as a whole "planning" constituted a central tenet of socialism. For the leadership and for center and right-wing Labourites, planning seems to have been almost an end in itself. An economy which was planned in the national interest would be more efficient than an economy based upon competition for profits. This had been the message of Fabian socialists since the 1880s. It was held to be one of the lessons taught by World War II. "In the hour of the nation's greatest need," George Tomlinson told BBC listeners during the 1945 election campaign, "it was state intervention that enabled us to survive." Five years later, party leaders continued to stress the utilitarian benefits of a planned economy. As Herbert Morrison argued in "The Last General Election and the Next," a memorandum he prepared for the NEC and government ministers gathered at Dorking over 19–21 May 1950:

> We should sharply emphasise the difference between having a plan and having no plan. The Conservatives believe in economic drift, in letting things go their own way. That would mean queer street . . . If we are to get through 1952 with full employment and increasing productivity and prosperity, we must have controls. . . We need these to secure the proper degree of capital investment and export and, above all, full employment.

Morrison was capable, of course, of arguing for socialism in less arid terms. Increasingly, however, it seemed to the Labour Left that the government thought planning, state intervention and socialism were all the same thing.[2]

Left-wing Labour did not doubt that the goals Morrison had listed were desirable. It believed, however, that the most important value of planning lay elsewhere. Early in 1946 Ellis Smith became the first junior minister to resign from the government. "We have got to have a plan for a return to prosperity," he wrote in explanation of his resignation, "and our plan must be based upon Socialist principles." For the Labour Left, but not necessarily for the rest of the party or its leaders, this meant that the plan must favor the working class, not merely an abstract notion of efficiency or utility. "Sound economics and social justice are interchangeable terms," R. T. Milroy, USDAW's acting general president, informed delegates to the union's annual conference in 1948. In Labour Left eyes, the true object of economic planning was the facilitation of justice. This meant applying Labour's wartime slogan, "fair shares for all," to the postwar era. Taxation, for example, must be used not only as a means of raising revenue, according to Milroy, "but as a method of ensuring that any necessary sacrifices are shared on terms of social equity. . . There must be a price policy and a profits policy, and sharing the sacrifice must mean some sacrifice of the shares." Where Fabian notions infused the government approach to planning, the Labour Left insisted that the "national plan" it so ardently desired must have, above all, a redistributive purpose.[3]

Redistribution meant more to the Labour Left, however, than simply higher living standards for the working class. It meant redistributing the prerogatives of power. This was one reason why the Labour Left objected so profoundly to the government's approach to nationalization. To party leaders and their supporters, nationalization was primarily an aspect of planning, an additional means of directing the economy. To the Labour Left, however, nationalization meant restructuring the industries taken from private enterprise. Nationalization must lead to industrial democracy, a railwayman warned in his union's journal on 31 August 1945, or else "the change from capitalist to public ownership . . . is not likely to make much difference." Possibly there was something perfunctory about the calls for workers' control which the parliamentary Labour Left issued. But as Charles Butler put it in the May 1947 issue of the *Tobacco Worker*, "Practically a quarter of our life is spent in the factory." For labor, democratic practices at the workplace were at least as important as in the political realm. Thus the trade-union Labour Left insisted with real passion that industrial democracy was an essential aspect of socialism.

Of course, political democracy was crucial too. "I do not believe there can ever be socialism without democracy or democracy without socialism," Sydney Silverman avowed in *Tribune* on 11 June 1948. The Marxist notion of a dictatorship of the proletariat held little attraction for the Labour Left. Of course, social justice could not be achieved unless the rights of capital were restricted. This was fundamental to socialist thought. As Crossman had put it during the run-up to the general election in 1945, "Labour will retain the wartime controls on finance and Big Business. . . This will mean less profits for Big Business and less freedom for the financiers and speculators. For you it will mean full employment and security." In a similar vein, Mikardo had spoken at Buscot of "forcing" nationalization upon various firms. Yet probably no one on the Labour Left disagreed with Acland's affirmation in 1951 that "We believe in laws which allow critics to organize themselves so as to be able (if sufficiently supported) to turn out the whole of our Government and put another in its place with different ideas from ours."[4]

For the Labour Left a crucial question during the postwar era was how to reconcile the need for government controls with the maintenance of individual liberties. As Crossman put it in the *Glasgow Forward* for 11 October 1947, "before we start discussing the pros and cons of any particular Socialist policy, we have to weigh it against those ideals of liberty and social equality." The negative lessons taught by the Soviet experience were only one impetus to Labour Left interest in this issue. The undemocratic and bureaucratic aspects of the society being shaped by the Attlee governments were another. At the fourth Buscot conference Crossman delivered a paper, "The Next Fifty Years," in which he asked, "Should it be our aim to distribute power, not to concentrate it further? . . . Should we assume the inevitability of planning, and take steps to ensure democratic checks on the planner and popular participation in its execution?" Cole, the "ancient, unrepentant guild socialist," answered affirmatively. He still believed the key to avoiding bureaucracy and totalitarianism lay in "democracy everywhere." Bob Edwards had offered the ILP a similar prescription in 1946. He thought there should be

workers', technicians' and consumers' control at every level of production, administration and distribution in the nationalised industries; the decentralisation to a district basis of the publicly owned industries . . . and the complete independence of the workers' Trade Unions so that at no point do they become auxiliaries of State Power.

This adamantine insistence upon the participatory and egalitarian aims of their movement remains a distinguishing mark of the Labour Left and one of its most important contributions.[5]

The Labour Left believed that a planned economy could redistribute wealth and power, thereby bringing complete democracy and moral regeneration, the ultimate goals of socialism, within reach. Here the influence, or at least the vocabulary, of Common Wealth is apparent. Acland, who joined the Labour Party in September 1945, continued to call for "a new motive for living to replace the now exhausted and inoperative doctrine of 'every man out for his own self-interest.'" Driberg held that "people of all kinds . . . seek some design and pattern in their lives. Socialism provides the pattern and the purpose." The entire Labour Left agreed that values of mutuality and solidarity were as fundamental to their vision of socialism as the increased efficiency and higher living standards promised by Morrison. As the editor of the trade-union journal *New Dawn* put it on 21 August 1948, "Only the development of socialism offers any opportunity for the growth of moral values different from those of the jungle, and a conception of human relationships wider than that of dog eat dog." Or, to cite Cole again, this time in the *Glasgow Forward* of 1 November 1947, "Socialism is to be regarded not solely as a political or economic doctrine, but also as a 'way of life' . . . Socialism is fully as much ethical as economic." Or, as the secretary of the "Keep Left" group, Jo Richardson, put it, socialism was

> not a system of economics but a system of ethics, not a piece of machinery but a way of life. Its fulfilment depends not merely on socialising things, but also on a revolution in men's minds. It cannot reach its full fruition until people are willing to absorb themselves wholeheartedly into the community of their fellows, and until they are moved not by the motivation of selfish interests but by the incentive of service to all mankind.

To critics, or to those who doubted the possibility of changing human nature, the young Frank Allaun responded confidently, "Oh yes you can." Once people had believed that slavery was natural. "Today it is regarded as abhorrent and immoral. So will the exploitation of one man by another be regarded in the future."[6]

The Labour Left believed, too, that socialism must be international. The third force movement demonstrated left-wing Labour's real commitment to the principle. It would be fair to say, however, that some members of the Labour Left were more internationalist than others. Crossman always concentrated upon the European aspects of the third force while patronizing non-Europeans. "The Malayans are a tame people," he once wrote dismissively. Such chauvinism, however, was uncommon. Much more typical was Driberg's memorial to the government, signed by more than sixty Labour Members, protesting British support of French and Dutch imperialism in

Indonesia and Indo-China; or Leslie Hale's defense of "the so called ju-ju murderers in the Gold Coast"; or Geoffrey Bing's defense of a condemned man, also in a Gold Coast trial, who had been accused of murdering his brother; or, quintessentially, Fenner Brockway's unswerving and long-standing commitment to the anti-imperialist struggles of Asians and Africans. The internationalism of the Labour Left was one source of its opposition to Bevinism. Where the Foreign Secretary attempted to uphold Britain's traditional imperial role, the Left's deep-seated anti-imperialism helped it to discern, quicker than Bevin, that the effort was beyond the country's strength.[7]

The Labour Left was no less realistic when it came to consider how the socialist transformation which it so ardently desired might be achieved. Fears of counter-revolution expressed in the 1930s by men like Cripps and Strachey, who now belonged to the government, had not been laid to rest. In their flat on Millman Street, "Swingler, [Harold] Davies and I often discussed whether British democracy could stand the strain of a Labour Government that meant business," George Wigg recalled. The three spent their lives attempting to prove that it could, though in the end Wigg thought that his country's institutions had not been severely tested during 1945–51. He wrote bitterly, "There are those who claim that Attlee betrayed the social revolution. He did not believe in social revolution." Many on the Labour Left, however, did believe in it. Basking in the glow of his party's great electoral victory, Laski informed the American correspondent Edward R. Murrow, "We're revolutionaries in the sense that we want by the rational processes of democratic government to reorganise the central principles of our civilization." He added, "and we think we've got a chance of doing it." This was hardly a ringing endorsement of the inevitability of gradualness. Nor were all Labour Left trade unionists noticably more sanguine about the prospects of a peaceful socialist transformation. "In this country . . . an endeavour is being made to achieve a better and more equitable system of society by non-violent means," the *Railway Review* editorialized on 7 December 1945 with remarkable detachment. "The advent of the Labour Government is part of the evolutionary change and leads up to the revolutionary climax which is our next major step." The journal carefully neglected, however, to consider how "the revolutionary climax" would be accomplished.[8]

Yet Labour Left preference for the constitutional path to socialism was deep seated. Mrs Katherine Bruce Glasier, one of the movement's surviving pioneers and the wife of a founder member of the ILP, remembered Eleanor Marx telling her

> that on more than one occasion Marx had declared to her his belief that the British people had it in them to achieve a democratic Socialism without bloodshed. Eleanor spoke of Engels too, and said that he had told her how sorry he was that Marx had not lived to see the tremendous progress made towards democratic Socialism in Britain. . . She told me that she had quite lost faith in revolutionary methods and would support Keir Hardie's ILP if it ever took shape.

Interviewed in the House of Commons, the veteran Red Clydesider David Kirkwood seemed to believe that the peaceful transition had occurred already. "I've been fifty-five years now in politics and I can mind the time when there wasn't a single Socialist legislator in Parliament. Look at Westminster now." The old man paused and went on, rolling his r's with withering scorn, "And you ask for r-r-r-revolutions!"[9]

Along with such sentimental observations the Labour Left was capable of hard-headed calculation. As Jack Tanner explained to the annual conference of the AEU in 1949, "so long as there is a possibility of a peaceful transition to a society of equal opportunity, in which poverty is eliminated, and which gives a better life for all ... then I am going to back it with every means at my disposal." A year later he was warning assembled delegates that "we should be fools and worse to abandon the way of constitutional advance so long as it remains open to us." Kingsley Martin developed a complementary argument for adhering to the parliamentary road, so long as it remained open. While acknowledging that class struggle was "an essential instrument of social analysis . . . *how* the class war is won is obviously also of the utmost importance." Martin believed that Labour must fight for socialism "by means which are in themselves good, and which will make our Socialist victory worth while when we have won it."[10]

Characteristically the Labour Left equated "good" methods of fighting for socialism with democratic practices and fellowship. For many this meant consciously attempting to recreate the kind of movement which the early socialists had developed. Three left-wing MPs—Norman Dodd, G. D. Wallace and Richard Acland—hoped to revive the mood and mode of agitation employed by the socialist pioneers. They suggested "Operation Victory," during which socialist speakers would cycle, like the original Clarion Club members, to speak at open-air meetings. They would be serenaded by a "Victory Socialism Choir" and choose a "Socialism Victory Queen." The only new twist was that the proceedings would be filmed and distributed to constituencies where meetings did not take place. Ellis Smith developed a similar plan. "Everywhere I go," he reported, "I hear people saying, we must revive the pioneering days, we must recapture the comradeship, the spirit of living for a cause." This would be the purpose of the Socialist Fellowship. "We will sing songs again," Smith predicted hopefully.[11]

Yet "Keir Hardie and Robert Blatchford and William Morris ... were products of a situation it is impossible to recall," Cole wrote less romantically—but more sensibly than Smith or Dodd. He favored instead the hard-headed attempt at Buscot to work out socialist priorities in a world transformed by the decline of British power, the development of Soviet communism and the invention of the atomic bomb. Incongruously, the champion of "democracy everywhere" hoped that Fabian experts would guide the socialist movement. The eminently practical Crossman was even less attached to traditional means of carrying on an agitation than the Oxford don. The Member for Coventry East argued that "an informal talk with a Minister may achieve a lot more than a long speech in the House." He had learned to despise the confrontational tendencies of many on the Labour Left. "If you're trying to get someone above you to change his mind its very stupid to assume that he's a villain and abuse him publicly. Your best bet is to assume that he's on the side of the angels and then indicate to him what a dreadful thing it would be if he wasn't." The Labour Left was as divided about the best way to work for socialism as it was about everything else.[12]

On one issue, however, all sections of the Labour Left agreed; their views were popular with the voters and, if accepted by the government, would enable it to keep power. Repeatedly and poignantly they invoked *Let Us Face the Future* as the model of a left-wing election manifesto, urging the government to return to the policies outlined in that document. They claimed that the triumph of the Bevanites in the constituencies section elections at Labour's annual conference in 1951 was a truer reflection of rank-and-file sentiment than were ballots dominated by the trade-union bloc vote. And they pointed with pride to the small number of casualties suffered by Labour Left Members during the general elections of 1950 and 1951. Yet party leaders turned as deaf an ear to this Labour Left claim as to most of its other prescriptions.

III

Why, during 1945–51, did the Labour Left fail to convert the rest of the party to its interpretation of socialism? Why did it so signally fail to change specific government policies to which it had principled objections?

Historians of the Attlee governments have emphasized the weakness of the Labour Left both inside Parliament and out. One aim of the present volume, however, has been to indicate the significant strength of the Labour Left in the constituencies, and in some unions, and its far from negligible presence in the PLP. To reiterate only one example of its representation in the parliamentary party: 142 Labour Members, a good third of the PLP, did not vote for British entry into NATO. Not all the abstainers opposed the Atlantic Pact. Some were absent due to illness or pressing business. It seems fair to say, nevertheless, that it was not simple lack of numbers which rendered the Labour Left so powerless.[13]

Nor can it have been another explanation often advanced by scholars, that the Labour Left failed to carry its policies because it recognized their unpopularity with the general electorate and therefore felt inhibited about campaigning for them. No doubt pressure on the Labour Left to tone down its rhetoric was intense before both the 1950 and 1951 general elections. Yet there was no let-up in the battle between consolidators and fundamentalists in the first instance, and in the second, Bevan chose to lead the gravest Labour Left rebellion of the period. This is not to suggest that politicians on the Labour Left ignored electoral considerations. In fact, however, the Left generally argued that its policies, if adopted by the government, would be popular and ensure victory at the polls. And this study has sought to show that the Labour Left fought for most of its goals with tenacity and intelligence. The history of the Labour Left during 1945–51 bears little resemblance to the Sherlock Holmes story in which the significant thing was that the dog did not bark.[14]

Historians and critics of the Labour Left have argued more tellingly that Labour's left wing has been doomed to impotence because historically it has concentrated on Parliament, while neglecting to build a radical mass base in the working class. Yet one is struck by the close relationships which developed between MPs and local activists in the constituencies we have examined in detail. Geoffrey Bing helped to build a socialist constituency in Hornchurch. As the Gateshead CLP attested, Zilliacus developed an important local following. Even Platts Mills was "generally well liked" by Finsbury CLP, according to Labour's London organizer.[15]

It may be pointed out, in addition, that it was during 1945–51 that the Labour Left cemented its hold over the CLPs. From this period on, the constituencies section of the NEC always contained a majority of left-wingers. It was during the early postwar era too that the constituency Labour parties began developing methods of communication with one another in order to maximize their impact on Labour's annual conferences. When the government attempted to curtail the circulation of messages between CLPs, it faced concerted and effective resistance. It is true that the Labour Left did not attempt to offer its own candidates to local parties when vacancies occurred in the PLP. Yet the weight of the evidence offered in this study indicates significant left-wing strength at the constituency level which was due, in part, to coordination between parliamentary Members and local activists. In this respect it is wrong to fault the parliamentary Labour Left for neglecting the world beyond Westminster.

A like point may be made about the various Labour Left pressure groups. The "Keep Left" group frequently has been represented as an elite debating society far removed from the hurly-burly of the class struggle. In reality it was not oblivious to the need for extra-parliamentary action. What, after all, was the purpose of its famous pamphlets except to bring before a mass constituency the demand for a "more drastic Socialist policy?" As for the Socialist Fellowship and Victory for Socialism groups, both represented conscious attempts to create a base outside Parliament for the Labour Left. What is more, with prominent Labour leftists like Foot, Driberg, Crossman and Hughes writing weekly in mass-circulation newspapers, the charge might easily have been not that they were overly concerned with events in Westminster, but rather that they were neglecting their parliamentary duties in order to create support for left-wing policies through their journalism.

It remains true, however, that connections between Labour Left politicians and trade unionists were tenuous (though one is obliged to point out that Walter Padley of USDAW and Bob Edwards of the Chemical Workers entered Parliament themselves in 1950 and 1955 respectively, thus personifying the very links historians have thought to be missing). The Labour Left confronted particularly difficult problems in the trade unions. As we have seen, the trade-union Left often was dominated by communists. It proved most difficult for the Labour Left to build a specific following in the unions separate from them. It was not so much lack of interest in the trade unions as lack of opportunity which limited Labour Left influence among them.

If previous explanations for the weakness of the Labour Left want force, at least for the 1945–51 period, to what may left-wing Labour's general lack of success be ascribed? The evidence presented in this study suggests several factors which may help account for the Labour Left failure to influence events more decisively.

There were, to begin with, structural impediments to the influence of the Left within the PLP. Of course, as we have seen, at first the Labour Left optimistically believed that Attlee's government would need no prompting from it. On 5 August

1945, immediately after the great general election victory, Driberg wrote, almost apologetically, in *Reynolds News*, "Some of us may suffer for a time from 'opposition mindedness'—a hangover from the years of frustration." At that early date he intended to give the government unstinting support. Even six months later, on 5 January 1946, the *New Statesman* believed that "the Labour Whips have never had an easier time... [This] is the tribute paid to a leadership which, taken all in all, has surpassed expectation." The government, however, took nothing for granted. On 30 August it created seventeen subject groups, and encouraged participation in them as an outlet for the energies of Labour Members with specific interests and concerns. When later the Labour Left discovered grievances, these groups were the instruments most readily at hand for publicizing them. The External Affairs Group, for example, became a megaphone for backbenchers dissatisfied with Bevin's foreign policy. Its powers, however, were purely advisory, and, as we have seen, the Foreign Secretary quickly learned to disregard its exhortations. The subject groups may have siphoned off the energies of Labour Left critics. They provided no leverage for shifting government policies.

More promising, perhaps, were the weekly meetings of the PLP. Yet, as "Phineas" observed in the *New Statesman* on 10 August 1946, hitherto these had "so completely failed to provide a possibility of serious discussion that most Members do not bother to attend." Later, when Maurice Webb was appointed PLP chairman, attendance improved, but the meetings were if anything even less satisfactory to the Labour Left. Now the *New Statesman* complained, "a meeting of several hundred Members is too unwieldy for serious discussion." Laski might, at the end of the fuel crisis, exhort "the critics . . . to make the institutions built for criticism work efficiently." He meant the PLP weekly meetings. Yet a further and inherent difficulty had been revealed. So long as Labour formed the government, any important issue formally raised at a party meeting was bound to be treated by the leaders as a matter of confidence. Unless the Labour Left was prepared to push dissension to the ultimate conclusion if need be, and demand the dismissal of ministers whom it no longer trusted, its members always would find it difficult to resist government appeals for loyalty.[16]

Then there was Labour's National Executive Committee. On this body the Left was, if anything, more powerless than in the regular gatherings of the PLP. It was always outnumbered and outvoted. This remained true even during the 1950s, after the Labour Left had learned to coordinate its vote for the constituencies sections of the NEC. Kingsley Martin's description of Laski's dilemma as an NEC member holds for all left-wing Labourites who gained election to the committee:

> In private conversation and on public platforms he promised more than he could perform; in the Executive he could do no more than put forward his proposals and, finding himself hopelessly outnumbered, propose a compromise which would be accepted more or less in the form he suggested and which was then binding on him . . . Year after year he allowed himself to be reluctantly responsible as a Member of the Executive for a policy which he denounced in private and which, because of his Party loyalty, he just managed to avoid denouncing in public.

Eventually Laski resigned from the NEC. This, however, was an impossible recourse for the Labour Left as a whole, unless it wished publicly to renounce all hope of influencing the larger party to which it belonged. Much as one may respect the values and goals to which Laski dedicated himself, he was in the last analysis the Walter Mitty of the Labour Left.[17]

Some left-wing Labourites believed that the right-wing majority on the NEC was due to the intimidating presence of government ministers. As representatives of the Cabinet, their first loyalty was to the government whose advocates, naturally, they became. The NEC, however, even if it was composed of the leaders of the Labour Party, owed its primary allegiance to Labour as a whole, not to the government. A St Marylebone Labour councillor, Nat Whine, circulated a memorandum in November 1947 which argued that the solution was to prohibit government ministers from belonging to the NEC. This prescription gained few adherents who were not already on the Labour Left. Whine's memorandum changed nothing.[18]

The ultimate sanction of the Labour party over its leaders resided in the annual conference. Yet here, too, the Labour Left lacked leverage. Attlee's was the first Labour government to provide anything like a credible performance. At conference the platform inevitably was invested with a prestige its critics could never equal. It was not, however, the government's matchless aura which accounts for Labour Left powerlessness. As with the PLP weekly meetings, so at conference Attlee could treat any significant issue as a matter of confidence. It was difficult indeed for the Labour Left to convince delegates that their duty was not to present a unified front to the outside world. This proved particularly true for the trade-union delegates, who possessed an overwhelming majority of the votes. The Labour Left never managed to overturn at conference a decision which the government deemed important.

It was not, however, for lack of trying. Every year a growing number of CLPs registered their discontent with government policies. Every year coordination between them, and between the Labour Left MPs, improved. It was lack of time, as much as anything else, which stymied their efforts.

We must remember that many Labour Left MPs were neophyte politicians in 1945. As Woodrow Wyatt recalled years later, "I was barely able to take in the fact that I had gone straight from the Army to Westminster, as indeed had many of my colleagues." At first, such Members lacked the necessary skills, if not the self-confidence, to challenge the booming, extroverted Dalton, the massive Bevin, the master political tacticians Morrison and, though at the time they themselves did not appreciate it, Clement Attlee. Their early manifestations betray their lack of weight. Wyatt himself wrote impatiently in the *New Statesman* on 8 September 1945, "In 1929 I believe that new and young Labour MPs, like I myself am now, were told to give the Labour Government a chance, to give them time. . . What is the use of having an orderly revolution if it turns out not to be a revolution at all?" Wyatt objected to government ministers demanding patience and more time from the "young Turks" on Labour's back benches. Ironically, however, the young men in a hurry were the ones who really needed time if they were to become an effective political force.[19]

Yet time was the one thing which the Labour Left did not have. It demonstrated in eight short months, from November 1946 to July 1947, a remarkable capacity for learning the methods of intra-party warfare: organizing the famous amendment to the Address from the Throne; forcing the government to back down on the length of National Service through judicious combination with Labour's pacifist contingent; and presenting with real verve and impact in *Keep Left* alternative policies to the government's, even though, as the *Daily Herald* of 2 May noted in some surprise, the average age of its authors was only thirty-five. Two months later, during the convertibility crisis, it came as close to defeating the government as it dared. Already, however, the cold war was closing off options, hardening people's minds, exposing incoherencies and disagreements within the Labour Left. The result of the Marshall Plan, of the Russian response to it, of the communist coup in Prague, of the division of the world into two hostile blocs and of the cold war in all its many forms was to freeze the growth of the Labour Left, and to shatter it into pieces.

Diverse and multifaceted as the Labour Left was, its strength depended upon the mutual respect and good faith of its members. These were destroyed by the cold war. In the trade unions, where left-wing effectiveness depended upon cooperation among communists and non-communist leftists, red-baiting on the one hand, and the refusal of communists to disavow Soviet practices on the other, brought a short-lived popular front between the two Lefts to an end. By 1951 former allies were separated by a wide and seemingly unbridgable chasm. In the PLP the gulf between "hard" and "soft" Labour leftists was somewhat less stark since both were members of the same political party. It was an effective barrier to collaboration between them, none the less. Brockway and Smith resigned from the Socialist Fellowship because they found it impossible to work with a "hard" Labour leftist like Tom Braddock. Hale and Wigg resigned from the "Keep Left" group when its most important members agreed to support the government's defense estimates. Mikardo gave up his directorship of *Tribune* newspaper because he could not accept the anti-communist rhetoric of Michael Foot and Jennie Lee. Mackay's Europe Group disintegrated into warring factions. It took the relinquishment of office by Bevan, Wilson and Freeman to reinvigorate and make possible some kind of reunification of the parliamentary Labour Left.

Until the three Cabinet ministers made that decisive gesture, the Left in the PLP never had wanted to coalesce in a single powerful organization. It could not have done so if it tried. For all that many of its members were deeply alienated by government policy, most left-wing Labourites sought only influence during this period, not outright power. No parliamentary "rebellion" was complete until the rebels had protested their innocence of organizing against the leadership. This was as true for the "hard" as for the "soft" Labour Left. As Emrys Hughes put it on 8 May 1948 in the *Glasgow Forward*, after being carpeted by Morgan Phillips for signing the Nenni telegram:

It is utter nonsense to talk about the 21 of us as a subversive group. We had never met before the Executive circularised us. We are a cross-section of MPs who may, at one time or another, have criticised the foreign policy of the Government from different angles.

Hughes might as well have been speaking of the group who abstained from voting on the November 1946 Address from the Throne, or of the signatories of the various fusion telegrams, or of the MPs who came together to found "Keep Left," or Socialist Fellowship, or to revive Victory for Socialism. Most of these men and women saw themselves as the keepers of Labour's conscience rather than as an alternative leadership of their party.

Consider, for example, the Member for Devonport, Michael Foot. "A lean, tall shy youth [whose] conspicuous personal qualities are seriousness, sincerity and devotion," according to one contemporary description, Foot was already a superb journalist, a master of political invective whose pen could flay the Tory Members, "Squeezem and Blockhead," or rally the Labour Party faithful to heroic effort. Few political columnists could match Foot's fierce, passionate, inspirational prose. "Let us not forget," he cautioned readers in a typical passage,

> this government and this Parliament are summoned to display the tireless energy of Francis Place, the burning anger against injustice of William Cobbett, the sublime hopefulness of Tom Paine, the rugged daring of the Chartists, the unity of the men who downed tools in 1926, the faith of the handful who met [to found the Labour Party] forty years ago.

In what role was a man with such talents most useful to his party? One suspects that Foot himself preferred to be a spur, a voice, exhorting the government to live up to its heritage, and the people to support it. Probably he did not even conceive that he could be the future leader of the Labour Party.[20]

A host of other Labour Left MPs fall roughly into the same category. They were keepers of the flame more than party politicians. Emrys Hughes, for example, was "perhaps the nearest thing to a pure Keir Hardie Socialist in the present House of Commons," according to Driberg. But he had always the air of the wide-eyed boy who blurted out that the emperor had no clothes, an important role but not with sufficient gravitas for a future Cabinet minister. Someone like Sydney Silverman appears temperamentally unsuited for a leadership position. He was, as Woodrow Wyatt put it, not unkindly, "the most individualistic person in Parliament. . . Whatever the Government . . . he would oppose it without fear on a variety of issues." Zilliacus was a similar figure. Many years later Foot termed him "a political saint." Successful politicians usually possess different attributes than do candidates for canonization.[21]

The Labour Left also had its share of conventionally ambitious men and women. Of them perhaps Richard Crossman was most able. Leslie Hale thought "he could still lead the Labour Party . . . if he can acquire the habit of taking decisions and standing by them." Crossman was indefatigable. In addition to carrying on the multifarious duties of an MP, he organized the amendment to the King's Speech in 1946, wrote the most important chapter of *Keep Left*, helped draft the follow-up pamphlet, *Keeping Left*, took over the editorship from G. D. H. Cole of *New Fabian Essays* and contributed weekly columns to the *Sunday Pictorial*, serving all the while as assistant editor to Kingsley Martin at the *New Statesman*. Yet this tireless figure was "always put[ting] stones in his own shoes," as Dalton observed to Attlee. He inspired mistrust even among allies. For example, Martin was

> never sure that [Crossman's] judgment is disinterested in its relation to his other ambitions, or that he will say the same thing to a different audience or person, or that he will keep silent . . . if gossip is attractive, or that he will stand by his colleagues in a tight place.

Martin considered that he had never "worked on the paper with anyone so brilliant but so impurely motivated." If this was the verdict of a close colleague, it is not hard to imagine the emotions Crossman inspired among opponents. Lester Hutchinson, the expelled Labour Member for Rusholme, thought him incapable "of holding one political opinion for longer than a fortnight." Attlee recalled the verdict of the warden of New College, Oxford, upon him: "Bad judgment, why he has no judgment at all." It was impossible for such a figure to play more than a secondary political role whatever his capacities until, by his own actions, he had erased these overwhelmingly negative first impressions.[22]

Other Labour Left MPs who might have aspired to cut a larger figure aroused distrust for different reasons. Hale confided to his diary that "one well informed Minister [Bevan or Wilson, perhaps?] says that George Wigg is the Parliamentary secret service agent of MI5, and he does not say it as a joke either." Ian Mikardo, whom Hale thought "one of the outstanding brains of the Party," missed promotion, according to Dalton, because he was Jewish. As for Tom Driberg, his personal life was held against him. In addition to being homosexual, he was thought to have some connection with the unsavoury Aleister Crowley, a practitioner of black magic who thought he was the great beast 666 foreshadowed in the Book of Revelations.[23]

With the exception of Silverman, these were all men who belonged to the "class of 1945." Whatever their qualities and talents, none had yet either the experience or stature to lead a dissident movement against the leaders of the Labour Party. There were in the PLP, of course, elder figures to whom they might have looked for leadership. Seymour Cocks, for example, had been prominent during the war as one of the few Labour Members willing to challenge Winston Churchill. He was more an agitator, however, than a statesman and in any case moved away from the Left after 1945. Then there was S. O. Davies, an admirable figure but a lone wolf rather than a leader. James Maxton, who headed the rump ILP in Parliament, was obviously a man of the past—anyway, he died in 1946. Such figures helped to define the goals and outlook of the postwar Labour Left, but they could not provide its leadership.

It would have been natural for the Labour Left to seek leaders among the men and women who had led the fight against Transport House during the prewar era. But Bevan, Cripps, Strachey, Shinwell, Wilkinson and Strauss all belonged to the government, or soon would, and thus had been neutralized by the doctrine of collective responsibility. Moreover, Wilkinson died in 1946, while Cripps, Strachey and Strauss moved sharply to the Right. Shinwell's reputation suffered irreparable damage after the 1947 fuel crisis. And Bevan was preoccupied by his epic struggle against the British Medical Association, which opposed the creation of a National Health Service. The Labour Left could challenge for leadership of the party only when it had credible substitutes for the front bench. This was impossible until after 1950.

"The real trouble," Hale thought, "is that the Left are left so completely without a leader." Although not the sole reason for Labour Left weakness during 1945–51, it was more important, perhaps, than it has been fashionable to say. At any rate, lack of leadership, which itself was due to a variety of deep-seated factors, combined with structural impediments in the party's organization and the unbearable pressures of the cold war to diffuse the immediate impact of Labour's left wing.[24]

IV

If during 1945–51 the influence of the Labour Left on events was small, the significance of its experience was great. The Labour Left response to the challenges and problems posed by Attlee's government, and by the cruel postwar situation, presented both the culmination of tendencies present on the Left in Britain for half a century and a prophecy of the future course of the British Left.

Since Labour's foundation in 1900 the Left had viewed the party with ambivalence. Beginning with the Marxist SDF in 1901 and ending with Common Wealth some forty years later, left-wing breakaways occurred sporadically. During 1945–51, however, left-wing Labour finally resolved, as Brockway put it on rejoining the party in 1947, that "this was the movement of the common people of Britain from whom a changed society will come." Brockway had learned to regard the Labour Party "as a process rather than as a machine." Crucial perception, it was the fundamental lesson taught by the postwar Labour Left. Labour's policies "may fall short of what one desires," Brockway acknowledged, but the parliamentary party was merely a part of the labor movement as a whole. As S. O. Davies had reminded Morgan Phillips, "Our Movement embraces millions of men and women, and not merely a few hundred Members of Parliament and a few dozen who may constitute from time to time our National Executive." Emrys Hughes made the same point after Labour's annual conference in 1950:

> There is no use remaining aloof and dividing yourselves into isolationists and sects. Yes, I know all you are likely to say about the "yes men" and the careerists and the office seekers and the ex-revolutionaries turned into the worst reactionaries. They come and go, but remember it's your movement, not theirs.

The editors of the *Railway Review* made the same point in even stronger language on 29 June 1951. "It is our Labour Party... The power to change policy is ours. The power to change leaders is ours." When Bevan resigned from the government, many thought he would break away from Labour altogether, as Mosley had done in 1931. The prospect does not appear to have occurred to him, or to any of his followers. The postwar Labour Left had resolved the long-standing dilemma of previous rebels, their direct ancestors, in Labour's favor.[25]

They struggled on three fronts to stamp their own identity upon the party. In the trade unions left-wing non-communists, building upon the experience of guild socialists and syndicalists, devised models for worker control of industry which testify to the Labour Left insistence upon autonomy and the rights of the individual. In the CLPs the Labour Left stood upon the shoulders of prewar activists in a battle to make Transport House accountable to the wishes of the rank and file, and to democratize both the NEC and annual conferences of the movement. At Westminster, Labour Left Members of the postwar era likewise built upon the efforts of their predecessors. They led the opposition to cuts in the social services, first during the 1947 convertibility crisis, and thereafter at Budget time every year. Their rallying cry was "never another 1931!" In a famous leader of 20 April 1951, *Tribune* levelled the charge of "MacDonaldism" against Gaitskell when he insisted upon the fees for spectacles and dentures. In its approach to the government's foreign policy, too, the Labour Left of 1945–51 carried on the struggles of prewar rebels. Advocacy of the third force was nothing less than a summation of the democratic socialist outlook, and of British Labour's long-held belief in its own redemptive mission.

Yet if the Labour Left visibly bore the weight of history in its critique of government policies, it was more than anything else forward-looking. Its greatest achievement was the outlining of a program for Labour which has proved a reservoir for the British Left ever since: practical plans for democratic control of industry, alternative methods to nationalization for controlling the economy in the interests of all citizens, unilateral renunciation of nuclear weapons, the socialist third force to balance between Russia and America. It is not surprising that the Labour Left failed to carry these policies during the six short years of Attlee's premiership. They encompass, after all, some of the most basic issues to confront the postwar world.

During 1945–51 Labour Left emotions ran the gamut, from exhilaration at the party's great general election victory, to disappointment with the government's rather cautious performance, to despair as the polarizing process of East–West tensions rolled inexorably forward and finally to a sense of possible resurrection under the leadership of Aneurin Bevan. That roller-coaster experience shattered or deferred the achievement of many Labour Left hopes. It smashed left-wing Labour's fragile unity, bringing many former critics into the government camp (until the advent of Bevan among the dissidents), while pushing a small number of intransigents into outright opposition. But the Labour Left experience of the early postwar era encompasses the complex task of modern democratic socialism, to combine social justice and liberty. It deserves to be considered as an important chapter in a story which continues to unfold.

Notes and References

1　For complete accounts of those great achievements, see, of course, Kenneth O. Morgan, *Labour in Power, 1945–51* (Oxford, 1984); Henry Pelling, *The Labour Governments*, 1945–51 (London, 1984); Alan Bullock, *Ernest Bevin: Foreign Secretary* (London, 1983).

2　*The Times*, 26 June 1945; for Morrison's memorandum, see Labour Party, Morgan Phillips papers, Dorking Conference file.

3　*Reynolds News*, 24 February 1946.

4　Labour Party, 1945 general election file, Richard Crossman election leaflet.

5　Bob Edwards, *The Only Hope Socialism* (London, 1946), pp. 4–5; *Glasgow Forward*, 15 June 1951; Richard Crossman, "The Next Fifty Years," paper presented to the fourth Buscot conference, preserved in BLPES, Hugh Dalton papers, 9/10/1.

6　*Reynolds News*, 23 September 1945, 19 March 1950; House of Lords Record Office, Benn Levy papers, file 20, 1951 general election, "Jo Richardson's election special;" *New Dawn*, 17 February 1951.

7　*Sunday Pictorial*, 22 August 1948; Bodleian Library, C. R. Attlee papers, dep. 24, ff. 123, 226, 247; Lord Hale papers, diary, 6 February 1950; *Hornchurch and Upminster News*, 27 January 1950.

8　George Wigg, *George Wigg* (London, 1972), pp. 110, 133; *Daily Herald*, 2 August 1945.

9　*Glasgow Forward*, 5 March 1949, 11 January 1947.

10　*AEU Annual Conference, 1949* and ibid., 1950, presidential addresses of Jack Tanner; *New Statesman*, 15 June 1946.

11　*Reynolds News*, 17 July 1949, 22 May 1949.

12　*Glasgow Forward*, 15 June 1951; BBC, Written Archives, Broadcasting House, "Inside Parliament," 31 October 1950, 14 November 1950.

13　For the weakness of the Labour Left, see Morgan, *Labour in Power*; Pelling, *The Labour Governments*; Bullock, *Ernest Bevin*; David Coates, *The Labour Party and the Struggle for Socialism* (Cambridge, 1975); Ralph Miliband, *Parliamentary Socialism* (London, 1972).

14　Coates, *Labour Party and the Struggle for Socialism*, p. 201, for example.

15　Coates, ibid., and Miliband, *Parliamentary Socialism*, make this argument.

16　*New Statesman*, 25 January 1947; *Reynolds News*, 13 April 1947.

17　Kingsley Martin, *Harold Laski, A Biographical Memoir* (London, 1953), p. 190.

18　Whine's "Memorandum defining the relationship between the Labour Party and Labour government" is preserved among the papers of the Labour Party. However, I have used the copy which Laski sent to Felix Frankfurter: Library of Congress, Washington, DC, Frankfurter papers.

19　Woodrow Wyatt, *Into the Dangerous World* (London, 1952), p. 105.

20　*Toronto Star*, 16 November 1946; *Daily Herald*, 15 February 1946.

21　*Reynolds News*, 22 May 1949; Wyatt, *Dangerous World*, p. 146.

22　Hale diary, 9 January 1950; Dalton papers, 9/18/2, Dalton to Attlee, 15 April 1951; Sussex University, Kingsley Martin papers, Box 25, file 5; *Daily Worker*, 3 February 1950; Dalton papers, 9/18/22, Attlee to Dalton, 16 April 1951.

23　Hale diary, 29 April 1951, 9 January 1950; Morgan, *Labour in Power*, p. 460; interview with Mr E. R. Millington.

24　Hale diary, 9 January 1950.

25　*Daily Herald*, 8 January 1947; *Labour Forum*, October–December 1947; see above, page 116; *Glasgow Forward*, 14 October 1950.

Appendix 1   *The Labour Left in Parliament*

THE FOLLOWING CHART lists the Labour Members who signed the fusion telegrams, the open letter to Attlee and a number of Labour Left pamphlets, who belonged to the various Labour Left groups and who opposed the government in the House on a variety of key issues. The list is not exhaustive, but it is suggestive. It demonstrates that, except for the issue of conscription, most of the pacifist contingent in the House rarely supported the Labour Left. Strikingly, it lists 145 Labour Members, more than a third of the PLP. Thus it provides further evidence of substantial Labour Left strength on the back benches during 1945–51.

	Anglo-American loan, December 1945	First German telegram, March 1946	Open letter to Attlee, October 1946	Crossman's amendment, November 1946	Anti-conscription, April 1947	*Keep Left,* May 1947	Secon tel Dece
R. Acland (Kent, Gravesend)							
H. R. Adams (Wandsworth, Balham and Tooting)				X			
G. Aligham (Kent, Gravesend)					X		
S. S. Allen (Chester, Crewe)				X			
A. Anderson (Lanark, Motherwell)					X		
H. L. Austin (Lancaster, Stretford)		X		X			
W. H. Ayles (Southall)					X		
J. Baird (Wolverhampton East)							
A. Balfour (Stirling and Clackmannan West)							
P. Barstow (Yorkshire, West Riding, Pontefract)				X			
J. R. Battley (Wandsworth, Clapham)				X			
G. Bing (Essex, Hornchurch)						X	
A. R. Blackburn (Birmingham, King's Norton)	X						
E. Braddock (Liverpool Exchange)		X		X			
T. Braddock (Mitcham)	X				X		
A. Bramall (Bexley)			X	X			
F. Brockway (Buckinghamshire, Eton and Slough)							
T. J. Brown (Lancaster, Ince)				X			
D. Bruce (Portsmouth North)		X	X	X		X	
T. W. Burden (Sheffield Park)					X		
H. W. Butler (Hackney South)					X		
J. Callaghan (Cardiff South)	X		X				
B. Castle (Blackburn)	X						
R. Chamberlain (Lambeth, Norwood)							
D. Chater (Bethnal Green)							
G. R. Chetwynd (Stockton-on-Tees)		X		X			
F. S. Cocks (Nottingham, Broxtowe)	X				X		
V. J. Collins (Somerset, Taunton)	X			X	X		
L. Comyns (West Ham, Silvertown)							
T. F. Cook (Dundee)		X			X		
G. Cooper (Middlesbrough West)	X						
Viscount Corvedale (Paisley)					X		
W. G. Cove (Glamorgan, Aberavon)	X	X	X	X	X		
R. H. S. Crossman (Coventry East)			X	X		X	
Harold Davies (Stafford, Leek)		X	X	X		X	
Hayden Davies (St Pancras South-West)				X			
R. J. Davies (Lancaster, Westhoughton)					X		
S. O. Davies (Merthyr Tydfil, Merthyr)				X	X		
H. J. Delargy (Manchester, Platting)	X						
W. Dobbie (Rotherham)							
N. Dodd (Dartford)		X					
T. Driberg (Essex, Maldon)				X			
M. Edelman (Coventry West)	X			X			

…ist civil …nts, 1948	Nenni telegram, April 1948	Nenni "goats"	Socialist Europe Group pamphlet	Socialist Fellowship, 1949–50	Labour Independent Group, 1949–50	*Keeping Left,* 1950	VfS, 1951	Early Bevanites, 1951
						X	X	X
	X							
	X	X		X				
	X							
	X							
	X	X						
	X	X					X	
	X	X		X				
				X				
				X		X		
						X		X
				X				
			X					
	X	X						X
	X		X	X		X		X
						X	X	X
	X	X						
	X	X	X					X
	X							

	Anglo-American loan, December 1945	First German telegram, March 1946	Open letter to Attlee, October 1946	Crossman's amendment, November 1946	Anti-conscription, April 1947	*Keep Left,* May 1947	Secon… / tel… / Dece…
S. N. Evans (Wednesbury)	X						
W. J. Farthing (Somerset, Frome)							
M. Follick (Leicester, Loughborough)	X					X	
M. Foot (Plymouth, Devonport)	X		X	X		X	
J. C. Forman (Glasgow, Springhorn)					X		
W. Foster (Wigan)					X		
E. Fernyhough (Jarrow)					X		
C. S. Garley (Battersea South)					X		
H. E. Goodrich (Hackney North)			X				
B. Ayrton Gould (Hendon North)							
J. R. Grenfell (Glamorgan, Gower)	X				X		
E. Grierson (Carlisle)							
J. Griffiths (Carmarthen Llanelly)		X					
W. D. Griffiths (Manchester, Moss Side)			X	X			
J. Haire (Buckinghamshire, Wycombe)				X			
L. Hale (Oldham)							X
S. Hastings (Barking)							
M. Hewitson (Lanark, Northern)			X		X		
J. H. Hudson (Ealing West)					X		
E. Hughes (South Ayrshire)							
H. L. Hutchinson (Manchester, Rush Olme)		X					
A. J. Irvine (Liverpool, Edge Hill)							
G. Jeger (Hampshire, Winchester)							
S. W. Jeger (St Pancras South-East)		X					
W. John (Rhondda West)					X		
C. Kenyon (Lancaster, Choney)					X		
D. Kirkwood (Dumbarton)		X					
G. Lang (Chester, Stalybridge and Hyde)					X		X
F. Lee (Manchester, Hulme)							
J. Lee (Stafford, Cannock)	X		X	X			
N. H. Lever (Manchester, Exchange)							
B. Levy (Buckinghamshire, Eton and Slough)	X		X	X		X	
A. Lewis (West Ham, Upton)				X			
M. Lipton (Lambeth, Brixton)							
F. Longden (Birmingham. Deritend)					X		
J. D. Mack (Newcastle-under-Lyme)							
R. W. G. Mackay (Hull North-West)		X	X	X		X	X
J. P. W. Mallalieu (Huddersfield)						X	
J. Mann (Lanark, Coatbridge)					X		
L. Manning (Essex, Epping)		X					
W. McAdam (Salford North)							
H. G. McGhee (Yorkshire, West Riding, Penistone)			X	X	X		
J. McGovern (Shettleston, Glasgow)					X		
F. Messer (Tottenham South)			X		X		
I. Mikardo (Reading)				X	X		X
E. R. Millington (Essex,							

...ist civil ...ts, 1948	Nenni telegram, April 1948	Nenni "goats"	Socialist Europe Group pamphlet	Socialist Fellowship, 1949–50	Labour Independent Group, 1949–50	*Keeping Left,* 1950	VfS, 1951	Early Bevanites, 1951
	X							
	X							
								X
							X	X
				X		X		X
	X	X						
	X	X			X			
	X							
				X				
								X
	X	X						
						X	X	
	X							
	X	X						
								X
			X					
	X							
							X	
							X	
						X	X	X

	Anglo-American loan, December 1945	First German telegram, March 1946	Open letter to Attlee, October 1946	Crossman's amendment, November 1946	Anti-conscription, April 1947	*Keep Left,* May 1947	Secon... tel... Dece...
Chelmsford)				X	X	X	
E. Moeran (South Bedfordshire)							
W. Monslow (Barrow-in-Furness)					X		
R. Morley (Southampton)					X		
P. Morris (Swansea West)					X		
J. D. Murray (Durham, Spennymoor)					X		
W. Nally (Wolverhampton, Bilston)					X		
M. W. Nichol (Bradford North)					X		
M. Orbach (Willesden East)		X					
A. M. F. Palmer (Wimbledon)				X			
B. Parkin (Gloucester, Stroud)		X		X			
F. Paton (Nottingham, Rushcliffe)					X		
W. Perrins (Birmingham, Yardley)				X			
J. F. Platts Mills (Finsbury)		X			X		
H. E. Randall (Lancaster, Clitheroe)					X		
J. Rankin (Glasgow, Tradeston)					X		
J. Reeves (Greenwich)			X	X			
R. Richards (Denbigh, Wrexham)					X		
M. Ridealgh (Ilford North)					X		
G. O. Roberts (Caernarvonshire)					X		
C. Royle (Salford West)					X		
R. Sargood (Bermondsey West)					X		
T. Scollan (Renfrew Western)		X					
S. Segal (Preston)				X			
E. Shackleton (Preston South)				X			
C. Shawcross (Lancaster, Widnes)			X	X			
P. Shurmer (Birmingham, Sparkbrook)							
J. Silverman (Birmingham Erdington)		X			X		
S. Silverman (Nelson and Colne)			X	X	X		
C. Skeffington-Lodge (Bedfordshire, Bedford)							
C. Smith (Essex, Colchester)		X		X	X		
E. Smith (Stoke-on-Trent, Stoke)							
H. N. Smith (Nottingham South)	X						
L. J. Solley (Essex, Thurrock)		X		X	X		
R. R. Stokes (Ipswich)	X				X		
B. Stross (Stoke-on-Trent, Hanley)		X		X			
S. Swingler (Stafford, Stafford)		X				X	
I. O. Thomas (The Wrecken)					X		
T. G. Thomas (Cardiff Central)					X		
S. Tiffany (Northampton, Peterborough)		X			X		
J. Timmins (Lanark, Bothwell)					X		
A. C. Usborne (Birmingham, Acock's Green)	X				X		
W. Vernon (Camberwell, Dulwich)				X	X		
S. P. Viant (Willesden North)					X		
W. Warbey (Bedfordshire, Luton)	X			X			
T. E. Watkins (Brecon and Radnor)					X		
P. L. Wells (Kent, Faversham)					X		
G. Wigg (Dudley)						X	
C. Wilcock (Derby)	X						

...ist civil ...nts, 1948	Nenni telegram, April 1948	Nenni "goats"	Socialist Europe Group pamphlet	Socialist Fellowship, 1949–50	Labour Independent Group, 1949–50	*Keeping Left,* 1950	VfS, 1951	Early Bevanites, 1951
	X						X	
	X	X	X					
	X		X					
	X	X			X			
	X	X						
	X	X						
	X	X	X				X	
			X					
			X					
				X				
	X	X			X			
			X					
	X		X	X		X	X	X
	X							
	X	X	X					
	X	X	X				X	
		X						
						X		

	Anglo-American loan, December 1945	First German telegram, March 1946	Open letter to Attlee, October 1946	Crossman's amendment, November 1946	Anti-conscription, April 1947	*Keep Left,* May 1947	Seco... t... Dec...
L. Wilkes (Newcastle-upon-Tyne)		X	X				
F. T. Willey (Sunderland)		X					
D. J. Williams (Glamorgan, Neath)						X	
T. Williams (Yorkshire, West Riding, Don Valley)							
W. R. Williams (Heston and Isleworth)						X	
W. Wyatt (Birmingham, Aston)			X	X		X	
V. Yates (Birmingham, Ladywood)					X		
K. Zilliacus (Gateshead)		X		X	X		

Communist civil servants, March 1948	Nenni telegram, April 1948	Nenni "goats"	Socialist Europe Group pamphlet	Socialist Fellowship, 1949–50	Labour Independent Group, 1949–50	*Keeping Left,* 1950	VfS, 1951	Early Bevanites, 1951
	X		X					
						X		
X	X	X			X			

Appendix 2   *CLPs Demanding an Emergency Conference*

THIS LIST HAS been compiled from Morgan Phillips's constituencies files. Quite possibly it is incomplete.

Altrincham and Sale
Ashton-under-Lyne
Aylesbury
Barnstaple
Basingstoke
Bassetlaw
Battersea
Bebington
Bedford
Bethnal Green
Birkenhead
Birmingham Aston
Birmingham Borough
Birmingham Perry Bar
Birmingham Small Heath
Birmingham Stechford
Blackpool South
Bolton Borough
Brecon and Radnor
Brighouse and Spenborough
Bristol North-West
Bristol West
Bromley
Cardiff Borough
Cardiff North
Chelmsford
Chislehurst
Coventry Borough
Coventry East
Coventry North
Dagenham
Derbyshire North-East
Dorset South
Dudley

Ealing South
East Grinstead
Edmonton
Enfield
Eton and Slough
Finchley
Folkestone and Hythe
Fulham East
Fylde North
Glasgow Camlachie
Glasgow Maryhill
Grimsby
Hackney South
Harrow Central
Hayes and Harlington
Hertfordshire South-West
High Peak
Holborn and St Pancras
Hull City
Huntingdon
Ilford South
Islington East
Kidderminster
Kirkcaldy Burgh
Lanark City
Leicester City
Leighton Borough
Lewisham West
Liverpool Exchange
Liverpool West Derby
Manchester Moss Side
Manchester Wythenshawe
Monmouth
Newbury
Newcastle-under-Lyme
New Forest and Christchurch
Newport
Nottingham North-West
Nuneaton
Oxford City
Paddington North
Rochester and Chatham
Rotherham
Rother Valley

Ruislip–Northwood
St Pancras North-East
Salford City
Sheffield Brightside
Spelthorne
Streatham
Swansea Labour Association
Thurrock
Tottenham
Twickenham
Walthamstow East
Wandsworth Central
Warwick and Leamington
Wellingborough
Wembley South
Westbury
West Ham North
West Ham South
Willesden East
Windsor
Woking
Wolverhampton North-East
Wolverhampton South-West
Woolwich
Yarmouth

Select Bibliography

Manuscript Collections

PUBLIC RECORDS

Cabinet: CAB 128 (Cabinet Conclusions 1945–52); CAB 129 (Cabinet Papers, 1945–52).
Foreign Office: FO 371; FO 800 (Ernest Bevin papers).
Home Office: HO 45.

PRIVATE PAPERS

Richard Acland papers (Sussex University).
A. V. Alexander papers (Churchill College, Cambridge).
Lord Ammon papers (University of Hull).
R. Page Arnot papers (Univesity of Hull).
C. R. Attlee papers (Bodleian Library, Oxford).
Beaverbrook papers (House of Lords Record Office).
Jim Cattermole papers (Warwick University, Modern Records Centre).
G. D. H. Cole papers (Nuffield College, Oxford).
Sir Stafford Cripps papers (Nuffield College, Oxford).
Richard Crossman papers (Warwick University, Modern Records Centre).
Hugh Dalton papers (British Library of Political and Economic Science).
S. O. Davies papers (University College, Swansea).
Tom Driberg papers (Christ Church Library, Oxford).
Rev. Stanley Evans papers (University of Hull).
Felix Frankfurter papers (Library of Congress, Washington, DC).
Victor Gollancz papers (Warwick University, Modern Records Centre).
Antony Greenwood papers (Bodleian Library, Oxford).
Reg Groves papers (Warwick University, Modern Records Centre).
Denis Healey papers (Labour Party, Walworth Road).
Emrys Hughes papers (National Library of Scotland, Edinburgh).
Harold Laski papers (Labour Party, Walworth Road; and University of Hull).
Benn Levy papers (House of Lords Record Office; and Sussex University).
R. W. G. Mackay papers (British Library of Political and Economic Science).
Kingsley Martin papers (Sussex University).
Herbert Morrison papers (Nuffield College, Oxford).
Philip Noel-Baker papers (Churchill College, Cambridge).
D. N. Pritt papers (British Library of Political and Economic Science).
Morgan Phillips papers (Labour Party, Walworth Road).
J. W. Raisin papers (Labour Party, Walworth Road).
Lord Stansgate papers (House of Lords Records Office).
Reginald Sorensen papers (House of Lords Records Office).
G. R. (Lord) Strauss papers (British Library of Political and Economic Science).
Edgar Young papers (University of Hull).
Konni Zilliacus papers (Gateshead Public Library).

Austin Albu papers: private papers in his possession.
Lord Hale papers: private papers in his possession.

John Platts Mills papers: private papers in his possession, and correspondence with the author.

Stephen Solley papers: private papers in his possession.

PAPERS OF ORGANIZATIONS

Coventry Borough Labour Party papers, 1945–51 (Warwick University, Modern
    Records Centre).
Coventry East CLP papers, 1945–51 (Warwick University, Modern Records Centre).
Coventry North CLP papers, 1945–51 (Warwick University, Modern Records Centre).
Hornchurch DLP (Greater London Record Office.
Fabian Society papers (Nuffield College, Oxford).
Labour Party, Walworth road:
    General Election files, 1945, 1950, 1951;
    National Executive Committee minutes, 1945–51;
    Policy Committee minutes, 1945–51;
    International Department archive, 1945–51;
    Annual conference reports, agendas, etc., 1945–51;
    Labour Peace Fellowship;
    Holborn and St Pancras South CLP papers, 1945–51;
    Numerous miscellaneous files.
National Council on Civil Liberties papers (University of Hull).
New Statesman papers (City University, London).
North Lambeth CLP (British Library of Political and Economic Science).
PLP minutes of meetings (BLPES, microfilm 199).
PLP Liaison Committee, minutes of meetings (BLPES, microfilm 199).
Union of Democratic Control papers (University of Hull).

OTHER PAPERS

BBC Written Archives (Broadcasting House London; Caversham Park, Reading).
"Parliamentary Profiles" (courtesy of Andrew Roth; Bridge Street, London).
Dictionary of Labour Biography (courtesy of Professor John Saville; University of Hull).

Published Sources

TRADE UNIONS

Amalgamated Engineering Union, annual conference reports, 1945–51; *Monthly Journal*,
1945–51.
Chemical Workers' Union, *Chemical Worker*, 1945–51.
Civil Service Clerical Association, annual conference reports, 1948–9; *Red Tape*, 1945–51.
Electrical Trades Union, annual conference reports, 1947, 1949–51; *Electron*, 1945–51.
Fire Brigades' Union, annual conference Agendas, 1946–47; conference report, 1947;
Firefighter, 1945–51.
National Federation of Building Trades Operatives, annual conference reports, 1945–9.
National Union of Foundry Workers annual conference reports, 1945, 1947–51.
National Union of Mine Workers annual conference reports, 1945–51.
National Union of Railwaymen, annual conference reports, 1945–51; *Railway Review*,
1945–51.
National Union of Tailors and Garment Workers, annual conference agendas, 1947, 1951.
National Union of Tobacco Workers, *Tobacco Worker*, 1947–51.

Trade Union Congress, Annual Conference reports 1945–51; special conference reports, March 1948, November 1948, January 1950.

Union of Post Office Workers, annual conference reports, 1947–8; *Post,* 1945–51.

Union of Shop, Distributive and Allied Workers, annual conference agendas, 1945–51; annual conference reports, 1946–9; *New Dawn,* 1945–51.

NEWSPAPERS

Coventry Evening Telegraph
Coventry Standard
Coventry Tribune
Daily Herald
Daily Worker
Gateshead Herald
Gateshead Post
Glasgow Forward
Hornchurch, Dagenham and Romford Times
Hornchurch and Upminster News
Illustrated Hornchurch Chronicle
Labour's Northern Voice
Newcastle Weekly Chronicle
New Statesman
Reynolds News
Romford, Hornchurch, Upminster Recorder
Socialist Outlook
Sunday Pictorial
The Times
Tribune

PERIODICALS

Herald of Peace
Labour Forum
Labour Pacifist Fellowship Bulletin
Left Forum
Left News
One World

PAMPHLETS

Acland, Bruce, *et al., Keeping Left* (1950).
Donald Bruce, *Challenge to Britain* (1948).
Bruce and Foot, *Who Are the Patriots?* (1949).
Bevan, Freeman, Wilson, *One Way Only* (1951); *Going Our Way* (1951).
Cocks, Mackay, Edelman, *Europe's First Parliament* (1949).
G. D. H. Cole, *Labour's Second Term* (1949); *Weakness through Strength* (1951).
Richard Crossman, *Socialist Foreign Policy* (1951).
Crossman and Foot, *A Palestine Munich?* (1946).
Crossman, Foot, Mikardo, *et al., Keep Left* (1947).
Bob Edwards, *The Only Hope Socialism* (1946); *Socialist Policy for Today* (1948).
Michael Foot, *Still at Large* (n.d.).
Emrys Hughes, *Arms and Mr Bevan* (1951).
Labour Independent Group, *Crisis and Cure* (1950).

Labour Party, *Cards on the Table* (1948); *European Unity* (1948); *Feet on the Ground* (1948); *Labour Believes in Britain* (1949); *Let Us Face the Future* (1945).

Harold Laski, *Russia and the West* (1947); *Socialism as Internationalism* (1948).

R. W. G. Mackay, *Heads in the Sand* (1959).

Ian Mikardo, *The Second Five Years* (1948); *The Labour Case* (1949).

Walter Padley, *Britain: Pawn or Power?* (1947); *Problems of the Peace* (1945).

"Saint Just", *Full Speed Ahead* (1951).

Silverman, Warbey, *et al., Stop the Coming War* (1949).

Socialist Fellowship, *From Labour to Socialism* (1950).

William Warbey, *Can Britain Recover?* (1947).

Warbey and Wilkes, *Palestine: The Stark Facts and the Way Out* (1948).

Leonard Woolf, *Foreign Policy: The Labour Party's Dilemma* (1947).

Konni Zilliacus, *Britain, USSR and World Peace* (1946); *Dragon's Teeth* (1949); *Why I Was Expelled* (1949); *Yugoslavia and the Cold War* (1949).

BIOGRAPHIES AND MEMOIRS

(Place of publication London unless otherwise stated.)

Attlee, Clement, *As It Happened* (1954).

Bevin, Ernest, *The Life and Times of Ernest Bevin,* Vol. 2 (1967).

Blackburn, Fred, *George Tomlinson: A Biography* (1954).

Blackburn, Raymond, *I Am an Alcoholic* (1959).

Brockway, Fenner, *Outside the Right* (1963).

Brockway, Fenner, *Towards Tomorrow* (1977).

Broome, Vincent, *Aneurin Bevan* (1953).

Bullock, Alan, *Ernest Bevin: Foreign Secretary* (1983).

Cole, Margaret, *The Life of G. D. H. Cole* (1971).

Cooke, Colin, *The Life of Richard Stafford Cripps* (1957).

Crick, Bernard, *George Orwell: A Life* (1980).

Crosland, Susan, *Tony Crosland* (1981).

Crossman, Richard, *Palestine Mission: A Personal Record* (1947).

Dalton, Hugh, *Memoirs, 1945–60: High Tide and After* (1962).

Donoughue, Bernard, and Jones, G. W., *Herbert Morrison: Portrait of a Politician* (1973).

Driberg, Tom, *Ruling Passions* (1977).

Duff, Peggy, *Left, Left, Left* (1971).

Eastwood, Granville, *Harold Laski* (1977).

Foot, Paul, *The Politics of Harold Wilson* (1968).

Foot, Michael, *Aneurin Bevan,* 2 vols. (1962, 1973).

Griffiths, James, *Pages from Memory* (1969).

Harris, Kenneth, *Attlee* (1982).

Hoggart, Simon, and Leigh, David, *Michael Foot* (1981).

Horner, Arthur, *Incorrigible Rebel* (1960).

Hughes, Emrys, *Sydney Silverman, Rebel in Parliament* (1969).

Lee, Jennie, *This Great Journey* (1963).

Lee, Jennie, *My Life with Nye* (1980).

Manning, Leah, *A Life for Education* (1970).

Martin, Kingsley, *Harold Laski, A Biographical Memoir* (1953).

Morrison, Herbert, *Autobiography, 1893–1950* (1960).

Pimlott, Ben, *Hugh Dalton* (1985).

Shinwell, Emanuel, *Conflict without Malice* (1955).

Thomas, Hugh, *John Strachey* (1973).

Toole, Millie, *Mrs Bessie Braddock* (1957).
Vernon, Betty D., *Ellen Wilkinson* (1982).
Wigg, George, *George Wigg* (1972).
Williams, Francis, *A Prime Minister Remembers* (1961).
Williams, Philip, *Hugh Gaitskell: A Political Biography* (1979).
Williams, Philip (ed.), *The Diary of Hugh Gaitskell, 1945–56* (1983).
Wright, A. W., *G. D. H. Cole and Socialist Democracy* (Oxford, 1979).
Wyatt, Woodrow, *Into the Dangerous World* (1952).

OTHER PUBLISHED WORKS

(Place of publication London unless otherwise stated.)

Addison, Paul, *The Road to 1945* (1975).
Ady, P., and Worsick, G. D. A. (eds.), *The British Economy, 1945–50* (Oxford, 1952).
Anderson, P., and Blackburn, R. (eds.), *Towards Socialism* (1965).
Anderson, Terry, *The United States, Britain and the Cold War, 1944–47* (Columbia, Mo., 1981).
Barker, Elizabeth, *Britain in a Divided Europe, 1945–1970* (Oxford, 1972).
Barker, Elizabeth, *Britain between the Superpowers* (1983).
Bealey, F., and Pelling, H., *Labour and Politics, 1900–1906* (1958).
Beer, Samuel, *Modern British Politics* (1965).
Burridge, Trevor, *Clement Attlee, A Political Biography* (London, 1985).
Butler, David, *The British General Election of 1951* (1952).
Cairncross, Alec, *Years of Recovery, 1945–51* (1984).
Calder, Angus, *The People's War* (1971).
Campbell, John *Aneurin Bevan and the Mirage of British Socialism* (London, 1987).
Chester, D. N., *The Nationalized Industries* (1951).
Chester, Sir Norman, *The Nationalisation of British Industry, 1945–51* (1975).
Coates, David, *The Labour Party and the Struggle for Socialism* (Cambridge, 1975).
Cole, G. D. H., *A History of the Labour Party since 1914* (1948).
Cook, Chris, *A Short History of the Liberal Party, 1900–1976* (1976).
Cowling, Maurice, *The Impact of Labour, 1920–24* (1971).
Crossman, Richard (ed.), *New Fabian Essays* (1952).
Dow, J. R. C., *The Management of the British Economy, 1945–60* (Cambridge, 1964).
Eatwell, Roger, *The 1945–51 Labour Governments* (1979).
Epstein, Leon, *Britain—Uneasy Ally* (Chicago, 1954).
Fitzsimons, M. A., *The Foreign Policy of the British Labour Government* (Notre Dame, Ind., 1953).
Fleming, D. F., *The Cold War and its Origins 1917–1960* Vol. 2 (1961).
Gaddis, J. L., *The United States and the Origins of the Cold War, 1941–7* (New York, 1972).
Gardner, R. N., *Sterling–Dollar Diplomacy* (New York, 1969).
Gimbel, John, *The Origins of the Marshall Plan* (Palo Alto, Calif., 1976).
Gordon, M. R., *Conflict and Consensus in Labour's Foreign Policy, 1914–65* (Stanford, 1969).
Gowing, Margaret, *Independence and Deterrence: Britain and Atomic Energy, 1945–52* (1974).
Gupta, Partha Sarathi, *Imperialism and the British Labour Movement, 1914–64* (1975).
Harrington, W., and Young, P., *The 1945 Revolution* (1978).
Harrison, Martin, *Trade Unions and the Labour Party since 1945* (1960).
Haseler, Stephen, *The Gaitskellites,* (1969).
Hill, Douglas (ed.), *Tribune 40* (1977).
Howell, David, *British Social Democracy* (1976).
Hunter, Leslie, *The Road to Brighton Pier* (1959).

Jackson, Robert, *Rebels and Whips* (1968).

Jenkins, Mark, *Bevanism: Labour's High Tide* (1979).

Jones, Bill, *The Russia Complex: The British Labour Party and the Soviet Union* (1977).

Kaufman, Gerald (ed.), *The Left* (1966).

Kavanagh, Denis (ed.), *The Politics of the Labour Party* (1982).

Kolko, Gabriel, *The Limits of Power: The World and the United States Foreign Policy, 1945–54* (New York, 1972).

Laski, Harold, *The Crisis and the Constitution* (1932).

Le Feber, Walter, *America, Russia and the Cold War* (New York, 1980).

Lyman, R., *The First Labour Government* (1957).

Martin, David E., and Rubinstein, D. (eds.), *Ideology and the Labour Movement* (1979).

Marwick, Arthur, *British Society since 1945* (1982).

McCallum, R. B., and Readman, A. *The British General Election of 1945* (Oxford, 1947).

McKibbin, Ross, *The Evolution of the Labour Party, 1910–24* (Oxford, 1974).

Meehan, Eugene, *The British Left Wing and Foreign Policy* (New Brunswick, NJ, 1960).

Miliband, Ralph, *Parliamentary Socialism* (1961).

Milward, Alan, *The Reconstruction of Western Europe, 1945–51* (1984).

Morgan Kenneth O., *Labour in Power, 1945–51* (Oxford, 1984).

Northedge, F. S., *Descent from Power, British Foreign Policy 1945–73* (1974).

Ovendale, Ritchie (ed.), *The Foreign Policy of the British Labour Governments, 1945–51* (Leicester, 1984).

Pelling, Henry, *The Origins of the Labour Party* (1954).

Pelling, Henry, *Britain and the Second World War* (1970).

Pelling, Henry, *The Labour Governments, 1945–51* (1984).

Pimlott, Ben, *Labour and the Left in the 1930s* (Cambridge, 1977, London, 1987).

Pritt, D. N., *The Labour Government, 1945–51* (1963).

Rogow, A. and Shore, P., *The Labour Government and British Industry, 1945–51* (Oxford, 1955).

Rothwell, Victor, *Britain and the Cold War, 1941–1947* (1982).

Shonfield, Andrew, *British Economic Policy since the War* (1959).

Sissons, M., and French, P. (eds.), *Age of Austerity, 1945–51* (1963).

Skidelsky, Robert, *Politicians and the Slump* (1967).

Swartz, Marvin, *The Union of Democratic Control in British Politics during the First World War* (Oxford, 1971).

ARTICLES

Hughes, Billy, "In defence of Ellen Wilkinson," *History Workshop,* vol. 7 (Spring 1979), pp. 157–60.

Jackson, Scott, "Prologue to the Marshall plan: the origins of the American commitment for a European recovery program," *Journal of American History,* vol. LXV (March, 1979), pp. 1043–68.

Pelling, Henry, "The 1945 general election reconsidered," *Historical Journal,* vol. 23, no. 2 (June 1980), pp. 399–414.

Pimlott, Ben, "The Socialist League, intellectuals and the Left," *Journal of Contemporary History,* vol. VI, no. 3 (1971), pp. 12–39.

Rubenstein, David, "Ellen Wilkinson reconsidered," *History Workshop,* vol. 7 (Spring 1979), pp. 161–9.

Rubenstein, David, "Socialism and the Labour Party: the Labour Left and domestic policy, 1945–50," Independent Labour Publications, Labour Party Discussion Series no. 3 (n.d.).

Saville, John, "May Day 1937," in Asa Briggs and John Saville (eds.), *Essays in Labour History,* (London 1977), pp. 232–84.

Schneer, Jonathan, "Hopes deferred or shattered: the British Labour Left and the third force movement, 1945–49," *Journal of Modern History,* vol. 56, no. 2 (June 1984), pp. 197–226.

UNPUBLISHED THESES

Calder, Angus, "The Common Wealth Party, 1942–45," D. Phil. thesis, Sussex University, 1968.
Wood, Jonathan, "The Labour Left in the Constituencies," D. Phil. thesis, Warwick University, 1982.

Index